S&L HELL

S&L HELL

The People and the Politics behind the
$1 Trillion Savings and Loan Scandal

KATHLEEN DAY

W. W. NORTON & COMPANY

New York   London

FIRST EDITION

The text of this book is composed in Century Old Style with the display set in
Century Old Style Bold. Composition and Manufacturing by The Haddon
Craftsmen Inc.
Book design by Susan Hood

Library of Congress Cataloging-in-Publication Data
Day, Kathleen, 1953–
S & L hell : the people and the politics behind the $1 trillion
savings & loan scandal / by Kathleen Day.
p.   cm.
Includes bibliographical references and index.
1. Savings and loan associations—United States—Corrupt
practices. 2. Savings and loan associations—United States—
Deregulation. 3. United States—Economic conditions—1981—
I. Title. II. Title: S and L hell.
HG2151.K63 1993
332.3′2′0973—dc20   92-22154

ISBN 0-393-02982-4

W. W. Norton & Company, Inc., 500 Fifth Avenue, New York, N.Y. 10110
W. W. Norton & Company Ltd., 10 Coptic Street, London WC1A 1PU

1 2 3 4 5 6 7 8 9 0

To Charles
and to my parents
and to Rebecca

Contents

CONTENTS

Introduction: Socialism for the Rich

The savings and loan debacle is the costliest scandal in the country's history. Bailing out the S&L industry will cost taxpayers at least $500 billion over the next few years and more than $1 trillion over the next several decades, once the cost of borrowing the money is added. That's more than $4,000 for every person in the United States, an amount that is equal to several times the government's deficit.

How could such a catastrophe have occurred? Some sort of shake-out in the industry was inevitable; by 1980 the day of the mom-and-pop thrift immortalized in Frank Capra's *It's a Wonderful Life*—the film whose heroic portrayal of an S&L executive has become painfully easy to parody—had passed. But the industry fell far harder (and far more expensively) than it had to.

In fact, the most remarkable thing about the collapse of the S&L industry is that so many of the major participants—the regulators, politicians, and S&L operators themselves—chose to do nothing as they watched problems mount and taxpayer liabilities grow. That choice was dictated by a variety of motives: greed, political self-interest, and even (sometimes) misguided good intentions. Whatever the motives, this collective interest in hiding the debacle made it certain that the industry's final fall would come with an enormous bang, one that would force administrations that professed a free market philosophy essentially to nationalize a majority of the nation's thrifts. As a result, the industry in many respects became one of the best examples of socialism in the U.S. economy.

Throughout the book, readers will find examples of an economic phenomenon in which a borrower gets so far in default that the lender has no choice but to throw good money after bad in the hope the debtor will one day recover and repay his debts. In this case the debtor is the thrift industry, borrowing on the good name of the U.S. government.

Other treatments of the S&L crisis have offered a range of explanations for the industry's problems: the influence of organized crime, a conspiracy on Wall Street, imperfections in the market, and so on. All of these—to which, perhaps, the roles of greed and ambition should be added—may have played some part. But while the temptation is great to offer the debacle as a paradigm for the failures of regulation, this book doesn't advance a grand theory. Instead it tells the history of the scandal through the stories of the principal players. It is a history sadly lacking in heroes. If there are some obvious lessons for the future to be learned from these stories, I've left them for the reader to draw.

I sincerely believe that banking establishments are more dangerous than standing armies.

—*Thomas Jefferson*

A nation's economy cannot be healthy when a basic element in it is sick.

—*Wall Street financier Bernard M. Baruch*
shortly before the 1929 crash

That's where the money was.

—*Willie Sutton, when asked why he*
robbed banks

S&L HELL

Part 1

AMERICA IN MINIATURE

—

The secret of life is honesty and fair dealing. If you can fake that, you've got it made.

—Groucho Marx

1

Ohio

March 14, 1985: A balding six-foot-seven-inch man sat scrunched in his seat as the United Air Lines jet taxied for takeoff from San Francisco International Airport. Suddenly a message over the intercom made the passenger even more uncomfortable. "We have to return to the terminal," the pilot said. "There's some guy on this flight named Volcker and he has a phone call." So much for the anonymity sought by Federal Reserve Board Chairman Paul Volcker.

Volcker's staff in Washington, D.C., agonizing over whether to recall the flight, felt they had no choice. Trouble was brewing in Ohio. Shock waves were washing through the Midwest and the world. Two weeks earlier, on March 4, the Securities and Exchange Commission (SEC) had closed down a small, fraud-ridden government securities dealer in Fort Lauderdale, Florida, E.S.M. Government Securities. The action had a domino effect.

E.S.M. owed millions of dollars that it could not pay to Home State Savings Bank of Cincinnati, and the losses might be fatal to the Ohio thrift. When the *Cincinnati Enquirer* broke news of Home State's losses on March 6, lines of depositors formed outside the thrift in a run that threatened to spread to other institutions. Depositors had panicked on news that Home State could fail and that its collapse threatened to deplete the $130 million Ohio Deposit Guaranty Fund, an industry-financed and -operated but state-regulated fund that covered deposits at seventy of Ohio's three hundred thrifts. Though the fund's name and seal gave the impression it was backed by the full faith of the Ohio treasury, it was not.

If the panic continued, it could spread beyond Ohio, upsetting an already fragile banking system, one rocked a year earlier by the $4.5 billion federal bailout of banking giant Continental Illinois of Chicago.

The American dollar—which had been climbing despite the best efforts of Volcker and Treasury officials to keep it down, making American goods more expensive around the world—fell overnight on the news of Ohio's problems. The tumble was a classic sign of anxiety among investors, fearing for the safety and security of the U.S. banking system. One of Volcker's jobs was to help maintain public confidence in the system. What if people couldn't take their money out of Home State when they asked for it? Who knew how many other panics might result? The reputation of the United States as a benchmark of financial security worldwide could evaporate, spreading havoc throughout the world. That prospect, no matter how remote, simply would not do.

With such thoughts in mind, the Federal Reserve Board's chief counsel, Michael Bradfield, dialed the White House switchboard and described the emergency to one of its operators. In seconds she patched him through to officials at United Air Lines' headquarters in Chicago, who summoned the plane's return. Back in the terminal Volcker telephoned his staff to learn that Ohio Governor Richard Celeste, with a full-blown emergency on his hands, had threatened to fly to Washington and camp out on the Fed's doorstep if he couldn't talk to Volcker. Depositor runs on savings and loans in Ohio indeed were spreading, and Celeste was about to declare the first broad bank closure since President Roosevelt's bank holiday in 1933 during the Great Depression. Knowing the decision would be the toughest of his career, Celeste wanted to inform Volcker personally and enlist the Fed's support.

Volcker called the governor. "The situation is out of control," Celeste said. "I'm desperate for help." Volcker said an airplane full of people was being held up for him. Could the conversation wait until he got back to Washington? Celeste sweated out the next few hours drinking milk and eating several boxes of Girl Scout cookies. With his advisers, who included his father and a leading Ohio thrift executive, he went over and over the possible consequences of each of his three main options: Let the runs play themselves out, limit withdrawals, or declare a bank holiday and keep the thrifts closed until a permanent solution could be found.

Finally, late that night, Volcker called back. His first observation, Celeste recalls, was this: "The system can stand one failure. It can't stand a second failure."

His second: "The Fed's ability to help is limited." The central bank could make sure the thrifts had enough cash to meet withdrawals, but that was about it.

The third: "Governor, I want to tell you one of the first lessons of bank regulation. No matter how bad things look from the outside, when you get inside it always looks worse." A bank's losses are always bigger than it at first lets on, and the cost to the government is always more than is at first expected.

The fourth: "Whatever you do is a decision you have to make. I'm sorry, I can't help you make the decision."

Volcker asked one favor. If Celeste closed the thrifts, would he please avoid the phrase "bank holiday"? The term harked back to the Great Depression and conjured up images of consumer losses and of an emergency out of control. No need, Volcker said, to create an artificial connection in the public's mind between Ohio's savings and loan problem and the mainstream banking industry, though he and his staff understood all too well that if Celeste mishandled Home State, the trouble could infect the rest of the banking system. And if that happened, Celeste's head cold would become the Fed's pneumonia.

For better or worse, the central banker has the largest single voice in determining government strategy for maintaining public confidence in the nation's financial system. That is true whether the institutions are commercial banks, which traditionally have been business-oriented, or specialty banks such as savings and loans, also known as thrifts, which traditionally have focused on consumers wanting home loans. On any given day, no bank in America, indeed in the world, has the cash on hand to pay off all its depositors. An institution holds only enough dollars and coin to meet daily withdrawals, normally a tiny fraction of deposits. The rest of it is invested in loans or government securities that thrift and bank executives hope will earn a profit. From time to time circumstances arise that drive withdrawals upward—a rumor of trouble at a savings bank perhaps. The resulting crunch in the bank's cash reserves might force a bank to deny a customer his or her money, at least right then and there. This scenario is anathema to the central bank. When consumers can't get their money, no matter what the reason, they are apt to panic. Matters worsen after the evening news broadcast, when additional depositors who see the story decide to withdraw their money. The situation can easily deteriorate into a mob mentality. One regulator who oversaw the government take-over of an ailing Texas bank recalls the dark blue limousine that pulled up and disgorged a man clutching a shotgun and a suitcase. The man marched into the bank, demanded his deposits (an amount reaching into six figures), and drove off.

Short-circuiting a chain reaction of fear is one of the Federal Reserve

Board's most important jobs. When the threat of a depositor run occurs, the central bank moves into action, funneling enough extra cash to meet the unusual demand so that the afflicted institution remains liquid. The Fed in effect guarantees that no matter what the circumstance, tellers can look customers in the eye and hand them their money. It's a situation where the stroke of a computer key just won't do. Crisp green dollar bills, not electronic transfers, are required. The Fed stands ready to fly planeloads of U.S. currency anywhere in the country, planes met by Brinks trucks that deliver bags full of money to besieged banks. When the federal government succeeds in its role as lender of last resort, customers no longer withdraw their funds.

But on the night of March 14, 1985, the problem was more local than national.

"Good luck," Volcker said. Governor Celeste hung up the phone.

He was in uncharted territory.

Celeste assumed his political career would be ruined no matter what he did. As he signed the order temporarily closing dozens of thrifts, officials in Washington pondered the big picture, praying that fate had not selected Governor Celeste of Ohio to be the man at the center of a meltdown of America's banking system.

Most of the seventy thrifts that had been insured by the state-regulated insurance fund remained shut for several weeks rather than the seventy-two hours Celeste originally intended. By and large, only those that could qualify for federal deposit insurance were permitted to reopen. In the meantime, the Ohio legislature passed a law backing S&L deposits in thrifts insured by the state-regulated fund. And Volcker publicly vowed that the Fed would provide reopened thrifts with any cash needed to meet withdrawals. Confidence was restored.

Nationally, top thrift executives insisted that Home State and the weaknesses it exposed in the Ohio thrift system were far from the industry norm.

So did the White House. President Ronald Reagan, when asked about the Ohio situation, said: "This is not a major threat to the banking system. There is no other problem of that kind anyplace else in the country that we're aware of."

2

Maryland

Selma Sweetbaum didn't like what she was reading. The Baltimore newspapers were filled with stories about the Ohio banking crisis and similarities between the state-regulated but industry-operated deposit insurance system there and the one in Maryland.

Sweetbaum, a trim, energetic woman in her fifties, worked with "older adults" at the Jewish Community Center of Greater Washington, located in a Maryland suburb outside the District of Columbia. Her office overlooked the playground for the JCC's day care center. From her window in March 1985 she could see the brick back wall of a branch of a Maryland savings and loan, First Maryland, a thrift insured by the state deposit insurance system. She knew that many members of the center banked at First Maryland.

Sweetbaum had just taken charge of her ailing mother's savings, placing the money in another Maryland thrift, Old Court Savings and Loan, to be withdrawn as needed for her mother's medical and living expenses. When news of the Ohio problem hit the Maryland newspapers, Sweetbaum fretted on her mother's behalf. She also was besieged with questions by senior citizens at the center who stopped by her office. Was their money safe? Maryland, after all, had a state-sanctioned insurance fund backing deposits, just as Ohio did. The fund managers gave the impression to depositors, through advertisements and use of a seal that resembled the state seal, that thrifts insured by the fund were state-insured—that is, backed by the state treasury—when in fact they were not. Like many depositors, Sweetbaum thought of First Maryland and other state-chartered thrifts as state-insured.

Every year the center invited the state's elected officials for a round table discussion with the seniors. The session, well attended by politicians and citizens alike, this year took place in the weeks shortly after the Ohio crisis. "This is a savvy group," Sweetbaum says. "The question on everyone's lips was 'Is my money safe in a state-insured thrift?' The politicians answered, 'Yes, no question about it. Maryland's thrifts are a healthy bunch. And anyway, your money is insured.' "

Armed with that assurance, Sweetbaum advised her charges not to worry. "Your money's safe," she told them.

She was not alone. Others also were asking questions about Maryland S&Ls in 1984 and early 1985. Seena King of Bethesda, Maryland, wrote on January 8, 1984, to Maryland Governor Harry Hughes questioning the soundness of the state-regulated deposit insurance fund. Was not the state deceiving depositors about the safety of their money? The state's chief S&L regulator, Charles Brown, passed the letter to another state official with the note "Mrs. King asked many questions which I found rather difficult to answer." On March 5 the governor's chief of staff, Ejner J. Johnson, sent a reply that "was upbeat and reassuring, designed to encourage Mrs. King to deposit her money" in a state-chartered thrift, a special state-appointed investigator of the Maryland crisis later wrote in a report to Governor Hughes.

On December 20, 1984, Maryland resident Kenneth A. Richer called the state regulator's office to express concern about Old Court Savings and Loan. "Old Court is in fine financial shape," a state official told him.

"Then how can Old Court afford to pay one to one-point-five percent higher interest than anyone else?" Richer asked.

"Because it has eliminated the middleman in its real estate deals by having its own real estate division," the Maryland official said. "Old Court is even less vulnerable to changes in local housing markets than other institutions."

April 13, 1985: A few days after Volcker's plane was recalled, it was the Federal Reserve Board's turn to place an urgent call. Governor Hughes was on vacation in Florida that Saturday night when the telephone rang. The Federal Reserve official apologized for disturbing him, but Volcker had insisted that important news be relayed to the governor as soon as possible. Old Court Savings and Loan of Baltimore was borrowing unusually large sums of cash from the central bank, a sure sign that the institution's depositors were pulling out. As often happens when a deposit institution runs into trouble, the public sensed it before the regulators did. Many Old Court depositors seemed to know the thrift was headed for disaster. In the few months preceding the telephone call from Volcker's office, electronic withdrawals from Old Court had totaled $630 million in what is known as a silent run; no depositors stood in lines, but the computers were very active. If news of massive withdrawals leaked out, a full-scale, customers-lined-up-at-the-door panic would ensue, providing television cameras a powerful visual image—the first requirement of any story vying for airtime. Regulators feared TV attention. TV would beget more lines. Suddenly a story that might have been buried on the business pages—and ignored by most—would be piped into millions of living rooms at dinnertime.

The situation in Maryland, Volcker believed, could blow up any day. It hardly mattered that the Maryland thrift regulator, Brown, and the head of the state-regulated deposit insurance fund, Charles Hogg, just days earlier had promised the governor and concerned members of Congress that Maryland faced no threat in the wake of Ohio. For Hughes, the message of the Fed's phone call was clear. The central bank was worried. Hughes should be, too.

Both Maryland and Ohio used a state-sanctioned, industry-run system rather than the federal deposit insurance system; this fact made an unstable situation worse. Neither Maryland nor Ohio technically was the federal government's ward—though Volcker's staff, in contrast with federal thrift regulators at the Federal Home Loan Bank Board in Washington, understood that a loss of confidence in banking at any level fell in everyone's lap. Maryland officials to this day speak almost reverently of the hand-holding and help the Federal Reserve Board provided.

Old Court, the subject of the Fed's concern, was owned by Jeffrey Levitt, a young Baltimore lawyer who had purchased it in 1982. In retrospect, it seems curious that the state allowed Levitt to husband other people's money. According to a special investigator's report, sent to Governor Hughes on January 9, 1986, Levitt in 1982 "was well known as the person responsible for a major portion" of trouble at another Maryland thrift, First Progressive, where he had been an attorney. (In 1985, just three years after Maryland granted Levitt permission to buy Old Court, state prosecutors charged, among other things, that he had stolen money from First Progressive to finance the purchase.)

Fresh out of law school, Levitt was thrown off the state parole board—an almost unheard-of sanction—for soliciting business from inmates during inspection tours of prisons. He also incurred a one-year suspension from practicing law for lying in a Baltimore City Superior Court hearing. Even Levitt's own lawyer, William Hundley, admits Levitt was a slum landlord who violated housing codes with such regularity that Fridays in Baltimore housing court were known as Levitt days.

State regulators nevertheless permitted Levitt to take control of Old Court.

In fact, they encouraged it. Regulators Brown and Hogg believed at the time that Levitt "had turned himself around," according to the special investigator's report.

As head of Old Court Levitt and his wife, Karol, lived like royalty. From October 1982 until May 1985 the Levitts used depositors' money to buy, among other things, $400,000 worth of jewelry, an $18,000 putting green at their Florida house, three Thoroughbred racehorses, two Ocean City condominiums, a $200,000 apartment in New York City, seventeen automobiles, a Rolls-Royce golf cart with a TV and tape deck, and dozens of sterling silver serving trays.

"Who did they think would come over for dinner, the Sixth Fleet?" *Washington Post* columnist Tony Kornheiser once asked in a profile of the couple.

The excess reached every aspect of the Levitts' lives. A waitress in a Baltimore restaurant reportedly watched Jeffrey and Karol eat six desserts each after finishing a full meal. Both Levitts were enormously fat, adding to the conspicuousness of their consumption.

In January 1985, years into Jeffrey Levitt's management of Old Court, state regulators finally began to worry about his style and its damage to the thrift. Insurance fund chief Hogg attempted to correct the mismanagement situation at Old Court by introducing Levitt to Huell E. Connor, a psychiatrist who specialized in helping, to use Hogg's words, "people with newly acquired wealth."

The problem, however, was not that Levitt's wealth was "newly acquired." The problem was that the wealth was stolen. He was robbing the bank. By the end of 1985 state prosecutors would know that Levitt had bilked Old Court of nearly $15 million. But even in 1984 Hogg, Brown, and many industry executives had known about abuses at Old Court: self-dealing, excessive lending to one borrower (the most egregious example being to Jeffrey Levitt himself), lack of proper loan documentation. In early 1985 the regulators prepared a letter citing the problems and ordering Levitt to promise to stop the practices, but for weeks the memo was not shown to higher-ups in the Hughes administration or to the public.

May 1985: Two months after the governor of Ohio declared a bank holiday and one month after the Fed's telephone call, at 1:00 A.M. on Monday, May 13, Maryland Attorney General Stephen Sachs, Governor Hughes's chief of staff Johnnie Johnson, a handful of other state officials, and *Washington Post* reporter Paul Valentine milled about the living room of Judge Martin B. Greenfeld's home in Baltimore. They drank coffee, talked to Mrs. Greenfeld, and patted the Greenfelds' dog, Gus, a frisky wheaten terrier that caused a welcome diversion during an uneasy situation. Hours earlier Sachs and the governor's staff had determined that Old Court's problems were so bad that the state had to take over the thrift immediately or risk being guilty of complicity in what looked like massive fraud on Levitt's part.

Judge Greenfeld soon opened court in his dining room to hear oral arguments on why Old Court should be closed. Then, after retiring alone to the kitchen to read the state's arguments, he signed an order allowing the state to seize control of the thrift later that day. A few days later, in an announcement that remains controversial, Sachs told the public that his office had launched a criminal investigation into Old Court.

That seizure and official acknowledgment that criminal activity might have caused Old Court's demise ignited runs at other Maryland thrifts. Depositors were withdrawing cash at a rate of $4 million every hour. Hughes, against the better judgment of several advisers, had only days earlier gone ahead with a visit to Israel, on the theory that canceling his plans would alarm depositors. Now it didn't matter. On May 13 Hughes cut short his trip and arrived home the next day to proclaim "a state of public crisis." He immediately limited withdrawals at more than a hundred thrifts to $1,000 per person a month.

In the following months more than a dozen savings and loans were seized, with access to billions of dollars in deposits essentially frozen while state and federal officials tried to sort out the mess. As it turned out, Levitt was not a singular phenomenon. Maryland had to boot dozens of savings and loan industry executives from their jobs because of misconduct ranging from gross incompetence to out-and-out thievery. But no one came to epitomize public sentiment better than Jeffrey and Karol Levitt, whose oversize frames and outsize life-style seem to embody all that had gone askew in the state's savings and loan industry.

Even after Maryland had taken over Old Court, Hogg and Brown decided to allow the S&L to continue its practices. Ads touting "the Old Court advantage" of high interest rates continued to run. The ads didn't mention that the thrift was paying such high rates because it was desperate for cash or that to pay such high rates, it had to invest deposits in highly speculative projects. Old Court was gambling with other people's money, and doing so under the state banner. Maryland Attorney General Sachs heard the ad on the radio while driving home soon after the takeover. As soon as he got in the door, he telephoned Hogg. "You'd better get that fucking stuff off the air or I'm going to sue you," he said. Hogg argued that pulling the ads would undermine confidence among consumers. Sachs held his ground: It was a sham to ask depositors to pour more money into such a shaky institution. It was one thing that the state's top officials had been screened from the mess by Hogg and Brown. But now the governor knew. Such shenanigans had to stop.

Within a few days the ads were pulled. But the damage had been done; scores of new depositors had been lured inside the sick thrift.

In the fall a second savings and loan shock wave hit Maryland. In September 1985 a Maryland thrift named Community Savings and Loan was seized by the state hours after its major subsidiary, a real estate tax shelter company called Equity Programs Investment Corporation, or EPIC, filed for bankruptcy. The collapse of EPIC single-handedly rattled the nation's housing market. EPIC's business was to buy homes and lease them back to builders and also to bundle the mortgages into limited partnerships that provided tax shelters for investors all around the country. None of the investors ever expected to see the property EPIC owned. Neither did the thrifts and banks from coast to coast that lent EPIC millions of dollars, using the tax shelter's inventory of homes as collateral.

When EPIC collapsed, lenders were left holding hundreds of condominiums and houses built only with tax breaks, not housing demand, in mind. A lot of that housing had gone up in markets already oversupplied, such as Austin, Dallas, and Denver. EPIC's failure led directly to the bankruptcy of the third-largest private insurer of home loans in the country—Ticor Mortgage Insurance of Los Angeles—which had unwisely insured too many loans on EPIC property. And of course, it led to the collapse of Community Savings, which in turn compounded consumer worry about thrifts in Maryland and sparked a second round of runs. The state was forced to take over additional thrifts, in which it found more evidence of fraud and mismanagement.

Months earlier Volcker's staff had sent into Maryland a battalion of federal thrift regulators, who set up shop in a hastily rigged "war room" in Baltimore's regional Federal Reserve office. As they consulted blackboards, computer printouts, and audit reports in an effort to monitor every thrift in the state, they were within sight of one of the city's most prominent landmarks: a stone clock tower with a face bearing the words "Bromo Seltzer" instead of the numbers 1 through 12. Some thought it an appropriate symbol as the list of hopelessly insolvent thrifts grew rapidly during the spring of 1985 and then again in the fall.

Linda Nusinov already had worked for several failed Maryland thrifts when she began her tenure as a consultant at Ridgeway Savings and Loan by trying to determine when the S&L's financial statement had last been balanced. A rough balancing of a bank's books entails adding up deposits and interest and then subtracting withdrawals. Nusinov began the process by hand, trying to add up the deposit and withdrawal slips one by one.

"You're wasting your time," one of the thrift's top officials said.

"Why?" Nusinov asked.

"Well, some of the deposit tickets aren't there."

"Why aren't they here?"

"Well, sometimes the directors make a deposit and they take the ticket with them as a receipt."

"And you have nothing?"

"No."

Nusinov finally figured the mess out, in part by sending letters to customers asking if the thrift's records matched theirs. To her surprise and relief, little money was missing. After reconciling the accounts, she put them on a computer; now proper interest would start accruing, and the balancing of the books could be handled automatically.

Next she decided to tackle the individual retirement accounts, the IRAs.

"They're over there," said the office manager, pointing to an office refrigerator where the thrift's few employees stored lunches and snacks.

Beside it Nusinov found a brown paper grocery bag filled with the IRAs— every IRA application and check the thrift had ever received, none processed or cashed. Some were two years old. Why hadn't the office manager processed the accounts? "She didn't know how and was too afraid for her job to ask," Nusinov recalls. When a customer asked about his IRA account, employees apparently bluffed their way through an answer. Nusinov had never seen anything like it.

But more appalling than the condition of the thrift was the fact that state regulators had performed regular audits of Ridgeway and never caught any of its many problems. Their incompetence amazed Nusinov. "The state had been out there to audit?" Nusinov says. "How? This was beyond me. How did the state do a regulatory audit? I never got an answer."

3

Just Deserts

As Jeffrey Levitt shuffled in and out of the Baltimore courthouse during his arraignment in late 1985 for bank fraud and theft of nearly $15 million from Old Court, former depositors spit on his squat 230-pound body. They hissed and booed and shouted like a lynch mob in the old West.

Levitt's wife, Karol, also was a public target, despite her less direct role in bilking depositors and setting off the statewide banking panic. She became a target of jokes about her physical appearance.

> "Here she comes, North America."
> "What did Karol Levitt wear to a Halloween party? She put on a white sheet and went as Alaska."
> "What does Karol Levitt call a beached whale? Sushi."
> "Know what they found during an autopsy of Karol Levitt? Jimmy Hoffa."
> "How did they get Karol Levitt in jail? They greased the bars and threw in Hostess Twinkies."

When Jeffrey was sentenced in July 1986 to thirty years in jail, he already had been there for six months. Karol, too, had served a dozen consecutive weekends. (Her husband's lawyer, Hundley, says she spent the time sitting on a stool, fists clenched, eyes closed.) Why? Because the couple had exceeded the $1,000-a-week spending limit a judge had imposed pending Levitt's trial and a sorting out of what money belonged to whom. The Levitts ignored the order, writing checks willy-nilly for country club fees, jewelry, clothing, and restaurant outings.

When Levitt appeared for sentencing, the man many of his high school peers had thought the least likely to succeed arrived many pounds thinner than in his glory days. He wore an outfit of yellow pants, madras shirt, and Dock-Siders–sans–socks more befitting a backyard barbecue with young Republicans than a court hearing. He was rumpled and harmless-looking, almost like a child. The leg irons that checked his gait were a humiliating and no doubt gratuitous touch that represented the state's concession to the hordes of angry depositors who filled the courtroom. "If I did what the public wanted, the Levitts would be hanging from the rafters in front of the courthouse," a judge in the case said.

In his own defense Jeffrey pleaded he was a first-time offender.

. "The biggest first offender the state has ever seen," the judge replied.

Hundley delights in telling a Levitt story involving the late Edward Bennett Williams, one of the best-known criminal trial lawyers in America. Williams's clients included the likes of Teamster President James Hoffa, New York mobster Frank Costello, stock swindler Robert Vesco, and political wheeler-dealer Bobby Baker.

Levitt first asked Williams to be his lawyer, Hundley says. But Williams couldn't take the assignment; he'd already agreed to defend one of Levitt's business associates at Old Court, Jerome Cardin. To accept both men as clients might pose a conflict should either defendant have to testify against the other. Williams recommended Hundley.

Cardin paid Williams a very large retainer (some say $1 million) and was upset that Williams was not handling the case personally but had handed it to a junior partner in his firm. The junior partner tried hard, but he couldn't get Williams to appear personally on behalf of Cardin. The junior partner turned to Williams's friend Hundley for help.

At the same time Levitt was pushing Hundley to set up a meeting with Cardin and Williams to discuss issues of mutual importance. Levitt had the idea that a codefendants' session could help everyone involved, if only to raise public awareness of his defense.

Hundley went to Williams and said, in his raspy, matter-of-fact voice, "Ed, you know, it would really help matters if you could appear with Cardin and Levitt."

To which the lawyer for Frank Costello and Jimmy Hoffa answered: "Bill, do you know what these guys *did*?"

"Needless to say," says Hundley, "we never had the meeting."

———

29

Maryland residents were, to say the least, unhappy about the fiasco. Many never forgave Governor Hughes, who found the months after closing Old Court the most trying of his career. State investigators later called the crisis inevitable, though without Old Court's failure and the ensuing fear among depositors, months or even years might have passed before the industry crashed. In a convoluted way Levitt did consumers a favor. The longer the abuses went undetected or uncorrected, investigators say, the more expensive the cleanup bill for taxpayers.

Consumers failed to see a silver lining in Levitt's excesses. They picketed the state legislature in Annapolis. They loudly and persistently denounced Hughes, heckling him all over the state. They voted him down in his bid for the U.S. Senate in the fall of 1986.

The bill presented to Maryland taxpayers for repayment to depositors eventually reached $185 million. The sum was hefty, but far less than the $7 billion—a sum equal to Maryland's budget—that Hughes aide Johnnie Johnson originally had feared. Depositors were repaid their principals in full, but many had to wait until 1989 for the final installment. In the meantime, all lost interest on the money.

Even so, it was better than 1960. A Maryland savings and loan crisis then had bilked some forty-six thousand depositors of as much as seventy cents for every dollar deposited. Maryland's speaker of the House of Delegates, A. Gordon Boone, went to jail and two U.S. congressmen were convicted for obstructing a federal investigation into the mess. After 1960 the state's system for regulating S&Ls was revamped with the promise that no thrift crisis would recur. This was the system in place when Old Court collapsed.

Attorney General Sachs was widely condemned by the industry and even by some Hughes officials for his decision to tell the public not only that the state had found evidence of criminal wrongdoing but that it was going to do something about it. Looking back, Sachs remarks that "all the arguments that say, 'Well, you don't recklessly make moves because the financial markets are sensitive'—of course, that's all true. But it doesn't gainsay any of that to say that when you see a cesspool, you should try to clean it up." The special investigator of the state's crisis concluded that while Sachs may have sparked a few runs in the short run, he saved taxpayers millions of dollars over the long haul. Voters didn't see it that way. Sachs lost his bid for governor in the fall of 1986.

4

Moral Hazard and the
Slippery Slope

How did Maryland, a state with a relatively robust economy despite its history of sordid and corrupt politicians, incur a thrift catastrophe twice in twenty-five years?

To start, S&Ls exerted too much control over industry oversight. "The state legislature consistently enacted legislation created by industry-dominated boards or commissions and often bowed to the influence of special interest groups representing the savings and loan industry," state investigators of the 1985 crisis concluded. In a reorganization bill of 1980, for example, which revamped the entire savings and loan regulatory framework, the ability of the industry to operate under looser rules received more favorable attention than did the safety of depositors.

That was no surprise. The commission that drafted the 1980 legislation was chaired by the secretary of the thrift industry lobby association and was dominated by thrift executives.

On top of inadequate regulation came a series of economic changes that the thrift industry was ill prepared to meet.

In the late 1970s thrifts blamed soaring interest rates for their sagging profits and for their inability to compete against full-service banks and brokerage firms. They complained about restraints on what they could pay to lure depositors and on investment restrictions. By the early 1980s Maryland's thrift executives had used the high interest rates of the marketplace and the

31

deregulation-minded policies of the Reagan era to persuade Maryland's legislature to give them greater freedom to run their business. As state-chartered thrifts, they argued, they could not compete unless deregulated along the lines of federally chartered institutions. From 1980 to 1982 federally chartered thrifts, backed by the Federal Savings and Loan Insurance Corporation (FSLIC), were given a green light to expand out of their traditional focus on home lending into new areas such as commercial lending.

Unless state-chartered thrifts had advantages over their federally chartered competitors, owners might be tempted to switch to a federal charter. That would leave state thrift regulators with little to do. Thus state regulators joined the thrift industry to lobby elected officials in Annapolis. Maryland legislators, like state officials across the country, were persuaded to keep the state's thrift statutes one step ahead of federal laws.

Many S&L executives viewed Maryland's new law as a government-insured license to gamble. The Maryland government, not the thrifts, would have to pick up the pieces and pay off depositors if things went wrong. Suddenly thrifts could invest in everything from shopping centers to high rises—not only by making loans to others but by actually taking an ownership position in such projects. At the same time, because of deposit insurance, consumers assumed they didn't have to watch over a thrift's shoulder because the government was doing it. Market discipline went out the window, replaced in theory by government oversight.

The result was a phenomenon economists call the moral hazard: If an S&L's gambles paid off, its owners won big. If it lost the gambles, taxpayers picked up the tab. Either way executives such as Levitt could not lose. There was no incentive—from the threat of losing either their own or customers' money—to be conservative. To the contrary, the more an S&L operator lost, the greater his incentive to take even riskier chances. This aspect of the moral hazard is sometimes called the slippery slope.

When Maryland's elected officials softened laws governing the industry, they failed to recognize what many regulators have come to recognize as a central truth: When rules are relaxed, oversight must be strengthened. Deregulation requires more cops.

Levitt, for example, strayed not only far from home lending but also far from common sense. He used Old Court deposits to buy lots in New York on which to build Jiffy Lube franchises—sites unseen. He relied solely on telephone descriptions from an Old Court employee in New York. "When we interviewed the man, he said he thought it was like money raining down," says Governor Hughes. "He told us, 'I'd just call up over the phone and say, "Look, I've got a good site here and it's gonna cost a half a million dollars," and the next day there'd be half a million dollars on my desk.'"

The Maryland thrift industry's hold on a minimal regulatory structure was such that in effect, no government checks operated on Levitt and others like him. The deposit insurance fund, though regulated by the state, was financed by member thrifts. Insurance fund chief Hogg therefore viewed himself as working for the industry, not the public. As problems developed, he spent his time lobbying government officials to keep the trouble quiet. Charlie Brown, the chief state regulator, was viewed by Governor Hughes and other officials as someone who acted as a cheerleader for the industry rather than for consumers. His efforts to discipline the industry were so soft in the view of his colleagues as to draw comparison to his comic strip namesake.

Says Sachs: "We were being told every time an investigator went to call on somebody, every time a subpoena went out for documents, the word would come back, 'You can't do this. You're going to cause a panic.' It was clear to us that if someone had created a panic two years before or four years before or five years before, the world would have been better off."

Maryland's special investigator's report for the governor winnowed to three the major factors leading to the state's crisis: "A total absence of regulation of savings and loan associations; individuals in the industry who took advantage of that absence of regulation to expropriate depositors' money for their own use; and a hopelessly flawed system which permitted the industry to make and enforce its own rules."

The state-regulated insurance fund was "totally dominated by the savings and loan industry and was obsessed with protecting the industry rather than protecting the safety of the deposits." The state regulator "failed to carry out regulatory responsibilities to control this conduct because he too saw himself as a protector of the industry.

"Almost without exception [the state regulator] took no action, paralyzed by the fear that regulatory sanctions of any major association would result in publicity that would denude the industry he felt bound to protect, leading to a loss of public confidence and the industry's demise.

"These activities were frequently facilitated by association lawyers, accountants and appraisers." For example, the respected eighty-seven-year-old Baltimore law firm of Venable, Baetjer & Howard represented both Maryland's deposit insurance fund and many of the state's thrifts. The law firm advised the insurance fund on rules and regulations even as it advised thrifts that were violating them. The conflict of interest that arose was obvious, though the law firm claimed it kept the interests of the funds and the S&Ls separate. In 1987 Venable, Baetjer & Howard agreed to pay the state of Maryland $27 million, settling a $450 million lawsuit claiming that malpractice and conflicts of interest by the firm had helped spark the thrift crisis. In agreeing to the settlement, the firm denied any wrongdoing and said it was merely trying to avoid lengthy and costly litigation.

In the months immediately following the fall of Old Court in early 1985, federal thrift regulators would turn up their noses at their state counterparts like Hogg and Brown. No federally insured institution would be allowed to fall into the sort of disarray found at the state-chartered thrifts and the fund that insured them, they claimed. Maryland regulators recall these condescending remarks with bitterness. Some persistent rumors even pin the less-than-helpful attitude of some federal thrift regulators on a streak of anti-Semitism. Levitt and many other notable crooks in the state's scandal happen to be Jewish. While the rumors are impossible to confirm or to refute, they pop up again and again in conversations with Maryland officials. As it turned out, Old Court, Community, and Ridgeway were not anomalies. Riddled with crooks, speculators, and incompetent employees of many ethnic and religious backgrounds—including a preponderance of white Anglo-Saxons—they were typical of the problems that plagued the industry during the 1980s.

The report to Governor Hughes credits many for creating the crisis, saying, "It is a history without heroes." Jeffrey Levitt made the same point on the humid summer day when he pleaded for a lenient sentence. "I was surrounded by attorneys and regulators," he told the judge. "Nobody questioned it." Today former Maryland officials like Hughes reflect on the state's crisis without embarrassment or regret. In light of what followed, they chuckle at the new meaning the state's thrift crisis gives to Maryland's tourism slogan, "America in Miniature."

President Reagan's March 1985 statement reassuring the nation that Ohio's S&L problems were unique remained his only public utterance on the thrift crisis during eight years in the White House.

Part II

IT'S A WONDERFUL LIFE

The story of the building and loan . . . is a story of self-help, of democracy, of an institution attuned to the weekly wages of the masses. In the words of one of our leaders . . . "the history of building and loan is not a record of accumulated personal wealth nor political power nor large affairs. Through a century, no man has ever accumulated a fortune in the business. Thousands have served as officers and directors through a whole generation without financial reward. They have made a record of self-sacrifice and devotion to a high ideal."

—From H. Morton Bodfish's preface to History of the Building and Loan, *published in 1931 by the United States Building and Loan League*

5

"The American Home: The Safeguard of American Liberties"

Before Jeffrey Levitt and scores like him gained notoriety, America's most famous savings and loan executive was George Bailey, who, with his uncle Billy, ran the Bailey Brothers Building and Loan in Bedford Falls. Bailey steered the tiny thrift through the troubled years of the Great Depression and saved it from the grasp of the town's commercial banker, an evil and heartless man who forever hoped the thrift would die.

Bailey ran the Bedford Falls thrift the old-fashioned way: He took the money customers deposited and lent it to home buyers. Over the years Bailey Brothers financed almost all of the middle- and working-class houses in Bedford Falls.

One day Bailey faced a run on his thrift. A crowd of worried customers demanded their money. Runs on small institutions were common in the 1920s and early 1930s; there was no federal safety net, either from the Federal Reserve or from deposit insurance.

"You're thinking of this place all wrong, as if I had the money back in a safe," Bailey frantically told the angry crowd that had lined up to empty their savings accounts. "The money's not here. Why, your money's in Joe's house . . . and a hundred others. You're lending them the money to build and then they're going to pay it back to you." Bailey, who had been on his way out of town minutes earlier to begin his honeymoon, took the $2,000 he had saved for the trip and used it to provide the cash for the minority of customers who remained unconvinced. The tactic worked. The thrift stayed open, averting a panic that would have shut it down and left Bedford Falls in the clutches of its commercial banker.

Disaster struck a second time, however, a few years later on Christmas Eve, when absentminded Uncle Billy misplaced all of Bailey Brothers Building and Loan's cash. A thrift examiner suspected fraud. The possibility of disgrace and jail loomed. This time depositors came to the rescue. Thankful for Bailey's good works through the years in providing home loans to the community, they took up a collection to make good the loss. Bailey was saved. Even the examiner, moved by the loyalty of Bailey Brothers' customers, made a donation. It was the nation's first S&L bailout.

George Bailey sounds too good to be true. And he was, of course, being a character played by James Stewart in Frank Capra's film *It's a Wonderful Life*. But even so, there really were some George Baileys when Capra made his film in 1947, and S&L executives have lovingly cultivated the George Bailey image ever since.

Like all bankers, thrifts act as middlemen, matching people who have excess cash with those who need to borrow. Matching savings and borrowers began centuries ago, when medieval bankers entrusted with gold realized that they could lend some of it out at a profit before the owner would want it back. Credit systems hastened economic development. The more efficient the match, the more quickly an economy grew.

In this country's early years, banks followed the practice in England by lending money for short periods and generally shunning borrowers who wanted long-term loans, such as those seeking mortgages for houses. The idea was that banks needed the ability to convert their loans and other assets into cash quickly so as to meet withdrawals from short-term deposit accounts, generally held by businesses. As a result, commercial banks in the nineteenth century and in most of the twentieth made comparatively few home loans. (Not until the 1960s, when commercial banks began to lose business clients to securities firms, did they focus on consumer lending, from home loans to credit cards.)

That left the home loan market to another English creation, a specialty bank called a friendly society or building and loan, the forerunner of today's savings and loan, or thrift. (These British institutions had not been without problems. Banks established specifically to attract savings from the common man were so vulnerable to owner-operator embezzlement that Parliament established a special committee in the nineteenth century to investigate the problem.)

The first S&L in the United States was formed during Andrew Jackson's presidency. It was the Oxford Provident Building Association, founded in 1831 in Frankford, Pennsylvania, near Philadelphia, by a group of textile workers who wished to pool their money to help one another buy homes. Depositors owned and operated such early building and loans, and the codes of conduct were strict. Oxford's bylaws, for example, included the right to fine the association's treasurer fifty cents for every board meeting he missed. During the hundred years after Oxford's founding, scores of similar institutions sprang up, invariably with high hopes for giving regular working people a chance to buy into the good life. In 1869 a 109-page book entitled *Workingman's Way to Wealth* described in the most enthusiastic of terms building and loans and how to use them. An article in *Scribner's Magazine* in 1876 entitled "A Hundred Thousand Homes: How They Are Paid For" included a typical building and loan advertisement:

> FOURTH OF JULY! INDEPENDENCE DAY! Young man and Woman, stop and reflect! The money you fritter away uselessly will make you independent. Today sign the magna charter of your independence, and, like our forefathers, in about eight years you will, in a great degree, be independent by saving only thirty-three cents each day. In that time you will realize $2,000, or have a home and be independent of the landlord. Let this, indeed, be your day of independence, by subscribing for shares in the new series, now issued, in the State Mutual Savings Fund, Loan and Building Association.

Some thrifts lent only to people with money on deposit in the institution, making borrowers and lenders one and the same. Others lent to anyone who was creditworthy. Most were started by groups of ethnic immigrants, such as newly arrived Germans or Italians. The new arrivals realized that while few among them could afford a home by himself, if they pooled money there would be enough for a few people at a time to borrow and build. As the loans were repaid and savings deposits increased, the next person could have his turn. Over time, thrifts grew to the point where lender and borrower might not know each other, but like the customers of the Bailey Brothers, they invariably lived within the same community.

Thrifts early developed a rudimentary secondary market for home loans. A so-called primary mortgage market exists when a consumer and home loan banker shake hands on a loan. Once an S&L makes the loan, however, it may want to sell it to recover cash that can be lent out on another home loan, perhaps at a greater profit as interest rates rise. The reselling of the loan is called the secondary market because it is once removed from the original loan.

Decades ago the secondary market worked like this: A thrift would find itself holding too much cash relative to home loans while another thrift in the same neighborhood or close by would have the opposite problem; it held too many loans and too little cash. The two would agree to swap assets. The cash-poor institution would sell its loans at a discount to raise money and the cash-rich institution would snap up the bargain-priced loans.

As more politically sophisticated businessmen entered the thrift business at the turn of the century, a subtle change ensued. They soon realized that the image of S&Ls as institutions vital to the nation's well-being could pay off in favorable treatment by the government. These executives understood how to couple a unified voice in Washington and state capitals with the political clout of bankers selling home loans.

The precursor of today's largest thrift lobby group, the U.S. League of Savings Institutions, was created in 1892 as the U.S. League of Local Building and Loan Associations. At its first convention in Chicago in June 1893, the league's members adopted the motto "The American Home: The Safeguard of American Liberties" as championed by the league's founder and first president, Seymour Dexter of New York. (The slogan appeared on the organization's letterhead until 1992, when the group changed its name, in part to try to improve its image.)

Dexter was a master of the patriotic homily. Decrying the "American citizen that will sell his vote or betray a public trust, or seek to induce another to do so," he once said that his "idea of a board of directors is one that keeps on meeting, week after week, for nothing save the gratification felt down in their own hearts that they were helping to make home-owners and good citizens. . . . It is a firm conviction with me that the future of the Republic depends upon the question whether we can make this nation a nation of home-owners or not."

Dexter went on a quest to find a rendering of the ideal American home. According to the *Omaha Bee* in August 1897, the drawing he chose from many submitted by various artists "represents a comfortable modern home surrounded by a large lawn in which children are at play. In front of the home is seen a mother and baby carriage, and a little daughter running to greet her approaching father. In the distance, half concealed by the foliage, is a picture of a New England school house, a square, two-story building, with its typical belfry. In front is the stars and stripes floating from a flag staff. The spire of a church rises in the distance, and in the background is a collection of houses, forming a characteristic village scene."

When the time came to lobby for government subsidies for S&Ls, however, Dexter and his successors had a more hard-boiled view of life. The league fought its first important battle shortly after its founding, when it took on the relatively new national thrifts that—in contrast with the community institutions that belonged to the league—took deposits from all over the country via mail; these nationals operated far-flung branch networks across state lines. The league argued that the business practice of nationals was unfair to community S&Ls because it brought competition from outside the region. Further, in the league's view, nationals were unsafe; they defeated the serve-the-community purpose of thrifts and thus enticed executives more interested in lining their own pockets than in serving local financial needs.

Never mind that the traditional local thrift had its own problems. The savings institution model was not all that thrift executives imported from England. Some of the fraud and incompetence associated with the English industry came, too. While local thrifts generally increased numerically in the second half of the nineteenth century, their ranks fell from 1897 to 1902, mostly because of failures in Chicago, St. Louis, and Cincinnati that league officials at the time blamed entirely on "extravagant, dishonest and incompetent management."

The league secretary reported to members at the time: "Many associations had recklessly borrowed large sums of money without authority of law, had hypothecated their securities as collateral with banks and trust companies, overvalued the real estate upon which they had made advances and during the hard times were compelled to acquire ownership. . . ." Still, savings institutions with problems represented a small percentage of the traditional industry, the league argued.

The credit panic of 1893, when several nationals fell into financial difficulty, seemed to confirm the league's arguments. The league pointed to the few nationals run by swindlers to argue that all nationals should be shut down; consumers could not tell the difference between well-run state thrifts and sham national institutions. The argument persuaded many state lawmakers, who banned nationals from their states. The five thousand or so state-chartered savings institutions were thus spared the competition. Furthermore, most states left thrift oversight to the industry's local lobby group, usually a state chapter of the league, an arrangement that gave the industry nearly complete say over its own regulation.

Despite some temporary dips, the number of thrifts grew steadily, reaching an all-time high of 12,500 in 1925. The number of commercial banks had peaked five years earlier at more than 30,000. Then came the crash of 1929, the Great Depression, and an onslaught of bank failures that led President Franklin D. Roosevelt to declare a national bank holiday in March 1933, just days after his inauguration. At first many thrifts, which offered long-term savings accounts, avoided the runs that plagued commercial banks. But they did experience large and steady withdrawals as consumers turned to their savings to maintain buying power during the economic downturn.

More than seventeen hundred thrifts failed during the Great Depression. Depositors lost $200 million, about a third of the value of their deposits. Unable to meet burgeoning demands for withdrawals, many otherwise healthy thrifts simply froze their depositors' accounts in place. Fearing loss of their savings and desperate for cash, many customers sold their passbooks at a loss on the black market.

The S&L failures and drawdown in savings accounts left fewer and fewer dollars available for home loans. An alarmed Congress and Presidents Herbert Hoover and Franklin Delano Roosevelt gave the S&L industry several pieces of legislation designed to maintain the flow of funds for housing. Not that the two presidents had the same goals in mind. Both White Houses worked with Congress to create new federal agencies devoted to housing. But ironically, the Republican, Hoover, representing the party of competition and big business, opted to favor S&L special interests over competition—all in the name of promoting homeownership. The Democrat, Roosevelt, representing the party dedicated to helping the little guy, chose to foster competition in housing finance. FDR had some luck translating his view into law. Hoover, the league, and congressmen sympathetic to the industry had more, crafting a system that regulated thrifts for the next fifty-six years—until a successor Republican, George Bush, had to dismantle and then reform it.

To enhance the thrift industry's access to funds from Wall Street investors, Hoover in 1932 signed a bill to create the Federal Home Loan Bank System, which included twelve regional Federal Home Loan Banks and, for oversight, the Federal Home Loan Bank Board in Washington. The regional Home Loan Banks (known derisively during Roosevelt's tenure as Hoover creations) borrowed money at cheap government rates and lent the money to thrifts at below-market rates. Thrifts were supposed to pass the savings on to customers.

Congress intended the regional banks to subsidize healthy thrifts during periods when the thrifts found it hard to attract new deposits. They were designed to insure that thrifts had cash for home loans during good times and bad. The regional government banks were never intended to act as lenders of last resort to prop up corrupt, poorly run, or bankrupt savings and loans the government decided it could not afford to close.

Getting federal deposit insurance—at first opposed by the league—wasn't as easy. Dozens of attempts had been made to legislate a federal deposit insurance fund from the late 1800s through the early 1900s. None had passed. Congress, however, had consistently endorsed two fundamental principles in the legislation that so far had failed to become law: The industry should pay premiums for insurance, and the government, as the guarantor, should act as a watchdog for the public. It fell to Hoover's successor, FDR, to sign into law the bill creating federal deposit insurance. Roosevelt initially had opposed the insurance program, predicting it would not work. But eventually he backed it, using it as a bargaining chip with the league to win support for other legislation he wanted but that had been opposed by the thrift industry.

In 1934 FDR approved the National Housing Act, creating the Federal Savings and Loan Insurance Corporation, generally known by the abbreviation FSLIC (pronounced "fizz-lick" by thrift insiders), as the arm of the bank board insuring savings accounts at thrifts up to $5,000. Based on Congress's earlier framework, the insurance program was a government-sponsored, government-run system funded by the industry through a federally collected fee, which was the same—a percentage of assets—for all thrifts. Commercial banks had been given deposit insurance provided through the Federal Deposit Insurance Corporation (FDIC) a year earlier.

The thrift industry breathed more easily. Deposit insurance was intended to stop runs or at least to curtail them. Specifically, deposit insurance was designed to put smaller institutions on an equal footing with the larger ones, which usually enjoyed greater public confidence and therefore greater stability. Often the confidence was justified. In times of trouble a wealthy bank owner could act as a combination lender of last resort and insurance fund by putting his own money at risk as a cushion against losses or as a reserve to pay out against in times of high withdrawals.

Smaller institutions, like the one portrayed in *It's a Wonderful Life,* often had no such line of credit to draw on during an emergency. Most of the runs that spurred the creation of federal deposit insurance occurred in rural areas, where banks and thrifts didn't have the name, clout, or public trust enjoyed by their big-city cousins.

Despite the obvious advantages of deposit insurance, a few early thrift executives understood a risky side effect, the moral hazard. One thrift executive noted a few years after the FSLIC was created:

> Deposit insurance plans have developed as a means of combating a universal lack of confidence in financial institutions which has adversely affected the sound banks otherwise able to survive the acute financial crisis . . . [but] insurance may tend to eliminate differences among associations. It may reduce the incentive for good management because, on the one hand, some institutions may become dependent upon insurance, and because, on the other hand, sound and efficiently staffed institutions may be penalized for the careless policy and poorly trained personnel of others. Further, the public may become indiscriminate in selecting the association with which it wishes to deal.

Roosevelt reluctantly had backed deposit insurance in exchange for the league's support of another part of the 1934 National Housing Act: the Federal Housing Administration. The FHA, a pet Roosevelt idea, was to provide federal insurance against default by low-income home loan borrowers and, in the process, evenly distribute the availability of home loans throughout the country. The threat of default had long discouraged insurance companies and commercial banks from becoming mortgage lenders in rural regions where other lenders were scarce, regions where, perhaps, there were few thrifts or where thrifts found it hard to garner deposits in sufficient quantities to service all the mortgage demand. Banks and insurance firms, reluctant to lend in unfamiliar territory, generally stuck to the region they knew around their headquarters. Often the familiar ground held an oversupply of lenders.

FHA loan guarantees greatly expanded the home-lending services of mortgage brokers—intermediaries matching home buyers with lenders of all types, be they thrifts, insurance companies, or banks—and thereby brought more lenders into the market. An insurance company in Connecticut might have extra cash to lend on home loans but little mortgage demand in the local market. At the same time home loan demand in Nebraska might exceed the resources of local thrifts. The Connecticut firm would gladly lend money in Nebraska if the federal government guaranteed the loans against default. That made it easier for mortgage brokers to roam the country matching up clients. Thrifts hated the FHA program; it might give insurance companies and other potential competitors an incentive to cut into their business. But their fears initially proved unfounded. FHA-backed loans didn't catch on. So in 1938 Roosevelt pushed through additional legislation to enhance their value. Over vociferous objection by the thrift industry, Congress created a quasi-government company called the Federal National Mortgage Corporation, better known today as Fannie Mae, to buy FHA loans from lenders, providing fresh cash for new FHA loans. Fannie Mae held on to the loans or sold them to other financial institutions. This established a small secondary market in home loans, one more sophisticated than any run by the thrift industry. Thrifts acting alone could buy and sell only loans that originated in their communities and even there had no organized way to match buyers with sellers. In contrast, originators of FHA-backed loans could buy or sell them to lenders across the country via Fannie Mae.

The league and its members protested that the FHA and Fannie Mae posed unfair competition for the savings and loan industry. Although thrifts were allowed to make FHA loans, they largely avoided them, saying FHA red tape was too cumbersome. Instead they stuck to traditional home loans and left the government-guaranteed loan business to the mortgage brokers.

———

Roosevelt pushed another piece of key thrift legislation in the early 1930s, creating a dual thrift system by empowering the bank board to charter and regulate federal savings and loans. These federally chartered thrifts—in many respects like the nationals the league had hounded out of business thirty years earlier—were to be set up in markets underserved by state institutions. Like the nationals, these federally chartered S&Ls could take deposits by mail. But otherwise the early federals acted just like state-chartered S&Ls: They stuck to home lending.

The dual system created a double standard. For years the bank board was stingy in granting new federal charters. Applicants were required to show that new institutions were needed and would not create "undue injury" by way of competition to existing thrifts. Moreover, institutions licensed by the federal government through the bank board had to carry federal deposit insurance. Thrifts licensed by the state could choose federal or state insurance, although most state-chartered thrifts eventually elected to put the federal sticker on their doors. Even so, the state institutions still were regulated primarily by the state, not the federal government. As a result, in time federal taxpayers came to guarantee depositors against loss from lending practices prescribed by state, not federal, law. For decades this potential conflict between federal and state jurisdiction posed no problem. But beginning in the 1960s and snowballing in the 1980s, ambiguity in the dual regulatory system magnified the moral hazard. If abuses arose at the state level, the federal government, though obligated to bail out the state thrifts, could not change the law to correct lax state rules. The bank board's only recourse—to revoke deposit insurance—seemed a radical move, one regulators rarely undertook for fear of frightening consumers and igniting runs.

S&Ls had many friends during the 1930s but also some powerful enemies in the commercial banking industry. League officials, knowing they faced an uphill battle to win their legislative goals, adopted a public relations and lobbying strategy of embracing the patriotism Dexter so clearly and cleverly outlined years earlier. But they updated the patriotism to the times. During the Great Depression that meant using a line established by H. Morton Bodfish, the league's chief executive during the 1930s and detailed in *A Business Reborn: The Savings and Loan Story, 1930–1960,* a history of the S&L industry written and published by the lobby group: "Obviously the best way to get any legislation through Congress in 1932 was to show how it would help the victims of the Depression. People who were losing their homes were among the most easily dramatized of the unfortunates. So the possibility of the proposed new [Federal Home Loan] Bank System alleviating foreclosure problems was given decided emphasis."

45

During the Roaring Twenties real estate had bred speculation; credit flowed far too easily as the stock market soared. The market crash in 1929 ushered in a sober and bleaker decade. Business failures, particularly bank failures, grew. Joblessness rose. In popular culture the plight of the little man replaced the 1920s idolization of big business. Regard for commercial, full-service banks ebbed as more and more banks failed and took consumers down with them. Tales abounded during congressional testimony about the sordid involvement of banks with the stock market during the go-go days. It didn't help that banks lent primarily to businesses and not to consumers. As the depression wore on, S&L executives increasingly billed themselves as bankers to Main Street. And indeed, the thrifts themselves were relatively tiny: In 1935 the nation's 10,825 savings institutions had $16.9 billion in assets, while the nation's 15,488 commercial banks had $48.8 billion. Around that time the league estimated that of 4,000 members, only 125 had assets of $5 million or more. Thrifts emblazoned words like "Dime" and "Emigrant" on their doors, seeking to attract small, steady savers of the working and middle classes.

Although thrifts cultivated this little-guy image, their ambitions among politicians were anything but home-spun. "Savings and loan representatives maintained headquarters in some unpretentious suites in the Willard Hotel in Washington—a spot from which the dome of the United States Capitol is visible and from which the Capitol itself was less than 10 minutes ride. . . . The White House was only two blocks to the west. The comings and goings of savings and loan representatives from far and near, with assignments to see this person or that person of influence in the legislative or executive branch, were part of the fascinating pattern of those days," the league history of 1930–1960 says.

Several themes have prevailed in league ideology from its earliest days: First, subsidies and tax breaks provided by the government—that is, taxpayers—accrue naturally to an industry that plays a special role in the American Dream. Second, the government's responsibility is essentially to deliver these entitlements and then disappear, leaving the industry to run its affairs without interference. Third, the industry congratulates itself for winning almost everything it has wanted from Washington, including the creation of the Federal Home Loan Bank System, through savvy lobbying by the U.S. league. Several league-sponsored histories make it clear that the S&L industry always considered itself different from other industries and therefore deserving of special treatment. Winning politicians to that view, thrifts became hooked on special treatment.

Despite little support from Roosevelt and opposition from commercial bankers during the 1930s, "practically every plan or general proposal of the

League was adopted by the government in full or in modified form and thrown into the breach to stabilize the situation and prevent a sweeping collapse," according to one early member of the Federal Home Loan Bank Board.

For example, several members of Congress thought that oversight of the regional Home Loan Banks and oversight of nationally chartered thrifts ought to be divided. It was unwise, they argued, to entrust the same agency with the duty of both policing the industry and extending it credit. Agencies, like any bureaucracy, are self-perpetuating, the congressmen argued. Thrift regulators were unlikely to close S&Ls if they could quietly prop them up through a transfusion of cash. Separating duties would have checked such temptations.

But at the league's urging, the idea of separation was quashed, and the bank board system assumed its wide oversight charter. The industry, as a result, had only one agency to lobby on every issue. Such concentration pretty well assured the league an unusually strong influence over its federal regulators. "The far-reaching consequences of this decision need hardly be elaborated; most observers nowadays concede that it was well for the savings and loan business that the machinery was set up in this fashion," the league wrote in 1962. Commercial banks, by contrast, had three federal agencies regulating and providing insurance for them: the Comptroller of the Currency, the Federal Reserve Board, and the Federal Deposit Insurance Corporation. While this setup had its own problems, competition between the agencies provided a kind of checks and balances that at least prevented bankers from becoming overly influential with any one agency. No such constraint held back the league's political influence.

Insurance and federally subsidized borrowing from the twelve regional Federal Home Loan Banks were very good things for the thrift industry, but no better than a traditional S&L perquisite: From the late 1890s savings and loans were exempted from any excise or income tax. As a league history puts it, "Congress has recognized the distinct value of the building and loan associations to the community and to the nation in developing a sounder citizenship and has consistently given them special consideration on account of their benevolent and helpful purposes." This tax-exempt status was maintained until 1951, but even when some taxes were imposed on thrifts, the burden was lighter than on banks and other companies. The differential, while narrowed further over the years, continues.

Indeed, the league had established such political might that the Roosevelt administration was forced to hide its plans to increase the supply of housing during World War II by instituting a plan to coordinate national housing policy. Bickering during the early years of the war between thrifts and the providers of FHA loans had stunted housing growth. Roosevelt accordingly

47

created the National Housing Agency on February 24, 1942, placing all hous-
ing-related agencies, including the bank board, under one roof. Roosevelt
aides crafted the legislation creating the new agency in secret, according to
Hilbert Fefferman, one of its architects, to avoid near-certain opposition by
the league. Not surprisingly, the league bristled at the final proposal, display-
ing extreme unhappiness at having the federal S&L regulatory agency answer to officials other than its own. "[The] superimposing of the National
Housing Agency upon all the [bank board's] operations resulted in genuine
alarm at 101 Indiana Avenue, headquarters of the Board. Savings and loan
leaders were shocked and apprehensive and they protested," says the
league's history of the period, which goes on:

> The Federal Home Loan Bank Board was reduced by this new consolida-
> tion to a role of minor importance in Washington and was made to march in
> harness with two other programs which were far from sympathetic to its
> objectives. One of its new teammates, the FHA, was still regarded principally
> as the sponsor of mortgage lending institutions in competition with savings
> and loans.
>
> The other teammate, the public housing program, was aggressively work-
> ing for greater use of public funds for increasing sectors of the residential
> building of the nation—an objective which could never be compatible with
> the basic reason for the existence of savings and loans associations.

Shortly after the war the league got the bank board moved out from under
the wartime agency and back into its traditional interaction with the thrift
industry it regulated. "The achievement in 1955 of independent status for the
Federal Home Loan Bank Board was a tribute to the perseverance of savings
and loan leaders," the league history states with pride. "Independence for the
Board had been the prime savings and loan legislative goal for many years."

In return for its privileges, S&Ls were allowed to sell only one product: home
loans. And their clients weren't expected to be the Rockefellers. This was the
pivotal idea behind the thrifts' social contract. Congress would give special
breaks to a private industry so that it could promote homeownership for the
masses.

Thus during the 1930s was set into law the dual system of banks that until
then had existed largely through market mechanisms. One set of institutions—savings and loan banks—catered to homeowners, and the other—full-
service banks—catered to business and consumers seeking shorter-term
credit.

In terms of their public image S&Ls made the most of their near monopoly.
In the grandiose terms of an early thrift executive, as told to league chief

Bodfish, "the biological family became the legal family and this form of organization has apparently led to the greatest industry, foresight, and general well-being, as contrasted to other forms of organization, such as communal promiscuity, clans, or the patriarchal family which long were the dominant forms. . . . We have here in the monogamous family and in private property deep-rooted in the heritage of the race the basis for the future of the building and loan. . . . The building and loan . . . therefore rests securely upon the very cornerstone of our social order."

During the same period, a third set of financial institutions was cordoned off by law in reaction to the market crash. Investment banks, in business to raise money in the stock and bond markets, were cut off from the commercial banking industry and given a separate regulator, the Securities and Exchange Commission. Interestingly, S&Ls were not prohibited by federal law from engaging in investment banking, as were commercial banks, but were kept out of such activities by regulations at the state and federal level— regulations that could be easily withdrawn by regulators without congressional consent.

6

The Golden Age

Between 1925 and 1945 the number of thrifts fell from a peak of roughly 12,500 to about 6,700. In the same period the number of banks fell from about 30,000 to 14,000. The decline reflected the large number of institutions that failed after the crash and during the depression and the mergers that ensued as the turmoil tapered off, the economy stabilized, and banks and thrifts became more conservative in their business strategies.

Then good times reigned. For the next twenty years, beginning with a veteran-driven home-buying boom at the end of World War II, the thrift industry prospered. Prospering with it was Dexter's idealized notion of the community savings and loan as occupying a special niche in the social order.

Even during this "golden period," however, small clouds hinted at dangerous weaknesses in the thrift regulatory system. In the early 1940s regulators in Washington grew wary of the loans some thrifts in the Los Angeles region were making, particularly loans on tract housing. The thrifts chaffed at the second-guessing from Washington and offered a nominee to become president of the Federal Home Loan Bank of Los Angeles who they believed would be sympathetic to their view. The presidents of the twelve regional banks, the government's chief supervisory agents in the field, were nominated by a board of directors made up primarily of thrift executives from the region; the bank board in Washington had to approve the choice, though traditionally the approval amounted to a rubber-stamping. But in the Los Angeles case the bank board rejected the nomination and picked its own man.

Adding insult to injury, the bank board in 1945 took the unprecedented step of merging the regional bank in Los Angeles into the regional bank in Portland and then moving the institution to San Francisco. In effect, the Los Angeles bank was merged out of existence. "California thrifts were really up in arms now," recalls William McKenna, a Los Angeles-based thrift lawyer who represented the federal government during the controversy. The S&Ls believed, correctly, that moving the regulator out of town would reduce their influence. That, of course, was the objective of the bank board, at the time still under the wing of the National Housing Agency.

Then bank board officials took over the Long Beach Federal Savings and Loan Association, booting out its president, Thomas Gregory, citing unsafe lending practices. Gregory, who wielded considerable clout with the congressional delegation from California, was controversial even within the S&L industry. According to McKenna, many thrift executives in Southern California agreed with Washington's assessment of Gregory. But those sentiments didn't mitigate the far stronger antipathy many of the executives had toward Washington. By and large the industry in Southern California applauded when Gregory sued the federal government and persuaded members of Congress to hold hearings on the affair in 1949 and 1950, during which the bank board got a thrashing from some of Gregory's political allies on Capitol Hill.

The first congressional hearing generally went in Gregory's favor. The second didn't exonerate the regulators completely—they still were taken to task by Gregory's friends—but lawmakers in general concluded that the bank board's actions in Southern California had been appropriate, according to McKenna. In 1956, a year after the bank board regained its independence, the agency ignored that conclusion and restored control of the Long Beach Savings and Loan to Gregory. But the wound festered between California and Washington over federal regulation. In 1960 the bank board seized Long Beach Savings a second time, sparking a third congressional hearing on the issue. By then tension finally had begun to ease as Southern California thrifts concentrated on a local housing boom. But the years of tension between California and Washington, D.C., have never been entirely forgotten in the industry. They were recalled by McKenna and others years later when the acts of a Southern California thrift named Lincoln again pitted regulators at the regional bank in California against those at the bank board in Washington.

Several serious outbreaks of fraud and speculation also marred the postwar boom. In the mid-1960s, according to Joseph Muldoon, an attorney who worked at the bank board at the time, the local mob had infiltrated the Chicago S&L industry and bilked it for easy money.

Fraudulent appraisals and payoffs were prevalent in the Cook County thrift world. Muldoon recalls reading an appraiser's report that valued a site with a shopping center at more than $2 million. Driving out to the site one cold winter day, Muldoon found an eighty-acre cornfield covered only by snow.

The state's looser oversight had bred the fraudulent activity, but the federal government ended up paying the cost of the mistake when the S&Ls had to be closed and depositors made whole.

Also clouding the bright picture the industry drew of itself were speculators. In the early 1960s in Nevada promoters took over several state-chartered thrifts and began building apartments despite a sluggish state business climate and housing demand. As apartments sat vacant, many of Nevada's thrifts drifted into insolvency. The federal government feared that a shutdown of the institutions would ripple next door into California, where many large thrifts also were feeling pinched as the industry raised rates in their clamor for deposits to feed a construction boom. So the bank board instead set up a "blue-ribbon" task force to steer the thrifts out of trouble while keeping them open. Nevada's thrift industry survived, but just barely and thanks to luck, not the blue-ribbon panel. The deus ex machina arrived when an economic upturn, fueled in large measure by Howard Hughes, hit Las Vegas. The ensuing boom stimulated a housing demand, saving the state's S&Ls.

About the same time, California officials were so lenient in granting S&L charters that the state found itself with an overpopulation of thrifts. It was not, as the industry likes to say, just because California was home to the largest housing demand in the country. Several big California thrifts failed during the 1960s, largely because of mismanagement, but the state remained at the center of power for the thrift industry, just as New York ruled commercial banking.

In 1967 Robert Gene ("Bobby") Baker, who had been secretary to Lyndon Johnson when he was Senate majority leader, was convicted of tax evasion, theft, and conspiracy to defraud the government in connection with $99,600 that he had received from California S&L executives five years earlier. The government claimed Baker was transporting stolen money. The thrift executives claimed they gave the money to Baker to make campaign contributions. According to Baker and his attorney, Edward Bennett Williams, the money was intended for Senator Robert Kerr, a millionaire oilman and Democrat from Oklahoma, after the senator had helped the thrift industry kill a proposed tax amendment.

Baker told the tale in his 1978 book *Wheeling and Dealing: Confessions of the Capitol Hill Operator,* describing himself as the go-between arranging a payment of $400,000 from the league to Senator Kerr in exchange for the lawmaker's promise to kill the amendment, which would have cost the thrift industry about $43 million a year. According to Baker, the deal was arranged by the league's chief lobbyist, Glenn Troop, at the behest of top thrift executives from California. Troop and Baker, the closest of friends, socialized and vacationed together. Baker even dedicated his book to Troop, among others.

"Bobby, we'll do anything to kill that bill. Anything!" Baker said Troop pleaded over lunch.

Baker checked with Kerr and then told Troop the senator's price. Troop's response: "Tell your man he's got a deal." But according to Baker, the industry didn't keep its end of the bargain. Later, when Kerr killed the bill, Troop told Baker that the industry could pony up just $200,000, and that only in installments.

"Bobby, I'm embarrassed," Baker quoted Troop as saying. "My people say they can't come up with more than $200,000 in hidden cash without robbing their own companies and they aren't about to do that. . . . We're not trying to be cute or embarrass you; it just can't be done. Here's what we can do: $100,000 now, or as soon as we can get the cash together. Plus another $100,000 in 1964, and that's it."

Senator Kerr didn't live to see all the money; he died a year before the second payment was due. Baker concludes his chapter on the incident with a rueful note. While thrift executives denied the allegations, he said, "I would go to jail over that money."

Troop fared far better. He continued as a lobbyist and, when he died in 1982, received a rare honor for someone in his profession: Members of Congress and staff eulogized him in a crowded, standing room only Senate caucus room.

Effective on the Hill, the league's hold on the bank board also remained as strong as ever. Just how thoroughly the industry controlled agency policy was evident to Stephen McSpadden, now an attorney on the House Committee on Government Operations. In 1970 he spent one summer during law school interning at the bank board. McSpadden worked on one project, preparing the bank board's contribution to a HUD guide telling small businesses and minorities what housing finance programs were available at thrifts, banks, and government agencies. After he returned to school, McSpadden learned that his material had been printed up with the rest of the booklet. But when league officials saw it, they hit the ceiling. The industry did not want to make it easy for consumers to know the ABCs of what the law required thrifts to offer in the way of special loans to communities and minorities, an area most thrift executives considered unprofitable. The bank board agreed to delete its entry and sent agency personnel to tear the offending pages one by one from each booklet before HUD distributed them to the public.

Despite such lapses, large and small, these were the industry's golden years, a time when long-term interest rates remained higher than short-term rates. This disparity produced what was called the 3-6-3 rule: Pay 3 percent interest on deposits; charge 6 percent interest on loans; leave the office to play golf at 3:00 P.M.

Thrift executives, it seemed, just couldn't lose.

Other economic factors were kind, too. Inflation was low enough to keep home buyers buying but high enough to mask any mistakes S&L executives might have made by overvaluing the property used as collateral for the loans. For example, if a thrift lent $100,000 for a house really worth only $80,000, it would lose money if a borrower defaulted, forcing repossession and resale of the house. It would lose money, that is, unless inflation rose fast enough to inflate the value of the house to $100,000 before the S&L stepped in. More often than not, S&Ls could ride their mistakes into profits, thanks to a mild but steady rise in the cost of living.

Deposit insurance kept pace. To keep up with inflation, it was raised in 1950 to $10,000, in 1966 to $15,000, in 1969 to $20,000, and in 1974 to $40,000. There had been an attempt in the 1950s to cut up the bank board system by separating the deposit insurance function from the chartering and regulatory agency, but largely through the efforts of the league, the effort died.

This was the good life, for the country and the bankers. Problems in Illinois and out West were aberrations, soon to disappear. Dexter would have been pleased. America truly had become a nation of homeowners. In the 1920s, 43 percent of all homes were owned by their occupants. By the mid-1970s the portion had risen to nearly 65 percent. The thrift industry's role in this rise had been enormous. Before 1920 the industry held less than 20 percent of all home loans by dollar amount. By the 1960s and 1970s that amount had doubled.

7

The Social Contract Unravels

For seventy-five years thrift executives profited wagering they could
make more on mortgages than they paid on savings accounts—until the
middle of the 1960s, when subtle economic winds began to shift. The first
sign of this change was a breakdown of the lines separating different kinds of
banking institutions. Until the 1960s commercial banks and savings and
loans had not competed head to head; they had coexisted peacefully, each
offering different advantages to depositors. From 1933 to 1966 banking
regulators had imposed a ceiling on the interest that commercial banks, but
not thrifts, could pay depositors. The rule, called Regulation Q, intended to
dull competition among commercial banks, was an outgrowth of the depression. Cutthroat competition in the 1920s was widely believed to have contributed to the many bank failures of the 1930s. Banks, it was thought, had paid
too much interest in a desperate attempt to attract deposits and then found
they could not make enough on loans to pay the promised yield to consumers.

Regulation Q gave thrifts a leg up on commercial banks in the interest
game. To attract customers and give them a reason to save with an S&L,
thrifts for years gladly paid a quarter to half a percentage point more than
commercial banks. It made up for the thrifts' inability to offer checking accounts.

For years this carefully balanced system worked, providing enough customers for everybody. Some savers put their money in banks at the lower

interest rate because it was convenient to save at the institution where they had a checking account. Others preferred to take advantage of the higher rates thrifts offered. As long as inflation was low and interest rates stable, as they were prior to the 1960s, the incremental difference in earnings was not enough to induce many customers to switch.

All this amity came to an end in the 1960s, when inflation rose in response to increasing government spending. As thrift rates rose in tandem, commercial banks began bumping up against the interest rate ceilings of Regulation Q and seeking ways around it. Banks needed to lure more deposits that in turn could be invested in higher-yielding loans.

A credit crunch in the middle of the decade pushed interest rates high enough for consumers to become sensitive to differences between banks and thrifts. As millions switched to higher-paying accounts in savings and loans, banks screamed. Congress responded in 1966 by slapping Regulation Q on S&Ls as well, although it still allowed thrifts to offer a rate a quarter of a percentage point higher than commercial banks.

About this time some thrift executives began to seek government help in expanding their businesses out of their communities, where the flow of new deposits was sometimes too low to support the demand for new home loans or where housing demand was insufficient to absorb the thrifts' cash. Thrifts needed a way to tap into regions where the opposite problem might prevail. The twelve regional Home Loan Banks provided some relief to S&Ls, infusing cash with low-cost loans. But cash-short thrift executives wanted access to even cheaper supplies of money, and thrift executives with too much cash wanted a convenient way to invest in home loans outside their area. They began, in short, to pine for the very thing they had criticized years earlier: a government-sponsored corporation like Fannie Mae.

This was a turnabout for the league. Having fought the creation of Fannie Mae under the Roosevelt administration, it now asked Congress to provide it with a similar corporation. As with Fannie Mae, the idea would be to match cash-heavy S&Ls with loan-heavy S&Ls and thus create a formal secondary market where home loans could be bought and sold efficiently.

True to its charter, Fannie Mae was buying and selling only FHA-backed loans, not the conventional home loans that made up the bulk of thrift investments. Some in Congress suggested expanding Fannie Mae's charter by allowing it to buy and sell all types of home loans, but that logical policy didn't suit the league. It wanted a corporation controlled by the three-man Federal Home Loan Bank Board in Washington, the same board that supervised the regional Federal Home Loan Banks and the FSLIC. The industry's reasoning was simple: Gaining a corporation inside the bank board system would add to the league's political and economic clout.

In 1970 Congress granted the league's request, creating the Federal Home Loan Mortgage Corporation, affectionately known as Freddie Mac, to be run by the Federal Home Loan Bank Board. Freddie Mac would buy and sell conventional home loans from thrifts—and only thrifts.

In a seemingly contradictory move, however, Congress in the same legislation expanded Fannie Mae's charter beyond government-insured mortgages so that it could buy and sell any type of home loan. With a stroke of a pen, Congress established two governmental corporations with the same function, the major difference being that only thrifts could take advantage of Freddie Mac's services without paying a special surcharge. It is a testament to the league's political might that it could convince lawmakers to commit millions of dollars to duplicate efforts.

Like Fannie Mae, Freddie Mac bought home loans with federally subsidized money, cash that thrifts then lent to home buyers on mortgages that carried current and presumably better rates than the older home loans the S&Ls had booked when inflation was low. Freddie Mac worked just fine, but the economy wasn't cooperating. Inflation continued to climb during the 1970s, outpacing the relief that the regional banks, or Freddie Mac, or any other division of the Federal Home Loan Bank System could bring. A thrift, for example, holding a home loan yielding 6 percent would sell it to Freddie Mac for a discount, relend the proceeds from the sale for a home loan yielding 7 percent, only to find the market rate had risen to 8 percent. By 1979, when Volcker decided to use high rates to contain inflation, the situation had become critical. Market rates rose to double digits. Freddie Mae and Fannie Mae dampened the deleterious effect of rising rates but couldn't erase them.

Attempting to cope with rising interest rates during the 1960s and 1970s, thrifts lobbied Congress and regulators for permission to expand out of home loans and into shorter-term, more profitable investments.

In the years of generally stable rates, home loans had been a low-risk investment. Repayment was all but assured. Even when strapped, borrowers kept up with mortgage payments. But home loans presented a high risk indeed when rates were unstable. A thrift could not make money if it had to pay depositors ten cents on the dollar while earning only six cents in long-term mortgages booked years earlier.

In response to this squeeze, Congress in 1964 allowed S&Ls to venture out of real estate into college and other education loans. Eight years later, in a step that put thrifts in head-to-head competition with commercial banks, Massachusetts thrifts used a loophole in the banking laws to introduce an interest-bearing checking account called a negotiable order of withdrawal (NOW) account in an effort to attract short-term funds. Although customers were restricted to a few withdrawals a month from the account, the service proved so popular that Congress approved the accounts nationwide in 1980.

Thrift problems were compounded in the mid-1970s by the Arab oil embargo and the surge in inflation and interest rates that followed from it. Energy prices soared faster than the economy could absorb them, pulling along an inflation that shot into the double digits in the late 1970s and early 1980s. In 1981 the prime rate stood at a twentieth-century high—21.5 percent.

And while interest rates were high, fundamental changes took place in financial service marketing. Merrill Lynch and other Wall Street brokerage and securities firms started to hype mutual funds and money market accounts, which could offer customers a market rate of interest. Because the rates that banks and thrifts could pay were capped by Regulation Q, depositors pulled hundreds of billions of dollars out of the banking system and put it in the new accounts. For the first time, banks and thrifts faced competition from outside the banking business in the fight for deposits, and the brokerage firms were winning the battle.

Inflation, however, was only one of the engines that drove the revolution in financial services in the 1970s. The other was computer technology, which made the execution of sophisticated, complex transactions move with a speed and ease unimaginable only a few years earlier. Microchips enabled anyone with a desktop computer to enter the world of financial services, as buyer or seller. Companies found they could borrow money directly from each other for short periods, issuing IOUs known as commercial paper, instead of borrowing from a bank, and do so quickly and efficiently through computers. The commercial paper market sprang into being almost overnight. This was good news for business borrowers, who could raise money more cheaply without the help of a bank, but it was a disaster for bankers, who lost many of their best loan customers. In 1970 the commercial paper market totaled $35 billion in outstanding loans. By the mid-1980s it had increased nearly tenfold, to $330 billion.

Squeezed between the money markets luring their depositors and the commercial paper market taking away their loan customers, banks scrambled for new business and found themselves face-to-face with the savings and loan industry. Thanks to Fannie Mae, commercial banks no longer worried about the risk of getting stuck with low-yield, long-term home loans in periods when interest rates on deposits were rising—a worry that had kept banks away from the mortgage business for so long. At the same time the rise in the 1960s and 1970s of private mortgage insurance companies virtually eliminated the already low risk of home loan defaults. Thus it seemed to banks that the two main obstacles to home lending—interest rate swings and defaults—could be averted.

Banks entered the mortgage business with a vengeance, but not merely with an eye on home loans. They wanted to capture the entire consumer credit market. Mortgages would be the centerpiece of the strategy: Hook a consumer with a home loan and then sell that captive client everything from a Visa card to a revolving line of credit on his or her checking account. Banks also began to eye expansion into commercial real estate and into two areas from which they had been excluded by law—securities and insurance. And they were looking to expand geographically beyond state boundaries, where they had been penned by federal and state laws.

Computers helped enormously in this process. Without previous experience a New York bank easily could set up a securities division, with computers doing much of the work to assess risks in the new market. And it could easily set up a loan office in California that technically did not qualify as a bank under federal law because it didn't offer checking accounts. (Federal law that regulates companies that own banks defines a bank as an institution that both offers checking accounts and makes commercial loans.)

Banks were not alone in wanting to expand the list of financial products they could sell. Real estate companies, insurance and securities firms, even department stores longed to expand into every aspect of the financial market. Instead of having to bear the expense of setting up a new office or of having to hire consultants, a company could sell insurance or real estate or make business loans merely by installing a desktop computer and proper software.

Even companies that were not traditionally in the finance business entered the arena aggressively. Sears, Roebuck hoped to offer consumers everything from socks to stocks. The Ford Motor Company wanted to sell everything from Mustangs to car and home loans. Financial services were becoming the fad of the 1980s, as high technology had been the fad of the 1970s.

In short, inflation and technology created de facto deregulation, blurring the once-clear distinctions among banks, thrifts, and other financial institutions and rendering many federal banking laws ineffective. That inevitably led to a call for the formal tearing down of walls erected in response to the crash of 1929.

As banks ventured more aggressively into mortgage lending and thrifts increasingly sought special treatment to remain afloat, some regulators and industry leaders began to think and speak about an old question with renewed appeal: Was there any longer a need for a federally subsidized housing finance industry? Had market innovations made the thrift industry an anachronism?

8

Government Sunshine, Hot Money

So matters stood in 1979. Hundreds of thrifts, humming a happy tune, were nonetheless looking into an abyss, whether they knew it or not.

As inflation raged out of control in 1979, Fed Chairman Volcker, charged with restoring order to financial markets, picked higher interest rates as his weapon of choice. The nation's central banker, Volcker controlled a faucet that could lower or raise the amount of money in the system, a process that simultaneously helped set the price of money. No one imagined that Volcker's strategy would push interest rates as high as 21 percent (as it did in 1981), but many thrift executives understood the devastating effect his policy would have on their business. Their worst fears came true, and then some.

Higher interest rates at the end of the 1970s caused a flight by depositors out of banks and thrifts, now prisoners of the interest rate caps designed to save them from competition for deposits. The once-stabilizing effect of Regulation Q now worked in reverse. Savers flocked to put their money into unregulated and uninsured but higher-yielding money market and mutual fund accounts. These accounts, which held only $3 billion in 1977, jumped to $50 billion in 1979, to $100 billion in 1980, to $200 billion in 1981, and to $233 billion in 1982, when the amounts began to taper off with inflation. Banks and thrifts watched with alarm as their deposits melted away. What could be done? One palliative, the thrifts thought, would be to cap the rates allowed by the unregulated accounts, in effect extending Regulation Q to portions of the securities industry. This was a course the thrifts urged on the regulators and on Congress.

Instead Congress took a giant step in another direction, toward financial services deregulation, a concept gaining currency even before Ronald Reagan recaptured the White House for the Republicans. Several blue-ribbon commissions and government studies in the 1960s and 1970s had reached the conclusion that interest rate caps should be eliminated and thrifts given broader freedom. In March 1980 the idea became law when Congress voted to phase out interest rate ceilings at banks and S&Ls over six years.

The league vehemently opposed lifting the interest rate caps. Commercial bankers, in general, favored it. To gain the league's support (and bowing to the popularity of the instruments with the public), Congress and the American Bankers Association sweetened the legislation by allowing thrifts to offer NOW accounts nationwide. Lawmakers also allowed thrifts to borrow from the Federal Reserve Board—a first. Now the industry could borrow from two sources: the Federal Home Loan Banks and the Federal Reserve System. (No change was made for full-service banks. They could borrow only from the Federal Reserve.) At the same time Congress allowed thrifts to expand their investments, permitting up to 20 percent of thrift assets to be placed in any combination of consumer loans, commercial paper, and corporate bonds, while continuing to bar commercial banks from the securities arena. The league, so successful in getting its way in years past, lost a major battle to keep interest rate caps in place. But many thrifts, particularly the larger ones in California, saw the move to deregulation as inevitable. They used the elimination of the rate caps to bargain for powers that would make S&Ls look more and more like commercial banks.

A revolution lay in these amendments. Under the guise of promoting homeownership, but in reality throwing the thrift industry a bone to win the powerful lobby's support for the bill, members of the House and Senate Banking Committees granted thrifts permission to expand into a host of new areas: credit cards, commercial and general consumer lending, interest-bearing checking accounts. The new activities went a long way toward breaking the social contract that in theory was the justification for the thrift industry's existence.

But there was more.

The biggest bone, one that proved too big for the system to swallow safely, was a decision to raise deposit insurance to $100,000 per account from $40,000 for both the FSLIC, which insured thrifts, and the FDIC, which insured commercial banks. This increase, far outstripping the rise in inflation, gave visible sign that S&Ls were abandoning their role as banker to the little guy. Depositors with $100,000 tend to be well-to-do, sophisticated investors who often have professionals managing their money. This was no longer Main Street. It was Wall Street.

On the surface the decision by the lawmakers to increase the limit seemed to come from nowhere. Despite numerous hearings before the Senate and House Banking Committees in 1979 and 1980 on possible changes in banking regulations, there is only one written record of any discussion of raising deposit insurance. That occurred in February 1980 before a House Banking subcommittee chaired by Fernand J. St Germain, a Democrat from Rhode Island. At that time a spokesman for the Federal Reserve Board endorsed raising the limit to $100,000. But Irvine H. Sprague, the chairman of the FDIC, said he favored raising the limit to $60,000 and would endorse the $100,000 only if, in effect, the premiums banks paid for insurance were increased.

When the Senate passed its version of the banking bill in October 1979, there had been a small debate on the floor about deposit insurance. Senator Alan Cranston, Democrat from California, introduced an amendment seeking to raise the deposit insurance limit to $50,000 from $40,000. Cranston was followed by William Proxmire, Democrat from Wisconsin and chairman of the Senate Banking Committee, who rose to say that because of inflation, he thought the insurance limit should be raised even higher, to at least $60,000 and possibly even to $100,000.

"The FDIC is making a study as to whether something higher is justified," Cranston responded. "I would have no objection to going somewhat higher."

"Let us make it $50,000," Proxmire said, "with the understanding that, perhaps early next year, we can get information from the FDIC and make it correspond to the increase in inflation."

Senator Jake Garn of Utah, the ranking Republican on the Banking Committee, agreed with Proxmire, saying that "we do need to move to make it higher. It represents no additional cost to the insurance funds and, in the past, when the FSLIC insurance has been raised, it has brought more savings in."

With this brief discussion the senators agreed to raise the limit to $50,000 and revisit the issue during conference with the House.

More often than not in banking legislation, the major and most controversial issues are resolved during the murky process of a conference committee, a forum where House and Senate members meet to reconcile differences in legislation produced by the two chambers. Until the mid-1970s most conference committee meetings were closed to the public. Then resentment against powerful committee chairmen combined with the spirit of reform following Watergate to produce the sunshine-in-government movement. Congressional rules were changed to require that conference committees be open to the public unless closed by special amendments. Few members of Congress wished to be associated with closed sessions, so they became the exception.

But lawmakers quickly found a way to circumvent the sunshine law. On controversial issues, members simply adjourned the conference committee and retired to a back room, there to settle their scores in private and agree on upcoming votes.

In theory, and usually in practice, too, a bill emerging from conference is a compromise between the House and Senate versions; nothing new has been added. Financial legislation, however, is different, often emerging with provisions that contain dollar amounts higher than either chamber originally approved. While the public generally doesn't care much about banking legislation, some of the richest and most powerful lobbies in the country care a great deal. And during the conferences, when last-minute deals done behind closed doors are at a peak, they do some of their best work.

The House version of the 1980 banking legislation contained no mention of increasing deposit insurance. Under normal procedures, then, the conferees for the two chambers would be limited to raising insurance to a maximum of $50,000, as the Senate's version mandated. That's not what happened.

House and Senate conferees working on a compromise bill alternate between Banking Committee rooms in the two chambers. The House Banking Committee room is a stately chamber, wood-paneled with carpeting and thick velvet curtains dyed a deep peacock blue. The Senate Banking Committee room is starker and more formal, without carpeting or velvet curtains, but with white stone carvings of the zodiac along the ceiling. In the spring of 1980, as the conferees labored in the Senate chamber one afternoon, Senator Cranston secretly proposed raising the limit to $100,000, according to Richard Still, a lawyer on the House Banking Committee at the time.

There had been no meaningful hearings, no public discussion of the issue except for the exchange before the House subcommittee and the brief mention on the Senate floor weeks earlier. Neither of the original bills mentioned $100,000. But to members of the conference, the proposal came as no surprise. California S&L executives wanted the $100,000 limit and had been lobbying hard to get it. They were having trouble raising deposits and believed that consumers would accept a lower interest rate in return for an increased federal deposit guarantee. California thrifts, further, wanted to go after the market of well-to-do savers who deposited money in chunks of $100,000 or more. The thrifts had a batch of $100,000 certificates of deposit near maturity. They worried that customers would move their money if it were not fully insured.

Leaders within California's thrift industry enlisted two key lawmakers to their cause: Senator Cranston, a longtime ally, and Representative St Germain, one of the most powerful members of the House Banking Committee and a key member of the conference, one who was fast establishing himself as a friend to the industry. Dean Cannon, head of the California thrift league, and top executives from several major California thrifts led the effort, personally wining and dining St Germain on the issue, according to a congressional aide close to the lobbying effort. The California thrifts also enlisted Glenn Troop, the lobbyist from the league who allegedly had worked out terms of the bribe for Senator Kerr years before.

The chairman of the House Banking Committee was Henry Reuss of Wisconsin, a strong-willed man who had bucked the seniority system during the years of Watergate reform to grab the chair from Wright Patman of Texas. Reuss had an appetite for things intellectual and concerned himself with what he thought were the big-picture issues of the House Banking Committee, issues like international debt and interest rate controls. He deferred to St Germain, who had helped him in his coup against Patman, on specific issues about banks and savings and loans. (In the fall of 1980 failing health forced Reuss to relinquish chairmanship of the House Banking Committee to St Germain, giving the Rhode Island Democrat a title befitting the power he exercised over banking and thrift legislation.)

According to aides involved in the conference, lawmakers had checked with bank regulators prior to the meeting and agreed to raise the insurance limit to no more than $60,000 or $80,000, amounts exceeding the $50,000 limit in the Senate bill but still far less than the $100,000 the California S&Ls wanted. On this afternoon, however, Cranston suddenly proposed raising the ceiling all the way to $100,000, according to congressional aides and industry officials. Still says he watched Cranston pass a handwritten note to St Germain that read, "$100,000," with the number underlined. St Germain understood the message to be Cranston's shorthand way of saying that he would vote in favor of St Germain's pet amendments if St Germain would back the $100,000 limit, Still says.

In fact, league and thrift lobbyists already had won the support of St Germain, who understood the power that California thrifts wielded within the lobby group and therefore over the industry's future contributions to his campaign. As one aide close to the discussions put it, "Cranston talked to Freddie [St Germain], but St Germain was already on board." But St Germain also was a savvy politician, one adept at winning publicity that advanced his well-cultivated image as a consumer advocate. In this case, his "pet" concern was to fight for interest-bearing checking accounts at banks and thrifts. The issue was the most interesting one to reporters covering the bill, the one that would most immediately affect nearly all consumers and therefore receive the most ink and airtime. By playing his cards right, St Germain could get accolades from consumer groups for pushing the new NOW accounts even as he did the league's bidding on deposit insurance.

(When NOW accounts were first introduced in the 1970s by thrifts in New England, the league opposed them, arguing that giving checking accounts to S&Ls would be the first step in getting rid of interest rate caps. It feared the government could argue that if thrifts looked like banks, why should they be able to pay more on deposits? But when the lobby group realized that Regulation Q would be lifted with or without its consent, it decided it might as well get NOW accounts for its members. So St Germain, too, changed his mind, endorsing the checking account-like instruments.)

After Cranston's note was passed, the conferees adjourned for a moment.

What happened next is a matter of dispute among politicians scrambling to distance themselves from the S&L debacle. Since there is no written record, it is impossible to check whose version of history is correct.

According to one version, Cranston, Garn, and Proxmire from the Senate, and St Germain and Reuss from the House, retired to the nearby office of Proxmire aide Kenneth McLean.

By telephone the lawmakers informed banking regulators of the new deal. Deposit insurance would be increased more than twofold to $100,000 unless there was strong objection. Cranston, Garn, and St Germain wanted it. Their respective committee chairmen—Proxmire and Reuss—were going along. The chief thrift regulator, the bank board chairman Jay Janis, said he, too, was for it. But according to those in the meeting, Federal Reserve Board officials said they would agree to the increase only if the FDIC, the insuring agency for commercial banks, signed on. Cranston and Proxmire had said on the Senate floor they would weigh the FDIC's opinion heavily, but when FDIC Chairman Irvine Sprague told the group huddled by the telephone that afternoon that he was not happy with the proposal, they ignored his warning. What could he do? There had been scant publicity on the issue, nothing good enough to use as a blocking tactic, and the major political players had lined up behind it. The league had won, virtually in secret.

Years later Sprague described in the *American Banker,* a trade publication for the financial services industry, what happened that fateful day: "I begged, literally begged, Senators Bill Proxmire and Jake Garn to hold the figure down to $75,000, which would have kept it in line with inflation. . . . Finally, as the House-Senate conferees were meeting, I got a call from Proxmire, with Garn and Freddy St Germain on the line."

"Can't you live with $100,000?" Proxmire asked.

"I can live with whatever the Congress does," Sprague says he replied. "But you are making a big mistake."

Sprague recalled his chagrin when they ignored his warning. "They did it. The savings and loan lobby won. They had made a massive effort, including big campaign contributions, to get the $100,000 insurance. Bank board Chairman Jay Janis of Florida led the fight. Sen. Alan Cranston of California, where S&Ls are a potent force, was a strong ally."

Having informed the regulators of the decision, the conferees reconvened in their public forum. St Germain told the senators that the House would adopt the Senate provision on deposit insurance but also presented an amendment to raise the limit to $100,000.

Carolyn Jordan, Cranston's chief banking aide, insists that Cranston was in no way responsible for raising the limit to $100,000. She cites as proof St Germain's submission of the amendment that actually did raise it to that amount. But others on both sides of the aisle and from both chambers vividly remember the back room politicking that preceded the submission. St Germain submitted the amendment only after Cranston had signed off on the interest-bearing accounts.

Senator Garn flatly denies that he participated in any back room meeting. Nor does he recall any objections to the $100,000 proposal from Sprague. He says he didn't actively push for the change but concedes he favored it and voted for it during the conference. (Accounts to the contrary so troubled the senator that ten years later he had a staffer spend considerable time trying to discover if there was any record of the back room meeting that could be used to refute the claims.) According to Garn, during the open conference a lobbyist for the FDIC was asked for the agency's view. The lobbyist said the agency backed the $100,000 figure. Though Sprague acknowledges he got a telephone call from his lobbyist during the conference in addition to the one he received from the members of Congress, Sprague says that he told the lobbyist that the agency only reluctantly agreed to the $100,000.

Senator Proxmire says he can't recall the details of the circumstances surrounding the California thrifts' big win on deposit insurance, though he defends $100,000 as an amount that inflation eventually has justified.

The recollection of Proxmire aide McLean is that "nobody considered it to be a big deal" at the time, though he concedes, "We kind of regarded it as a cookie, a crumb for the dumb thrift lobby. Maybe in retrospect that was a mistake."

For investment firms like Merrill Lynch, which handled brokered funds, this was no crumb. A goodly amount of investment firms' time and talent is spent managing brokered deposits (sometimes called hot money)—blocks of $100,000 or more that are shuffled among banks and S&Ls. For a fee these professionals place and yank this money at a moment's notice in search of the highest interest rate offered by a federally insured institution. With the increase in deposit insurance, brokers no longer needed to fret that a bank or thrift offering the highest rate was in shaky condition. If the institution failed, the government would make the depositors whole, a key selling point the securities firms could use to pitch their services to consumers.

McLean defends the role of the 1980 insurance increase in boosting the brokered funds market. In his view the increase merely gave the market a head start of several years toward an inevitable modus operandi: a big business in its own right providing cash-hungry thrifts and banks with deposits. Others disagree. To them such a head start was critical in feeding unsafe banking practices by making too much money too easily available to poorly run thrifts. In fact, almost immediately thrifts desperate to lure cash became addicted to brokered deposits.

The 1980 deregulation of interest rates, coupled with higher deposit insurance and inflation, meant that thrifts overnight found themselves holding too much high-cost money and chasing too few high-return, safe investments to put it in. Too much money and too few good investments—a classic economic problem. Banks and thrifts had to do something. Banks ventured into third world loans. Thrifts would take a few years longer to find their nemesis. To pay depositors without losing money, and to curtail the deterioration of net worth—the difference between an institution's assets and liabilities and its cushion against losses—thrifts had to find some high-paying investments.

"Few appreciated the potential adverse consequences of deregulating an industry that was deeply in the red and had nothing to lose," says William S. Haraf, a visiting scholar at the American Enterprise Institute.

Certainly not President Jimmy Carter, who signed the deregulation bill into law on March 31, 1980. "This morning we are assembled in the White House to take action which will have far-reaching, beneficial effects on our Nation. Not only will it help to control inflation, but it will also strengthen our financial institutions, our thrift institutions and commercial banks, and in addition to that it will help small savers . . ." the president said at the signing ceremony. "It's another step in a long but extremely important move toward deregulation by the Federal Government of the private enterprise system of our country. We've already had remarkable success in deregulation in the airline industry. . . . As you know, under existing law, which this bill will change, our banks and savings institutions are hampered by a wide range of outdated, unfair, and unworkable regulations. Especially unfair are interest rate ceilings that prohibit small savers from receiving a fair market return on their deposits. It's a serious inequity that favors rich investors over the average savers."

He then thanked Bill Proxmire, Jake Garn, Henry Reuss, and Fernand St Germain, who attended the bill-signing ceremony, for their major contribution in getting the legislation passed.

Nine months later, in this climate of rapid change and low net worth in the thrift industry, Ronald Reagan, the prophet of deregulation, took office.

9

Lincoln . . . The Beginning

I t was called Lincoln Building and Loan in the 1920s, when it was chartered in Los Angeles by the state of California. Named after the president,
it displayed a picture of "Honest Abe" on its logo. In the beginning Lincoln
was small, and during the depression, like many S&Ls, it fell on hard times
that forced it to give up a storefront office for a loft. It employed one or two
people, part-time. In the 1930s one of the shareholders, Roy P. Crocker,
bought out some of his partners, acquiring a controlling share in the thrift for
a sum Crocker's son Don describes as very modest.

When World War II came, much changed. California's economy boomed,
and with it Lincoln's fortunes. Migration brought housing demand, and
homes galore began to pop up in sunny Southern California. Lincoln moved
to street-level offices, opened its doors five days a week, and began to open
branches in the Los Angeles metropolitan area. In those day, of course, thrifts
paid interest rates that were a bit higher than those of banks.

In the 1950s aggressive California thrifts like Lincoln discovered a wonderful way to raise cash. They put ads in newspapers in the Midwest, where
consumers had few basic investments that matched the rates offered by rapidly growing savings and loans in the West. For every dollar spent on adver-
tising in the *Christian Science Monitor,* a thrift could collect hundreds of
dollars in new deposits, a tidy return. In 1958 Roy Crocker had a heart attack
that forced him to leave Lincoln's day-to-day operations in others' hands. The

new managers aggressively sought funds from out of state and poured the money into California real estate development.

As interest rates rose in the 1960s, savings and loans kept pace by upping the price they would pay for deposits. Regulation Q, which capped commercial bank rates, still tied the hands of banks, which watched helplessly as consumers withdrew funds and walked them across the street to the local savings and loans. When Congress put savings and loans under virtually the same interest rate cap in 1966, it dried up the river of money from the Midwest. With thrifts everywhere paying the same rate, why should a saver in St. Louis or Cleveland put his income anywhere but in the neighborhood savings and loan?

Lincoln, like the rest of the industry, protested the cap on interest rates and, when it was first imposed, felt the pinch. But eventually, like most of the industry, Lincoln came to love its chains. The cap dried up deposits, but it gave thrifts a federally mandated leg up on the rates banks could pay. "The cap on interest rates was like a drug because it eliminated competition as far as cost of deposits, and so you competed in tricky ways," Don Crocker says. Thus was born the "toaster and blanket" era as thrifts competed for customers by giving away gifts instead of the higher yields on savings they had been used to. California passed a law saying thrifts could spend no more than $2.50 for a gift. But, as Crocker says, "It's amazing what you could buy in those days with $2.50." One thrift, Mutual of Pasadena, offered rosebushes in honor of the Rose Bowl. Glendale Federal gave away oranges. Lincoln specialized in educational items, like books and globes.

Just as Lincoln and others were getting used to the interest rate caps—indeed, even coming to depend on them—a downturn in California real estate stalled some of Lincoln's construction investments. The thrift faced hard times. "Things had gotten pretty tough. They were losing money, and they were in these troubled loans, and deposits were flowing out. Borrowings from the Federal Home Loan Bank were increasing," recalls Don Crocker, who after graduation from Stanford Law School in 1958 went into private practice. Among his clients was his father's thrift. In 1970 Lincoln's management asked the younger Crocker to head the company and steer it out of trouble.

When Don Crocker came to Lincoln, he found a company near the breaking point. Lincoln had borrowed so heavily from the Federal Home Loan Bank of San Francisco that it was all but buried in interest payments. Under the younger Crocker, the thrift embarked on a plan to slow down its aggressive lending policy—a policy that had required calculated borrowing from the regional Federal Home Loan Bank—and instead to concentrate on working its way out of debt. In a few years, Crocker says, Lincoln emerged as a thrift ready to start expanding once again. The institution set about building up a branch network of twenty-six offices in the Los Angeles area, none more than two hours' drive from Lincoln's headquarters in downtown Los Angeles at Hope and Sixth streets.

"We took great pride in making full disclosure during this whole period to our stockholders as far as exactly what was happening," says Crocker. "There were no secrets. I'm a great believer that if you admit what your problems are and address them head-on, that's the best way to manage problems, and to hide them is almost a sure way to make them worse."

In the early 1980s Lincoln faced the interest rate squeeze. Historically, thrift executives had worried only about underwriting risk—the chance that land or homes used as collateral for mortgage loans would prove to be worth less than the face value of the loan. Now, with double-digit interest rates and with deregulation of what thrifts could offer, thrift executives faced a new and more frightening worry: interest rate risk.

Like the rest of the industry, Lincoln entered the 1980s with a portfolio of low-yield home loans made in the days of single-digit interest rates in the 1970s—6 to 8 percent for the most part. Like the rest of the industry, it was being forced to pay high interest to attract and keep deposits—15 percent and more in many cases. Like most of the industry, Lincoln was unprofitable and close to insolvency. Its net worth was vanishing, ravaged by economic changes that happened too quickly for executives to counter.

On the eve of the 1980s Lincoln, like the thrift industry as a whole, appeared on the brink of bankruptcy.

Part III

FINANCIAL COCAINE: 1981–1983

Christmas is a time when kids tell Santa what they want and adults pay for it. Deficits are when adults tell the government what they want and their kids pay for it.

> *—Richard Lamm, former*
> *governor of Colorado*

If you can't eat their food, drink their booze, screw their women, take their money, and vote against them, you don't belong here.

> *—Advice to new assembly*
> *members from Jesse Unruh,*
> *former Speaker of the*
> *California Assembly*

10

Clash of the Titans:
Don Regan and
the Thrift Industry

R onald Reagan came to the presidency pledging to cut federal spending
  and to get government off business's back. He categorically opposed
government bailouts for industry, whether in Silicon Valley or the Rust Bowl.
But as his transition team arrived in Washington in 1981, its members circulated a memo among themselves about the thrift industry. It warned that
"the new Administration may well face a financial crisis not of its own
making. . . . Confidence in the entire financial system could evaporate."

President Reagan made public mention of the thrift crisis only once, and
that halfway through his tenure, but behind the scenes administration officials took the thrift industry's woes seriously from the start. The topic came
early to the attention of Treasury Secretary Donald Regan when he took
office in January 1981.

Federal banking regulators under the Carter administration, afraid that an
erosion of confidence in thrifts could spill into the mainstream banking industry, had grappled with the issue for months. Led by Fed Chairman Paul
Volcker, they had tried to craft legislation addressing some of the problems.
The Fed team continued the quest as President Reagan took office.

A few weeks into the new administration the group invited Roger Mehle,
President Reagan's new assistant treasury secretary for domestic affairs, to
one of its regular meetings at the Federal Reserve Board. Mehle had been put
in charge of thrift policy by Regan.

For a few uncomfortable moments Mehle sat quietly as particulars of the proposed legislation were mentioned. Then he rose. "I don't think that I should be at this meeting," he said, and walked out. The Carter administration might have allowed Volcker to take the lead over Treasury in trying to solve the thrift crisis. But Mehle felt certain that Regan—and the White House—would want to set policy on their own. He was right.

The White House quickly placed the S&L question before a cabinet council, one of a number of such committees by which President Reagan forged policy on important issues. The Cabinet Council on Economic Affairs, chaired by Regan, handled financial issues, including the thrifts. Its members included top executives from the White House, the Council of Economic Advisers, and the Office of Management and Budget. All the top administration officials—or their representatives—came to the meetings, held every few weeks or so in the Roosevelt Room of the White House. David Stockman, head of the Office of Management and Budget, or his representative, Lawrence Kudlow, attended. So did Vice President George Bush or one of his surrogates—C. Boyden Gray, Richard Breeden, or Craig Fuller. Richard Darman regularly sat in on behalf of the White House chief of staff, James Baker III. While the president occasionally might attend a cabinet council meeting, in general the council took recommendations to him, recommendations that almost always were accepted.

No one on the cabinet council headed by Regan doubted the complexity or the seriousness of the thrift problem. Noted economists such as Alan Greenspan, chairman of the Council of Economic Advisers under former President Gerald R. Ford and an economic adviser to President Reagan in the early days of the administration (and the chairman of the Fed after Volcker), publicly estimated in early 1981 that nine out of ten thrifts were losing money and that if liquidated, the troubled portion of the industry would find that it had a whopping negative net worth, that its obligations exceeded its assets by $100 billion.

The cabinet council set up a subcommittee, a thrift working group of a handful of people headed by Mehle, Regan's assistant, to recommend a course of action. The group included Kudlow from the OMB, Stockman's sharp and outspoken assistant, and Edwin J. Gray from the White House, whose official title was Deputy Assistant to the President and Director of the White House Office of Policy Development.

Despite his impressive title, Regan, Baker, Darman, Stockman, and other heavy hitters in the early Reagan years considered Gray a political hanger-on and a lightweight, a man who had obtained his job in the White House as a reward for loyal campaign work. To many in Washington, that Gray was nominally in charge of White House domestic policy, including housing, meant little. His appointment to the thrift group seemed logical, though: Before the campaign Gray had been a top executive at the Great American Federal Savings & Loan Association, a San Diego thrift headed by President Reagan's good friend Gordon Luce.

Today memories vary regarding these council subcommittee meetings. Gray says he rarely attended and usually sent his assistant, Shannon Fairbanks. Fairbanks says she remembers attending only occasionally. Several participants say Gray was there regularly, adding that his contribution was unremarkable except for one odd characteristic: At unexpected moments he would blurt out statements such as "I support the president's program. I know what the president wants. I am loyal to the president." Gray's colleagues found the outbursts puzzling. Their attitude was "That's nice, Ed, now let's go get on with the meeting." Members of the working group assumed that Gray, with his close ties to Luce and many other top S&L executives, was a source of leaks to the industry about the doings of the thrift working group.

As the working group's effort got under way, the federal banking regulators, led by Volcker, unveiled their proposed bill. Among other things, it called for expanding the FSLIC's line of credit to the U.S. Treasury to $3 billion from $750 million and allowing healthy banks, thrifts, or securities firms to buy ailing thrifts across the nation. The regulators pushing this plan included the three commercial banking agencies—the Office of the Comptroller of the Currency, the Fed, and the FDIC—as well as the chairman of the bank board. All were holdovers from the Carter administration.

The thrift industry liked the proposed hike in Treasury backing for the thrift deposit insurance fund. But the industry opposed the legislation as a whole because it called for interstate and interindustry mergers. S&L executives argued that allowing securities firms or commercial banks, particularly those from out of state, to take over thrifts would hasten the demise of an S&L industry distinct from other financial service businesses. (Actually, thrifts themselves were pushing for broader powers so they could resemble and compete with securities firms, banks, and insurance companies, but the thrifts wanted to do so while preserving the S&L industry's special status.) Mergers might start people wondering why a separate thrift industry was necessary at all.

The league offered a different solution: The government should buy low-yield home loans from S&Ls and warehouse them until the economic climate improved and restored their value. At that point the government would sell the loans in the secondary market or simply hold them until consumers paid them off. The industry also wanted the government to provide federal subsidies to home buyers. The programs carried an estimated cost of at least $10 billion in the first year alone.

Regan and Mehle disagreed with the league on both counts. They reasoned that the White House could not endorse any increase in the FSLIC's line of credit to the Treasury. In the president's view, the deficit inherited from Carter's White House already was too large. And President Reagan had pledged that the new administration would balance the budget. As for interindustry mergers, Regan and others in the new administration actively favored the idea of merging S&Ls into banks. Selling a troubled institution to a healthy one was often less expensive for the government in the short run than liquidating it and paying off depositors. Selling a thrift bypassed the expensive initial cash outlay necessary to reimburse customers. Instead accounts were transferred to a new institution, without any federal expenditures and often without interruption of service.

Only so many healthy S&Ls were around to absorb ailing institutions. Banks, on the other hand, were more plentiful. They might be enticed into taking over sick wards in exchange for a relaxation of other federal restrictions.

But the Reagan administration also valued the political support of the thrift industry, centered as it was in the president's home state. Nine of the nation's ten largest thrifts were in California. They controlled nearly a third of the industry's assets, far more than those in any other single state. And nearly all the top executives were Republicans—Reagan Republicans.

As governor of California Reagan had included in his kitchen cabinet Ed Gray's old boss, Gordon Luce of Great American Federal in San Diego, one of the largest and most influential S&Ls in the country. Luce was so close to Reagan that a cartoon appearing in the *Los Angeles Times* on April 5, 1984, pictured the White House with a sign on the front gate reading, "Great American Savings & Loan Assn. of San Diego, Washington Branch."

To avoid offending Reagan's friends, the Treasury declared itself neutral on the merger issue in public, even though internal memos prepared at the time show that the administration not only liked the idea but counted it among its major tactics to plug the industry's hemorrhaging.

The industry knew where the White House and Treasury actually stood. It had a friend in the White House by way of Ed Gray—and, it thought, in the president himself. But it also had a nemesis: Regan, head of the cabinet council charged with resolving the thrift crisis. Regan came from Wall Street, and Wall Street, the thrift industry knew, considered S&Ls dinosaurs run by Babbittesque executives with a penchant for polyester pants, white shoes, patent leather belts, and government subsidies.

Treasury's lack of respect for S&L operators was bolstered by a deep-seated belief in free markets that ran counter to thrift industry tradition. If a bank wanted to specialize in home loans because of market demand, that was fine with Regan. But he viewed specialization promoted by government subsidies as inefficient and unnecessary. The secondary markets created by Fannie Mae and Freddie Mac, the government-sponsored companies that bought home loans from banks and thrifts, had matured significantly in the late 1970s and early 1980s. By buying home loans, Fannie Mae and Freddie Mac eliminated much of the interest-rate risk faced by banks and S&Ls holding home mortgages. That made it attractive for commercial banks to stay in the home loan market year-round and thus, in Regan's mind, rendered thrifts obsolete.

Regan, the former head of Merrill Lynch, had shown his bias against thrifts early on, the industry thought, by appointing Mehle assistant secretary and then head of the cabinet council's thrift working group. Mehle, an avowed free marketer, also had worked in Wall Street's securities industry. He was not likely to favor massive industry bailouts that raided the U.S. Treasury to keep alive an outmoded industry.

League leaders, including the association's chief economist, Dennis Jacobe, sat down with Mehle in early 1981 before his Senate confirmation hearing on his nomination as an assistant secretary of the treasury. In Mehle's mind the talks went well, with a friendly discussion about deregulation and free markets, followed by a cordial good-bye. But as soon as the league officials walked calmly out the door, they launched a campaign to derail the nomination. Robert Dole of Kansas, who headed the Senate Finance Committee and was to conduct the confirmation hearings, found stacks of letters on his desk from thrift executives in his home state declaring their dislike for Mehle, even though none of the executives ever had met him. Here was the league's formidable grass-roots lobbying machine in action.

One of Dole's aides showed the letters to a stunned Mehle, who was not used to the ways of Washington. The aide laughed at the complaints and told Mehle not to worry. He proved to be as good as his word. The confirmation went through smoothly.

Mehle was an odd mix. A graduate of the U.S. Naval Academy, Fordham Law School, and New York University's Stern School of Business Administration, Mehle could be almost annoying to colleagues in his thoroughness when preparing reports and background material for Regan and the White House. Many saw only Mehle's serious side. Yet it was Mehle who instructed his fellow Treasury officials in the art of flinging food—a skill acquired at the Naval Academy—during lunch in the treasury secretary's small, history-rich dining room when Regan wasn't there. As Mehle explained it, one popular maneuver at the Naval Academy was to stand behind a victim's chair, ask the other diners at the table if they had any extra bread, peas, or whatever, and then get out of the way as the requested items were hurled in great quantity in the victim's direction. Mehle denies that food fights took place at the Treasury. But some participants swear a few mild bouts of bread throwing did take place. In any case, they say, Mehle's enthusiasm in describing the finer points of roll tossing endeared an otherwise all-business-like man to several Treasury staffers.

To the league, Regan and Mehle were public enemies one and two. When the attempt to derail Mehle's confirmation fizzled, the lobby group tried to contain the damage by challenging Regan directly. At first the appeals rested on political arguments.

On May 8, 1981, the league president, William O'Connell, sent a letter to Regan protesting statements the treasury secretary had made a week earlier in the Senate regarding free markets and thrifts. Many feared, O'Connell wrote, that Treasury had simply "written the savings and loan business off.

"A great majority of savings and loan people, were, of course, supporters of President Reagan last year and many participated actively in his election campaign. For those people your public expressions have been particularly distressing and disappointing," O'Connell added.

This admonishment failed to move the combative Regan. Just three weeks later, on May 29, 1981, in a front-page story in the *Los Angeles Times,* Regan was quoted as labeling the league's $10 billion bailout plan "nothing but a massive raid on the Treasury and I can't see that.

"First of all, you've got to find out what is the problem," the ex-Marine said. "Well, the thrifts are losing money, so what? Every time a company loses money, is the federal government supposed to go in and make it whole? I don't see that."

In response, O'Connell wheeled out the big guns, writing directly to President Reagan on June 1. O'Connell complained about the "seemingly callous attitude on the part of a number of Treasury Department officials toward the fate of the savings and loan business." And he went on to declare himself "appalled" to find that Regan's commentary "continues, as evidenced in the front-page comprehensive interview in Saturday's *Los Angeles Times:*

> The article reports an attitude on the part of Secretary Regan that traces its roots back to Marie Antoinette.
> He says he is "unalterably opposed to an industry suggestion that the federal government bail out the savings and loans by buying up the old low interest mortgages that are draining their profits."
> We have never asked for a bailout, Mr. President. Never once have we

suggested any direct financial aid from the government. What we are trying to do . . . is to find a broad range of effective measures short of having to use any tax dollars.

This appeal was disingenuous, of course. While they might not have used the term "bailout," O'Connell and other league officials had asked for government financial assistance. Even so, the pressure from the thrifts forced Regan to back down, at least publicly. A few days after the *Los Angeles Times* story appeared, the number two man at Treasury, Deputy Secretary R. T. McNamar, flew to the Beverly Hills headquarters of Great Western Savings Bank. There he met with the California thrift leaders to reassure them that the administration *was* concerned and, contrary to Regan's comment, was hatching a plan to help the S&Ls.

The next day the *Los Angeles Times* followed up with a second front-page story under the headline REGAN SWITCHES STAND, NOW HAS PLAN FOR HELPING S&LS. Regan in truth had no firm plan, though his aide, Mehle, was working on one. Regan reiterated that no need existed for a direct bailout, but he had softened his stance considerably from "So what?"

O'Connell now offered a suggestion. To avoid further friction between the industry and Regan, a savings and loan advisory committee ought to be set up for the Treasury similar to one created a year earlier for the Federal Reserve Board. The 1980 law had given thrifts borrowing privileges at the Fed for the first time. As lender to the industry and as the nation's lender of last resort the Fed had begun to take note of the alarming problems besetting S&Ls. They, in turn, had begun to lobby the Fed through the advisory committee.

At the Fed the S&L advisory committee astonished—and offended—some officials because the league so obviously set its agenda. O'Connell frequently participated in meetings between the committee and the Fed, to the quiet disgust of several Fed governors. O'Connell's presence confirmed in their minds a growing worry: The S&L industry was too cozy with its regulators at bank board; it would expect to develop the same close relationship with officials at Treasury.

Treasury officials declined the advisory group. They thought it was inappropriate. Hearing the industry's opinion—and reading O'Connell's vituperative letters—was one thing; asking for its advice on a formal, regular basis was quite another. Besides, Treasury officials had little regard for the industry's leaders, a sentiment they made clear during policy meetings at the White House and with commercial bankers and other financial executives. The Treasury had not fully decided how to cope with S&L problems, but it had concluded that thrift executives were mediocre businessmen looking for government handouts to mask their shortcomings, not solutions that were in the public's best interest or to the president's best political advantage. One prominent bank industry lobbyist summed it up this way: "Apparently any idiot could get an S&L charter—and some did. . . . Donald Regan . . . had little use for thrifts . . . or, more broadly, for any specialized financial institutions."

The extreme free market approach of the Treasury and OMB rang throughout most of the business community, swept up in deregulation. The *Wall Street Journal* led the way with an editorial about thrifts on June 8, 1981: "Indeed, the whole idea that we need specialized institutions to deal in home mortgages probably deserves re-examination." But the short-term problem remained: What to do about a sagging industry until interest rates came back down and it could diversify out of its niche as home mortgage provider into more profitable lines of work? Regan and Mehle believed that however the administration resolved the question, it would do better without the league's contribution.

In the summer of 1981 Shannon Fairbanks, Ed Gray's assistant, hosted a buffet dinner at her Washington home for the President's Commission on Housing, a group many OMB officials regarded as a shill for the S&L industry. Fairbanks had worked in the Reagan campaign, and her husband, Richard, was a major player in Republican politics.

Several leading California thrift executives, including Reagan's friend Luce, were there. So was the Housing Commission's chief, William McKenna, whose law firm represented most of the country's top thrifts as well as the California Savings and Loan League, the state affiliate of the national league.

Fairbanks had asked Lawrence Kudlow to speak to the group about how Stockman and the rest of the White House budget staff at the OMB regarded the thrift industry.

Kudlow was reluctant but agreed. After dinner, with many guests still sipping the white California wine that was de rigueur in the nation's capital that season, the crowd moved into the den to hear from Kudlow. He was frank: The government couldn't afford to give the S&Ls any special subsidies, and even if it could, it wouldn't because the administration didn't think any business deserved them. Kudlow bluntly said what Regan, Stockman, and many other Reaganites thought: Thrifts were overprotected, oversubsidized and poorly run. The industry had outlived its usefulness, and the prospect of keeping it alive with government help was neither feasible nor desirable.

Fairbanks looked white with shock. She had not expected such harsh words from Kudlow, a man she considered her friend. Her guests were outraged.

"Why should we give you subsidies?" Kudlow asked. "Have you looked at the car industry lately? The steel industry? We're not giving them any special treatment. Have you looked at the timber industry? The manufacturing sector? They're not getting any special treatment. Why should you?"

"Because housing is important," McKenna shot back.

"Do we mean all housing or do we mean California thrift-related housing?" Kudlow said.

There was dead silence.

McKenna and company fumed. But in the end Kudlow didn't matter to them. Even the Treasury's support wasn't crucial. McKenna and the league knew how to make an end run around the nation's budget keepers. They would go to their friends in Congress, particularly to Senators Jake Garn, Alan Cranston, and Donald Riegle (like Garn and Cranston, a leading member of the Banking Committee), and to Representatives St Germain and Frank Annunzio. These politicians were not among the largest recipients of league largess for nothing.

And of course, the league would continue to milk its traditional source of power, the bank board.

11

The Utah Connection

Past presidents had given the league carte blanche to select the head of the bank board. Now, with enemies in the Treasury and tough times ahead, the California thrifts and the league took care in choosing their candidate for the bank board chairman. Ultimately they looked to Utah, where an economist in his early forties who specialized in housing and urban issues seemed the perfect choice.

Richard Pratt, a thickset man with blue eyes, went to New Zealand at nineteen as a missionary for the Mormon Church. He spent a year there as a circuit preacher, riding his rounds on bicycle. In his spare time he became a heavyweight wrestling champion.

Pratt first met league executives while he was a Ph.D. candidate in finance and urban economics at the University of Indiana in Bloomington from 1964 through 1966. The league sponsors a thrift executive training program at Indiana. To make money while earning his doctorate, Pratt tended bar at the program's parties and chauffeured thrift executives around town. He impressed industry people as a smart, good speaker, one possessed of a good, if off-color, sense of humor. (A typical Pratt joke, told at a conference on housing years later: "I haven't been to church for quite a while until today, but it's always good to get back, I guess. I do feel like the dumbest guy in class; it reminds me of a quiz show I watched where the question was 'Where does a gentleman kiss a lady?' and I missed all of the first three answers. So I'm way behind. [The Fannie Mae chairman and chief executive] David Maxwell said

82

one day that my only redeeming social value was my scatological sense of humor; somehow I don't see that as high praise, but I guess it's what one has to go with—whatever strengths one has.")

A few years after leaving Indiana, Pratt became chief economist for the U.S. league and a consultant to the California league. Later he opened his own financial consulting firm in Utah and taught business at the University of Utah in Salt Lake City.

Pratt describes himself as a devout free marketer, an "Ayn Randian" capitalist even though he admits he has never read one of the political philosopher's books. To thrift executives who wanted to play up to the Reagan camp with rhetoric about laissez-faire government but at the same time preserve their special government protections, Pratt seemed ideal.

In addition to industry support, Pratt had the backing of his home state senator, Jake Garn, who became chairman of the Senate Banking Committee when the Republicans captured the Senate in 1981. Garn was a darling of the Reagan-Bush White House. A tall, gaunt Mormon with sharp features and a nearly bald head, Garn often expressed disgust at his fellow lawmakers and the entourage of lobbyists and reporters who populate Washington. He brushed them aside with a sweep of a hand, calling them "the assholes of this town." He had a special distaste for the House of Representatives, whose members he looked down on with a withering and quite public contempt—a contempt directed in no small way at Fernand J. St Germain. During conference meetings with representatives to work out banking legislation, Garn often rolled his eye, tightened his pencil-thin lips in disgust, and expressed utter boredom by holding his chin in his hand and staring into space while his colleagues nattered on.

Quick to judge others, Garn is just as quick to find excuses for himself. He is proud to have been the administration's strong ally in the Senate, especially in efforts to deregulate thrifts. But he was no White House puppet. He says he believes he is one of the few politicians in Congress who say and do exactly what they think is right and who don't care what others think. But in the same breath he admits that he is troubled to hear that even his most ardent admirers in the banking agencies call his record on thrifts abysmal.

Garn's sanctimoniousness, large ego, and shining pate earned him the moniker the Screaming Skull among lobbyists and congressional aides. But he also became a folk hero to many colleagues by riding to space in the shuttle and donating a kidney to a sick daughter.

With Garn's backing, Pratt was a shoo-in.

During Pratt's tenure as the league's economist from 1967 through 1969, he befriended several top thrift executives in California. One day in early 1981, while sitting in his office at the University of Utah the telephone rang. Anthony Frank, chairman of First Nationwide in San Francisco, a thrift owned by the National Steel Company but soon to be purchased by the Ford Motor Company, asked, "How would you like to be chairman of the Federal Home Loan Bank Board?"

"That would be great," Pratt said. Frank was more than a friend. He belonged to the inner circle of influential California thrift executives. Pratt knew that only the president could offer him the job, but he also knew that having Frank and the other major California thrift executives behind him was tantamount to a nomination.

Despite support from the league and from Garn, Pratt didn't want to take any chances. Several desirable appointments within the Federal Home Loan Bank System had fallen through at the last minute. So he asked William O'Connell at the league for advice on whom he should contact in the administration. O'Connell told him to call Ed Gray at the White House. Gray's office would decide for President Reagan who would get the job. Gray, Pratt was told, would rely heavily on advice from those in the industry, including William McKenna, the San Francisco lawyer.

Gray told Pratt to come for an interview. "Can you be here tomorrow?" Gray asked.

Pratt flew to Washington the next day. He arrived midmorning at Gray's office, only to wait for several hours. Late that afternoon Gray interviewed Pratt for fifteen minutes, then sent him out to dinner with his assistant, Shannon Fairbanks, and with McKenna. McKenna himself had been the league's first choice to head the bank board, but he had declined, citing health reasons and the possibility of a conflict of interest with his duties at his law firm. Although McKenna had no official job in the White House, Gray considered him its unofficial spokesman on housing and thrift policy. Pratt already knew McKenna from Pratt's days at the league and as a consultant to the California league.

During dinner Fairbanks and McKenna discussed various thrift issues and told Pratt he had the job if he wanted it. At the time McKenna was still senior partner in his firm and thus representing the California thrifts. In a sense, more than just William McKenna and Shannon Fairbanks spoke. In essence it was the industry's California contingent asking Pratt to be the nation's chief thrift regulator.

To Ed Gray, McKenna's presence at dinner seemed natural enough. "He was the understood thrift expert for the White House. He was considered the housing expert," Gray says. Indeed, Gray often consulted with McKenna, along with his old boss Luce and the league's O'Connell. But for others, McKenna's presence at the dinner was hard to fathom. In the banking world it would be as if a lawyer for Citicorp, Chase Manhattan, and Chemical had taken Alan Greenspan out to dinner and, after screening him, had over coffee and dessert offered him the chairmanship of the Federal Reserve Board.

Pratt accepted on the spot.

After Pratt was sworn in, he appointed McKenna chairman of the Federal Home Loan Bank of San Francisco, which supervises the industry in California, Arizona, and Nevada. Before assuming the chairmanship of the regional bank, McKenna retired from his law firm. But he continued to keep an office there and to draw a salary. He also remained under a contract that required him "to advise and consult with" his partners. As chairman of the San Francisco bank McKenna would oversee allocation of federally subsidized credit to all the S&Ls his firm represented. He also would have a large voice in picking the chief supervisor for the region—the chief supervisor of both the thrifts McKenna's firm represented and the smaller S&Ls that were competitors to his firm's clients. These were not conflicts of interest, McKenna and other industry leaders later argued. Rather, these ties enabled McKenna to maintain a good understanding of developments in the thrift business.

For chief counsel of the bank board in Washington, Pratt hired Thomas Vartanian—after McKenna had approved him. Pratt had no formal obligation to McKenna, but he thought it good politics to make sure the chief lawyer for the board met with approval from the California crowd.

Pratt and Vartanian had met in Utah in 1980, when they found themselves on the same side of a case involving a bank merger. Vartanian, a recent graduate of Brooklyn Law School's night program, was an attorney in the Office of the Comptroller of the Currency, one of three federal agencies that regulate commercial banks. Pratt, an expert witness for the government, was impressed with how hard Vartanian worked, with how well prepared he was.

Vartanian, a devout Catholic, almost had become a priest before he married and went to law school. He likes to tell a story about the Utah bank case, which brought him west for the first time. When a Utah resident described himself as LDS—short for the Mormon Church's formal name of Church of Jesus Christ of Latter-Day Saints—Vartanian assumed the letters stood for "learning disabled student" and said he was sorry to hear that.

"Well, about ninety percent of us here are," the man replied to a puzzled Vartanian.

Vartanian and Pratt quickly came to admire each other's work. When Pratt called McKenna to say he wanted Vartanian to be the bank board's chief counsel, McKenna was less than enthusiastic. Brooklyn Law School? Night school no less? Thirty years old? Not from a law firm? McKenna wanted someone with more prestigious credentials, more experience, more clout. But he agreed to meet the young man anyway.

Vartanian flew to Los Angeles. An interview scheduled to last only a few minutes ran from midmorning through a late dinner. McKenna called Pratt the next day. "If you don't hire him, I will," he said.

Vartanian got the job.

To head the bank board's deposit insurance arm, the FSLIC, Pratt picked Brent Beesley, another youngster, only in his early thirties. Beesley had made a fortune in real estate in his late twenties and early thirties. Pratt knew Beesley by reputation as an good commercial banking lawyer.

"Head of what?" Beesley asked from his law office in Salt Lake City. Having no idea what the FSLIC was, Beesley looked it up at the University of Utah library. But he took the job, and he and Pratt developed an abiding friendship. They had many interests in common besides finance. Both men love to motorcycle, wrestle, and fly planes. Both are Mormons (giving rise to the phrase "Morman Mafia," which many lobbyists used to describe the bank board under Pratt). Both have a free market approach. Each enjoys a good challenge, in sports or in business. And that's exactly how they regarded the task facing them in the thrift industry.

Pratt, Beesley, and Vartanian ran the bank board from early 1981 through mid-1983. Pratt, the intellect, set the overall strategy. Beesley was the innovator, figuring out how to change rules to keep the industry afloat. And Vartanian had the job of facilitator, seeking the legal justification for changes in bank board policy and later becoming the agency's chief lobbyist on Capitol Hill in favor of giving the industry both more freedom and more government help.

President Reagan's S&L team was now in place.

12

The Plan

A t a cabinet council meeting in the spring of 1981, not long after Pratt was picked to run the bank board, Mehle summarized the thrift industry's troubles. Industry pleas for help amounted to scare tactics to get a handout, he said. S&Ls already had a plan for a $10 billion loan subsidy and for the warehousing of old loans. Now they wanted the government to increase deposit insurance on retirement accounts to $500,000 as a way to help thrifts lure large chunks of money into their branches.

Keeping President Reagan's no-bailout philosophy in mind, Mehle counseled holding the line. Yes, the industry was losing money, and its net worth was falling, pushing many institutions into technical insolvency. But that didn't matter in the short term as long as thrifts had the cash flow to meet withdrawals and there were no depositor runs. In other words, the thrifts could muddle through as long as all their depositors didn't demand their money at once and thus create a situation guaranteed to demonstrate that the thrifts' obligations exceeded their assets.

Once interest rates came down, Mehle argued, the pressure would ease and profitability would return to a large portion of the industry, helping restore its net worth. That would allow the administration to embark on a longer-term program to remedy the industry's fundamental problem of overconcentration in home loans. The solution: a regimen of deregulation enabling the industry to diversify out of home loans and thus become less vulnerable to interest rate volatility. Thrifts, in short, could become commercial banks.

"The industry's problems are not as severe as thrift executives and the league have portrayed," Mehle said. "This is an earnings problem, not a cash flow problem."

George Bush, who had decided to attend the day's cabinet council session, looked puzzled. He raised his hand. "If that's the problem, how come my friends in the S&L industry tell me things are so dire?"

"Well," Mehle said, "your friends probably own stock in the S&Ls, and net worth does affect the value of stock." Any thrift executive who had his money tied up in thrift stock—and that was many thrift executives—would see the value of the stock decline as net worth fell. For executives who used their S&L stock as collateral for loans or other investments, the decline posed a double whammy. Their investment was souring, and in addition, they likely were being called upon to ante up cash as additional collateral when the value of thrift stock underpinning a business deal declined.

But Mehle had a plan, one with three main components. The first was to merge sick thrifts whenever possible into healthy thrifts or banks. The second was to push deregulation, give thrifts powers equal to that of banks (even though S&L executives were generally not considered as smart as commercial bankers) so that eventually there would be no separate S&L industry vulnerable to interest rate swings. Deregulation would be accomplished through the lifting of interest rate ceilings, as mandated in the 1980 law and implemented through a committee chaired by Treasury Secretary Regan, the Depository Institutions Deregulation Committee. And it would be facilitated through rule changes issued by the bank board and through legislation that the administration planned to push in Congress.

The third and most controversial component of Mehle's plan was called forbearance. Federal law required banking regulators, including the bank board, to close insolvent institutions. Forbearance, a way to get around the law, stipulated that government regulators leave insolvent institutions open by using looser accounting rules, rules that made a thrift's net worth appear greater than it was. Basically this was a way of letting hundreds of S&Ls claim solvency when they were broke.

The centerpiece of forbearance called for the bank board, through the FSLIC, to issue government notes that insolvent or near-insolvent thrifts could count toward net worth. If, for example, a thrift's obligations to depositors and other creditors exceeded its assets by $1 million, then the government would issue a note for, say, $3 million, so the institution could appear to have the resources to meet its obligations and still have $2 million left as a cushion. Making institutions appear solvent would buy them time to grow out of their problems. Under the plan the deposit insurance fund would give thrifts notes, and the fund would promise to pay cash if the institution were ever liquidated. In exchange, the FSLIC got an IOU from the thrift promising to build up its reserves to the point where the government note was no longer needed to help the thrift meet net worth requirements. Once a thrift's net worth reached a safe level, the FSLIC would tear up the IOU and the thrift would tear up the FSLIC note.

The idea for the notes hit Mehle one weekend afternoon in May 1981 while he sat at his desk at the elegant old Treasury Building next to the White House. Mehle had been poring over financial information about the thrift industry to determine whether conditions were as dire as the league claimed. After several hours he discerned a pattern. While the industry's net worth was falling, its deposits were rising. S&Ls countrywide, in fact, had plenty of cash to play with in their daily operations.

Deposits were rising because the industry had begun to offer the newly allowed higher than market rates to attract new business. But Mehle didn't worry about that. In the short term the practice seemed safe.

The possibility of using government notes to help thrifts had been kicking around for some time. But until now proposals involved notes to be issued by a new government agency or, as House Banking Committee Chairman St Germain suggested at the league's behest, directly by the Treasury. Either way the notes would count as an obligation to taxpayers and so would appear on the budget and increase the deficit. For the new Reagan administration, that course was out of bounds.

But, Mehle realized, the note idea could be tailored to the White House's needs. Only the FSLIC's cash outlays counted in the budget; if the FSLIC fund issued the notes—although really government IOUs—the effect on the budget would be nil. The notes would boost the net worth of sagging thrifts all over the country but not add a dime to the deficit—unless, of course, the thrifts failed and the notes had to be replaced with cash.

The wizards of Wall Street likely would detect such budget trickery immediately as they toted up the federal government's liabilities. But for the time being, the notes seemed heaven-sent. Mehle called Pratt at home. Could Pratt meet him at the bank board as soon as possible? Pratt, arriving in shorts and running shoes, agreed to the idea right away. The White House liked it, too. Reagan economic adviser Martin Anderson commended Regan and Mehle for devising such an "elegant" solution to the problem of propping up the industry without appearing to spend any money. Lower-level officials at the OMB—the full-time bureaucrats—objected that FSLIC notes should be placed on the budget, noting that failure to do so amounted, in the words of one, "to spending without counting." But political appointees higher up the agency's ladder overruled the objection, preferring to adopt Mehle's interpretation of what should and should not count on the budget.

On the theory that the league and industry would be less receptive to a Treasury-generated plan, Pratt and Mehle decided Pratt would peddle the idea for the FSLIC notes as the bank board's own.

But McNamar, Regan's right-hand man, leaked news of the plan almost immediately, causing friction between Mehle and Pratt, who thought he had been double-crossed. After some verbal skirmishes in the press over which agency set thrift policy, the cabinet council formally adopted the plan.

And as expected, Wall Street immediately ridiculed it. "They'd issue a piece of paper that says I owe you some money if you need it and I'm doing it this way because I don't have enough money. How dumb do they think people are?" the *Wall Street Journal* quoted one investment banker as saying on June 4, 1981, shortly after McNamar's leak.

The industry was skeptical, too. Anthony Frank, Pratt's friend at First Nationwide in San Francisco, warned that if thrifts signed on for the program and failed, the FSLIC would have to replace the notes with cash. Quite likely there wouldn't be enough money in the FSLIC till, and the government would be forced to take over scores of thrifts, operating them much as it operates the U.S. Postal Service. "The policy outcome will be nationalization" for the bottom third of the industry, Frank predicted at the time. (By coincidence, Frank left First Nationwide in 1988 to become postmaster general.)

Economists and (privately) some officials in the Treasury and the White House budget office also criticized the plan, calling it financial sleight of hand. Regan and Mehle looked at the problem upside down, they thought. Traditionally bank regulators have considered it safe to allow institutions long on net worth but short on cash to stay in business. The rationale has been that such institutions are fundamentally sound. They have value, real assets. The Fed, as central banker, agrees to lend cash to those institutions to avert a cash shortage that could trigger a run. The Fed assumes the chances are high the institution will regain its balance and repay the loan to the government. Conversely, the Fed traditionally has frowned on lending cash to institutions with little or no net worth. The law requires regulators to close institutions whose net worth is zero. If left open, they present unfair competition to healthy institutions; moreover, losses tend to grow at insolvent thrifts that are left open, exposing deposit insurance funds to ever-greater liability once an insolvent institution fails, as most inevitably do.

Regan and Mehle adopted the opposite view. They decided a thrift with no underlying value—that is, no net worth—could stay in business safely so long as it had enough cash to meet withdrawals and other daily demands. The strategy amounted to a gamble that rates would come down soon enough and thrifts would diversify responsibly and quickly enough for the industry to restore itself to health without any effect on the budget.

Regan and Mehle—indeed, many officials in the administration—knew the plan was a gamble. But given the prohibition against raising the deficit, they saw no option. And to many it seemed a reasonable gamble: Interest rates were so unusually high they had to come down. In the meantime, why close every insolvent thrift when no S&L, well run or otherwise, could make a profit in such an environment? Still, it was a risk; if interest rates remained high, the condition of insolvent thrifts probably would deteriorate further, and forbearance would add to the ultimate cost—and budget outlay—of shutting them down.

Despite the risk, Mehle's proposal was adopted. It had a clear advantage over the alternative of closing down thrifts: It didn't require tax dollars. It bought the industry and, perhaps more important, the administration time. The bank board had authority to issue notes without additional legislation from Congress; in fact, Pratt used some notes in 1981 to aid several troubled institutions. But everyone thought that the program would stand a better chance of political success if Congress explicitly endorsed it with a vote. Such an endorsement would short-circuit the competing plan offered by St Germain on behalf of the league that would have required direct guarantees from the Treasury. Further, Democrats in Congress could not then accuse the administration of accounting gimmickery and financial hocus-pocus. Congress's hands would be dirty, too.

The Net Worth Certificate Program, as it was called, was included in a proposed bill written by the administration. Senator Garn was asked to sponsor it. (Pratt originally asked the cabinet council to endorse a bill to guarantee deposits through a direct line to the Treasury—the league's version of the aid package. But when he realized the administration never would support such a proposal, he threw his support behind the next best thing, the FSLIC notes.)

Despite some industry pooh-poohing, the friends Bush had spoken of during the cabinet council meeting on the S&L problem appreciated the significance of the notes. The IOUs could restore a thrift executive's personal net worth by boosting the value of his ailing S&L. This 1981 "bailout" program saved many thrifts from closure, and that in turn saved many thrift executives from financial strain, if not bankruptcy.

There were some constraints. The administration stipulated that thrifts receiving the notes could pay no dividends to stockholders, that money had to be plowed back into the thrift until net worth was restored and the notes retired.

For the next ten months Regan and Mehle worked to implement their plan, all the while praying for interest rates, hovering in the upper teens, to fall.

13

Racing Past Congress

When Pratt, Beesley, and Vartanian took office, the thrift industry was a mess. Technically it had failed. Of the country's four thousand thrifts, the three bank board officials estimated that only forty or fifty—at most maybe one hundred—were solvent. Even these struggled. Beesley recalls that most of the big California S&Ls, touted as the industry's largest and healthiest, were hurting. Pratt, echoing Greenspan's analysis, publicly estimated that if all insolvent thrifts were liquidated, the FSLIC would fall as much as $100 billion short of the amount needed to pay off depositors, a figure he later revised upward to $178 billion, or about $350 billion in 1990 dollars. As it was, they remained open only because depositors had not panicked and demanded their money all at once.

Nineteen eighty had been the first year in FSLIC history that its expenditures to handle problem cases exceeded its income from insurance premiums paid by the thrifts it insured. When President Reagan took office the next year, the deposit insurance fund had resources of $8.5 billion to back thrifts with deposits of $600 billion to $700 billion. Pratt—and the administration—knew they had to stem the drain or risk big budget outlays. "In 1982 the bank board saw no survivors in the event that the then present financial conditions continued or worsened," according to Pratt.

California, Illinois, and New York emerged as key problem states early on. Just four weeks into the Pratt regime the bank board had to close a Chicago

S&L, the Economy Savings and Loan Association, and pay off depositors. It was the first liquidation and payout in ten years. (During that time failed thrifts had been merged into stronger S&Ls, and accounts transferred.) Beesley talked with depositors the day the FSLIC closed Economy Savings. The scene remains among the most vivid memories of his tenure.

"They lined up. The line went around the block. They were so real. There were people who had their life savings in there. If we hadn't been there, they'd have lost it," Beesley said. "I got a testimony of the value of deposit insurance in the lives of real people that I never forgot." The experience is one that tempered his free market philosophy and led him to appreciate some government interference—particularly a federal guarantee sticker on the doors of thrifts.

Pratt, whose staff was in the field monitoring the problem—and who, unlike Regan and other officials at the Treasury and OMB, devoted full-time to thinking about thrifts—had a keen sense of the impending crisis. And he made no attempt to hide it. When Volcker asked the size of the problem during a meeting with Pratt one day in late 1981, the cigar-chomping Fed chairman nearly choked on the $100 billion answer, spewing out a cloud of smoke that filled the meeting room at the Federal Reserve Board. The numbers were staggering.

In late 1981 Gray arranged for Pratt to brief top White House advisers, including staff from the Treasury and the White House budget office. The meeting took place in the Roosevelt Room of the White House, where Theodore Roosevelt's Nobel Peace Prize sits on the mantel above the fireplace. Instead of making his case, Pratt received a pounding. Why, the OMB's Kudlow asked, did he make so many gloom-and-doom speeches to the industry? Yes, there was a problem, but what good would talking publicly about it do? The officials told Pratt to shut up and handle the problem quietly while they all waited for the administration's plan to work. Furthermore, whenever possible, Pratt was to avoid dealing with insolvencies by closing thrifts and paying off depositors. Use FSLIC notes. Use forbearance. Use anything that didn't swell the deficit.

Pressure from the administration to keep thrifts open became intense; even so, the Pratt bank board occasionally shut down an S&L. When one such defunct savings and loan sued the agency, Mehle, while a Treasury official, took the remarkable step of testifying as an expert witness against the bank board. His argument: As long as an insolvent thrift—that is, one whose liabilities equal or exceed its assets—can pay its bills, it should not be closed.

Mehle made clear that he was testifying as a private citizen, not on behalf of the Treasury, and that he was speaking generally, not in reference to any specific thrift. Still, he hoped his appearance would reassure the public by sending the message that just because a thrift appeared to be insolvent, that didn't mean it couldn't meet its short-term obligations. But considering Mehle's prominence in setting White House thrift policy, his appearance also sent a message to the industry, a message that in Pratt's mind undermined the bank board's ability to get tough with recalcitrant thrifts.

Meanwhile, Mehle, Kudlow, and their colleagues had become unwitting allies of the industry they disdained. Although thrifts had lost the first round of the battle for a direct bailout, they liked the idea of being allowed to diversify without having to play under the stricter rules of commercial banking. And the no-bailout decree carried a silver lining. Had the Treasury stepped in with direct dollars to solve the crisis, the money surely would have been used to close insolvent thrifts rather than prop them up. Without the Treasury's cash, the bank board could not afford to close ailing thrifts. And the more thrifts there were, scattered among the nation's congressional districts, the stronger the lobbying efforts of the league.

Time was of the essence in 1981, for a large number of thrifts were verging on collapse. Pratt and Beesley kept a list of "dog" institutions ranked by severity of sickness: those that never would recover, those that probably wouldn't, those that might still get well, and those that surely would if given a little time. The bank board's typewriters didn't have any way of representing a dog pictorially; one key, however, looked something like a fire hydrant. Next to each thrift's name officials typed one or more hydrants, symbolizing a one-dog mess, a two-dog mess, and so on to a four-dog mess, hopeless. There were hundreds of hopeless cases, possibly thousands.

As Pratt saw it, after his browbeating at the White House, he had four options: He could close the worst cases, though this would cost the government lots of money up front; he could sell them to healthy bidders, though this option was limited by the relatively small number of buyers; he could merge ailing institutions together (but this amounted to a cosmetic remedy because two failures rarely added up to one success); or he could allow thrifts to operate despite their insolvency by using trick accounting—a delaying tactic.

While federal law mandated the closing of insolvent thrifts, the law also offered a loophole: It gave the FSLIC authority to assist troubled institutions or to sell or merge them if doing so was cheaper than closing them and paying off depositors. While paying depositors usually was costlier than a merger in the short run, it often proved the least costly once a thrift's assets were sold to help offset the government's initial cash outlay to depositors.

Since Reagan's people wanted short-term expenditures kept to a minimum,

FSLIC officials sought ways to slant the computation in favor of mergers and sales. It began to estimate the cost of S&L liquidations without deducting the money the government would recover from the sale of repossessed assets, thus inflating the cost of a shutdown. Or it failed to estimate the additional cost a merger could entail should the blended institution fail after incurring additional losses. The math, calculated as it was, led to very few closings. Instead, Pratt "sold" struggling institutions to healthy buyers—other thrifts, commercial banks, or nonbanking companies. But the price was high.

Federal law, for example, prohibited commercial banks from crossing state lines without permission from the state being invaded. Over the years local bankers had made sure their state legislators barred outsiders. The federal law did not apply to thrifts, but traditionally S&L regulators had elected to impose similar geographic limits. The restrictions could be (and under Pratt were) removed by the bank board for purchasers of troubled S&Ls.

The league had long opposed interindustry mergers, and now it fought Pratt's approach—unless the buyers were thrifts. A major challenge arose almost immediately. In 1982 Pratt agree to sell Fidelity Savings and Loan, a struggling S&L in San Francisco, to Citicorp, the nation's largest commercial bank company. Even as bank board officials closed the deal by shaking hands with the Citicorp chairman, Walter Wriston, the California S&Ls howled and hounded Pratt. Within a few days he relented. Now Wriston complained. Pratt reopened the bidding to give the California S&L executives a chance to match Citicorp's offer. When they couldn't, Citicorp won the thrift for keeps.

The Pratt bank board cast a wide net, welcoming bids for ailing thrifts from a spectrum of companies: securities dealers, insurance underwriters, utility companies, retail clothing and appliance stores. Federal law generally prohibits nonbanking businesses from owning commercial banks. Sears, Roebuck, for example, cannot own a full-service commercial bank, the rationale being that general commerce should be separated from banking to prevent conflicts of interest. If Sears owned a bank, it could, in theory, withhold credit from its competitors at K Mart or could provide itself dangerously easy credit terms. But the law says nothing about whether Sears can own a thrift, though traditionally the Bank Board imposed regulations that mimicked the policy applying to commercial banks, thus barring retailers from owning S&Ls. Pratt's bank board waived these regulations, as it was empowered to, without congressional approval.

The board eliminated still other ailing thrifts through mergers that clumped together several sick institutions in the hope that a single, healthier institution would emerge. Though such a strategy threatened to make one larger problem out of several smaller ones, Beesley thought the gamble worth taking. Mergers avoided depositor payouts and slowed the rate at which dollars were being sucked from the FSLIC's dwindling reserves.

During Pratt's two-year tenure at the bank board, 1,000 S&Ls disappeared. Many were merged or bought privately without government aid. But a large chunk, nearly half, was transferred to new owners with the assistance of the bank board. By comparison, from the time it was created in 1934 until 1980, the board had resolved only 165 problem thrift cases.

Despite the flurry of activity during Pratt's chairmanship, however, little changed. While hundreds of S&Ls were eliminated as single institutions through mergers or acquisitions, few were actually closed or pulled from the market. Many industry analysts judged that the policy amounted to little more than rearranging deck chairs.

So it went in 1981 and 1982 with the bank board's use of sales, mergers, and the occasional depositor payout. It was the fourth option, however—the juggling of accounting standards—that ultimately proved most significant. As an industry joke that played on a Mark Twain remark put it, for the thrift industry in the 1980s there were lies, damn lies, and accounting. Accounting principles are supposed to provide investors—and regulators—with a standard they can use to compare firms and judge business performance. When Pratt realized the government couldn't afford to shut down and wouldn't be able to sell off all the insolvent S&Ls, he changed the language and the rules. He changed the standard by which the industry was measured.

Pratt's predecessors already had lowered the financial standards the industry had to meet. At the urging of the league and with the blessing of the leaders of the Senate and House Banking Committees, Pratt continued the process. (Privately Vartanian argued against allowing thrift rules to deviate from the norm, wondering, "How will you ever push them back into the mainstream?" But he was overruled and so had to find the legal justification for the lower standards and argue the case for them on Capitol Hill and in public.)

First, Pratt further lowered the amount of money that thrift owners or investors were required to have at risk—an amount called capital or net worth. Capital is the cushion an institution has on hand to absorb bad loans or other mistakes. If investors must provide the cushion with personal funds, they likely will behave more prudently than if they have nothing at risk. In the 1970s Pratt's predecessors at the bank board had lowered net worth requirements to 4 percent of liabilities, which meant that owners and investors had to have only $4 of their own money at risk for every $100 of deposits.

Pratt, at the league's suggestion, lowered the S&L capital requirement to 3 percent.

Commercial banks, by contrast, were held to a higher standard—$6 for every $100 in outstanding loans. It was a far tougher for two reasons: The percentage amount was greater, and in healthy institutions the loan pool exceeded the pool of deposits and thus provided a larger base from which the size of the capital requirement is calculated.

Next, Pratt relaxed the definition of what constituted capital, embracing assets of dubious value. He not only lowered the net worth requirement but made it easier for thrifts to meet the lower standard. FSLIC chief Beesley took the biggest step in this direction by introducing a concept bearing the sleep-inducing name of supervisory goodwill. Since its inception, this type of goodwill has raised all sorts of ill will among reputable accountants.

Imagine someone buys a widget manufacturer for $1 million even though he knows that if he were to break the company up and sell its tangible assets—its inventory of widgets and widget parts, its office desks and chairs, its paper clips and pencils—the lot would fetch only $800,000.

Why would he pay an additional $200,000? Because in theory the company is worth more than the sum of its parts. The business is a going concern, has established a customer base, is earning profits, and so on. Under the accounting rules most businesses use—known formally as generally accepted accounting principles, or GAAP (pronounced "gap")—the $200,000 represents a new asset for the company once it is sold. It is listed under the heading of "goodwill."

Though not a tangible object a person can touch like a car or desk, goodwill has a value that can be measured. In this case, it measures exactly $200,000—the number of dollars paid in excess of the company's tangible, kick-the-tire worth.

But if the buyer resells the company for only $600,000, he will have to write off—erase—$400,000 in assets all at once to reflect the decline in market value: the $200,000 booked in goodwill from the initial purchase plus $200,000 in additional lost value on assets.

Beesley put a twist on the concept of goodwill. He decided in late 1981 that if the bank board melded two ailing institutions, the new thrift could add up its soured loans—loans worthless as assets—and count them on the positive side of the balance sheet ledger under the heading of "goodwill." Such a maneuver is technically permissible under generally accepted accounting principles, but in practice it almost never occurs. People in the business of making money will rarely pay more for a company than they know it is worth.

Beesley's arrangement worked this way: Suppose a thrift had a negative net worth of $100 million—its liabilities exceeded its assets by that amount—because its liabilities were $300 million and its good assets were $200 million

97

($100 million was written off as worthless when, perhaps, borrowers defaulted on repayment of loans). Suppose a buyer agreed to assume the liabilities and the assets of the S&L—all $300 million. He had, in effect, agreed to make up the missing $100 million. Under normal accounting rules, that entitled him to add $100 million to the asset side of the ledger, in effect, restoring full value to the $100 million in soured loans.

In the real world, the buyer would seek offsetting benefits—cash, notes, or other incentives, like the waiver of federal banking laws—equaling $100 million. And Beesley was there to provide that, albeit in a way uniquely satisfying to the buyers of the ailing thrifts. To put it plainly, he issued FSLIC guarantees insuring the buyers against loss. Under that system the soured loans were restored to full value, at least on paper, under the heading of "goodwill" and thus contributed to net worth. The word "supervisory" had to be added to the "goodwill" heading because such transactions would not take place in the private sector in the absence of the government guarantee.

Everybody at the bank board seems to have liked the notion of supervisory goodwill as a ploy to keep thrifts alive. Beesley actively promoted the technique, encouraging ailing and healthy thrifts alike to take advantage of it. An S&L merger specialist at the time remarked to the *Wall Street Journal,* "I've never seen a government agency undertake such hokum with such relish."

Beesley defends supervisory goodwill, arguing that it is no more deceitful or inaccurate than the goodwill used in generally accepted accounting rules. He has a point—but a limited one. Under generally accepted rules, companies state the value of their assets as the price the companies paid for them. Because of inflation and other economic shifts, the value of any given asset deviates over time from the price originally paid. The stated values on a company's books often are years out of date. A table, a chair, a home loan, or any other asset could be worth more than its stated value or far less, just as most automobiles lose value year by year. Generally accepted accounting rules deal with changing values through a process called depreciation, the formal recognition each year that an asset like a car or other piece of machinery is worth less now than it was last year. Depreciation doesn't work for assets like loans, however, which are booked at full value until paid off or until a borrower falls so far behind that the lender is forced to revalue the loan, writing it down or possibly even writing it off.

This inability to depreciate loans created giant headaches for Beesley by producing misleading balance sheets. Time and again a thrift's books would show that while the institution's capital was gone, its assets nonetheless equaled its liabilities. In theory that meant the S&L's assets could be sold to pay off all obligations to depositors and other creditors. Nothing would be left over, but neither would any government money be required.

Real life was quite another matter because many loans carried on the books at face value proved to be worthless. Beesley invariably found that a thrift's liabilities far exceeded its resources, often by many tens of millions of dollars. Depositors could be paid off only by dipping into the FSLIC. When the FSLIC ran out of money, the next step would have to be the pockets of taxpayers.

"It just outraged me that the accounting system was so inaccurate," Beesley says. "The numbers were just almost fraudulent." That was what Volcker meant when he warned Ohio's Governor Celeste that no matter how troubled a financial institution looked from the outside, it was always in worse shape once you got in and examined the assets.

To Beesley, the creation of regulatory accounting, with its special kind of goodwill and other goodies, was no more misleading than the rules most companies, including S&Ls, already used. To critics who accused him of accounting alchemy—creating valuable assets out of rubbish—he argued that you cannot corrupt a corrupt system, but you can use it to your advantage. That was what he and Pratt were doing.

The Pratt regime initiated several other accounting tricks to jack up S&L paper values. Normally, if an S&L sold a loan for less than the loan's original worth, the thrift would have to reflect the loss in its earnings statement right away. But the Pratt bank board, after meeting with top California thrift officials, put in a new wrinkle. It allowed the thrift to continue carrying the loan (which the S&L didn't even own anymore) at its full value and write it off (depreciate it) slowly over several years. This was called a deferred loan loss, and it had the effect its name implied: It masked losses for years, postponing them into the future in the hope that some big profit would roll in.

Yet another cloaking device Pratt put in place in the early eighties involved real estate values: If an S&L building could be sold for more than the thrift paid for it (even though the S&L had no intention of selling it), Pratt permitted the thrift to estimate the profit from such a sale and book the profit as though the transaction had actually occurred. This neat trick was titled appraised equity.

These practices—supervisory goodwill, deferred loan losses, appraised equity—deviated so far from GAAP that bookkeeping for thrifts had to be given a new name: regulatory accounting principles (RAP). Cynics quickly dubbed it creative accounting principles (CRAP) and pronounced it worthless.

"We knew they were accounting tricks. We laughed about it," says a former OMB official who attended cabinet council meetings. "But we thought it would be a short-term remedy. What else could we do?"

From 1980 to 1982 reporting under the relaxed rules indicated the industry's net worth fell from $32.3 billion to $25.4 billion. In reality, net worth fell to $3.7 billion or less, hardly an adequate cushion for an industry with $700 billion in assets and a tendency toward wild growth that within a few years would push assets to more than $1 trillion.

While mergers and phony accounting bought time, deregulation was meant to be the long-term solution. Pratt inherited the first phase of deregulation, legislative changes wrought by the 1980 law. He wasted no time in implementing phase two, the regulatory changes that needed no approval from Congress.

Before Pratt had passed a year in office, the bank board permitted thrifts to invest in futures options and to buy and sell securities. (Both activities generally were off limits to commercial banks because they were considered too risky.) The board also permitted federally chartered thrifts to sell adjustable rate mortgages nationwide—a move the California thrifts had sought for years. Such loans, outlawed by many states for state-chartered institutions, forced consumers to absorb some of the interest rate risk that thrifts traditionally shouldered. (National banks had been granted similar authority in 1980 but, because of restrictive state laws, had not pushed to use it.)

As part of their deregulatory approach, administration officials implemented another change that, paradoxically, increased the number of thrifts. Until 1980 bank and thrift regulators judged applications to form a new bank or thrift on the basis of community need. Reaganites at the Treasury and in the White House had other ideas. They thought the market should decide whether there were too many banks or S&Ls. Pratt and his counterparts at the Comptroller's Office accordingly decided to approve any new application for a bank or thrift charter as long as the owners hired competent management and proposed a sound business plan. Let institution owners bear the risk; the market, not the government, should decide such matters. Unfortunately, phony accounting and the administration's decision to avoid closing insolvent thrifts prevented market forces from working. Thrifts remained in business whether good, bad, or ugly. The new charters didn't foster market discipline or efficiency. They just bid up interest rates by increasing the demand for deposits in an already overcrowded market.

This artificial competition was heating up even as the secondary mortgage market created by Fannie Mae and Freddie Mac—the government corporations that bought mortgage loans from thrifts—was becoming more efficient, and the need for a separate housing finance system was increasingly being called into question by scholars and Wall Street executives. Fannie Mae and Freddie Mac had started repackaging the home loans that they bought from financial institutions into securities that investors the world over clamored to buy. The efficiency of the secondary market in supplying fresh cash to lenders meant that more mortgage makers could meet America's need for home loans, but efficiency also lowered the profit any single institution could make on a loan; as more and more institutions offered to sell home loans to Fannie and Freddie, the price thrifts could fetch for the loans began to shrink.

Lost profit had to be made up in volume and in new business loans. Supply and demand were calling for fewer institutions with larger market share. But administration officials, who tried to apply free market theory to a system distorted by deposit insurance and phony accounting, couldn't hear.

Here and there skeptics tried to make themselves heard. "We ... have some doubts that diversification by savings and loans will help alleviate their earnings and liquidity problems in the short run" because companies venturing into new businesses usually lose money at first, Richard F. Syron, special assistant to Fed Chairman Volcker, wrote to Mehle in August 1981. "Expanding the powers of savings and loans raises a number of difficult and complex public policy questions, including the treatment of the industry in relation to other financial institutions and whether specialized lenders should continue to be a feature of our financial structure."

Robert McCormick, an Oklahoma banker who was president of the Independent Bankers Association, a lobby group representing small and medium-size commercial banks, wrote to Treasury Secretary Regan on June 23, 1982: "If anything, giving thrifts these powers will diminish the safety and soundness of these troubled institutions over the short term as they scramble for on-the-job training in the slipperiest of economic times; times in which the origin of sound, profitable commercial loans is far from easy." Thrifts had not yet "digested" the new powers they were granted in the 1980 law, he warned.

And red flags waved to those who cared to see. In late May 1981, around the time Secretary Regan caused a flap by saying, "So what?" the Economy Savings & Loan Association of Chicago had gone under. It was here that Beesley had talked with customers and was moved by the peace of mind federal deposit insurance gave them. Especially ominous was the cause of the thrift's demise: risky investments and poor management, not the high interest rates the administration—and the industry—liked to name as the culprit.

A year before its collapse in early 1981 Economy had signed contracts to buy mortgages from other institutions, locking in certain interest rates. The S&L was betting that interest rates would fall, and it would make millions of dollars in profits. But rates didn't fall. They went up. Economy lost its shirt. Its contracts required that it buy home loans that yielded lower than market returns. No one at the bank board seemed concerned that the moral hazard was kicking up. Nor did Pratt or anyone at Treasury wonder if desperate thrifts would be any more responsible with the new powers granted them by deregulation.

The effects of deregulation received a dramatic and largely unanticipated boost by a change in the tax law, which President Reagan pushed through Congress in 1981 as his first major legislative effort. The change, which provided massive tax shelters for real estate investments, was a disaster. It fueled a frenzy in financial competition as thrifts, banks, and insurance companies outbid one another to lend the money for shopping centers, condominiums, and other developments, many of which were built solely with tax breaks, not consumer demand, in mind. The frenzy helped push up real estate prices to artificially high levels. That prompted calls for further deregulation so that thrifts could take a direct ownership position in these seemingly lucrative projects. Soon thrifts held mortgages on hundreds of worthless properties all over the country.

The 1981 tax law exacerbated the thrift crisis in another way. Budget counters realized that the law cut federal revenues to an extent that, if unchecked, would produce a deficit within a few years four times larger than the highest deficit during the Carter administration. Prior to the 1981 tax law no administration official had favored the use of tax dollars to close the nation's bankrupt thrifts. By 1982, as the impact of the lost taxes became known and tax dollars became even scarcer, the idea of going to the budget to solve the crisis became wholly unthinkable. Suddenly the Reagan administration had a deficit of its own making, not one it could blame on Democrats. Now what had been a guideline became holy writ: Don't close thrifts if they can be kept open by any means.

All along, in the early eighties, Pratt kept the Senate and House Banking Committees, as well as the White House, abreast of his rule changes. They in turn supported his efforts. At the end of speeches Pratt routinely thanked White House aide Ed Gray for supporting the new rules, saying that the bank board could not have acted but for the support Gray helped generate within the administration.

The changes also were bolstered by the president's overall push for deregulation and in particular by a 1982 report of the president's Special Commission on Housing, which was headed by McKenna and included the president's thrift industry friend Luce on its board.

Among the recommendations of the avowedly Republican panel ("We are not a bipartisan commission," McKenna told a reporter in 1982): "Encourage free and deregulated housing markets" and "rely on the private sector." The report advocated deregulation so that S&Ls could diversify out of home lending and compete more directly with banks and with securities and insurance firms. A few pages later, the report championed the role of thrifts in housing and advocated tax breaks for them. Most important, it advocated leniency from regulators in shutting down sick S&Ls.

The report infuriated officials in the OMB. They saw it it as a ploy by Luce and McKenna to win presidential approval for regulatory and legislative changes sought by the California thrift industry. These changes amounted to more freedom without more accountability. Besides, in the eyes of the OMB, no industry deserved special treatment.

"We had been forewarned that there was this commission coming, a phony-baloney group whose purpose was to get breaks for the industry," recalls a top aide to OMB director Stockman. "McKenna, the ubiquitous Bill McKenna, headed it. I mean McKenna was everywhere during this period, at every meeting, trying to figure out ways to get the industry subsidies. He gives new meaning to the phrase 'tunnel vision.' I mean he didn't have a clue how things had changed. And the industry's attitude was a nonstop 'gimme, gimme.' "

Thrift executives regarded McKenna, nicknamed Red for the color of his hair, as the patriarch of their industry. He was name partner in the law firm of McKenna, Conner & Cuneo, which, from its offices in Los Angeles, San Francisco, and Washington, represented the major S&Ls in the country, particularly the big shots in California. Not only did the firm dominate representation of the West Coast thrifts individually, but it was chief counsel for the California Savings and Loan League, the state affiliate of the U.S. League of Savings Institutions. Dean Cannon, who heads the California league, once said McKenna succeeded because when no one else could think of a legal strategy to get the industry what it wanted in state capitals or in Congress, he could think of two or three. And McKenna had been faithful, his firm remaining at the forefront in the formation of thrift industry policy, local and national.

In McKenna's view, blame for the S&L mess resided with members of Congress, state legislatures, and courts that, over the years, voted in favor of consumers on issues such as adjustable rate mortgages and whether home sellers have the right to transfer their mortgages to the buyers of their homes, rather than in favor of the thrift industry. The industry, he says, time and again fought unsuccessfully to shift to consumers much of the risk—and, therefore, the cost—inherent in the interest rate-sensitive, government-protected industry. His attitude might be expected. For decades McKenna has been *the* S&L lawyer. Traditionally, a majority of petitioners from California thrifts to the regional Federal Home Loan Bank in San Francisco or its parent agency in Washington have hired McKenna's firm.

Devoted Catholic, Republican, and Irish-American, McKenna graduated in 1936 from Providence College in Rhode Island and in 1939 from Yale Law School. At Yale, he says, law professors instilled in him a crusading spirit about social issues. After law school he went to work as a lawyer for the bank board, then not even a decade old, helping the agency fight states that challenged the federal government's right to license thrifts. After a stint in the navy doing intelligence work during World War II, he rejoined the board, working there from 1947 to 1951. California was booming during this period, right at the heart of the postwar housing and thrift explosion. McKenna spent a lot of time there, becoming familiar with the names and faces of the industry.

Under President Eisenhower, McKenna set up the organized crime unit for the Department of Justice. In 1954 and 1955 he became an aggressive investigator of a front-page scandal in the Federal Housing Administration. As in the HUD housing scandal of the 1980s, a handful of men in the 1950s made millions of dollars in "windfall" profits from questionable transactions involving government-subsidized housing loans from the FHA. During congressional hearings, McKenna's outspokenness against the practices caught the ear of President Eisenhower. They met on several occasions to discuss the gravity of the problem.

Eventually McKenna went into private practice and within a few years he had built his reputation. His power within the thrift industry was immense, his imprint everywhere. Although officially never a member of the league, McKenna by all accounts wielded one of the strongest voices within the lobby group and among its leaders. Holding court in the lobby of the Clift Hotel in San Francisco just outside the well-known Redwood Room in the mid-1980s, he described himself as a humble bit player in thrift politics, someone with strong opinions but relatively little power. Former Reagan administration officials chuckle at that characterization.

McKenna doesn't pull punches. Housing, said the otherwise ardent spokesman for free enterprise, is too important an issue to leave to the vagaries of the market. Like the early founders of the league, he maintained that the nation's welfare and safety depend on homeownership.

"I don't think the free market should extend to whether or not a person can buy a home," he says. "It's terribly important to this country that a young family, whether with or without its first child, is able to buy a home. It's essential to our whole political system."

McKenna could have become more visible. Reagan wanted him to head the bank board, but McKenna declined for health reasons. He also told the *Los Angeles Times* in 1981 that the job might present conflicts of interest with his duties at his law firm, including the consulting agreement he signed upon retiring from active duty that same year. However, McKenna maintained his consulting contract with his law firm after he took the job as head of the regional Federal Home Loan Bank in San Francisco, arguably a job that rivaled the bank board chairmanship in power.

Officials at the OMB and Treasury were wary of McKenna, Luce, and Gray. They also had doubts about Pratt, despite his self-proclaimed instincts as a free marketer. He had, after all, been selected with the approval of McKenna and O'Connell. All were thought to care more about special interests than about true deregulation and consumer welfare. As Pratt sought to unshackle the industry, for example, he worked to shift cost and risk onto consumers. Thus in the fall of 1981 the *New York Times* ran a personal finance column under the headline FAILED PROMISES IN BANK DEREGULATION. It pointed out that the bank board imposed a penalty on consumers who reinvested funds from their low-yielding Keogh and Individual Retirement Accounts into newly authorized, higher-yielding ones. The new accounts cost thrifts more in interest payments; the more people kept their money in the old, lower-yielding accounts, the better for the industry.

True free marketers found this sort of protectionism anathema. Indeed, to some, deregulation went beyond loosening rules. It also meant getting rid of regulators. OMB chief Stockman meant to slash employment in all regulatory agencies, including the bank board, to support President Reagan's expensive desire to boost military spending while cutting taxes. The White House, through the OMB, pressured banking agencies to reduce their examination staffs. From 1980 to 1984, at the height of the deregulatory frenzy, all except the Federal Reserve Board complied.

During that period at the FDIC, the number of examiners dropped from 1,698 to 1,389. The Comptroller of the Currency let go of 310 examiners. The bank board cut 42 slots, bringing its total force to a low of 596 by 1984. Similar trends occurred at the state level. California's examination staff fell from 178 in 1978 to 44 in 1983 to oversee more than 100 state-chartered thrifts.

The examiners who remained, at both the state and the federal levels, generally were underpaid—often earning $14,000 a year or less—and too inexperienced (many were newly graduated from college) to understand the increasing complexities of financial fraud and incompetence.

Compounding matters, the federal government's front line against criminal activity—the Justice Department—was so woefully understaffed that it became impossible to prosecute bank fraud. Sparsely staffed U.S. attorneys' offices—which had one or two, perhaps half a dozen attorneys at best, devoted to major fraud of all types, not just that involving thrifts—couldn't keep up with hundreds of criminal referrals they received in the mid-1980s. Nor were the staffs of these offices adequately trained in the intricacies of financial fraud. Hearings by the House Committee on Government Operations criticized the Justice Department for failing to give bank and thrift fraud a higher priority. "For some prosecutors these cases have little, if any, appeal," concluded one report by the committee. "These cases are paper cases, which are not as sensational as a bank robbery, kidnapping, or an espionage case, but which, owing to the complexity of the criminal schemes devised, can be rather convoluted and therefore difficult to organize and try before a jury."

But lack of resources, rather than of "sensational" appeal, was the reason that few, if any, thrift cases were prosecuted by U.S. attorneys' offices around the country in the early 1980s. "The impact of inadequate resources, both in terms of FBI agents and assistant U.S. attorneys, is that some cases simply are not being investigated," the U.S. attorney for Wyoming, echoing statements by many of his colleagues, told the committee.

As a result, the government gave federally insured financial institutions new powers without providing the resources to detect and punish abuses of these powers. Pratt, to his credit, constantly fought Stockman to get more examiners. But his pleas were futile. Stockman's decision to cut bank board staff remains a glaring example of the penny wisdom and pound foolishness that prevailed during the Reagan years. The lack of examiners meant abuses in the thrift industry would not be detected and stopped until years after the damage had been done. Pushing the industry to expand into new fields and allowing it to follow lower standards while guaranteeing deposits up to $100,000 effectively privatized the industry's profits and socialized its losses.

As far as the industry went, that outcome was fine. It didn't mind the dirth of examiners. But it complained bitterly about Stockman's opposition to additional federal subsidies.

Through the early eighties Pratt seemed in conflict with himself. Even as he preached forbearance, he questioned the long-term viability of a federally subsidized housing finance industry. Like many of President Reagan's free marketers, Pratt thought that it was fine public policy to promote homeownership if that's what the government decided to do, but he questioned whether the savings and loan industry as it was structured was the best, most efficient way to do it. The S&L share of America's home loans was slipping steadily. Fewer Americans, in fact, could afford to buy a house.

Pratt knew very well how the league had hidden behind the apple pie image over the years. Now, as bank board chairman during the most tumultuous period in the industry's history, he believed severe economic changes were making a mockery of such ruses. He felt he had to speak out.

"This is a business, not a religion," he told industry executives. "I think a savings and loan is a business, and you ought to be in business to run an effective business. All this other stuff—the flags, the apple pies, the safeguard of American liberty stuff—is crap."

Pratt told the league at its eighty-ninth annual convention in 1981: "The savings and loan business as it previously existed . . . in my opinion died some time ago." It needed to be "reborn" by getting the religion of competition.

Beesley preached the same philosophy. "The economic history of the United States is replete with fascinating accounts of how entire industries and individual firms have adapted or failed to adapt to change in their operating environment," he said at the same convention, going on to relate a case study he had learned at Harvard Business School and never forgotten.

"In the nineteenth century there were two primary suppliers of glass lenses to the railroad industry," he said to row upon row of gentlemen who had followed the 3-6-3 rule for decades. "These marvelous lenses withstood a flame on the inner side and snow or sleet on the outer side. One of these two lens manufacturers hung on to its specialized product line and to its niche in the marketplace, and it followed the railroad lantern industry out of existence. The other company foresaw change in its environment. It did not fight the change or seek legislative protection, but it successfully began to develop new products and new markets. Today Corning Glass Works makes a wide variety of successful products, including sophisticated electronic components and heat-resistant materials for space vehicle reentry shields.

"The winds of change are blowing in the savings and loan industry at hurricane velocity. To those who sense some relief . . . I suggest you look around. We may just be in the eye of the storm."

A year later Beesley delivered a speech that harked back to the social Darwinism touted by business in the 1920s. Already nicknamed Dr. Doom by many in the industry, he cautioned healthy S&Ls against trying to keep all their brethren alive. "The winnowing-out process of the weakest market participants is neither unexpected nor unprecedented," Beesley told the league in the fall of 1982 in New Orleans, during its ninetieth annual convention. "Even as in the evolution of animal species, there is a natural tendency for the fittest to push out the weakest. It is salubrious, and it should not be thwarted."

Some in the audience understood and agreed with Beesley and Pratt. Others understood and disagreed. They wanted a return to thrifts that specialized in home lending, seeing such a return as the only way to retain entitlement under the social contract. Still others, the vast majority perhaps, had no idea what Beesley was talking about, but they didn't like the ominous tone.

Some of the California thrift leaders, like Anthony Frank at First Nationwide, began to speak of the day when distinctions between thrifts and full-service banks would disappear. Replacing the old order would be a new rivalry between consumer and business banks. The market, not government subsidy, would define the specialty of each.

But for all their speeches, Pratt and Beesley could not afford to follow their own line. They led the resistance against the laws of natural selection. Keeping insolvent thrifts alive became the rule.

14

The Grand Illusion

I nterest rates peaked at 21.5 percent in 1981. But when they began to come down in 1982, they didn't fall far enough fast enough to help the thrift industry. Treasury officials began to worry. The situation was getting worse, not better. The Mehle plan might fail.

Even with phony accounting the outlook worsened. About a third of the industry had become obviously insolvent, despite the host of artificial props. Pratt estimated that one new institution a day reached zero net worth. Some accused Pratt of employing scare tactics on behalf of the industry to gain the forbearance and other aid it wanted. A *Wall Street Journal* editorial said so. But concern was building. The *Los Angeles Times* published a chart showing how long it would take each major California thrift to become insolvent under various interest rate scenarios. Some had a few years left; some a few weeks or months. Industry executives remember the article well. Public awareness of the thrift crisis was growing. Bad headlines were scaring depositors away.

The Treasury began to develop its own disaster estimates. The work sheet of one top official estimated that if conditions of early 1982 continued, withdrawals from thrifts would outstrip new deposits in late 1983 or early 1984. If interest rates fell, the imbalance might be postponed until late 1984 or early 1985. If they rose, a cash shortage could hit the industry by the end of the year and spark runs all over the country.

Notes from a meeting between Regan, Mehle, and Pratt in February 1982 read:

Problems: Chicago—$15 billion in loses in '82
New York—whole industry
Mergers and Closings
82—can buy time
83—possibly can get through.

The next line of the document says simply: "bailout."

Treasury officials nonetheless assured President Reagan no bailout was needed. "The Working Group believes that FSLIC insurance fund is sufficient to meet projected needs," the group told the cabinet council in March 1982. Despite industry claims, the public had not lost confidence in the industry. No "silent runs" were occurring.

The S&L industry, continuing to pursue a bailout, kept trying to change the Treasury's mind.

On March 31, 1982, Regan wrote a memo to President Reagan in preparation for an April Fool's Day meeting between the president and leaders of the savings and loan industry. It outlined the administration's three-step approach, which it described as "a coherent short and long-term set of solutions to the problems."

Notes taken by an administration aide show the industry made these points to the president:

Q. What are the biggest problems?
A. Loss of confidence due to American press. . . .
In this recession, Main Street is having a harder time than Wall Street. Deregulation: Thrifts want deregulation in a responsible way. Bailout: 90 percent of industry free enterprise oriented and support President's goals, do not like government interference. Assistance: Some necessary on short-term basis to help housing and maintain confidence.
Goals: Encourage thrift and home ownership.
Housing will not come back without thrifts.

The S&L executives then suggested several solutions. One, attributed to Senator Richard Lugar (R-Ind.), involved a somewhat novel tax plan that would allow wealthy investors to buy mortgages from S&Ls and get tax write-offs on the losses. The estimated cost to the Treasury: $50 billion. Another was an accounting trick allowing losses to be booked as gains when one thrift bought another. Beesley, who talked frequently with industry leaders, already had started using this technique, calling it supervisory goodwill.

In April 1982 the league chairman, Roy Green, wrote Mehle disputing the administration's public position that the industry was not in crisis. "Seventy million dollars in deposits flowed out of a California thrift following an auditor's statement on the condition of the institution. This was only the tip of the iceberg: the most visible portion of an unmistakable 'quiet' run taking place at thrift institutions across America."

Around the same time the league resurrected the $10 billion warehousing plan it had pushed a year earlier, the plan that called for the government to buy and hold its bad loans until interest rates fell. Simultaneously it called for a reduction in the deficit that would bring down interest rates.

Industry spokesmen saw nothing inconsistent about a request that government both provide aid and cut the budget. But Senate Banking Committee Chairman Garn did. The simultaneous request represented "the great double standard that runs rampant in Washington. . . . That's why I'm not ready to jump on board some massive bailout at this time," he told the *Wall Street Journal*. Like the administration, he favored legislation that would restructure the thrift industry and make it more like commercial banking.

15

Storming the Hill

S enator Garn's views were important. The regulators had done all they could, and the action in 1982 now shifted to Congress. The administration wanted Congress to endorse legislatively its plan of forbearance, interstate mergers, and deregulation. The league, in contrast, pushed for more direct government subsidies, the plan it had been unable to sell to Treasury free marketers.

The league had allies in Congress. Foremost among them was Representative St Germain, the Democrat who had proved so helpful in raising deposit insurance to $100,000. Now chairman of the House Banking Committee, St Germain, known to most on Capitol Hill as Freddie, operated most comfortably in back rooms out of public view. St Germain graduated in 1948 from Providence College, William McKenna's school a decade earlier. He received a law degree from Boston University, returning afterward to Rhode Island, where he made the most of his name among a heavily French-Canadian population to win a seat in the state House of Representatives from 1952 to 1960. Then he went to Congress.

Many of St Germain's colleagues in the House disliked him. Some found his life-style too freewheeling. Many more resented the iron hand he used to run the Banking Committee. They regarded St Germain as a savvy politician but also as a ruthless autocrat who wouldn't share power, in many cases even refusing to fill in fellow Democrats about his planned strategy on a particular bill. For example, he was known to insist that banking regulators check with him before meeting with other members of the committee when major legislation was being considered. Representative Henry B. Gonzalez (D-Texas) is one of the few to complain publicly about such treatment—although even he waited until St Germain was voted out of office. St Germain ended up with many allies who feared him but few friends on the committee.

Part of St Germain's success stemmed from his self-proclaimed status as a consumer champion. Consumer lobby groups looked faithfully to him when they wanted Congress to make banks give fuller disclosure about loan rates or lending patterns in racially mixed neighborhoods, though few of the consumer provisions he proposed ever became law.

Curiously, however, officials from consumer organizations such as the Consumer Federation of America say that St Germain rarely, if ever, met with them directly, though he had plenty of time to talk with thrift executives or representatives of other financial industry groups. St Germain's chief of staff, Paul Nelson, occasionally met with consumer lobbyists, though he, too, seemed to spend more time with the industry. St Germain's day-to-day contact with consumers was left to aide Jake Lewis, who also was responsible for dealing with the press. That, lobbyists say, was no coincidence. Seeking publicity about his consumer work was one of St Germain's constant goals. Downplaying his ties to industry was another.

Like his House colleagues, many lobbyists, especially those from commercial banking who sought to lift regulations, disliked St Germain. They thought he favored other special-interest groups that wined and dined him. His proconsumer stand notwithstanding, St Germain was considered by lobbyists and fellow representatives as a best friend to the securities, insurance, and savings and loan industries, most of whose members opposed full-scale deregulation that would have eliminated the protectionist laws each industry enjoyed.

Commercial bankers went through the motions of paying homage to St Germain. They made campaign contributions and provided other perks, but their desire to expand into securities, insurance, and real estate fell on unsympathetic ears. They made their campaign and entertainment payments and paid their respects principally so that their bad relationship with St Germain wouldn't get personal; they wanted to be able to get in the door to plead their case, even if the exercise generally proved futile. And like many others, the bankers feared the congressman. They were, for example, loath to be the source of revelations about the extent to which St Germain was wined, dined, and provided late night entertainment by league lobbyists. If such disclosures only embarrassed St Germain but did not unseat him, the bankers would have to live with his rancor.

In short, lobbyists thought that St Germain benefited too much from the status quo to want to change it. The longer it appeared major legislation might pass, the longer St Germain and other members of the Banking Committee could collect honoraria and political contributions from the troops of financial services lobbyists wanting to influence the outcome of a bill. Stoking the expectation of action, but failing to act—that was how the Banking Committee's members drew money from industry groups.

St Germain had long ago mastered the art of seeming to move ahead on banking legislation while actually stalling. He would propose proconsumer legislation so radical that it stood no chance of passing. Or he would attach so many consumer provisions to a bill that the entire bill would die.

But St Germain was an astute parliamentarian who often proved he could be just as masterful in getting legislation through his committee as in stalling it; when he wanted action, he would force lawmakers to work without recess for hours and even all night if necessary.

In any event, most components of the financial services industry were content to live with the devil they knew. If St Germain were pushed aside, the next chairman might very well be worse. Representative Gonzalez, second in seniority to St Germain on the committee, was considered honest but peculiar, disorganized, and prone to stream-of-consciousness rambling. Another senior member, Frank Annunzio of Illinois, was too sick (he suffered from a heart ailment) to be a hands-on chairman and was said to leave management of the committee to his aide, Curt Prins, widely disliked by congressmen, congressional aides, and lobbyists as an arrogant, bigoted bully. A third possibility was Walter E. Fauntroy from the District of Columbia, considered to be more concerned with the District's parochial interests than with banking issues.

St Germain is a short, pudgy man with white hair and, except for an occasional ruddiness around the nose, a fair complexion. His sexual appetite and enthusiasm for fine food and drink were legendary in Washington. Lobbyists during St Germain's tenure as chairman joked that the Securities Industry Association took care of him Mondays, Wednesdays, and Fridays, and the league took over on Tuesdays, Thursdays, and Saturdays. "And on Sunday we all rested," quips one former league official. Sometimes other financial lobby groups took a turn, lobbyists say. But they insist that the league and its employee, James ("Snake") Freeman, were always on call. (Snake says his father gave him the nickname when he was a boy; to many who worked with him, it naturally suggested itself.)

Freeman was the league's chief lobbyist for the House Banking Committee, and that meant that his job was to take care of St Germain. A trim man with silver hair, a southern accent, and a preference for conservative dress, Freeman could often be seen leaning in a doorway leading from the House Banking Committee's hearing room to its back rooms, a doorway usually restricted to members of Congress and their staffs.

The accepted word among lobbyists on St Germain was that to get him to speak at a convention or meeting, trade groups had to pay for his travel and lodging, and the trip had to include limousine service, plenty of liquor, and entertainment. If any element were missing, the congressman was known to throw fits of verbal abuse and threaten not to speak—the kiss of death for lobbyists trying to show their rank-and-file members that they had the clout to get the House Banking Committee chairman to attend their gathering.

It is impossible to establish the truth of these assertions, and St Germain will not discuss whether he ever accepted prostitutes from the league or any of its state affiliates. But the stories abounded, and many lobbyists and government officials conducted their business with St Germain assuming the stories to be true. League President O'Connell, though never offering an out-and-out denial that the league paid for women, says he knew of no such arrangement and doesn't believe there was one. But he acknowledges that the stories were repeated so widely during his tenure as head of the organization (1979 to 1988) that he once called Freeman into his office and asked him point-blank. "Snake denied it to me," O'Connell says, adding, however, that "the league's a big place" and it would be "hard to follow every person's expenses." He denies reports from several former league employees who say they saw Freeman on several occasions withdraw thousands of dollars at a time from petty cash, sometimes asking that checks be cashed at that moment if the till didn't have that much in it, with the explanation that the money was needed for "the chairman."

O'Connell says that league records were well kept and detailed, and such requests would have aroused questions. (A Justice Department investigation of Freeman's expense accounts in 1987, however, found some sloppiness, such as expense slips for dinners with St Germain on days when Freeman was not in town.) "Somebody would have invited my attention" to such large withdrawals, O'Connell says.

O'Connell's predecessor, Norman Strunk, who joined the league in 1938 and ran it from 1959 to 1979, also worried about St Germain's reputation for "liking girls," as Strunk puts it. For that reason, Strunk says, several of his key staffers, including lobbyist Glenn Troop, advised him not to ask St Germain to league annual conventions because "it was just too much trouble" with "the girls and all." He says that St Germain attended only one or two conventions during Strunk's tenure. "To my knowledge we never provided any girls [to St Germain]," Strunk says. "But that doesn't mean we never did.

"I do know that at state [league] meetings there were girls for Freddie [St Germain] that I assume were provided by the state leagues," Strunk adds.

As for persistent rumors about Freeman's and St Germain's social relationship, Strunk says, "Frankly I was worried about it. We tried to back away from this stuff. . . . Freddie was very difficult. He was vain. He was demanding. He would insist on certain kowtowing. He would demand a great deal of social attention, and he would let you know when he needed campaign contributions."

The most frequently told tales of St Germain's amenability to subsidy involve Snake Freeman. The two often could be seen together eating and drinking the night away, accompanied by female companions (who observers say were not their wives) at the Prime Rib, a pricey restaurant popular with politicians and lobbyists in Washington. A grand piano with a see-through Plexiglas top sits in front of the bar.

How could St Germain afford to go there night after night on a congressman's salary and sup on a dinner that easily cost $100 or more with wine and drinks? Snake Freeman's credit card took care of it.

In fact, Freeman paid for hundreds of dinners over the years that the congressman failed to report on his financial disclosure forms.

A former official at the league who is now in the housing finance industry tells this story of his days as a league lobbyist. He was sitting in Snake Freeman's office one evening watching the television news about a personnel shakeup at the White House during the last days of the Carter administration. The telephone rang.

"Mr. Freeman's office," the league official answered.

"Is Mr. Freeman in?" a female voice said long distance from Los Angeles.

"No, he's not. Can I take a message?"

"Would you tell him Fifi called?"

The official says he decided to have a little fun, as a joke. He too had long heard the stories about Snake, St Germain, and the women and decided to fish for more information.

"I know why you're calling," he says he lied. "You understand the terms of the agreement?"

"Yes," he recalls she said. "I fly to Washington, and if I pass approval by Mr. Freeman and Mr. St Germain, then you will reimburse me for my expenses, and I will be on retainer with you."

"Yes, that's the normal condition under which we make these arrangements," the astonished official says he told her.

"Fine, that's what I was told."

"I'm sure we'll reimburse you for expenses because you sound like someone who will fulfill our needs," he said.

"I certainly hope so," she said, "because I can do anything."

The same league official says he once saw Freeman take $2,000 from the petty cash fund with the explanation that the money would be used to take St Germain deep-sea fishing.

"Deep-sea fishing?" the official asked.

"That's one thing to call it," he says Freeman replied.

St Germain's lawyer, Milton Semer, says he personally is not aware that prostitutes were provided to St Germain, but he does not categorically deny any were. Fred Webber, who succeeded O'Connell as head of the league in November 1988, after St Germain lost a bid for reelection, says he knows nothing about it. "It was before my time," Webber says, acknowledging he has heard the stories but refusing either to confirm or deny the movement of his troops before he took command.

The league also counted many friends in the ranks of the Republican-controlled Senate. Democrats Cranston from California and Riegle from Michigan were two. But none was more important than Republican Jake Garn of Utah, chairman of the Senate Banking Committee. League lobbyist Richard ("Rick") Hohlt, who once worked as a top aide to Senator Lugar, had the job trying to influence Garn. He dispatched his duty by concentrating on Garn's chief banking aide, M. Danny Wall.

Wall drank little, if at all, but he earned a reputation for taking all-expense-paid trips from the league and other lobby groups when he worked for Garn. He outdid many top congressional staffers in accepting lobbyist-subsidized junkets, once logging thirty in a single year.

According to Senate aides, Hohlt's telephone number at the league was listed first on Wall's speed dial telephone. Wall disputes this, saying the first number was that of Alvina, his wife. But since Alvina worked as Garn's personal secretary, that meant only that the first interoffice number was that of his boss's chamber. The first outside number was Hohlt's, Senate aides insist.

Representative St Germain and Senator Garn had little in common. St Germain was a ladies' man and a self-proclaimed protector of the little guy. Garn, a family man, championed business and free enterprise. But the two lawmakers held one view in common: They agreed that the thrift industry needed help.

While Garn and St Germain each favored policies the industry wanted, their differing perspectives meant that they pushed for different programs. St Germain wanted to preserve the industry. Though he favored some deregulation, he sought to maintain a semblance of the industry's original housing mission. The thrust of Garn's legislative proposal rested on forbearance—the official policy of encouraging regulators to tolerate problems and look the other way during hard times.

In 1981, after the Treasury's refusal to endorse the bill that had been proposed by Volcker's group, St Germain had proposed legislation to provide at least $7.5 billion in Treasury notes to prop up ailing thrifts. The White House objected to the scheme, which amounted to a direct cash outlay from the Treasury and was almost identical to what the league wanted.

In early 1982 St Germain devised a second bill; this one provided $8.5 billion in aid, but this time in Treasury guarantees, which he argued would not be a direct outlay from the Treasury. The bill also prohibited regulators from forcing mergers at institutions receiving the guarantees, another key initiative favored by the league. The White House still objected, arguing that expenditures under the second bill, like those under the first, would count on the budget. When Representative Chalmers Wylie, a Republican from Ohio, proposed an assistance proposal more to the administration's liking because it didn't directly tap taxpayer revenues, discussion of the provision was tabled on a motion by Representative Annunzio.

The Banking Committee approved St Germain's second $8.5 billion bill by a vote of 25–15, along straight party lines, on May 11, 1982. The full house passed it on May 20.

In essence, the House bill contained provisions favored by league President O'Connell: direct government aid and the preservation of as many thrifts as possible.

The legislation Garn forged during 1981 and 1982 was very different from St Germain's. That was no surprise: Regan, Mehle, and Pratt were instrumental in forming the administration package—a joint effort between the Treasury and the bank board—that became the centerpiece of Garn's bill.

Though Pratt and Regan both were free marketers, they found themselves bickering over what thrifts should and should not be allowed to do. Pratt fought hard to put language in the bill giving thrifts greater powers than banks. Regan and Mehle objected, arguing that while thrifts should be allowed more freedom, they should not be given a competitive edge over banks. Pratt responded by pointing to the financial success that California thrifts attained under the looser laws of that state in areas such as commercial real estate, suggesting that relaxing laws nationwide would have similar benefits.

"Real estate is the area thrifts understand best, and we believe that extending additional flexibility in this regard could have a beneficial earnings impact in the relatively short run. California state-chartered S&Ls which already have real estate equity investment authority similar to what we are proposing have been able to use that authority quite successfully," Pratt wrote to Mehle in the fall of 1981.

In the same letter Pratt protested Treasury suggestions that thrifts, which were subject to no dollar limit on lending to a single borrower, be subject to the same restrictions as commercial banks. He wrote: "[The bank board's] record of supervision in this area and that of insider transactions generally was instrumental in persuading Congress not to apply to thrifts a number of restrictive statutes enacted . . . in response to the Bert Lance affair. It would be highly ironic for an Administration dedicated to deregulation to seek to impose additional statutory restrictions on an industry's business practices in the absence of a demonstrated record of abuse." (In 1977 Lance resigned as President Carter's chief of OMB amid allegations of financial improprieties during Lance's years as a banker in Georgia.)

Pratt's letter also gave Regan and Mehle some political advice. He suggested they leave out of the administration's proposed bill any explicit language permitting banks to take over thrifts, arguing that such language would kill S&L industry support for the entire proposal. "Such support, in our view, is essential to the success of the legislation," Pratt said.

In the end Pratt won on the issue of giving thrifts greater commercial real estate powers, persuading the Treasury to include them in the administration proposal handed to Garn. And Pratt persuaded Regan and Mehle not to tamper with S&Ls' looser restrictions on loans to one borrower. The administration also took Pratt's advice and left out any provision regarding the merger of thrifts with commercial banks. Eventually the House Banking Committee, at the league's suggestion, put in language suggesting—but, significantly, not mandating—that healthy thrifts be given first crack at buying unhealthy S&Ls. The suggestion amounted to a placebo, but it helped the league save face with its members, who had favored language requiring that S&Ls be given priority in the purchase of ailing S&Ls.

Garn's proposal ended up containing the key provisions sought by the administration, the bank board, and the California thrifts: forbearance in the form of FSLIC notes (Mehle's IOUs that didn't count on the budget) and significant deregulation for thrifts. The first bill Garn unveiled also proposed raising deposit insurance for retirement savings accounts to $250,000, as the league wanted (actually, the lobby group originally favored $500,000), but because the Treasury Department objected to it, the provision was dropped before the Senate Banking Committee voted on the legislation.

"With fewer government restrictions, the financial system should respond more efficiently to changes in the economic and competitive environments for the benefit of everyone. This deregulatory effort is important to the administration not only because it comports so well with the President's regulatory reform program, but because the effort should be especially beneficial to consumers," Regan told the Senate Banking Committee during the fall of 1981, testifying in support of Garn's bill.

Regan's wholehearted endorsement rested on two assumptions. First, he assumed that there was plenty of business for which S&Ls, banks, and other financial institutions could compete head to head. Second, he assumed that S&L executives were sophisticated enough to take advantage of the new powers and the forbearance provisions with long-term profits in mind. At the time, few in Congress—certainly not Garn—took issue with those assumptions.

Today Garn tries to distance himself from the 1982 legislation by saying that its provisions were not radical and that in any case, he merely included administration proposals in his bill as a courtesy. But few buy the notion that a man as strong-willed as Jake Garn would serve merely as a conduit for the administration. Garn's party loyalty *is* strong—he claims he would not have run for a third term in 1986 if President Reagan had not asked him to do so—but not that strong. "The administration proposes. Congress disposes," Garn told Regan icily when the treasury secretary visited him in early 1981 to discuss bank and thrift deregulation legislation.

In fact, Garn had been fighting for deregulation in the financial markets for some time. He included provisions in his 1982 bill that would allow commercial banks to offer mutual funds and to underwrite certain types of bonds. Although the administration supported Garn on the provision, his colleagues on the Senate Banking Committee—notably Republicans John Heinz of Pennsylvania and Alfonse D'Amato of New York and Democrats Riegle, Cranston, and Proxmire—did not.

Heinz, D'Amato, Riegle, and Cranston acted in the interests of the Wall Street securities firms, which didn't want banks invading their turf. Proxmire's opposition stemmed from his populist sentiment that the separation of commercial and investment banking was a good idea: The separation protected the public from concentrations of power and from potential conflicts of interest in the lending of money and the selling of securities. In July Garn took the controversial banking provisions out, to the delight of thrifts and securities firms and the chagrin of bankers. He also removed the proposal to increase deposit insurance for retirement plans.

But he retained one politically charged provision that dealt with the right of thrifts to demand full payment of mortgages each time a homeowner moved, so-called due-on-sale provisions. These clauses have been written into housing contracts since the early 1960s to guard against uncreditworthy buyers who might take over a loan from a seller. But as rates soared in the late 1970s, thrifts found a new use for the clause, a way to unload unprofitable loans each time a home changed hands.

Forcing consumers to repay existing loans and take out new mortgages each time they bought a house helped thrifts retire low-yield loans and replace them with more profitable ones. By the same token, of course, it forced consumers to pay more for a loan on each purchase of a house. Realtors, whose livelihood depends on sales commissions, sided with homeowners and against the thrifts on the theory that anything that discouraged sales was bad.

McKenna, whose stated priority was to make homeownership available to as many people in as many economic classes as possible, had long been involved in the fight. His law firm led the drive for due-on-sale clauses. His logic? Sales lost because of the clause would be more than outweighed by the benefits afforded consumers by a healthy thrift industry. Before he joined the government, Pratt had assisted McKenna and the California league in court battles involving the legality under state law of due-on-sale clauses.

According to a former McKenna, Conner & Cuneo lawyer and several former bank board employees, the league virtually wrote most of the bank board policy that sought to preempt state law and allow due-on-sale clauses, often conferring first with McKenna's firm. Although lawyers with the firm deny it, several attorneys familiar with the issue say that McKenna's lawyers essentially ghostwrote the bank board's legal brief in support of the California thrift industry's position in the due-on-sale controversy.

The Reagan White House was divided on the issue, a division that highlighted the distinction between free market rhetoric and the interests of California thrifts. The Thrift Industry Working Group wrote to the cabinet council in late 1981, "This issue requires a balancing of state interests with the federal interest in preserving sound financial institutions." If the White House went along with thrift wishes on the due-on-sale issue—a stance that would ban consumers from transferring home loans to buyers—the administration would violate two of its own top objectives: limiting governmental interference in private contracts and returning regulatory responsibilities to the states.

If the administration and Garn had been true to their ideals, they would have let California and other states ban due-on-sale contracts at state-chartered thrifts. Instead they reached a compromise with the industry. With White House backing, and in a sharp departure from his usual states' rights stance, Garn included a provision in his bill that preempted state laws allowing consumers to transfer loans but gave states the option to override the preemption in three years.

The Senate Banking Committee unanimously approved Garn's bill on August 19, 1982. The full Senate approved it on September 24.

The league endorsed the measure. But the American Bankers Association, the largest lobby group for commercial bankers, dubbed it "a sweetheart savings and loan bill that leaves the commercial banking community at a greater competitive disadvantage than before. Little is left in this legislation which addresses the special needs of the banking industry."

House and Senate conferees worked quickly, reaching an agreement on September 29, five days after the Senate acted. The final compromise generally followed the Senate bill. To do otherwise would have risked a presidential veto. St Germain didn't want the responsibility of having killed what amounted to the first thrift industry bailout bill. Besides, Garn's bill contained the item St Germain most cared about: forbearance and aid for the industry. If the Senate's version of that aid was the only version the White House would accept, then St Germain would go along. All the other measures the Senate included—deregulation, relaxed rules—well, if the league endorsed it, St Germain could, too.

The highlights of the law included:

- Expansion of direct aid, mostly through Mehle's FSLIC notes, to ailing thrifts so that their cushion against loan losses—their net worth—would be overstated; regulators then wouldn't have to close the institutions. The law also made it easier for the deposit insurance fund to facilitate and provide aid for mergers of ailing thrifts; it suggested, but did not mandate, that healthy thrifts be given the first chance to bid on ailing thrifts.
- An increase in the proportion of assets thrifts could commit to business and consumer loans, and commercial real estate. Thrifts now could invest 30 percent of federally insured funds in consumer loans (up from the 20 percent permitted in the 1980 law). They could invest 40 percent in nonresidential mortgages (up from 20 percent permitted in 1980). And they could invest 10 percent in loans to business, up from zero, and another 10 percent in leasing activities. Thus the law enabled an industry created to specialize in home lending to invest 90 percent of its assets in commercial bank-type, or nonresidential mortgage, activities.

  Despite permitting these new freedoms, the law favored any thrift that kept 60 percent of its assets in home loans, cash, mortgage-backed securities from the secondary market, student loans, or certain government securities. If an S&L met the 60 percent "thriftness" test,

it qualified for tax breaks and also could branch across state lines—
two benefits S&Ls very much wanted. In effect, 60 percent "thriftness"
rather than 90 percent became the industry benchmark after the 1982
bill passed.

- Elimination of the minimum down payment requirement for consumer home loans. Here was the advent of 100 percent financing.
Down payments had been required in years past on the conservative
theory that fewer borrowers will default on mortgages if a sizable
portion of their own money is at stake.
- A preemption of state laws that had allowed homeowners to transfer
their mortgages to buyers of their homes—the controversial due-on-
sale provision.
- A provision making it tougher for the bank board to throw out management. Oddly, another provision gave the board greater authority to
seize state-chartered, federally insured thrifts. That authority was to
expire, however, in January 1987.
- Permission for S&Ls to offer regular checking accounts both to consumers and to companies already doing business with the thrifts. (The
NOW accounts authorized in 1980 carried restrictions on how often
withdrawals could be made.)
- A provision—pushed hard by the industry—that allowed thrifts to
drop "savings and loan" from their names and replace it with "savings
bank." The phrase was intended to link S&Ls in consumers' minds to
full-service banks. Gordon Luce was among the first to take advantage of the new law. In May 1983 he changed the name of Great
American Federal Savings and Loan of San Diego to Great American
Federal Savings Bank.

The 1982 law had one striking omission. Neither the House nor the Senate
versions advocated stronger oversight to make sure no thrift abused forbearance or new powers, whether those granted by the 1980 law, by Pratt's bank
board, or by the new legislation. As a consequence, S&Ls were freed from
decades-old restrictions without anyone looking over their shoulders.

The law was called the Garn-St Germain Depository Institutions Act of
1982, or the Garn-St Germain Act for short. Although this legislation would
allow the industry to move far afield from its original purpose of providing
home loans, both men wanted their names on it. "There is some poetic justice," a banking lobbyist bitter about the law wrote in a private memo years
later. "They insisted their names be tied to the bill. So they will be [linked]
together into history. Dante would be amused."

The 1982 act was the third and final step in a federal effort to deregulate the thrift industry during the early 1980s. The first step had been the 1980 law. It had lifted interest rate caps, increased deposit insurance coverage, and permitted thrifts to exercise broad new powers similar to those permitted commercial banks. Pratt had undertaken the second step by easing bank board regulations. No law had been required for that.

At a Rose Garden ceremony in late 1982, President Reagan signed Garn-St Germain into law, saying, "I think we've hit the jackpot."

Federal and state deregulation went hand in hand. In 1981 and 1982 state legislators cited the looser rules of the 1980 federal law to justify even more radical changes in state law; federal lawmakers in turn cited relaxed state law to justify loosening federal restrictions in 1982. It was a classic example of what lawyers and economists call a race to the bottom: States loosened their rules to prevent state-chartered thrifts from switching to federal charters, and federal regulators trotted to keep up.

Arizona, California, Texas, Florida, Ohio, and Maryland led the nation in state efforts to liberalize thrifts law. Many other states also followed Washington's lead: Louisiana, Illinois, New York, Michigan, Massachusetts.

In 1981 seven of California's ten largest thrifts, including the three largest, held state charters. By the end of 1983 nine of the ten largest were federally chartered. Funding for California's supervisory department diminished proportionately. Between 1978 and 1983 the department's staff fell from 178 to 44.

The remaining state thrift regulators, eager to justify the existence of their jobs, fought against the trend by pushing state legislators to give state-chartered thrifts even greater freedom than that held by federally chartered institutions. State legislators eagerly complied, and for good reason: Under California law, state corporations may contribute to candidates seeking state office. Federally chartered thrifts cannot. State-chartered thrifts had been a major source of campaign funding in local politics, and now the number of state-chartered institutions was shrinking.

In 1982 California State Assemblyman Patrick Nolan, a Republican from Los Angeles who received $154,000 in campaign contributions from thrifts in the 1980s, went the last mile. The California legislature passed the Nolan-sponsored, California league-supported legislation that permitted California thrifts, as of January 1, 1983, to invest their money any way they wished. According to people in the industry, it was a partner in McKenna's law firm, Norman Raiden, who virtually drafted the law for Nolan on behalf of the state league. Raiden, who was counsel to the state league at the time, denies the claim, saying he never advised or even commented to Nolan's office on the subject. In fact, he says he recalls that the state league was "neutral" on the Nolan bill. His recollection is not supported by the state league's literature.

Thrifts now didn't have to put a dime of their federally insured deposits into home loans; 100 percent of their lending could (and did) go into wind farms, junk bonds, restaurants, Nevada brothels—there were no limits. The law outderegulated the feds.

"The California Savings and Loan League is sponsoring this 'deregulation' or 'investment flexibility' effort as one of the more important goals to seek this year at the state and federal levels," the California league said in a memo on May 20, 1982, to state lawmakers about to vote on the Nolan bill. "Our members are unanimous. . . . The savings and loan industry has the intent and expertise to be the state's and the nation's primary housing lender. We must have the flexibility to remain viable."

Texas, meanwhile, had always left state-chartered thrifts to invest federally insured money any way they wanted. Until the 1980s, however, few thrifts took advantage of the freedom. They prefered to stick to home lending, a profitable business for them. But as oil prices soared, the state's economy took off. Interest rates followed, home loan profits dropped, and Texas thrifts began to take advantage of the little-used authority to speculate heavily in commercial real estate and other ventures outside the housing industry.

Washington's deregulation rhetoric helped foster the frenzy in Texas, and vice versa. While pushing the Garn-St Germain Act, Garn cited a study by Pratt and the bank board that found Texas S&Ls earned 2 percent more on nontraditional loans than they did on home loans. The report concluded that Texas thrifts on average earned more money than their federal counterparts. Loan portfolio diversity seemed to be the reason. The Texas institutions, the study pointed out, engaged in activities that went far beyond anything Congress was proposing.

Pratt, as the nation's leading thrift regulator, didn't merely allow FSLIC-insured thrifts to enter new businesses permitted by state and federal law. He encouraged thrifts to do so in the hope that new profit-making enterprises would restore them to health.

Hundreds of S&L executives, veterans as well as newcomers to the business, rushed to heed Pratt's admonition. Pratt and his crew "hawked" the thrift charter as the most liberal bank charter around. With it, Pratt preached, a thrift executive could offer more financial services than any commercial bank. Banks, which had been clamoring for permission to sell securities and insurance, knew the truth of this promise all too well.

Shortly before Pratt resigned from the bank board in the spring of 1983, his agency issued a rule interpreting the new Garn-St Germain Act as permitting federally chartered thrifts to invest up to 11 percent of their federally insured assets in high-yield, high-risk securities known as junk bonds.

Indeed, thrifts' powers became so loose that Citicorp studied the possibility of converting its entire banking operation to an S&L charter. The no-holds-barred ability of S&Ls to sell whatever financial service—or whatever product, for that matter—they desired was alluring. Citicorp eventually decided against the move on the ground that the tarnished reputation of the thrift industry outweighed the benefits of an S&L charter. However, Citicorp did buy several ailing thrifts in major markets, including California and Washington, D.C., where it might otherwise have been barred from buying a commercial bank.

16

The Revolving Door

A t long last interest rates fell in 1982 and 1983. But they did so ever so slowly. A third of the thirty-two hundred thrifts that had survived the interest rate spike remained in critical condition. Only lenient government policies allowed them to keep their doors open and creak along.

But it was also true that more than a thousand S&Ls began to look less sick, and the remaining third or so started looking downright healthy. Pratt had warned in 1981 of a problem reaching to $100 billion and beyond. That figure had been reduced by tens of billions of dollars, by some internal government estimates to as low as $30 billion. But a $30 billion payoff to depositors at hundreds of insolvent thrifts was no small headache, especially as the 1984 election approached. In fact, the difference between $100 billion and $30 billion was nil to Reagan's budget keepers. Either figure was too big to put on the budget. Now Regan and Pratt crossed their fingers. Perhaps the benefits of deregulation would kick in, allowing a phaseout of such government aid as FSLIC notes and forbearance.

In early 1983 Pratt, Beesley, and Vartanian left government. Pratt took a six-figure job as head of Merrill Lynch Mortgage Capital, the unit of Merrill Lynch that handles mortgage-related products and services for the S&L industry and federal agencies. Merrill Lynch was the leader on Wall Street in selling financial services such as brokered deposits to cash-starved thrifts that couldn't handle the new powers granted them by the Pratt bank board.

Vartanian became a partner in a major law firm—Fried, Frank, Harris, Shriver & Jacobson. He brought in millions of dollars a year in business from deals that involved the buying or selling of thrifts, including many that had run into trouble using the new powers put into place during his tenure as the bank board's chief counsel.

Beesley bought a struggling S&L in St. George, Utah.

17

Lincoln Continued . . .
Charles Keating

C harles Keating says he grew up immersed in S&Ls. More precisely, he grew up in Hamilton County in southern Ohio, which he says had scores of thrifts, more than one hundred. They were little thrifts, run by German-Americans and open one or two nights a week.

"My father-in-law was an S&L guy. He operated one night a week," Keating says. "He had three million dollars in assets. He made loans to his friends. And I grew up in the most intense S and L environment in the United States. They had as many S and Ls there as they did in Southern California for all those years. Everybody my mom and dad knew was a director in or a lawyer for someone in an S and L. It was just an S and L environment, and I knew S and Ls from the ground up. . . . You know, I bought them. I sold them. I did work for and against them as a lawyer."

Keating got a liberal arts degree from the University of Cincinnati, though he actually attended college for no more than six months; the university accepted as academic credit much of his World War II experience as a night fighter pilot in the navy. Then he graduated from the university's law school.

Keating went to work for the American Financial Corporation, which bought an Ohio S&L called Hunter Savings in 1959. American Financial was a multimillion-dollar diversified company based in Cincinnati that was owned by takeover artist Carl Lindner. In the 1970s Keating became one of Lindner's top executives, rising to be executive vice-president of the company. American Financial at the time also owned the *Cincinnati Enquirer,* where Keating's brother William was publisher. (Eventually the Gannett Company, Inc., bought the newspaper, and Keating's brother moved up the ranks of the media giant.)

In 1979 Keating had his first brush with federal regulators. The Securities and Exchange Commission charged in a civil fraud suit that Lindner and Keating had defrauded stockholders of Lindner's company and filed false or misleading information with the SEC. The case involved $14 million in loans that the SEC said were made on "preferential terms"—and without proper collateral or credit checks—to American Financial insiders, including Keating. Lindner and Keating, without admitting or denying guilt, settled the matter by signing a consent order promising to stop breaking SEC rules. Lindner also agreed to pay $1.4 million to American Financial.

Keating shrugs off his brush with the SEC. He says he signed the consent decree only because it was cheaper than proving his innocence in court. He wanted, he says, to avoid the expense of a protracted legal battle.

That same year Keating moved to Phoenix, where he had paid $300,000 to buy Lindner's financially stressed real estate and home building company. He then used this company to develop property in Arizona, California, and Colorado and to build a holding company he called American Continental Corporation. At first he succeeded in turning Lindner's troubled company around.

Keating, an avid college swimmer who still tried to get in a workout in the pool every day, was a longtime Republican activist. He was the campaign chairman for former Secretary of the Treasury John Connally's unsuccessful bid for president in 1980. And Keating was a longtime crusader against pornography. He has six children, five of them girls. Colleagues say that the attempted rape of one of his daughters intensified his passionate fight against smut. He collected a large portfolio of pornography, filed by subject matter, that filled several large file drawers at his law office in Cincinnati. Keating was President Nixon's appointee to the Federal Commission on Obscenity and Pornography. When the commission concluded that pornography was probably not a threat to society and that laws to censor it probably violated the First Amendment right of free speech, Keating gained national attention by suing to block release of the report until he could write a dissenting opinion.

Keating says that in 1981 President Reagan called to offer an ambassadorship to the Bahamas but then withdrew the offer when presidential aides discovered Keating's brush with the SEC through newspaper reports. Keating blamed the press for the incident, saying the SEC consent decree did not reflect on his character. "To keep people like me out of positions like that because of yellow journalism, I don't know what good it does," he told the *Arizona Republic.*

Keating says he put his pornography crusade aside for a while after he went to Arizona, where he became preoccupied with the real estate market. During an interview in the summer of 1989, when asked why he had wanted to get into the S&L business, he said: "I knew the business inside out, and I always felt that an S and L, if they'd relax the rules, was the biggest money-maker in the world. And indeed, that's what they did in California. . . . And the minute we saw that, that California relaxed the rules, we raised some money, paid off our bank debt," and went shopping with $50 million cash for a California thrift.

Helping entice Keating to the Golden State was California's new commissioner of S&Ls, Lawrence Taggart. Before becoming commissioner, Taggart had worked for twelve years at the San Diego thrift owned by President Reagan's confidant and thrift guru Gordon Luce. Taggart was sympathetic to the idea that less red tape, less government oversight, and much more freedom should be the order of the day. He and Keating were on the same wavelength.

When Keating went to California, he found a cornucopia of possibilities. Federal and state regulators in 1983 were pushing innovation: junk bonds, real estate, almost any new and risky venture. "They expected you to do it," he says. "They were encouraging of the diversifying." Federally insured money probably should not go to such enterprises, Keating says today, but that is not the issue. The point, he says, is that the rules said you could invest in such things. And the regulators said you should. For much of California's thrift business, the domination of home loans was a thing of the past.

Thrift regulators touted the advantages of a thrift charter. That, says Keating, was his attraction to the thrift business. Among the thrifts that caught his attention was Don Crocker's S&L, now called Lincoln Savings and Loan, in Southern California.

Part IV

A WOULD-BE HERO, PART I

Hell is paved with good intentions.

—English proverb

Now is the time to raise the cow's tail and look the situation squarely in the face.

—Texas proverb

18

The Puppet

When Edwin John Gray worked as press secretary to California Governor Ronald Reagan from 1967 to 1973, he garaged his car in the basement of the governor's office building. One evening he stepped into the governor's private elevator without noticing a handwritten sign taped on the control panel warning, "DO NOT GO TO BASEMENT." He pushed the button to the basement. When the doors opened, water from the flooded garage poured in. Those waiting floors above for the elevator heard Gray's screams for help.

Colleagues added the incident (which Gray denies) to a long list of Ed Gray stories. With his rumpled clothing, his disregard for some details and obsession with others, and his penchant for working until all hours, a few colleagues thought him clownish. Others viewed him as a workaholic. Still others saw him as an absentminded eccentric, who, though prone to emotional outbursts, was a likable fellow.

As the governor's top public relations man Gray could backslap and glad-hand with the best of them. He enjoyed parties and socializing. But even in the relatively carefree days in Sacramento, where his job was to make people like his boss, the outgoing Gray exhibited an unsettling intensity, a doggedness that often made him appear stubborn, unrelenting. Sometimes it made him unmindful.

Once the governor got a call from the state's general services office. Gray had checked out more than a dozen automobiles over six months and returned none of them. The state's fleet was running low. Eventually all of the vehicles were found in the parking lot of the Sacramento airport, where Gray had left them. Gray brushes off the incident as a minor point of forgetfulness, explaining that he often went to the airport alone but usually returned with Reagan in the governor's car.

When it came to serving Ronald Reagan, Gray could not work hard enough. Michael Deaver, assistant executive secretary to Reagan at the time and usually first to arrive at the governor's office in the morning, often found Gray fast asleep at his desk, where he'd worked on the details of a speech or some other project until the early hours of the morning and then dropped, too weary to go home.

Over the years many of Reagan's friends became Gray's friends. Deaver, Edwin Meese, and Edward Rollins came to look fondly on the sometimes befuddled, ever-eager Ed Gray. So did Gordon Luce, head of Great American Federal Savings Bank in San Diego and one of Governor Reagan's kitchen cabinet. Luce saw the light on in Gray's office until midnight many nights, and he often thought, "What a hardworking young man."

In 1973, in the midst of exchanging pleasantries, Gray told Luce how much he loved San Diego, with its fine weather and beautiful views of the Pacific.

"Ed, why don't you come to San Diego and work for me?" Luce asked.

"You know, I'm ready," Gray said.

So began Gray's career in the savings and loan industry. From then on two concerns dominated his life: Ronald Reagan and thrifts.

Gray grew up in Modesto, California, in a hardworking family of modest means. His father, who went no farther than the eighth grade, owned a hardware business catering to the local agricultural community. Gray, a champion debater, was graduated as the valedictorian of Modesto High School's class of 1953, an accomplishment he still lists on his résumé but plays down by saying, "Well, it was a small class."

He worked his way through Fresno State University as a radio and television announcer and technician, graduated in 1957, and then held a variety of journalism jobs, including a stint from 1961 to 1962 as a news editor in the Madrid office of United Press International.

But upon returning to California and getting married in 1963, Gray moved out of news and into public relations, joining the Pacific Telephone and Telegraph Company. In 1966 the company volunteered Gray to help with the Reagan inauguration. With characteristic determination and single-mindedness, Gray combed the state's Spanish missions to find the oldest Bible for Reagan's swearing in.

The governor's press officer soon asked Gray to join his staff. Gray told the official that he'd been a Republican for only a year and had not even voted for Reagan in the primary. It didn't matter, the official told him.

After joining Great American a few years later, Gray, like Luce, was active in California Republican politics. Great American had close ties with many of Reagan's strongest supporters. When Reagan ran for president and asked for his help, Gray couldn't resist. He took a leave of absence from the thrift from 1980 until the fall of 1982 to work in the campaign, then on the transition team, and, finally, at the White House. His friend Meese was there, too, as counselor to the president.

In Washington Gray seemed to many observers to be obsessively proud of his ties to Reagan. At social engagements such as embassy dinners, Gray bored listeners with tales of how close he was to the president, how long and how hard he had worked for him.

In the White House Gray served as deputy assistant to the president, first as director of the White House Office of Policy Development—the job he held when he interviewed Pratt for the bank board chairmanship—and then as director of the White House Office of Policy Information, responsible for articulating presidential policies. He helped create the president's Special Commission on Housing, the group that McKenna headed and that many officials in the White House budget office viewed as a Trojan horse sent by the California thrift industry to obtain presidential backing for their legislative and regulatory goals.

At Great American, Gray had seen firsthand how the interest rate squeeze had mauled the industry. In the White House Gray heard from men he respected, men like McKenna and O'Connell, that matters were getting worse. Gray tried to help. He became a vocal advocate for tax-exempt savings accounts for thrifts, for looser regulations that would give the industry breathing space, for the Garn-St Germain Act—all the initiatives that the U.S. League of Savings Institutions backed.

But despite Gray's ties to President Reagan and Reagan's friends, and despite his impressive title, few took Gray seriously. Many of the president's top advisers regarded Gray as nothing more than a political hanger-on who had won a place in the White House through loyalty, not brains. Gray had the president's ear through Deaver, Meese, Rollins, and others from California, but other key Reagan aides, like Baker, Regan, and Stockman, didn't give much credence to Gray. When they listened to Gray speak, they believed they heard Meese talking, or worse, McKenna, Luce, and the California thrift industry.

As Pratt implemented one new policy after another, he found Gray's interest in S&L matters, and his accessibility to Meese and the president, an enormous help in gaining acceptance from the administration for the bank board's actions. Treasury Secretary Regan, by contrast, often wouldn't return Pratt's calls.

"I couldn't do what I've done without the help of Ed Gray," Pratt frequently added in speeches to the thrift industry. "I thank him."

Gray's wife, Monique, hated Washington. To her relief, they returned to San Diego and Great American in September 1982. But in spirit Gray never left the capital. He spent much of his first six weeks at the thrift pushing for passage of the Garn-St Germain Act, which Reagan signed into law on October 15. A month later in New Orleans, at the league's annual convention, Gray's Potomac fever became obvious. Bank board Chairman Pratt recently had let his intention to leave be known, though he hadn't officially announced it. Thrift executive after thrift executive approached Gray to say they wanted him to take Pratt's place.

"It was embarrassing," Gray recalls. "I mean, I had just returned to my job, and there right under my boss's nose people were offering me another job." And it wasn't just another job. It was the pinnacle thrift regulatory position, one that all but guaranteed a prestigious six-figure job as head of an S&L or on Wall Street when it was over. The offer surprised and embarrassed Gray, but underneath he gloated, flattered at the attention.

Pratt urged Gray to take the job. League President O'Connell agreed. So did McKenna.

Meese did, too, and as a member of the senior staff personnel committee that dealt with White House appointments he formally recommended Gray for the position.

League lobbyist Rick Hohlt pushed two influential friends to help secure Gray's nomination: Senate Banking Committee Chief of Staff M. Danny Wall and Craig Fuller, chief of staff for Vice President Bush.

For his part, Luce says he never lifted a finger to help Gray win the appointment; he claims, in fact, to have tried to persuade Gray not to take it. "Ed, you can't be serious. That is a grueling, thankless job," he says he told Gray, to no avail.

"I want to be perceived as a manager. I want to be a manager and show I can do this job," he recalls Gray responding.

Within the industry, however, few believe that Gray could have obtained the job without Luce's blessing. According to former administration officials, Luce lobbied through Meese to land Gray the job. "He wanted one of his own there," a former White House senior aide recalls of Luce. He adds that in the early years of the Reagan administration Luce visited the White House every few months, making the rounds of senior staff and executive appointees, including Gray.

Only one powerful player held a different view: Regan, a Wall Street man, had disliked Gray from the earliest days of the Reagan administration. The animosity flowed in part from Regan's condescending attitude toward thrift executives as a class, but the rift deepened when Gray, as a White House aide in 1981 and 1982, fought to give thrifts additional tax breaks. Regan killed the idea and wrote Gray off as a tool of the thrift industry.

But in early 1983 the forces favoring Gray were too powerful for Regan. The White House still viewed the bank board chairmanship as a harmless spot where the president could park a pliable political loyalist, and Reagan offered Gray the job. He accepted, over the objections of his wife, although he promised her he would return to San Diego in two years. Meese swore him into office on March 24, 1983. Gray had what he long had craved: a leadership role. It didn't matter that the bank board chairman was little more than a cheerleader for the industry. At least he held center stage.

As Gray took his oath, he bathed in the glory of being out from under the shadow of a boss. That a nobody could climb to the top through hard work reaffirmed his rosy view of the American Dream. It was a simplistic, sentimental outlook, one shared by President Reagan. Gray reveled in his new position, describing it this way in the résumé he handed out as chairman: "In a broad financial context, Mr. Gray presides over one of the largest corporate financial conglomerates in the world, including the nation's savings institutions industry, the Federal Home Loan Banks and the Federal Savings and Loan Insurance Corporation and Freddie Mac whose total resources are equal to the combined assets of the following American industries: petroleum, private utilities and all retail trade."

Industry executives were pleased with their new chairman but a bit worried. Stormy times lay ahead, industry leaders knew. Gray, while as accommodating as could be, might not have what it took to hold the reins during a crisis. Gray's talent thus far lay in giving speeches and attending dinner parties, not in tending to the nuts and bolts of running an agency.

Industry leaders persuaded Gray to name as chief counsel to the bank board Norman Raiden, a senior partner in McKenna's law firm and counsel to the California league when California Assemblyman Nolan created his deregulation bill. In the industry's view, Raiden would be the agency's brains, keeping an eye on Gray and, in many important respects, running the agency in a manner key voices in California would like. Gray would immerse himself in public relations.

Gray also was flanked by his two colleagues on the bank board, both Reagan appointees, Mary Grigsby and Donald Hovde.

Grigsby, the board's Democrat, had been in the Texas thrift business for forty-two years, holding top positions as a thrift executive. She also was past president of the Texas Savings and Loan League and had been a director and member of the executive committees of the U.S. league and of a smaller industry trade group, the National Council of Savings Institutions. Widely considered to be far and away the smartest of the three board members, Grigsby also had a sense of humor about the sometimes uncomfortable role of regulating during hard times, once donning a Groucho Marx mask during a visit home to Texas.

Hovde, an avid golfer, was considered by Gray to care more about spending the afternoon on the fairway than about the impending thrift crisis. Before coming to the bank board in May 1983, two months after Gray, he spent two years as undersecretary of the Department of Housing and Urban Development. Before that Hovde had owned and operated a commercial and investment real estate brokerage and development firm in Madison, Wisconsin. In time, as Gray's relationship with the industry and many key White House officials soured, Gray's relationship with Hovde also broke down. At one point Gray locked himself in his office and forced Hovde to communicate with him by slipping notes under the door.

19

Into the Breach

From the beginning Gray established a tone and style that would be the hallmark of his tenure as the nation's top thrift regulator. One of his first acts was approval of a retreat for high-level bank board staff at the Boar's Head Inn in Charlottesville, Virginia. That wasn't unusual. Each year the three members of the board and the heads of the board divisions went off to discuss policy for the coming year. Sensitive and confidential financial information about the industry and individual thrifts was put on the table.

But Gray astonished his staff by arriving in Charlottesville with executives from two of California's (and the nation's) largest thrifts in tow: James Montgomery, chairman of the Great Western Financial Corporation, of Los Angeles, and Pratt's friend Anthony Frank, of First Nationwide of San Francisco. Montgomery and Frank were part of the California thrift clique. They were friends of McKenna's, used his law firm, were active in affairs of the Federal Home Loan Bank of San Francisco. Questioned months later by the *Wall Street Journal,* Gray explained, "I invited them because they are proven leaders in the industry. I wanted to hear their suggestions, especially on profitability."

"It's good for my company that Ed listens to me. Sometimes I talk with Ed three times in one week, though I may go for weeks without talking to him," Montgomery told the *Journal.* "We've had some influence on Ed's positions before they're public."

A bank board staffer saw it another way, commenting, "We were shocked that two thrift executives would sit in on the most important meeting of the year."

Staffers got another surprise when, back in their Washington headquarters, workers descended on Pratt's former office, a suite with a sweeping view of the Old Executive Office Building and White House grounds. Bypassing government purchasing procedures, Gray spent $47,254 on cosmetic changes, including $2,000 in new carpeting, $3,700 for a new kitchen door, $7,950 for a security entrance near his office, and $900 for gold-leaf lettering on doors around the suite.

For the final touch Gray hung a giant poster-size picture of himself with Ronald Reagan and George Bush. The picture, a blown-up snapshot, dominated the office.

News of the lavish office renovation prompted an FBI investigation. The inquiry also looked into an even more peculiar allegation: charges that Gray actually lived in his office, presumably as a way to avoid the expense of a Washington apartment. (Monique Gray had stayed behind in San Diego with the Grays' two daughters.)

Gray conceded he did "crash" on the office couch occasionally, following his long-standing practice of working on speeches until the wee hours. But he also had an apartment, a tiny place near the bank board that, because he was sending every paycheck home, Gray kept sparsely furnished. He says that when he stayed at the apartment, he ate on a shoestring—McDonald's hamburgers, the cheapest frozen pizza from Safeway, sometimes nothing more than a can of beans or corn for dinner. It was not easy making ends meet while maintaining two households on a government salary of $75,000 a year.

The FBI investigation went nowhere. Gray may have been kooky, but he was no crook. Even so, the somewhat bizarre incident, like the cars Gray left at the Sacramento airport, embarrassed President Reagan. And other aspects of Gray's life-style soon began raising eyebrows. Gray may have eaten modestly when in Washington, but as often as not he roamed the country and the world delivering speeches on the S&L industry, staying in one luxury hotel after another and living on restaurant food paid for by the Federal Home Loan Bank System or by the league or other trade groups. He often remained in Washington only a few days a month.

Gray believed in travel. During a two-month stretch early in his tenure, his calendar shows three days in Washington, with the rest of the time in Japan, Hawaii, California, Georgia, Florida, and New Mexico. He needed to get out among the troops, "to see the whites of their eyes," as he put it, to encourage S&L executives during hard times and to preach the benefits of Garn-St

Germain. Whatever Gray's motives, lavish travel and entertainment came to be the mark of his first few years in office, expenditures that seemed out of place for an agency that was presiding over a collapsing industry. And the spending seemed even more peculiar because it was funded by the industry.

The league paid for Gray's travel, lodging, meals, and entertainment whenever the bank board chairman attended league functions. While this was an arrangement of questionable legality and ethics, Gray's predecessors had supped at the league's table for decades. But Gray and his aide Shannon Fairbanks, who had left the White House to become Gray's chief of staff at the bank board, took the perk to new heights. In this Gray and the board were out of step with commercial banking regulators—Volcker at the Fed and William Isaac and then William Seidman at the FDIC—who would not have dreamed of allowing the bank executives they regulated to pick up an expensive tab, let alone one for an especially fancy outing of the sort routinely financed by the thrift industry.

The industry-funded regional Federal Home Loan Banks or Freddie Mac, the quasi-government company governed by the bank board, paid Gray's travel when board or league reimbursement was unavailable.

Gray's trips to Europe were typical. While in Paris on business in 1984, Gray couldn't figure out how to work a French pay telephone. Leaving his wallet in the phone booth, he went in search of instruction. The wallet was gone when he returned, but he didn't lose a penny of the missing $744 in cash and airfare discounts. The twelve regional banks reimbursed Gray for the entire amount.

A year later, in the summer of 1985, Gray made another trek to Europe, this time to sell bonds for Freddie Mac. The trip included free tickets to Wimbledon worth $1,040 for himself, his wife, and his two daughters, as well as hundreds of dollars in payments for limousines, fancy restaurants, and hotels, all paid for by Freddie Mac, which in turn was funded by the thrift industry.

During the same trip, on July 6, Gray, Hovde, Fairbanks, and several officials from Freddie Mac and the Federal Home Loan Banks of Boston and San Francisco attended a Freddie Mac-funded dinner in a private room at Lasserre, one of the most expensive restaurants in Paris. No prospective investors were present.

Gray's personal limousine expenses on the trip totaled $779.42 and included use of a car and chauffeur for ten hours to fetch Gray and his wife from the airport and take them sight-seeing in London on Friday, June 28. On Saturday Gray and his family used a car for fourteen hours while they attended Wimbledon. On Sunday the Grays used a limo and driver for a seven-and-a-half hour trip to the Windsor Castle area.

Freddie Mac did sell $100 million of its bonds a few weeks after the trip, a result that given Europe's appetite for U.S. securities at the time, the officials could probably have achieved from their desks in Washington or, at the least, with a smaller, more cost-conscious travel entourage.

Similarly, in 1985 Gray charged the industry via the regional banks for $9,000 to celebrate President Reagan's second inauguration, including a $1,207 liquor tab for a reception for the members of the league, people whom Gray and the rest of the bank board staff already saw frequently during the chairman's speech-making jaunts around the country.

The regional banks also paid for small personal items, such as beauty salon appointments and massages for Fairbanks and, in one case, a gag gift of exploding golf balls for board member Hovde. Others were bigger-ticket items—for example, a three-day San Francisco affair in August 1986, when Gray and his retinue ran up hotel and banquet bills of $12,324, plus $6,924 more for a cruise on San Francisco Bay.

Some of the largest expenditures came at regular meetings of the presidents and directors of the twelve regional banks. From 1983 through September 1986 bank board officials met, often with the same fifty people, in Hawaii; Palm Springs, Monterey, and Lake Arrowhead in California; at the Greenbrier resort in West Virginia; at the Tamarron in Colorado; and at the Boca Raton Hilton in Florida. Some of the costliest meetings took place in San Francisco and New York, hosted by the regional banks headquartered in those cities.

Entertainment at these meetings was lavish. At a bank presidents' meeting in the Lake Arrowhead Hilton Lodge in August 1985, for example, the bank board's chief counsel, Norm Raiden, and his wife hosted a cocktail party for the presidents and their spouses that the Raidens later billed to the banks. The liquor bill of $276 included a case of Moosehead beer and nine bottles of Johnnie Walker Red. The night before, the same people had attended a catered cocktail party costing $554. Sometime that day or the next, some persons attending the meeting took paddleboat trips costing $320 around Lake Arrowhead. The hotel bill for Gray, Hovde, and Grigsby totaled $4,902. When that conference ended, the president of the San Francisco bank, James Cirona, hosted a $5,256 dinner at the Sheraton Plaza la Reina in Los Angeles in honor of Gray.

Similarly, in January 1986 the board of directors of the San Francisco bank, with McKenna as chairman, met with the board of directors of the Atlanta bank in Hawaii for three days. Gray, his wife, and their two daughters attended the fete. So did Hovde. The hotel bill, paid by the banks, was $2,614. After the Hawaii meeting, Hovde and Gray flew to New York for the bank presidents' monthly meeting. Gray stayed at the Waldorf-Astoria in a room costing $649 a night. Room costs for other staff members averaged about $170. Gray stayed three nights, billing the banks for $2,088, including more than $1,000 in taxes, room service, and telephone calls.

In February San Francisco bank directors went to a three-day meeting at the Boca Raton Hotel and Club in Florida, again to meet with the board of directors of the Atlanta regional bank. Gray, Hovde, Fairbanks, and several other bank board officials attended, leaving the two banks with a bill of $5,441, including the cost of "box lunches for golfers."

But the regional banks didn't pay just for parties. They paid for bank board business that the board could not afford under its congressionally approved budget limitations. For example, in July 1985 Fairbanks ordered the banks to set up and pay for a one-day meeting by top board officials to "develop the major board priorities and goals . . . over the next six months." The regional banks arranged for top agency staff to drive forty-five minutes south of their offices in Washington to the Woodlawn Plantation, described in a bank board memo as "the home built by George Washington for his daughter." The cost: $368, including $29 for alcoholic beverages.

Requests for regional bank largess typically went from Julie Gould, Fairbanks's assistant, to the director of the regional banks' joint office in Washington, Austin Dowling, who maintained what bank board employees used to refer to as the imprest fund, or, sometimes, as the regional banks' slush fund. When asked about the arrangement, Dowling said that no one forced him to pay the bills but that paying for a reception here and there "made my life easier."

Of course, Gray's spare-no-expense attitude at the bank board simply took a page from the league's book. The league's chairman, each year a different thrift executive, and his wife (all the chairs were men) were treated like royalty. Perks included a chauffeured limousine, all-expense-paid trips across the country, stays in first-class hotels, and meals in top-of-the-line restaurants. The wife of one former league chairman is said to have been so depressed to see her husband's tenure end that she had to seek psychological counseling.

Even the bank board staff, no strangers to league officials and to the occasional free dinner or other perk, found Gray's behavior excessive. A Christmas skit by the board's legal department in 1986 included this dialogue between a travel agent ("T. A.") and Ed Gray ("E. G."):

T. A.: Good Morning Chairman Gray! Where will you be traveling today, sir?

E. G.: I'd like to go out and learn about the problems in the field.

T. A.: Very good, sir. We have a number of package tours available to you.

Option One is the Gnome Getaway. Freddie Mac gives you seven days of luxury accommodations in London and Paris with a sumptuous dinner at a Michelin four-star restaurant. And if your money is lost or stolen in a Parisian phone booth, it will be replaced within twenty-four hours by a bank board courier.

E. G.: No. I think I've already done that. What's Option Number Two?

T. A.: Option Two is provided by U.S. League Luxury Lines. This package offers four days in Hawaii, all expenses paid. Helpful U.S. league lobbyists are available to assist you in getting any regulation your pesky staff may be pushing.

E. G.: No. I think I've already done that, too. You said there was a third option?

T. A.: Yes, and it's a real beaut. The District Bank Boondoggle offers you six-hundred-dollar-a-night suites and fawning bank presidents trained to meet your ego's every need. A broad range of transportation is available, including chartered planes, yachts, and limousines.

E. G.: Well, that sounds awfully familiar.

T. A.: Nothing, I'm afraid, that would be suitable for a gentleman of your stature sir. There is, of course, the special Suffering Staff Safari.

E. G.: What's that?

T. A.: By government regulation you get a room next to the squeaky elevator of a fleabag hotel with a window that looks out through a blinking neon sign. Meals are included with your coach airline fare. Typical destinations include Harrison, Arkansas; Clovis, New Mexico; Mesquite, Texas; and Kalispell, Montana.

E. G.: I haven't done that before.

The skit went on to describe a contest among the regional banks on which could "put on the best spread" under the "District Bank Boondoggle." The winner was San Francisco, where McKenna was chairman and Cirona was president and chief regional regulator. A staffer acting as Gray sang a song entitled "Jim Cirona's Bank" to the tune of the Beach Boys' song "California Girls":

The New York bank is hip,
I really dig their Waldorf suite,
And the Atlanta bank
With the way they spend
They knock me out when I'm down there.

The Midwest Home Loan Banks
You know they really treat me right;
But Kermit's bank*

*Kermit L. Mowbray was president of the Topeka regional bank.

With the deals they do
They keep my lawyers up at night.

I wish they all could be Jim Cirona's
I wish they all could be Jim Cirona's
I wish they all could be Jim Cirona's bank.

The sun at Wimbledon was warm,
I couldn't help but tan,
I love a Dallas meeting on Hawaiian shores
By a palm tree in the sand.

I've been all around this great big world
And I seen all kinds of perks,
But I couldn't wait to get back to the states
Back to the richest bank in the world.

I wish they all could be Jim Cirona's
I wish they all could be Jim Cirona's
I wish they all could be Jim Cirona's bank.

Staffers not only resented Gray's high style of living but also found that the extent of his travel made work more difficult. Staff members sometimes had trouble tracking him down and often had to spend hours and hundreds of dollars preparing documents and sending them by courier across the country so that the three-member bank board could meet by telephone.

All this traveling occurred as the air was going out of the industry tire. In the second half of 1983, despite a decline in interest rates, nearly four of every ten thrifts lost money. Many more barely made a profit. At the same time one of every four was experiencing an erosion of its net worth, according to bank board estimates. But because the board and the industry used bogus accounting that made the problems look less severe than they were, the actual situation was much worse.

20

Empires of Hot Money

G ray's travel often took him to Texas. In June 1983, just a few weeks into his new job, Gray flew to Dallas for the annual convention of the Texas league. He arrived at the Dallas-Fort Worth airport clutching a speech entitled "A Sure Cure for What Ails You." In it Gray urged conventiongoers to take advantage of the new laws that provided novel ways to attract and invest money. In the evening he hobnobbed with executives at dinners and hotel suites around town, the public relations man playing his part in the industry's customary celebration of itself. He enjoyed himself. He was part of the party.

(On a similar swing through Dallas, trying to enlist the industry's support on a proposed regulation to limit the use of brokered deposits, Gray complimented an executive on a pair of gold cuff links bearing the emblem of the Federal Home Loan Bank System. The executive insisted Gray take them. He wore them often in the days ahead.)

On another evening of the 1983 Texas league convention Gray was puzzled. He sat cushioned in the back seat of a blue Rolls-Royce speeding toward the neon lights of the Dallas skyline, studying his dinner host, Spencer H. Blain, Jr., chairman and major stockholder of Empire Savings and Loan of Mesquite, Texas. Blain was no newcomer to the industry. He was a former vice-chairman of the regional Federal Home Loan Bank, who, at this convention, was being honored as the outgoing president of the Texas league. Gray couldn't reconcile the car with the man; no thrift executive in California that he knew drove a Rolls. A Mercedes maybe (that was the kind of car Gray drove). But not a Rolls.

The balding, button-downed Blain was a respected S&L executive when he joined Empire as chairman in March 1982 and later that year bought a controlling interest in the thrift. He had served in top executive posts at several Texas thrifts, including First Federal Savings and Loan of Austin. But his relations with executives there soured in 1982. So he quit his $120,000-a-year job in Austin to join Empire, a small, unremarkable thrift, in a position that offered only $30,000 a year.

Blain's new S&L was headquartered in a nondescript shopping center outside Dallas. Its driving force (and the reason Blain went to Empire) was D. L. ("Danny") Faulkner, a condominium developer who had joined with some partners to acquire the thrift in 1979. Faulkner was immediately generous. When Blain met Empire's board of directors for the first time, he sported a gold nugget bracelet and Rolex watch—all gifts from Faulkner. Blain seemed to sense that he wouldn't hurt for riches at Empire, despite his paltry executive salary. And he didn't. He earned $16 million on investments related to the thrift during his two years at its helm, according to the Justice Department.

After Blain bought Empire from Faulkner in 1982, the two remained close business associates, so close, the federal government charged later, that Faulkner and the former mayor of Garland, Texas, James Toler, effectively controlled much of Empire's lending. Their specialty was a transaction that thrift executives called a land flip, in which executives at different thrifts arranged for the same piece of land to be purchased over and over, jacking the price up on each flip to inflate its value. Each time the value went up, the thrift could provide a bigger loan to a new buyer. To thrifts, loans are assets. Because interest charges grow with the size of the loan, the bigger the loan, the bigger the profit an institution appears to book (and does unless the loan sours). The "next greater fool," in Texas S&L parlance, referred to the person who eventually got stuck holding the property, having bought it at an absurdly high price. Faulkner and Toler made millions of dollars from such deals, selling the land to buyers who used money borrowed from Empire.

Empire's tie to developers was not unusual in itself. Thrifts always had been closely associated with businesses that built and sold homes. But Texas law added a wrinkle. It permitted state-chartered, federally insured thrifts to take ownership positions in the projects they funded and to lend themselves as much money as needed. Empire, once a sleepy thrift making conservative home loans, pushed this power and its construction industry connection to the limit. Like many Texas S&Ls, Empire began to acquire a large appetite for the builder's fee it got at the start of a project and began to lose interest in whether the project itself made sense in the long run.

"No one will admit it now, but at the time the Federal Home Loan Bank welcomed these guys into the industry," L. L. Bowman, Texas thrift regulator at the time Gray ran the bank board, says today. He says the prevailing attitude among Federal Home Loan Bank regulators was, "Hey, if you've got money, come on in."

Faulkner's life-style stood out even in Texas. A seventh-grade dropout, former sharecropper, and house painter who claims he can neither read nor write, Faulkner routinely handed out Rolex watches as gifts. Sometimes he gave away Mercedes-Benz cars and mink coats. When his son married, he hired the Tulsa Philharmonic to play the theme from *Rocky* at the wedding and paid a uniformed guard to stand at a tollbooth and toss in quarters for guests driving to the reception afterward.

Every Saturday morning Faulkner's breakfast club met at the Wise Circle Grill east of Dallas, where dozens of politicians and developers munched on steak and eggs while Faulkner expounded on his business philosophy, turned a few deals, and handed out dozens of 14k gold stickpins bearing a diamond-studded *F*. Jaguars, Mercedeses, and Rolls-Royces filled the parking lot.

According to local newspaper reports, one local jeweler claimed he sold nearly $4 million in gold and diamond jewelry to Faulkner and his associates in just six months. When Faulkner threw himself a fiftieth birthday party in December 1982, guests at the event in the Fairmont Hotel in downtown Dallas included many local politicians, including Texas Attorney General-elect James Mattox. At the time Mattox had already received $200,000 from deals with Faulkner involving condominiums built along I-30 outside Dallas.

Gray knew little of this background as he rode along in Blain's Rolls. "Is this your car?" Gray asked Blain. "I don't know any thrift executive who drives a Rolls-Royce."

"Oh, well," Blain said. "We're just very profitable down here in Texas."

Gray knew that. The state's thrifts had been held up as exemplars during the debate on the Garn-St Germain bill. Still, the Rolls jarred Gray. So did the Rolex watch and gold nugget bracelets he saw throughout the evening. Even in free-spirited California few bankers wore jewelry, at least not so much. But Gray shrugged off these trappings of wealth as a loud but innocent aspect of a Texas culture that encouraged people to flaunt prosperity.

As the evening wore on, Gray attended a party for thrift executives that Blain hosted in a penthouse atop what then was called the Registry Hotel. Reporters for the *Washington Post* described the scene: "They hooted and hollered and danced around the ornate fireplace and the mock 18th century

French furniture. An odd, guitar-picking duo provided the music: L. Linwood Bowman III, the lanky, sedate Texas savings and loan commissioner, and chubby, ribald Durward Curlee, lobbyist for the industry that Bowman was responsible for regulating. The two crooned for more than an hour, serenading Gray with 'I'm Walking the Floor over You' and 'Lovesick Blues.' "

Bowman says he took Gray aside during the convention to alert him of rumors about Blain and shady business dealings at Empire. The thrift had embarked on a frenzied growth spree, doubling in size every few months. The spree was powered by higher than market rates to attract brokered deposits, money then plowed into a ghost town of condominiums on Route I-30.

Bowman says he instructed Gray in the art of land flips and daisy chains, a variation on land flips, in which thrifts sold and resold bad loans to each other to inflate their value. That gave rise to the industry saying "A rolling loan gathers no loss." The goal was to prevent regulators from realizing how many loans were not being repaid on time. Gray has a different recollection, saying Bowman mentioned, but only in passing, several troubled Texas thrifts, none of which Gray had heard of before.

Later regulators uncovered many instances of land flipping at Empire. When Blain bought the thrift in August 1982, he also bought some land for about $1 million. Six months later he sold it for more than $16 million. According to federal investigators, in a two-week period during November 1982, Empire and its partners inflated the price of another parcel of land from $3.2 million to $96 million by selling it over and over again.

Thrifts like Empire also made a special type of loan that looked healthy for as long as two years after it had soured. Under these loans, called acquisition, development, and construction (ADC) loans, a thrift lent a borrower a principal sum, but also enough to make two years' worth of interest payments on the loan. The thrift in effect paid itself interest and therefore earned no real profit. The arrangement was legal, and coupled with the other schemes, it kept the regulators at bay. Regulators didn't close profitable thrifts, even if they suspected the profits were phony. Regulators maintained they needed proof of trouble. With ADC loans, that could take years.

Other peculiar things were going on in Texas. Even as Gray tapped his feet to the honky-tonk melodies spun by Bowman and Curlee, Fannie Mae had decided to buy no more loans on Empire's I-30 condo project. They represented too big a risk. Fannie's reasoning was simple: Nearly half the completed condos on I-30 were vacant. Yet Blain and his Empire continued to build more, spurred by the paper profits they were booking.

Unsettling rumors circulated. Someone had been towing cars from a junkyard and parking them in empty driveways along I-30 to create an illusion of financial health. Any motorist driving by could see that something was wrong. Sign after sign announced desperation: NOW LEASING! TWO MONTHS FREE RENT! THREE MONTHS FREE RENT! NO DEPOSIT! LOW RENT! Row after row of apartments stood empty.

But a drive through the I-30 projects wasn't on Gray's agenda. He flew back to Washington and then out again, traveling to and fro, not giving much thought to Texas. Good-natured Gray didn't suspect that a large number of legitimate thrift owners, as well as many crooks, didn't share his vision of the Ozzie-and-Harriet S&L making home loans on Main Street. Besides, there was in his mind a safety net built into the thrift business. No sane business-man, he reasoned, would purposely run his own company into the ground.

Two months later, on a muggy August Washington afternoon, Gray met with the bank board's top staffers, who were gathered in the agency's sixth-floor conference room for their monthly meeting to brief the board members on the health of the industry. The staff members startled Gray with their report. The interest rate problem had largely disappeared, but in its place loomed an equally costly mess: bad loans. Scores of thrifts had rushed headlong into risky projects like shopping centers, condominiums, racehorses, fast-food restaurants—activities allowed by the new state and federal laws that carried a high chance of failure but also the potential for higher-than-average returns if successful. They had embarked on strategies of fast growth because they had a fountain of easy money: brokered deposits.

Also called hot money, brokered deposits, it will be recalled, are sums that securities firms such as Merrill Lynch collect from individuals and then de-posit in increments of $100,000 at whichever bank or thrift pays the highest interest rate. Of course, $100,000 is the maximum deposit amount insured by the federal government. In the early 1980s securities firms essentially used brokered accounts to enter commercial banking, offering clients the highest federally insured rate around. The firms collected one fee from their custom-ers for managing the money and another fee from the thrift or bank where they deposited the funds. Commercial bank regulators opposed the practice. Banks, they argued, couldn't sell securities, and securities firms shouldn't be able, through a back door, to offer federally insured deposits.

As it happened, while running Merrill Lynch, Donald Regan had overseen the pioneering use of brokered funds during the period of high interest rates in the late 1970s. Merrill Lynch nearly single-handedly developed it into a major Wall Street business. The firm continued to dominate the brokered funds market during the 1980s.

Until 1980 thrift regulations limited brokered funds to 5 percent of an S&L's deposits. In that year the bank board, chaired by Carter-appointed Jay Janis, lifted the cap, largely in response to the 1980 law that ushered in

152

deregulation and also pushed deposit insurance to $100,000. But Janis maintained a strict limit on finder fees paid by thrifts to hot money brokers. Further, the finder fee had to be counted toward total interest paid. Because brokers earn much of their income from fees, the restriction substantially dampened Wall Street's enthusiasm for the business.

In March 1982, however, the Pratt bank board voted to lift nearly all restrictions on brokered funds, although it did not disturb the limits on finder fees. That restraint was cut when the Depository Institutions Deregulation Committee (DIDC), formed in 1980 to oversee the phase-out over several years of interest rate caps and now chaired by Regan, voted on September 17, 1982, to lift the fee cap for professional money brokers like Merrill Lynch.

The hot money question had been the first, item on the committee's agenda that Friday afternoon. Pratt tried to prevent the committee from removing the limit. Volcker, too, was cautious. "I think that some recent experience in the banking world suggests that broker deposits are not the healthiest element of banking liability structure in any event. And I think that broker deposits have led to a lot of abuses in the past, and I'd just as soon let it stand the way it is," he said. "I do think the problem is that this encourages a kind of impersonal rate shopping and leads to highly volatile deposits. It does it to big [institutions] and it would do it for small ones. It's a question of whether it's good or bad for the banking system. I don't think you can adjust this by saying all regulation is bad."

But Regan was all for allowing the fees in unlimited amounts. "As far as I can see, it seems to me that what we have here is a classic case of whether or not we're going to let free enterprise work or not, be they thrifts or commercial banks, that they make the decision themselves whether they want to accept these funds," he said.

"What is the damage which is likely to occur from a thirty- or sixty-day comment period?" Pratt asked.

"It just makes it look to me, Mr. Pratt, as though you do not intend to allow other people to vote. You wish to have a popularity poll, something of that nature. Well, we've studied this issue. We've had a colloquy, we've had a discussion of it, and I'm perfectly prepared to go ahead and vote," answered Regan.

"Fine," said Pratt. "The chairman is in the chair."

The committee, with Pratt casting the sole dissent, voted in favor of unlimited finder fees.

The committee's vote fired the starting gun that set off a mad race. Desperate thrifts scrambled to offer the highest rate—and to pay the fattest fees to brokers—to attract money to invest in projects of questionable worth but of potentially high returns. In January 1982, nine months before the DIDC okayed the payment of higher fees, brokered deposits totaled $3 billion in the thrift industry. By January 1984 the figure had grown to $30 billion. The amount shot up 75 percent in the first six months of 1983 alone, a direction Gray decried as "growth for growth's sake." In the same two-year period the bank board detected a related trend: Half the thrifts that failed had brokered deposits that exceeded a third of their total deposit base.

Empire exemplified the trend. When Blain bought it in 1982, the thrift had deposits of $17.3 million. Less than two years later it held $308.9 million in deposits, 85 percent of it hot money.

In early 1983 Pratt left the bank board to join Merrill Lynch and regularly tromped up to Capitol Hill to argue in favor of brokered funds.

By the time Gray's staff alerted him to the brokered deposit problem in August 1983, William Isaac, chairman of the FDIC, already had noticed it. Isaac began a campaign to curb use of hot money at commercial banks. (Isaac's stance seemed to be a shift from a year earlier, when, as a member of the DIDC, he had sided with Regan and against Pratt in voting to allow higher fees to attract brokered deposits.)

Brokered funds, Isaac now argued, provided an unstable source of cash for desperate deposit institutions. Brokerage firms searched for the highest rate, pulling money in and out of institutions with even a quarter of a percentage point change. Isaac worried that the firms pulled these vast sums of brokered money in and out of banks and thrifts without regard to the soundness of the recipient institutions, and why not? The money was federally insured.

Alarmed by his staff's report, Gray joined Isaac in January 1984 in proposing a regulation to limit deposit insurance for brokered funds to $100,000 per securities firm. The securities industry dubbed it the sledgehammer rule, arguing that the culprit was not brokered funding but bank and thrift officials who misused such money. Wall Street accused Isaac of lobbying on behalf of the banking industry he represented. It chalked up Gray's reaction to his dislike for Regan.

The league says it supported Gray's effort, but in fact, it did so only on the condition that the restriction be phased in over seven years, a time frame regulators considered tantamount to no rule at all. The California league, representing the state where 63 percent of all brokered deposits were held, supported the proposed restriction with similar modifications. These lukewarm endorsements were overwhelmed by the opposition of individual S&Ls, especially those in California. The Texas league, with active members like Empire's Blain, also hated it. The National Council of Savings Institutions, the much smaller lobby group than the league, with members mostly in the Northeast, favored complete deregulation and also opposed the change. A newcomer to the business, Charles Keating, nearly single-handedly pushed the national council to oppose Gray on the issue.

Gray was scheduled to testify about his proposal before a House subcommittee chaired by Doug Barnard (D-Ga.) on May 14, 1984. He had written a speech endorsing restrictions on brokered funds but then had second thoughts. The night before the testimony, at a league dinner in Washington's Capitol Hilton, O'Connell told Gray that the lobby group, which had said it would back Gray on brokered funds, was changing its position. League officials, O'Connell said, had decided they would support only a scaled-down version of the proposal. Gray knew what that meant. It was, in his mind, lobbyist-speak warning him the industry would sabotage the agency's position even as it appeared to back the proposed regulation in modified form.

Depressed, Gray decided to abandon his speech. St Germain had told him on several occasions that no thrift legislation could pass without the league's backing. Gray was proposing an agency rule rather than congressional legislation, but the principle was the same. An unpopular bank board regulation needed at least informal congressional approval to ward off industry lawsuits challenging its legitimacy. Congressional support discourages challenges because it implies that if the courts strike down the disputed regulation, Congress will pass a law incorporating the regulatory standard.

But later that day, as Gray stepped out of his limousine at the House Rayburn Building, where the hearings were to be held, he ran into Leonard Shane, a California thrift executive and active league official. Shane told Gray that O'Connell was wrong, that a small but significant portion of the industry supported Gray's stand on brokered deposits. "You've got to give that speech," Shane told him.

Bucked up, Gray hopped into the waiting limo and drove back to the bank board to retrieve the original speech, which he then delivered.

"The list of horror stories resulting from the misuses of brokered funds by desperate financial institutions is growing as the weeks and months go on," Gray told the House subcommittee. "We are facing a potentially acute shortage of examiners. . . . Simply put, a large number of institutions have taken in more funds than can be safely employed in prudent lending, resulting in growth which is almost uncontrollable. . . . We . . . are seriously understaffed.

"The proliferation of federally insured, third-party money brokering has become a spreading cancer on the federal deposit insurance system," Gray concluded.

Merrill Lynch's Pratt, testifying later that afternoon, challenged Gray's denunciation of brokered deposits. Oversight by regulators, not new regulations restricting business, was the way to curb abuses, Pratt argued.

"The regulators have cited . . . problems with brokerage of insured deposits," he said. "No foundation or evidence has been presented for this view." In characteristic fashion, Pratt used humor to illustrate his point. The regulation proposed by the bank board and the FDIC "seems to be a bit like the drunk fellow who was looking for his key. When someone came by, they said: 'What are you doing?' He said: 'I am looking for my keys here under this light post.' The questioner said, 'Well, where did you lose them?' He said, 'Down the road about 200 yards.' The questioner said, 'Then why are you looking here?' He said, 'The light is better here.' "

Pratt, though not fond of Regan after their clashes over the thrift crisis in 1981 and 1982—he is said to refer to him as a dumb Marine—nonetheless, on returning to the private sector, had begun to accept the treasury secretary's view of Gray as a misdirected "reregulator." (Years later, after the extent of the thrift debacle began to unfold, Pratt conceded that Gray's instincts were correct [though not on brokered funds] and commended him for his tenacity in trying to rein in the industry.)

No one on the subcommittee asked Pratt, nor did he offer any explanation, about the regulatory failure of the bank board during his tenure that permitted thrifts like Empire to grow wildly. In fact, the subcommittee wrote a report generally favorable to the brokered funds industry.

In the Senate Gray and Isaac also were coolly received, especially by the senators most often identified as friends of the thrift and securities industries: Democrats Cranston and Riegle and Republicans Garn and D'Amato.

In a March 1984 hearing before the Senate Banking Committee, Cranston commented in language that might have been scripted by the thrift and brokered funds industries. "I think the question really is whether this rule in fact will stop behavior that you consider unwise," he said. "History seems to indicate that those that are intent upon doing such things find a way to do them, and I am concerned about a rule that would affect all the institutions when you're really after just a few."

"Cranston gave me hell," Gray recalls.

As Gray expected, the absence of congressional support led the thrift industry to challenge the brokered funds regulation. In June a federal district court invalidated the restriction.

On March 14, 1984, Gray eased into his leather chair in the bank board's airy boardroom to watch a videotape. Gray's staff had been warning him. He knew that at the board meeting later that morning the staff would ask the board to declare Empire insolvent and close it. It would be the FSLIC's biggest loss to date, an estimated $165 million, and the first major closing of an S&L because of fraud in fifty years. As Gray listened, his mind wandered up the street to Congress, where he was to testify on brokered deposits before the House subcommittee that afternoon. Gray the speech writer and public relations man had worked late and been up early preparing his remarks. As the staff members took their places around the oblong table in the conference room, Gray toyed with changes to his speech.

An assistant wheeled in a television and videocassette recorder and set them before Gray and his two fellow board members, Hovde and Grigsby. A staff member popped in a tape.

The camera, filming from an airplane, panned along Dallas's I-30. A narrator described the obvious: "Looking west toward downtown Dallas, we can begin to see the hundreds and hundreds of units that are under construction, none occupied.... Building after building ... all unoccupied.... Other mature projects, probably complete for a year, and no occupancy.... The problems of security, vandalism, fire control, completion—all are readily apparent from pictures like these.

"A project called Snug Harbor—vacant. On Faulkner Point North, numerous projects, numerous buildings, virtually totally vacant. No sales effort, no leasing effort, and across the street, more slabs and active construction. Notice the incredible waste, the total lack of contractor control.... Evidence of arson is already available.... In the distance, numerous projects, virtually 100 percent complete, no occupancy, and the land between the camera and the buildings is being prepared for more development.... This particular series of buildings made up one project, apparently totally vacant, with severe freeze damage inside of each unit."

Virtually all of the mess was the work of Empire.

The tape had an electric effect on Gray. His staff's warnings had come true. Easy money coupled with deregulation had wrought a fundamental change in the thrift crisis. Nightmare loomed, but interest rates were not the culprit. They had fallen from double digits in recent months, but still profits dragged and the cost of failures grew. In 1981 the industry lost a record $4.6 billion; in 1982, $4.3 billion.

Scarcely a banner year, 1983 nonetheless appeared to bring an improvement; the industry earned $2 billion, at least on paper. Even failures had dropped: fifty-three in 1983, compared with seventy-seven in 1982. Still, the numbers contained a troubling trend. The average thrift that failed in 1983 had $333 million in assets, an increase of 72 percent from the prior year. Though the deposit insurance fund usually had to pay out much less than that to depositors, the government's liability was growing. The FSLIC had assets of $8.3 billion at the end of 1983. It took in about $1 billion a year from premiums and investments in government securities. The arithmetic was simple: At the 1983 rate and cost of failure, the fund soon would run out of money. With only three places to get money—the industry, consumers, or taxpayers—Gray glimpsed rough times ahead. Empire offered concrete evidence of why. Just as Gray's staff had warned, what began as an interest rate squeeze had changed into a bad asset problem, one fueled by fast, imprudent growth.

Falling oil prices and interest rates had pricked the balloon of speculation that had taken real estate prices in Texas and other oil-producing regions sky-high. From 1975 to 1981 oil prices shot from $7.64 to $35.53 a barrel. Real estate prices shot up, too, as bankers came to believe the growth would never end. Many thrifts, like Empire, engaged in fraudulent transactions involving artificially inflated values and the snookering of "the next greater fool." But many honest thrift executives also got swept up in the go-go mentality, abandoning common sense to believe that even if a piece of land was over-priced today, dramatic appreciation would soon raise its value again. At the bank board it was called the "me too" syndrome.

Indeed, S&L executives lived in a dream. Many envisioned oil going to $50, even $100, a barrel. They approved loans on that basis, violating a basic tenet of good banking: Never lend on the expectation that prices will rise. In an attempt to emulate the high-roller practices of their renegade competitors, honest executives often ended up as "the next greater fool." Or they tried their own hand in ventures offering unrealistically high rates of return.

If oil prices—and real estate—had continued to rise forever, the bets might have paid off; Dallas would have continued to grow wildly to support the production of oil, and housing demand would have grown with it. But oil prices fell almost as fast as they rose. The bottom fell out of the real estate market in Texas and California and Colorado, leaving behind a glut of homes and commercial buildings. Many oil cities suddenly found themselves with a ten-year oversupply of office space.

Thrift executives joked about the bad times. In Texas the interest rate squeeze had been converted into a joke about an Aggie gas station owner who bought fuel at fifty cents a gallon, sold it for forty-five cents, and hoped to make up the difference on volume. In Southern California a Dallas gas station owner replaced the Aggie.

Consider the Lamar Savings Association, once Austin's fastest-growing thrift. Portly, eccentric Stanley E. Adams, Lamar's owner, filed an application to open a branch on the moon, picking as a site a crater in the Sea of Tranquillity. On Earth, Lamar was negotiating to build the tallest office building in China and, with Texas lobbyist Durward Curlee and others, to build a fitness center in Austin, where, in Curlee's words, executives could "take a holistic approach to mental finess, where your brain learns to accept unreality as real." Gray and his cadre of assistants in Washington knew by then that Texas needed no coaching in unreality.

Certainly Lamar took a holistic approach:

- From January 1983 to July 1985 Lamar's board of directors included University of Texas Finance Professor Robert Mettlen, who was also chairman of the Federal Home Loan Bank of Dallas.
- For several months in 1984 a man named Joe Settle became president of Lamar—after Gray had fired him as president of the Dallas bank and chief federal regulator of the region.
- One of Lamar's stockholders was Dick Jameson, chief of supervision of the Texas Savings and Loan Commission.
- Lamar's internal auditor, the person who reviewed audits and appraisals and served as the thrift's liaison to state and federal regulators, was Felix Charles Rheams. He began his professional career in 1963 as branch manager for a San Antonio thrift. Though he lacked a college degree or formal training as an accountant, he left five years later to become an examiner for the Federal Home Loan Bank in Texas.

  One of the thrifts Rheams examined was Lamar. In 1982 Lamar owner Adams hired Rheams away from the government, using a Lincoln Town Car and a $40,000 bonus as lure. Later, in a deposition, Rheams recounted that "Mr. Adams walked into my office one day and told me he was going to make me executive vice president. And I said, 'What for?' And he says, 'Well, I know you don't like titles, but I want you to be executive vice president.' I said, you know, 'You're the boss.' "

In 1988 federal regulators seized Lamar. It ranked among the ten costliest thrift cases in the period from 1980 to 1988, requiring $805 million from taxpayers to pay off depositors. According to a spokesman for the federal thrift regulatory agency, the bank board rehired Rheams as an examiner but then "encouraged him to leave" a short time later in 1988, when it realized that he was a defendant in the conspiracy lawsuit filed by the government against Adams and former Lamar officers and directors.

Empire's problem didn't all spring up during Gray's tenure, though the bank board failed to take action for a year after he took over.

When Blain bought Empire in 1982, Pratt was board chairman. Blain had failed to report the change in ownership to regulators, as the law requires. Pratt took no action. An examination report in late 1982 by the regional Federal Home Loan Bank (then in Little Rock, now in Dallas) unearthed improper appraisals and other defects in the thrift's lending policies. The report described Empire with adjectives like "imprudent" and "speculative" and recommended "immediate forceful supervision action." Using a best-to-worst scale of one to five, the examination gave Empire a three, mostly because the institution's records were a mess. The rating should have triggered a meeting between Empire's directors and federal regulators. Instead, bank board officials decided that because Empire appeared to be profitable, the matter could be handled by letter. They sent a letter to Blain in January complaining of violations. Although he did not respond for three months, regulators took no action.

Nor did regulators under Pratt react when accountants from Coopers & Lybrand couldn't make sense of Empire's books to meet a filing date of September 30, 1982. The accountants asked for one extension after another—nine in all. They completed the audit on October 14, 1983, more than a year late. Most remarkable, the auditors then issued what is known in the accounting trade as a clean opinion. That meant Coopers raised no warning and found no major problems with Empire's operation.

Part of the bank board's difficulty in detecting these problems resulted from a regulatory inefficiency that Congress had built into the Federal Home Loan Bank System in the 1930s to guard against overly zealous bank examiners produced by the depression: The system had two distinct sets of regulators with two distinct sets of bosses.

One set was the examiners. They acted as government accountants, reviewing a thrift's books much as an accounting firm in the private sector would do. These examiners were federal bank board employees working out of the twelve regional banks who earned government salaries that started at $13,000 to $14,000 a year. The institutions they reviewed often hired them away within two years of their starting days, meaning that the federal examiners were perpetually inexperienced.

When examiners discovered irregularities, they turned the information over to a second set of regulators called supervisors. Supervisors worked not only in the regional banks but directly *for* the banks—quasi-government entities run by industry-dominated boards of directors. Their job was to interpret and judge the facts that the examiners dug up. Because they technically did not work directly for the federal government, the supervisers were not subject to government pay caps. And because their salaries were ultimately controlled by the industry-dominated boards of directors of the banks, they were tied financially to those they regulated.

The imbalance in pay and status between examiners and supervisors, not to mention differences in whom they reported to, produced antagonisms and office jealousies that impeded prompt action. "You had an insane system," one senior executive at the bank board later told the *Washington Post,* "that guaranteed rivalries and things falling between the cracks."

Bowman, then Texas's chief thrift regulator, says he twice warned the bank board about Empire, once during a trip to Washington in March 1983 and once during Gray's visit to Dallas for the Texas thrift convention a few months later. The regional Federal Home Loan Bank president, Joe Settle, says he also warned Gray. Gray says Settle "never said a word. Period. End of statement." Gray acknowledges that Bowman mentioned Empire and some other thrifts in passing during the Texas league convention but claims Bowman never seriously alerted him to the problem.

Eventually Empire's difficulties became too great to ignore. On January 12, 1984, Bowman's state regulators seized control of the thrift, which they operated until federal officials at the FSLIC decided what to do. The FSLIC immediately set about trying to estimate the damage and decide whether to sell or close the institution. The decision was bound by a single legal mandate: Take whatever action minimized costs to the deposit insurance fund. Officials at the fund hired a consultant, who, after examining Empire, decided only a videotaped viewing of the condo wasteland would do the situation justice. The consultant grabbed his video camera, hired a World War II bomber pilot, and set off, eventually producing the tape of the I-30 fiasco that Gray watched the morning the bank board decided to close the thrift.

The tape lasted twenty minutes and forty-one seconds. As Gray watched the film unroll, he felt dumbfounded, disgusted. This was the sorry condition of the industry he was supposed to be regulating. Gray thought of his car ride with Blain, of the Rolls and the Rolexes.

The board quickly voted 3–0 to seize Empire and to ban Blain from the thrift industry.

The seizure of Empire set in motion more than a hundred fraud and racketeering charges against more than a hundred companies and individuals. In April 1987 Blain settled a civil racketeering suit with the FSLIC for $100 million. He contends he did nothing wrong, however, and has pleaded not guilty to the criminal charges. "I'm not ashamed of anything I've done, don't believe I've broken any laws, believe that the theory [with which] I operated Empire was sound," he said during a deposition in a related civil suit.

Blain, Faulkner, and five other associates were charged in Lubbock, Texas, in an eighty-eight-count indictment alleging criminal racketeering and conspiracy. In this S&L loan fraud case, one of the largest to go to trial, a mistrial was declared in September 1989 after six months of testimony when the jury deadlocked 11–1 in favor of conviction. In early 1990 a federal grand jury indicted Faulkner's daughter, Pamela Faulkner Tomalin, on charges of jury tampering. A few months later the federal government began retrying the case against Blain, Faulkner, and the others.

Left to clean up the mess in the meantime, the FSLIC demolished scores of condos along I-30, finding the bulldozer a cheaper remedy than fixing up the properties and trying to sell them.

––––

Within days after closing Empire, Gray showed the video to officials around Washington. He brought Paul Volcker to the bank board, where the Federal Reserve chairman just shook his head as he sat and watched.

Gray also traipsed to Capitol Hill to show the tape to House Banking Committee Chairman St Germain. St Germain's chief of staff, Paul Nelson, sat in. But the film didn't strike the politicians as it had the bank board officials and Volcker.

Gray recalls that St Germain and Nelson seemed to know the names of "Faulkner and others" involved with Empire, names Gray had learned only recently. "They didn't seem to be horrified," he says. His instincts were right.

"Gray's the regulator, not us," Nelson thought. "That's his job to stop this. Why am I watching this?"

Gray soon received another unpleasant message from Congress. Representative Barnard announced that in four weeks his subcommittee of the House Committee on Government Operations would hold hearings into the collapse of Empire and the failure of regulators to detect the mess earlier.

The decision by the slim silver-haired former banker to investigate alarmed Gray. In Washington's close-knit world of financial regulators and lobbyists, the decision also underscored the league's close relationship with leaders of the House Banking Committee, who normally would be the ones to investigate thrift failures. But Snake Freeman and other league leaders, according to financial industry lobbyists and congressional aides, had convinced St Germain to forgo hearings. It was not helpful, they argued, airing and drawing attention to the industry's dirty laundry.

In any event, the House Banking Committee didn't react. Government Operations, far less beholden to the industry, stole the show from St Germain. For Gray, the hearings became the final event—along with the Empire tape and revelations about brokered funds—that completed his metamorphosis from a rumpled and kindly flack into a rumpled but fire-breathing regulator.

The Empire fiasco supported Gray's arguments against brokered deposits—so much so that Representative Barnard suspected that Gray had timed the take-over of Empire to coincide with the hearings on brokered deposits that afternoon. Gray claims the timing was coincidental.

But the Empire fiasco also worked against Gray. He could now be truly labeled as unorganized, unfocused, and so preoccupied with world travel that he failed to run his agency. Gray became known as Mr. Ed after the talking horse on the television show. He was, his critics started to suggest, a buffoon, a man who talked about safety and soundness without detecting fraud right under his nose. The criticism stung.

Perhaps the insults motivated Gray. Perhaps the millions of dollars of building material rotting in the Texas sun along I-30 did it. Perhaps he feared the embarrassing lack of competence at his agency that Barnard's investigation surely would uncover. Perhaps it truly was Gray's disgust at the situation in Texas and the unavoidable conclusion it couldn't have become such a big problem if regulators hadn't been asleep at the switch.

Whatever the reason, Gray decided that removing Blain was not enough. Gray wanted the blood of a regulator.

On April 14, 1984, one month after the closing of Empire, the three bank board members—Gray, Hovde, and Grigsby—summoned Joe Settle, president of the Federal Home Loan Bank of Dallas, to a Hyatt hotel in Monterey, California.

The board members were in Monterey for a two-day meeting of Freddie Mac directors and executives. For the most part, the people attending the meeting lived in the Washington area and had offices around the block from one another. Usually such meetings were held in Washington, but this time Hovde, the avid golfer, had expressed a desire to play at Pebble Beach. Because the three bank board members also directed Freddie Mac, Hovde's desire became Freddie Mac's command. So thousands of dollars were spent on airfare, hotel rooms, and meals to accommodate Hovde and hold the meeting three thousand miles to the west. Two years later, when Congress denounced the trip as a boondoggle, Hovde returned $447 in green fees for a golfing group that included Shannon Fairbanks and her husband. The rest of the money was unrecoverable because it had been spent during a meeting on bank board business.

In this plush setting, just ten days before Barnard's investigative hearings into Empire would begin and Gray would be asked to account for the agency's regulatory lapses, Gray fired Settle. "We're not satisfied with the supervisory functions going on in your district," Gray told the unsuspecting bank president. "We've decided to replace you."

Technically the board of directors of a regional bank picked its chairman and president (who also served as chief regional regulator), but the bank board had to approve the president before he could don the additional title of principal supervisory agent. Preventing a president from also being the PSA, however, essentially precluded an effective term in office, making a resignation all but inevitable.

"It's only because of Empire, isn't it?" Settle asked.

"No, no, no, no," Gray said. "I specifically looked at other cases."

Giving the boot to Settle shocked the Bank Board system. It was the first firing in the system's fifty years. There were plenty of problem thrifts in other districts, especially California and Florida. Why didn't heads role there? And where had the Bank Board been, especially Gray?

As a replacement, Gray chose Roy Green, a full-time executive with the league who was strongly identified with the inner circle of thrift executives. As a Florida thrift official and league chairman from November 1981 through November 1982, Green had worked side by side with league President O'Connell to push for passage of Garn-St Germain. In April 1983 Green became a full-time staff member of the league, assuming the title of executive vice-president and director of operations.

The chairman of the Dallas bank, Robert Mettlen, was furious. Texas thrifts wanted to pick their own president. In part the Texans suspected that California thrifts would try to stifle competition from Texas. Mettlen and Gray got into a shouting match over the point in the lobby of a Dallas hotel, with Gray screaming, "You can send me any name you want as long as it's Roy Green's." The Dallas bank finally named Green in August 1984.

The bank board's Office of General Counsel poked fun at the episode during the staff Christmas party a few months later.

Chairman Ed was sorely vexed
When Empire went insolvent;
Said he, "The Board looks mighty bad,
How could we let this happen?
If we want to save our skins,
We've got to aim some low blows,
Go my loyal minions now
Bring to me a scapegoat!"

So the staff looked all about,
And fault they found aplenty;
In the end the blame was pinned
On sloppy supervision.
Ed he went to Congress then,
His scapegoat for to peddle;
Said everything is O.K. now,
I've brought the head of Joe Settle.

Gray's firing of Settle failed to soften congressional criticism. Representative Barnard's hearings into Empire, which began on April 25, 1984, revealed fundamental flaws and embarrassing failings by state and federal regulators.

Texas S&L Commissioner Bowman testified that he could not have moved against Empire sooner because its books had not reflected the problem he knew existed. On paper Empire appeared to be among the fastest-growing and most profitable thrifts in the nation. "This, of course, is an alarming thing to us because there is no Santa Claus," Bowman told congressional investigators. "But, by the same token, it makes it that much more difficult for us to walk in the front door and say, 'I'm sorry, Number 1, we're going to close you down.' "

(Although Bowman says he warned Gray about the perils growing in Texas, he also staunchly opposed Gray's proposals to limit risky investments by thrifts, writing a letter in December 1984 to the Bank Board stating, "My primary concern . . . stems from the hazard of allowing an examiner to interpret complicated accounting principles and arrive at an arbitrary conclusion. I have long espoused the philosophy that this responsibility rests solely with the private audit firm which performs the association's annual audit. . . .")

Empire represented the "Catch-22" regulators claimed to find themselves in throughout the 1980s. Congress repeatedly asked why a particularly horrendous thrift failure wasn't closed at an earlier, less costly stage. Regulators repeatedly replied that they couldn't move in sooner because the thrift looked profitable; it looked profitable because of fraud, but they couldn't move in to stop the fraud until the institution looked unhealthy.

In his testimony to Barnard, Gray freely admitted the bank board's fault in the affair. In so doing, Gray broke ranks with board chairmen before him, who never blamed the agency in public. Gray believes his admission of guilt diffused congressional anger and recalls that reporters attending the hearings thought so, too. "One newsman leaned over and whispered, 'You're a savvy old dog, Gray,' " Gray says.

The congressional panel, however, rejected the regulators' "Catch-22" defense. There was, for instance, the bank board's own 1982 examination report on Empire. It had been ignored for seventeen months, although it contained more than enough information for regulators to act against the thrift. They might not have prevented Empire's failure, but they could have reduced the cost to the government.

Gray's conduct looked particularly bad because he had moved the regional Federal Home Loan Bank from Little Rock to Dallas in September 1983, a move that disrupted oversight at a time when steady regulation was essential. For years the congressional delegations from Texas and Arkansas had fought over where to house the bank's headquarters to oversee thrifts in Texas, Arkansas, Louisiana, Mississippi, and New Mexico. Regional banks provided jobs and prestige, and state officials fought hard to keep, and woo, them.

In 1958, when the Texas Savings and Loan League voted—as it did every year—to lobby for the move, its president found a one-line telegram under his hotel door in Galveston. Signed by John L. McClellan, the powerful Arkansas Democrat who chaired the Senate Appropriations Committee, the message read, "You're whistling Dixie."

But eventually the Arkansas influence waned and that of Texas grew. The directors of the District 9 bank, coming as they did from the bank's entire five-state region, voted 11–2 to move to Dallas. In fact, when President Reagan nominated Gray to the bank board chairmanship, Senate confirmation was delayed by members of Congress with an interest in the question of moving the institution to Dallas. Just three weeks after taking office, Gray went along.

The move was a mess. Only eleven of the bank's forty-eight supervisory employees elected to make the move. Most of those were clerks; only two were supervisory agents. The two remaining supervisors divided the five-state region in half. Now each oversaw about 240 thrifts when 2 or 3 would have provided work aplenty.

The consequences of the move were not lost on Representative Barnard. "The committee finds that the move is a totally unacceptable explanation for allowing the supervisory responsibilities of the Bank Board to have been neglected," his subcommittee said in its formal report on the hearings. "The move cannot be given as an excuse for the FSLIC fund to suffer loss of approximately $165 million."

At the hearings a private-sector banking analyst testified that using only publicly available information about Empire and not the bank board's additional reports, he had been able to deduce that the thrift's violations were extreme. He dubbed Empire "the Penn Square of the thrift industry," after the Oklahoma bank that had failed two years earlier and, in a domino effect, forced the bailout of Continental Illinois. The implication stung: The problems at Empire were so obvious anyone could have seen them. So where were the federal regulators?

"I just don't understand why it was so hard to get your hands on this institution," said Representative John M. Spratt, Jr. (D-S.C.). "That's what I'm grappling with."

A humiliated Ed Gray left the hearing room. The committee members had made a mockery of his first twelve months on the job. And 1984 was almost half over.

21

Creation of a Failure

Thrift owner Mark Taper cut a legendary figure in the California industry. He is said to have come to California from England in the 1940s after making a fortune in real estate. (He is credited by California thrift executives with developing in England the first modern real estate brokerage system in which agents escort clients to houses.)

According to a thrift industry executive who worked for Taper for many years, when Taper first arrived at the Los Angeles airport with his family, he directed a taxi driver to take him to see the ocean. The driver went to Long Beach, where Taper took a suite on the top floor of what was then a swank hotel in the city's downtown. From there he set out to make a second fortune in America.

Taper opened a state-chartered, federally insured thrift called American Savings and Loan, which became one of the biggest in the nation, and he became a codeveloper in building the entire city of Lakewood, which borders Long Beach. He soon was an insider among California thrift executives. It was Taper who Bobby Baker said handed him the envelope with cash for Senator Kerr.

Taper was no highflier. He ran a very conservative company. Former employees say he used to rummage through office desks after hours, looking for excess paper clips, rubber bands, and pencils. Workers often arrived in the morning to find notes admonishing them to be more frugal with the company's assets. Years before the energy crisis Taper turned out lights when he left a room. At meetings with senior executives or officials from other thrifts, coffee and tea were considered a big expenditure. Once Taper served cheap Danish pastry to visiting S&L executives, who, knowing him and his habits, practically fell over in surprise.

Perhaps it was because of the economic slide that had hit the thrift industry in the late 1970s. Perhaps Taper was simply tired of the business. Whatever the reason, in 1982 Taper decided to sell his thrift, American Savings and Loan. He found a willing buyer in Charles Knapp, a former home builder who in the late 1970s had turned a small money-lending company called Budget Industries, Inc., into a thrift operation that he renamed the Financial Corporation of America. FCA was based in Stockton, a small, rough, and economically depressed town in northern California.

FCA's purchase of American made it the largest thrift in the state. But even before the acquisition FCA had embarked on a madcap growth spree in the early 1980s, funded by brokered deposits and high-risk real estate deals. FCA aggressively undercut the largest California thrifts by offering low, fixed-rate mortgages. Executives at the larger S&Ls, including Anthony Frank at First Nationwide and Herbert M. Sandler at World Savings of Oakland, didn't like this. They had grown fat on adjustable rate mortgages, which rose along with interest rates and thus helped stabilize S&L profits during economic ups and downs. Knapp's FCA practices gummed up their strategy by giving consumers a steady supply of cheaper mortgages. The S&L executives wanted him out of their business.

In January 1983 Taper and Knapp agreed on a deal, pending approval from state and federal regulators. Executives of the largest California thrifts went wild. They begged Gray, as the incoming bank board chairman, to stop the deal; although the state of California was the primary regulator of the two state-chartered institutions, the board had to approve the marriage because the resulting thrift would be federally insured. As soon as Gray assumed office, the bank board in Washington and the regional bank in San Francisco launched an extensive and highly unusual examination of American Savings, citing accusations by Knapp's competitors that he engaged in dangerous lending practices. But American, a state-chartered thrift, also was regulated by the state of California, whose chief regulator was Lawrence Taggart.

Taggart, like Gray, had worked as a top executive at Great American in San Diego. Taggart started his job as California thrift commissioner within weeks of Gray's becoming bank board chairman. Both men welcomed the other's appointment, thinking that their past affiliation at Great American would make cooperation between the state and federal government easy. It didn't.

As Gray grew disenchanted with unbridled deregulation, Taggart supported it even more strongly. Taggart approved 211 new thrift applications during his two years in office, or roughly 1 every two or three working days. At the time the state employed only forty-three examiners, who already had their hands full regulating the existing 105 state-chartered institutions.

Dean Cannon, head of the California league, praised Taggart. At the same time the California league and many in the industry expressed frustration with Gray, dubbing him the reregulator. Gray still cherished the notion of thrifts as home lenders. If thrifts abandoned home lending, he knew they could not long justify special treatment from the government. On this Gray and his enemy Don Regan agreed completely.

Gray wanted to preserve the specialization in home lending and the benefits that accompanied it. Regan wanted to do away with both. Taggart was somewhere in the middle. He favored giving thrifts greater freedom but also wanted to preserve their special status; in his view, that was what made the thrift charter better than a commercial banking charter in the era of deregulation.

Despite opposition to Gray's "reregulation" policies, many of the California league's biggest, most influential members sought to enlist Gray's help in trying to prevent Knapp from becoming a major player in the industry. Taggart, they found, wasn't about to block the deal. After months of looking, the bank board ultimately said it could find no reason to kill the deal between Taper and Knapp, and in August 1983 the two men completed the sale. But Gray continued to look for ways to get Knapp out of the business. Baffled by this incongruity—Gray had approved the deal but disapproved of Knapp—a senior league official said that many industry leaders believe Gray approved the deal at the request—implicit or explicit—of the White House. Taper, after all, was a friend of President Reagan's. Gray's decision let Taper sell his thrift at top dollar and leave the industry profitably.

Now a giant, Knapp transformed American into the country's largest S&L. He kept the thrift's headquarters in Stockton—a curious site for an S&L that size—although he appointed it with a gourmet kitchen, complete with a boar's head on the wall, and an executive suite that in the go-go 1980s would have appeared plush even on Wall Street. Knapp did move the headquarters of the thrift's parent, FCA, to Beverly Hills, however, a setting more in keeping with his own life-style.

Knapp's appetite for growth seemed unbounded, his methods unorthodox. He believed that he could tolerate 5 to 6 percent of his loans being delinquent or bad, a rate several times the industry average. Typical of the business practices at FCA were the company's buy-sell agreements. Builders have charged that FCA bought property from developers and then sold it back at a higher price, booking a fat profit in the process. In return, FCA promised to provide loans to the developers.

Knapp also began to play the stock market in ways that looked like preliminary steps in a take-over attempt. He bought large blocks of stock in the American Express Company, Merrill Lynch, and the Walt Disney Company. He said the purchases were intended only as investments, but with Knapp, regulators thought, you could never be sure.

According to Taggart, California's chief thrift regulator at the time, Knapp visited Washington shortly after buying Taper's thrift to see a very worried Paul Volcker. The Fed chairman expressed concern about the aggressive lending tactics used by the nation's largest thrift, tactics that could lead to the thrift's failure, put enormous strain on the nation's banking system, and force the Fed to act as lender of last resort to the thrift industry. At one point, according to Taggart, Volcker ushered Knapp into an elevator, closed the doors, and rode up and down, up and down, up and down. All the time Volcker warned Knapp about the damage that could be done by a thrift company as large as FCA and cautioned that the government would not stand idly by while Knapp bought major positions in such blue-chip companies as American Express, Merrill Lynch, and Disney.

During another trip at about the same time Knapp met with Gray in Washington in a cool fifteen-minute meeting. Gray says he told Knapp he wanted him out of the industry. According to Taggart, Knapp simply describes the meeting as bizarre and Gray as a man he couldn't talk to. Knapp flew home, Taggart says, thinking Washington was a strange place.

But Taggart got a clear impression that the bank board was going to target Knapp for discipline. "A very important turn of events happened on June 28, 1984," Taggart later told a congressional committee. "I was sitting back at the Federal Home Loan Bank Board, in their offices meeting with several of the directors. It was at a formal meeting. And they said, 'oh by the way Larry,' they said, 'do you know Charles Knapp?' I said, 'well, I met with him several times and I talked with him.' I said, 'why?' And they said, 'well, we are going to go out there and take him over our knees and teach him a lesson.' This was a very high official in the Bank Board.

"I said, 'you are going to do what?'

" 'We are going to go out there and teach him a lesson. He is growing too fast.'

"I said, 'have you ever sat down and talked with him about his business plan, or had lunch with him, or anything?'

" 'No, we have not. We are not going to give him the time.' "

Taggart warned the bank board officials to be careful. Interference with an institution as large as FCA, if bungled, could upset confidence in the industry as a whole and spark runs. All in all, he says, he believes "there was a hidden agenda there somewhere that the regulators weren't communicating to me or to Knapp."

For all the bank board's posturing, Knapp's downfall came at the hands of a more professional agency, the Securities and Exchange Commission. A few days after their investigation had begun, SEC examiners found what Gray's staff had missed despite months of searching: misstated profits. On August 15, 1984, the SEC forced FCA to restate its profits from its thrift subsidiary for the second quarter of the year, turning the company's reported $31.1 million gain into a $107 million loss.

The action sparked massive runs at American Savings. In six weeks nervous customers withdrew $6.8 billion in deposits. At the Fed anxiety ran high. Regulators forced Knapp to resign on August 28, 1984, just a year after they had approved his purchase of the S&L. But Gray allowed Knapp to leave with a $2 million severance fee, or golden parachute. Knapp tried to have David Stockman chosen by regulators as his replacement at the company, but Gray picked his own man—William Popejoy, another industry insider in California who had worked at American Savings years earlier when it belonged to Taper.

The California industry applauded Gray's choice—at first. Popejoy believes he was welcomed because "the club" thought he would do as they wished: stabilize FCA to restore consumer confidence, curtail the thrift's sale of fixed-rate loans, then break the company up and sell off the pieces to its competitors.

Popejoy and Gray had a different strategy in mind. Gray essentially decided that American Savings was too big to fail; its collapse would undermine confidence in the entire thrift system, not to mention all but deplete the thrift deposit insurance fund. So Popejoy put FCA on a risky path similar to the one Knapp had used. FCA would use interest rate spreads on securities and stock market options to try to earn—critics said gamble—its way out of its financial hole. In essence, Gray and Popejoy concluded that the only way to save FCA was to set it on the very course that Gray now was fighting industrywide, one that involved a risky strategy in the hope of winning large returns that would push the institution back up the slippery slope.

In the ensuing months, the number of problem properties at FCA climbed to the thousands. The computer printout list of the troubled real estate owned by the thrift was so thick "it makes the yellow pages look like a pocket diary," one financier who buys foreclosed properties told the *Los Angeles Times*.

In September, as things began to calm down, another blow hit the wobbly giant. Treasury Secretary Regan told a reporter for a thrift industry newspaper, *National Thrift News*, that the Treasury would not guarantee depositors holding more than $100,000 at FCA against loss in the event of a run. Regan had a reputation at the White House for speaking without thinking. His comment sparked a new run—$400 million in one day, an industry record.

Gray scambled to cope with the panic. He recalled a telephone conversation he'd had with Regan in August 1982, just as Gray was leaving the White House to return to Great American. "I'm not sure you're a team player," the treasury secretary had told him.

"You don't have to tell me about being a team player," Gray had shot back. "I go back with Ronald Reagan since 1966." Later Gray concluded that Regan was talking about Don Regan's team, not President Reagan's.

Regan's thoughtless remarks about FCA confirmed Gray's interpretation of that cryptic telephone call. Regan operated on his own. Furious, Gray wrote him a nasty letter, asking him to be more careful next time he said something about a troubled thrift. Regan shot back with a letter that said, in part, "I do not have to be reminded of my responsibilities in areas of concern to you, or, for that matter, any of the other areas of government in which economics and finance play a role."

The run at American put Gray in a bind. He couldn't close the institution. That would deplete the FSLIC. It might also provoke more and wider panic. In desperation, Gray turned to the instrument he had fought to eliminate, brokered funds. Gray contacted Dick Pratt at Merrill Lynch in New York.

Pratt agreed to place $1 billion of brokered money in FCA. But when he checked with his superiors, usually a routine matter, they vetoed the deal as too risky. Gray claims Pratt told him that Regan secretly ruined the deal, a serious charge because government regulations dictated that the treasury secretary have nothing to do with his former company. Regan, through a spokesman, has denied talking to anyone at Merrill Lynch. The spokesman said Regan checked his telephone logs for the period and found no record of any conversation with anyone at the company.

Regan's denial is accurate, according to a top industry official who was directly involved in the matter, but only to a point. Regan actually used an intermediary, one of his assistants, to make contact with lower-level officials at Merrill Lynch and sour the deal. The officials at Merrill Lynch then passed the word up the ladder to the people who, finally, passed it down again to Pratt.

Gray and Popejoy found brokered deposits from other firms, but the troubles at FCA were far from over. Another period of unstable interest rates would bring it down. And that was ultimately what happened. FCA became one of the most expensive casualties of the thrift debacle, by 1990 costing taxpayers an estimated $5 billion to bail out. (Most of that money was paid by the government to oil billionaire Robert Bass, who in 1988 had agreed to take the troubled thrift off the government's hands in exchange for many billions of dollars in tax breaks and other government subsidies. As usual in such cases, the "purchaser" of the troubled thrift paid no money to the government; instead the "purchaser" demanded cash and other hefty subsidies in exchange for assuming ownership of the money-losing S&L.)

Those responsible for the fiasco didn't fare badly. On December 31, 1984, Taggart resigned as California's thrift commissioner to become a consultant to the industry, including thrifts, like Keating's Lincoln, he had regulated. A little more than two years later he went to work for Knapp, who had formed an investment company, Trafalgar Holdings, Inc.

As for Knapp, after he was booted from FCA, he left his wife of sixteen years and went cruising on his 120-foot-yacht, the *Henry Morgan,* with a movie actress named Lois Hamilton, a striking blonde about fifteen years his junior whom he eventually married. "Lifestyles of the Rich and Famous" featured him after his departure from FCA as a "millionaire mogul" who spent his days making deals, yachting, and flying his planes. At one point it showed a painting of Knapp and his new wife locked in a passionate embrace.

Through Trafalgar, Knapp also began building another fast-growth empire. His tactics there have proved as controversial and questionable as they were at FCA. According to the *Wall Street Journal,* Knapp's Trafalgar pledged millions of dollars it didn't have in take-over battles, earning fees of hundreds of thousands of dollars for promising the cash. "Trafalgar is a house of cards," says Mark S. Dodge, who was a lawyer for Knapp at FCA and followed him to Trafalgar until quitting in late 1987. "Making commitments without the money—that seemed to be the business plan."

The FBI spent months investigating FCA, but Knapp has never been charged with wrongdoing. He and his wife continue to live a flamboyant life-style in Southern California, making appearances at fancy restaurants in San Diego and Beverly Hills. "I have, to my knowledge, done nothing illegal," Knapp says.

Taggart blames the government for the FCA fiasco, arguing that the techniques and investments Knapp used were permitted by law. He faults regulators in their handling of FCA and other thrifts that weren't part of the California thrift "club." Regulators were arbitrary and selective in which S&Ls they targeted, and prejudiced and unfair in how they went after whatever they targeted, he says. And he notes that Gray, who faulted Taggart publicly for being on a camping trip in the Sierras and out of reach when the government decided to take over American Savings, himself had just returned from his trip to Wimbledon.

"There's no due process in the system," Taggart says, "but there are plenty of double standards."

22

Misfits

G ray became increasingly outspoken in the wake of Empire's collapse and Knapp's departure. "New thrift powers were not intended by Garn-St Germain to transform thrifts into commercial banks," Gray had testified before the Senate Banking Committee in 1983. By late 1984 his tone had changed dramatically. Thrifts, he warned, weren't changing into banks. They were becoming monsters, using federally insured funds to go far beyond what banks could do. The industry now held $1 trillion in deposits—$1 trillion that the federal government insured with a fund that had dwindled to $2 billion, down from $8 billion a few years earlier. The FSLIC would have been billions of dollars in the red had Gray not kept "brain-dead" thrifts open until more money could be found.

"In a decision of great significance in December 1983," Gray wrote to Congress in October 1984, "Vice President [Bush's] Task Group on Regulation of Financial Services concurred, without a single dissenting vote, that savings institutions are unique and different from commercial banks and that they ought to be governed under a separate and distinct regulatory structure."

For that reason, he wrote, thrifts must be careful to stick to their intended purpose. "Asset diversification beyond the options provided for in the Garn-

St Germain Act create tremendous pressures on the FSLIC fund. When financing or investing in windmill farms, fast food restaurants, airlines, oil drilling operations and a myriad of other novel and risky endeavors for thrifts begin to undermine, as we are seeing today, the very finite resources of the insurance fund, the industry as a whole is shaken. We at the Board have no problem with any asset diversification authorities a state may wish to establish—if such states are willing to underwrite the risk of those institutions' activities."

Unfortunately Gray's new persona as white knight was undermined by his ethically dubious judgment and unsavory connections. In early 1984, for example, President Reagan nominated Gray's mentor at the White House, Edwin Meese, to be attorney general. Meese promptly was accused of numerous ethical lapses.

During Meese's confirmation hearings, senators called for an investigation into financial assistance Meese had received from six people who then secured appointments to federal jobs in the Reagan administration. Two of the six were Gray and his former boss at Great American, Gordon Luce.

In the late 1970s Great American had lent Meese $120,000 for a house in California. In 1981, when Meese came to Washington, the thrift lent him an additional $132,000 to buy a house in Virginia. Meese couldn't keep up with both loans on his government salary and for nearly a year and a half made no payments on the California house. Great American took no action. Instead it granted Meese another loan, this time for $21,000, even though he was $400,000 in debt and in default. President Reagan, meanwhile, had appointed Luce to be a delegate to the United Nations.

Independent counsel Jacob A. Stein, appointed to investigate the allegations, found that while Meese was White House counsel, he had recommended Gray's appointment and had attended the White House meetings when Luce's appointment was discussed. But Meese insisted that the loans and the appointments were unconnected, and Stein, concluding the investigation in September 1984, said he found no basis for criminal prosecution. Still, the matter embarrassed Gray, adding to the perception that he was a hack who had procured his job through political connections.

The Ohio and Maryland crises in mid-1985 also undermined Gray's image. Republicans and Democrats alike accused him of responding slowly, of letting the governors of the two states "twist in the wind" because they were Democrats. Even top members of Gray's bank board staff say they believe he might have acted more quickly had Republicans been on the line. Gray says he acted promptly and without regard to party affiliation. But the governors tell a different story.

When Governor Celeste had trouble reaching Gray, Representative Chalmers Wylie had to intercede. Then Gray became more helpful, though Celeste says the assistance was still grudging.

Governor Hughes of Maryland had an even harder time with Gray. "He wasn't much help. He was always traveling. He was always going somewhere. He was hardly ever in Washington, it seemed to me," Hughes recalls. "I couldn't reach him."

Gray, understandably, didn't want to give either governor the impression that the federal deposit insurance fund was going to bail out Ohio and Maryland by taking over responsibility for their deposits. Gray's federal fund had enough problems of its own. The governors say they understood that, but that Gray—and the entire Federal Home Loan Bank System—failed even to provide guidance and examiners until asked by the Fed to do so.

The exception, both governors say, was Frank Haas, head of the bank board office overseeing the regional banks. It was Haas, not Gray, who helped the states cut red tape and assisted the state thrifts in applying for federal deposit insurance, according to state officials, even as he made clear that the federal thrift system was not going to assume the cost of the states' problem.

Hughes's most frustrating encounter with Gray concerned the sale of the large, teetering Baltimore thrift called First Maryland, a state-chartered and state-insured S&L. One of Maryland's healthiest, federally insured thrifts had agreed to buy First Maryland in a deal that would have allowed the state simply to transfer the deposit accounts and thus give consumers access to their funds without interruption.

But examiners in the Federal Home Loan Bank in Atlanta—the same bank whose officials regularly traipsed across the country for meetings in the most opulent of settings and which has jurisdiction over Maryland—held up the sale pending an audit of the healthy thrift. Hughes said the examiners dragged their feet and finally vetoed the merger because they found what they said were "expense account abuses" of $50,000 at the healthy S&L. (Hughes will not give its name.)

The healthy thrift protested the finding, but executives said they would return the disputed $50,000 if that would speed the sale. Still, the examiners were not satisfied. Hughes, frantic as the crisis dragged on for days, finally decided to plead the case directly to Gray. Hughes located the bank board chairman in Manhattan and flew there in a state patrol helicopter. He met Gray in the offices of the Federal Home Loan Bank of New York and pleaded with him to speed approval of the merger. Gray was pleasant but made no promises, Hughes said.

Atlanta didn't budge. According to Maryland officials, an outside auditor finally determined that the expense account expenditures in question amounted to no more than $1,500 and arguably could be considered an appropriate charge. The money had been used to buy golf clubs and throw a retirement party for a longtime thrift employee.

But it was too late. Runs at institutions around the state forced Hughes to close First Maryland. "The result was we had to put First Maryland into receivership, and instead of all the depositors getting access to their money right away, it was frozen in receivership with the state," taking years to be fully repaid, Hughes said.

Hughes was angry over the incident, all the more so when he learned the extent to which Gray traveled and the officials in the regional Federal Home Loan Banks partied and wined and dined themselves.

All this—the indecision and ultimate failure on brokered deposits, the belated but frenetic activity on Empire, the personal embarrassments—contributed to a growing sense that Gray had a sort of split personality. He raised the alarm about the emerging problem with bad loans but dawdled when facing emergencies in Ohio and Maryland. He criticized the excesses of the Texas S&Ls while using the industry's dollars to travel the world on business trips of questionable value.

This duality—Gray's attempt simultaneously to regulate and to coddle the industry—was his tragic flaw as he tried to stem the growing crisis. Gray thought he was being tough. He even entitled the bank board's 1985 annual report to Congress "Better Examination, Supervision, and Enforcement: Tools for Ensuring Safety and Soundness."

The goal, as he saw it, was to impose stricter enforcement to save the thrift industry from itself. Thus he told the league's annual convention in 1985 that "failure to come to grips with [FSLIC's problems]—sooner or later—can only make the national thrift system as currently structured more vulnerable to measures which could, in time, seriously alter the character and structure of the thrift industry itself, as we have known it for a half-century." Gray, in a prescient moment, added that "the stakes for the future of the thrift industry are simply enormous. Removal of the FSLIC from our national thrift system would cut the heart out of the system. And, if this were to happen, others who traditionally have had far less sympathy for the role of thrifts in the national financial structure would end up making deposit insurance rules for all of your institutions."

But, Gray concedes, he didn't see at the time how his own conduct undermined his ability to discipline the industry. For example, when the regional bank presidents met in December 1985 for their monthly meeting, which Gray attended, the affair was typically elaborate. All stayed at the Ritz-Carlton Hotel in Laguna Niguel, south of Los Angeles in Orange County. The posh setting would have been shocking enough for their counterparts in the Federal Reserve System, but on the second day Gray did something even more unthinkable in the world of commercial banking: He brought league President O'Connell to the meeting and asked him to speak to the presidents.

"I assure you, you don't have the head of Citibank or the American Bankers Association come talk" when the Federal Reserve Board presidents meet, comments one Federal Reserve Bank president familiar with the Federal Home Loan Banks.

As the thrift problem changed from bad interest rates to bad judgment by managers, so did the industry's public argument about why the government should keep ailing thrifts open. In the early 1980s, everyone agreed, a spike in interest rates and an overconcentration by the industry in one commodity—home loans—had caused the problem. Now the industry was arguing a new economic plague had descended: falling oil and real estate prices. Prices would rebound, the industry argued, so thrifts should be given time to grow out of their problem. The culprits were regional depressions, not bad managers who had speculated beyond all common sense that oil and real estate prices would rise forever. Forbearance became a rallying cry of the league.

Privately, however, the league sang a different song.

According to notes that O'Connell took when he addressed the twelve bank presidents, he admonished them to be tougher regulators and warned that lack of supervision and management, not economic hardship, was the root of the problem—just the opposite of what he was telling Congress and the press.

"Let's not talk about the exotic items to illustrate the reasons for Federal Savings and Loan Insurance Corporation problems—windmill farms, Arabian horses, Wendy's franchises, etc.," he said. "The real problems are in real estate . . . because some institutions did not follow the basic principles of the business—loans to home owners, in the local lending area and with sound underwriting and appraisals."

The speech was telling. The industry knew that its costliest mistakes didn't stem from headline grabbers like sperm banks or options markets but from run-of-the-mill real estate. But even as O'Connell spoke, league lobbyists pushed Congress for forbearance, for time to get healthy, arguing that economic problems, not bad management, were to blame.

Gray says he brought O'Connell along to show the presidents, many of whom were undermining Gray's get-tough policies, that the industry supported his calls for tougher oversight. Today he regrets bringing O'Connell to the meeting, agreeing that it was the kind of action that bolstered the league's influence with the very people who were supposed to be cracking down on its member institutions. (The bank presidents already knew O'Connell well. In Chicago, for example, the offices of the regional Chicago bank were in the same building as the league's national headquarters.)

Gray's duality was reflected in the philosophy he brought with him as an old-time S&L executive. He wanted to preserve the industry's special role—and its many regulatory advantages. He therefore was ecstatic when Vice President Bush's Task Group on Regulation of Financial Services concluded in 1985 that a place existed for a separate thrift regulatory apparatus—so long as thrifts performed a service distinctly different from banks.

"Instead of a consolidated financial regulatory giant at the federal level, which several members [of the task group] had suggested earlier, the Federal Home Loan Bank System came out of the study fully intact," Gray said in the March–April 1985 issue of *Outlook,* a magazine published by the bank board. "... I am proud of the effort made by the Federal Home Loan Bank Board and those members of the thrift industry who effectively articulated to the task group staff the arguments that were compelling enough to result in the unanimous consent of the task force members to the continuation of the Bank System's separate, multifaceted role in the nation's financial system."

In fact, Richard Breeden, the task group's staff director, had considered proposing the abolition of a separate thrift industry, dropping the idea only after intense league lobbying. But the report does state strongly that if thrifts do what banks do, then the two types of institutions should be governed by the same rules and regulations. Gray, the optimist, saw the concession in terms more flattering to the industry than the White House intended. To him, it reaffirmed the thrift industry's housing mission. It reinforced his idea of apple pie thrifts and his commonsense reasoning that, if S&Ls strayed far from home lending, they would lose any right to special privileges.

Of course, preserving the industry's special role meant directing it back toward its traditional function as a provider of home mortgages while reining in the highest fliers. Gray wanted to do this but, like the good public relations man he was at heart, without offending anyone. The inevitable result—a result compounded by Gray's personal quirks—was that he made enemies on both sides. "He was not consistent," said one high-ranking Treasury official who worked closely with Gray and liked him. "He was two or three people at once."

Gray says that during this period he took particular inspiration from Winston Churchill, a statesman who fought alone against great odds. Working late at night, writing speech after speech on his trusty IBM Selectric 3 typewriter, Gray often pulled out *A History of the English-speaking Peoples* or listened to tapes of Churchill's speeches. Or Gray would ask himself,

"What would Ronald Reagan do in this situation? How would he make this decision?"

Several times a week Gray sought moral support from George Gould, who became an undersecretary of the treasury in 1985, or Volcker, or L. William Seidman, who took over from William Isaac as chairman of the FDIC in 1985. In telephone calls or over dinner, Gray spent hours complaining to these men about the obstacles placed in his path by the industry and Congress.

All of them sympathized. Gray was a nice man, basically a good man, they thought, but in a little bit—or maybe not such a little bit—over his head.

23

Mr. Gloom and Doom

In January 1985 Treasury Secretary Regan and the White House chief of staff, James Baker III, switched jobs. Gray's enemy, Regan, now sat in the White House and had the president's ear. But Baker, universally considered to be intellectually and politically more astute than Regan, took the reins of an agency that had more direct dealings with the bank board.

In early February 1985, shortly after the switch, Gray telephoned Ed Rollins, a Reagan adviser from California who had rejoined the White House staff after leaving to work on the 1984 campaign. Like Gray, Rollins harbored no love for Regan.

"We have a major crisis here, and I can't get anyone's attention," Gray said.

Rollins walked over to the bank board and spent three hours listening to Gray and Fairbanks outline the extent of the problem. Rollins carried the message back to Regan and his assistants.

Regan, too, had begun to recognize that thrifts no longer suffered from the interest rate squeeze, that instead they had a potentially devastating bad asset problem. Rates had been down for months now, and still, industry losses climbed. But as Regan sat nodding at Rollins's description of the mess, he dismissed the gloomy picture as one born largely of incompetence by thrift managers and bank board regulators, not economic forces. If Gray were replaced by a smart, well-organized leader dedicated to deregulation, the problems could be managed, Regan told Rollins.

Others in the White House had reached a similar conclusion. At a meeting a few months after the 1984 election, Baker, Darman, Stockman, and Rollins met for one of their regular get-togethers to discuss the campaign and the issues facing the administration in the second term.

The thrift industry loomed as a major economic worry. Its condition was growing more and more fragile.

"Who's minding the store?" Baker reportedly asked.

"Ed Gray," Rollins said.

"Oh, my God," said Baker. "I thought he'd gone back to California."

Baker, Darman, and Stockman had always held Meese and his friends, including Gray, in contempt, regarding them as mediocre minds and political embarrassments. The trio realized something had to be done. They needed a plan. They didn't harbor Regan's passionate dislike for Gray. Nor did they share Regan's simplistic reverence for free markets. But they decided that Gray, while well intentioned and certainly correct in many of his newfound criticisms of the industry, could not be left in charge.

As Baker and Darman set out to resolve the Ed Gray problem, so did Regan, in his own way.

Increasingly frantic, Gray introduced a package of regulatory proposals in early 1985. In February Gray announced that the bank board would impose a special assessment on the industry as of March 31. This special premium, equal to one thirty-second of 1 percent of deposits, would be collected on top of the regular deposit insurance fee and would be imposed every quarter the bank board deemed it necessary. Gray says that he levied the special assessment to force the industry, Congress, and the White House to heed warnings that the deposit insurance fund was on a collision course with bankruptcy.

In addition, Gray proposed limiting the percentage of federally insured deposits that thrifts could invest directly in shopping centers, racehorses, or commercial real estate. And he sought to bolster bank board enforcement tools by making it more difficult for thrift management to block disciplinary action through administrative proceedings or lawsuits challenging government intervention.

The industry attacked Gray on each issue.

"Ed, you're going too far," Gray says O'Connell told him the evening before he planned to unveil his direct investment rule to Congress. "There's only so much the industry can take at one time. If you do this, you're really going to hurt your career." O'Connell does not recall the conversation.

Only a few weeks earlier, Gray recalls, O'Connell had told him that he would be O'Connell's choice as next president of the league, a job that came with a salary in the $300,000 range and many perks.

In deference to the strong opposition to the direct investment rule, Gray softened the proposed regulation. Even so, support remained scarce. Alan Greenspan, at the time a private economist at his own firm, Townsend-Greenspan & Company, argued on behalf of seventeen client thrifts, including Southern California's Lincoln, that the watered-down rule was too harsh and not in keeping with free market principles.

Gray modified the proposed restrictions even further, and the league finally offered a lukewarm endorsement. This is not surprising, for the compromise had been worked out carefully: When a group from the league met in Chicago to discuss certain changes the lobby group wanted in the direct investment rules, three officials from the bank board flew in to join the meeting at the O'Hare Hilton. According to the *Wall Street Journal,* participants in the meeting said that by the end of the day the board officials "were essentially helping the League staff to draft the group's official comment letter" on the proposal—comments the bank board could then use to justify modifications to its proposed rule.

"As originally proposed and then reproposed . . . the Bank Board's approach [to direct investments], in our opinion, was far too rigid and restrictive and failed to balance properly the competing considerations involved," league official Gerald Levy testified to Congress in February 1985.

"Fortunately, the Bank Board showed itself to be very willing to listen to our concerns and those of other interested parties, and in the end" proposed a direct investment rule the league thought it could live with, Levy said.

Levy also testified that the league opposed most of the increased enforcement powers Gray recently had asked Congress to give the agency. As usual, Congress followed the league's lead.

Levy's testimony summed up a process that infuriated Gray's staff. "How the hell can you be a tough regulator when you keep going back to the league?" said Peter O. Stearns, the head of the FSLIC for the first two and a half years of Gray's four-year term.

In March 1985 Gray attended a private ski party-cum-thrift meeting held each year in Utah by Dick Pratt for about one hundred of the industry's top executives. When Gray tried to explain why he thought direct investments were a threat to the industry's deposit insurance fund, many in the audience yelled at him, groaning and booing each time he started to speak.

In addition to rules on brokered funds and direct investment, Gray offered a variety of other measures to rein in the industry, including a proposed limit that would have tied a thrift's growth to its net worth. Individual members of the thrift community—including Herbert Sandler at World Savings in Oakland and executives at Great Western in Los Angeles—supported some of these efforts. But mostly the industry bucked Gray's attempts.

As the industry fought Gray's requests for more enforcement powers, saying the bank board had sufficient authority under existing law to rein in the highfliers, some old-timers in the industry admitted—privately, if not publicly—that the tactic was a mistake.

Norman Strunk, O'Connell's predecessor who started at the league in the late 1930s, for years has consulted to the league and, for many in the industry, remains one of its wisest friends. Strunk saw the tension between Gray and the league mount and even wrote a memo to O'Connell cautioning the league about the pitfalls of arguing that the industry had acted responsibly when it came to highfliers. And he warned against the dangers of waging war with Gray in public. The memo said in part:

> I know that many in the business complained about some of the operations that later resulted in failures and losses . . . but even if the bad operations were identified as involving substantial elements of fraud, the supervisors would have been unable to respond to such finger pointing, or at least respond very quickly. . . .
>
> . . . When we participated in the writing of the supervisory law, hindsight shows that we probably gave the business too much protection against unwarranted supervisory action, thus protecting the crooks as well as the good guys and impeding effective supervisory action against reckless management. . . .
>
> In making a case that "the government" was basically responsible for the tragedy that befell the FSLIC, I think we have to be careful that we do not put all the blame on the [bank board], particularly the board under Ed Gray. Goodness knows, he called to everybody's attention the problems that were developing in the business—to a point that the business got tired of hearing about it—and, as we have discussed, there was widespread opposition to his regulatory initiatives.
>
> The brokers and their association customers killed the proposed reforms with respect to brokered money. There was widespread opposition to his initiatives with respect to the net worth regulation. There was vehement opposition by many with respect to his proposal for direct investments. . . .

Great Western and World Savings could have withdrawn from the league to protest its continuing effort to weaken or sabotage Gray's regulatory proposals, but they did not. Their contributions, among the largest in the country (league dues increase with the size of the institution), helped fund league claims that Gray was hysterical, exaggerating, trying to "reregulate." O'Connell was one of the first to dub Gray the reregulator.

———

In fact, by the early 1980s the thrift industry contained many interest groups. There was a division between the profitable and the unprofitable, a gulf that widened each year. The haves clamored for relief from fees imposed to support the have-nots. The have-nots clamored for more aid.

There also were ideological differences. Traditional thrifts wanted to stay in home lending. They by and large did not acknowledge that computers and high interest rates had changed their old-fashioned world forever. Young Turks wanted to turn their thrifts into full-service financial centers, offering everything from stocks and bonds to checking accounts, credit cards, and life and auto insurance.

And there were the crooks and highfliers who hid behind the gospel of free markets and states' rights to do whatever they could get away with.

O'Connell was in charge of keeping everybody happy.

O'Connell was a newspaper reporter for the *Chicago Daily News* from 1945 to 1948, when he left to form a consulting firm. The league became his major client. Thirty years later, in 1979, he became the group's president and chief lobbyist.

As the 1980s wore on and thrift failures grew, one of O'Connell's chief missions became holding on to league members. His manner helped in this. A slight man, bald, with pale skin and sharp features, O'Connell speaks in a soft voice. His low-key demeanor leaves the impression that even when he disagrees violently on an issue, he is unruffled, calm, friendly. As S&Ls fell into disarray over the future of the industry, O'Connell found he had to try to be many things to many people, favoring deregulation before one group, the industry's original housing mission before another. He told government officials that he was against brokered deposits but wanted time for those of his members who depended on them to wean themselves away. He said he was for cracking down on bad operators yet against giving the bank board new enforcement powers. He wanted tougher standards yet sought greater use of net worth certificates. He favored a reduction in the deficit even as he lobbied for more thrift aid. He insisted he opposed a taxpayer bailout as he begged for help for S&Ls in the form of Treasury-backed notes.

In the eyes of many in the administration and in Congress, double-talk by league officials often breached the lobbyists' cardinal rule: Stretch the truth, use it to your advantage, but don't withhold critical information or distort the truth too far, for such tactics will come back to haunt you, especially if a member of Congress relies on your statements and then is embarrassed by them.

O'Connell, whose job was largely public relations, also was handicapped by a view of the press that was formed in the 1940s, when business reporting often amounted to reprinting company press releases. As a result, he increasingly wrote angry letters to editors as newspapers and magazines gave the S&L industry critical coverage. Some editorial offices around the country began to find it hard to tell when O'Connell had a legitimate complaint.

For example, *Barron's* ran a long article in 1989 chronicling the thrift disaster and the industry's role in creating its own troubles. O'Connell wrote a long letter to the editor decrying "the great and irresponsible flight of fantasy on the part of the writer. . . ."

Barron's reporter John Liscio responded to the letter in a manner that summed up the feelings many in government and the news media came to have about the league in general and O'Connell in particular. "I made three attempts to speak with Bill O'Connell," Liscio replied. "Two were handled by the main receptionist at the U.S. League and one by its public relations director . . . we would have been happy to include his version of history in the story.

"We stand by ours."

Typically, as if to balance his annoying penchant for "reregulation," Gray followed his direct investment initiative with a proposal concocted by the league. Gray and the staff at OMB had stuggled for months over how many examiners the bank board could hire. Also at issue was whether they should be exempt from federal pay caps. Gray wanted more examiners, arguing that like a teeter-totter, the fewer rules there were to govern the industry, the more oversight was needed. OMB's staff, skeptical of Gray's judgment and suspicious of his industry ties, repeatedly turned him down. Besides, they kept telling him, deregulation meant he needed fewer examiners, not more.

This is not to say that the professional staff at OMB was completely unmindful of the need for federal oversight during turbulent times. In fact, Gray would have had even fewer examination slots if the OMB staff hadn't protected existing positions from Stockman's budget ax. After going to bat for Gray in this way, however, OMB staff members found that Gray didn't fill all the slots he had. Some staffers suspected that Gray was trying to score points with the president by keeping down the number of federal employees, as Reagan had promised to do during the campaign. Whatever Gray's motivation, the practice angered OMB officials, who say they felt ridiculous fighting tooth and nail to preserve positions Gray never filled.

Gray says he had an excuse. He couldn't fill the slots because civil service pay for these positions—$13,000 or $14,000 at the entry level—was too low to attract applicants. The salary problem had made it hard to attract top-quality people for senior bank board positions, too, Gray argued, though he had earlier found a way to circumvent the government salary cap of approximately $70,000. He "borrowed" personnel from the regional banks, which were not subject to the ceilings. This permitted him to pay those employees six-figure salaries. He also promoted civil servants to serve as "acting" political appointees. These people thus drew higher salaries while keeping the benefits of lower-paying but more secure civil service positions. Neither of these approaches worked for the run-of-the-mill examiners, however.

So McKenna and league President O'Connell hatched a plan that would allow Gray to hire more examiners *and* offer higher salaries. There was a one catch: The salaries gave the industry control over the examination force. When McKenna and O'Connell presented Gray with the plan, he immediately endorsed it.

On a spring day in 1985 Gray walked across the street from the bank board headquarters to the White House to meet Constance J. Horner, associate director of the OMB, for lunch, at which time, in a wood-paneled lunchroom amid presidential staff, he presented the idea as a fait accompli. For most of the meal Horner ate while Gray talked, giving his usual spiel about the growing horrors in the industry and the need to increase substantially his 750-person examination force, perhaps even to double it.

At the end of the meal, according to Gray, Horner said she could give him 30 more examiners. She warned, however, that because the bank board had failed to notify the OMB before closing several thrifts, Gray could be found guilty of violating a federal law that required advance notice of any action that could add to the federal budget. Because the amounts of money involved in the closings were so large, he might even be guilty of a felony. The astonished Gray interpreted the charge as a threat intended to intimidate him.

Then Gray dropped his own bomb.

Bank board lawyers, led by the chief counsel, Norman Raiden, had studied the issue and concluded the agency could transfer examiners out of the federal government and into the regional banks. The move presented some immediately apparent conflicts of interest, not the least of which was that it put the entire regulatory force under the thumb of the industry-dominated regional banks, a consequence that presumably had not escaped the notice of McKenna and O'Connell. (Today Gray concedes the plan was inherently flawed but insists he had no alternative.) Under the plan the examiners, like the supervisors, would report to each regional bank's president, who, in addition to running the bank's lending operations, was its top regulator.

Regional bank presidents are chosen by the bank's board of directors, made up largely of thrift executives or political appointees with strong ties to the thrift industry. Often, as in the case of Federal Home Loan Bank of San Francisco President James Cirona, or Chicago bank President Leo B. Blaber, Jr., for example, the presidents had another strong link to the industry: They were close to or active in the league.

S&L executives clearly viewed the plan as a way for the industry to control its regulators and further blur the line between itself and government. The supervisers, empowered to act on information gathered by the examiners, already had been paid by the regional banks for years. Because the thrifts in each regional district paid the operating costs of the banks in exchange for the right to use their services, the industry considered the banks their property, not the federal government's—although the banks were treated as federal agencies when it came to borrowing money from the public. Thus their status as government or private-sector institutions was murky at best. (Thrift industry executives used this ambiguity to their advantage. The banks called themselves government when they borrowed money, thus enabling them to pay lower rates, but private when they wished to keep information from the public and dodge requests under the Freedom of Information Act asking for details of political contributions or entertainment expenses for members of Congress.)

Thrift executives spoke of "our" banks, "our" supervisors. Now, with Gray's ready adoption of McKenna's brainchild, they could speak of "our" examiners.

At the time Gray saw only the pluses of the plan. Under it he could double the examination force and get better people by raising their pay. Horner saw only the negatives. She was horrified.

"You're going to have nongovernment employees regulating the industry?" Gray recalls her asking.

"Yep," Gray said. He thanked her for lunch and left.

(Horner has a different recollection of the lunch, though she would not talk about it until forced to during sworn testimony before the Senate Banking Committee in mid-1990. Her recollection, while hazy, was that she requested the lunch to warn Gray about the need to give the OMB advance notice before moving in on an S&L. Her goal, she said, was to give him a friendly prodding, not to threaten him. She said she does not recall Gray's mentioning a plan to change the status of the examiners by moving them out from under the pay cap. Privately, however, other OMB officials say Horner not only learned of the plan from Gray but was dismayed by it.)

On July 7, while Gray and entourage were in Europe on bank board business, the regional banks took over responsibility for the examiners and immediately boosted their starting salary to $21,000, an increase of 50 percent. By the end of 1985 the force grew to 1,000 from 750. By mid-1986 it had doubled to 1,500. Of course, these new examiners were, as the league had advocated, indirectly working for the institutions they examined.

As Gray battled to rein in the industry and stem its losses, the bank board's ethics problems persisted. This time Gray wasn't the target. In 1985 the

House Energy and Commerce Committee and its powerful leader, John Dingell (D-Mich.), launched an investigation into potential conflicts of interest by Norman Raiden, Gray's chief counsel and the agency's top ethics officer.

Before joining the bank board, Raiden had advised a variety of thrift clients, including Beverly Hills Savings and Loan of California, on the legality of a business strategy that permitted the Los Angeles S&L to grow from an institution with $400 million in assets to one with nearly $3 billion in just three years.

The accounting methods that Beverly Hills used to make itself appear to be solvent were, in the words of Representative Ron Wyden (D-Ore.) during a hearing on the S&L's problems, "imaginative" at best.

In 1984, while Raiden was at the bank board, massive loan losses forced the board to seize Beverly Hills. (It became one of the most expensive failures in thrift history, costing taxpayers nearly $1 billion.)

Dingell's investigation was prompted by Raiden's failure to disqualify himself from several matters involving Beverly Hills. The committee ultimately issued a report saying that Raiden acted improperly by signing documents affecting the thrift. In his congressional testimony Raiden said that "almost immediately" after coming to the bank board, he was advised of the ethics rules that applied and decided that while at the agency, he "wouldn't handle any matter handled by me or by my firm for a client as of Nov. 30, 1983." But he didn't send out a memo or other formal notice informing his staff of his decision, according to congressional aides who investigated the matter.

Dingell's staff then presented Raiden with several bank board documents concerning Beverly Hills that bore his signature. Raiden said, "I don't think anything I signed was anything other than a ministerial document." But he acknowledged that he had signed an opinion letter from the board interpreting the agency's rules as they applied to Beverly Hills and its business practices.

Earlier in the day Gray testified, "I consider Mr. Raiden to have the highest possible ethics." After he had confirmed that Raiden was the bank board's ethics officer as well as its top attorney, Dingell leaned over his desk and asked, "Isn't that a little like putting the fox in control of the henhouse?"

Gray, who became the agency's chief ethics officer in cases involving the chief counsel, reviewed the matter and cleared Raiden, who always has maintained he acted properly. At the end of 1985, as Dingell's congressional hearings wound down, Raiden returned to McKenna, Conner & Cuneo.

In 1986, shortly after Raiden arrived back at his law firm, Gray's legal staff wrote a draft memo discussing the role played by the McKenna firm in Beverly Hills' financial problems. The bank board's legal staff gave the law firm a copy of the draft to review. The firm asked that its name be removed from the report, arguing that it had acted properly. The board staff disagreed but nonetheless deleted the firm's name before making the memo public.

When asked at a congressional hearing in 1987 why the firm's name had been deleted, William Black, a member of Gray's legal staff, said he could not discuss the matter because the bank board was investigating the firm.

Shortly after that testimony Black went to work for the regional bank in San Francisco, where McKenna was chairman. His job as chief counsel paid nearly double what he'd earned at the bank board.

Gray describes Raiden in laudatory terms, though the revolving door between the California industry, the bank board, and the regional bank in San Francisco helped foster a perception that the industry controlled the regulators and that some law firms, accounting firms, and troubled thrifts received special treatment based on whom they knew.

No legal action has been taken by the government against McKenna, Conner & Cuneo.

By 1985 many in the administration wanted Gray to leave. As that wasn't in the cards for one so long a friend of Ronald Reagan, however, Stockman and Baker reportedly decided on a diplomatic approach that would lower the tempers of all concerned and allow the White House to become more active on the thrift crisis.

In the spring of 1985 the White House sent M. Kathryn Eickhoff, associate director for economic policy at the OMB, to see Gray and Fairbanks and extend an olive branch. In Eickhoff's view, Horner and Gray had behaved childishly. By now Gray wouldn't return Horner's calls. Eickhoff didn't express her sentiments, of course. Her job was to figure out how bad the situation really was.

She asked Gray and Fairbanks to lunch. They invited her to the board conference room, where, as she munched on tuna sandwiches, she heard Gray's story.

The year was proving a banner one for the industry, deceptively so. Earnings stood at $3.8 billion, up from $1.1 billion in 1984 and just short of the industry record of $3.9 billion in 1979. The profit was possible because since 1979 the industry's deposit base had soared as it lured money to invest in high-yield, high-risk projects. The record earnings were the paper profits it was earning on those investments. Of course, the profits would evaporate if the loans soured and had to be written off.

The FSLIC fund's income also rose in 1985, to $2.4 billion, compared with $1.3 billion in 1984. The increase stemmed almost entirely from the special assessment Gray had imposed. But despite the increased revenue, the fund lost ground. A mounting caseload of failed thrifts, and the increasing costliness to the government of the thrifts that did fail, reduced the fund by $1.1 billion in 1985. The fund ended the year with reserves of $4.56 billion, down from $5.61 billion in 1984.

Eickhoff knew the situation actually was much worse. As a private economist before joining the OMB, she had worked with Alan Greenspan in his consulting firm monitoring the mounting problems in the thrift industry and had frequently worried about what was happening. Now she wanted to try to figure out how much worse. Why not, Eickhoff suggested, do a study of the thrift problem and draw up long-range plans for the FSLIC?

Working with Fairbanks to obtain bank board data on the industry, Eickhoff's OMB staff estimated the cost of closing or selling all the problem thrifts to be from $15 billion to $25 billion. The numbers were never officially released. But OMB officials knew them. Presumably so did Gray and Fairbanks.

The bank board didn't like the numbers. Fairbanks says she doesn't remember the study, but Gray does, and he says he thought the OMB figures represented a worst-case scenario and therefore were too high. The board's official guess was that the cost then of disposing of all the officially recognized insolvent thrifts hovered in the range of $4 billion to $6 billion. After discussions with the OMB, however, Gray increased the agency's estimate to $8 billion. Even that low-ball number was troubling; although dramatically lower than the $30 to $100 billion figures bandied about earlier in the decade, an $8 billion expenditure would have depleted FSLIC resources, making a taxpayer bailout of the fund inevitable. As one OMB official said, "It didn't matter if the estimate was $4 billion or $6 billion or $15 billion, the net worth of the industry was zero."

Nevertheless, at Senate hearings in late summer 1985, bank board member Hovde testified that because of falling interest rates, the industry would record a profit and that 90 percent of all thrifts soon would be in the black. Yet at the same time failures were expected to continue at a record pace. Gray's explanation of this so-called paradox of the S&L industry was that most thrifts were getting healthier while a few, say, 10 percent, were getting sicker. This gap between the haves and have-nots occurred, Gray said, because while lower inflation helped the vast portion of the industry, a few S&Ls had transformed their interest rate problem into a bad loan problem.

This was, in retrospect, a wildly optimistic view. Many thrifts, perhaps half the industry or more, were engaging in unsound lending practices. If Hollywood had done a remake of Capra's *It's a Wonderful Life* in 1985, Jimmy Stewart's speech to the angry crowd at the thrift's door would have had to be rewritten. "The money's not here," he would have had to say. "Why, your money's in racehorses, a bordello in Nevada, a share in the Dallas Cowboys, a nitrogen-cooled tank filled with vials of buffalo semen, vacant shopping malls, unneeded condominiums, Rolls-Royces, golf courses, prostitutes to pay off regulators, credit cards. . . ."

It therefore is not surprising that there were dissenting opinions to Gray's optimistic outlook, even on his own staff. A group of four economists at the bank board issued a report in May 1985 saying that the FSLIC needed at least $16 billion to close the 434 S&Ls that were insolvent under generally accepted accounting principles. The FSLIC's reserves were less than $5 billion.

And as two of the authors, R. Dan Brumbaugh and James Barth, point out today, even the $16 billion figure was low because it included only officially recognized problems—known insolvencies—and thus specifically excluded an estimate of additional insolvencies that surely would emerge from another 850 thrifts that regulators knew were weak.

Those numbers—434 broke and 850 nearly so—showed that at least a third of the $900 billion thrift industry remained in trouble. That assessment contained staggering implications for the budget, not to mention the future of the industry.

Gray approved the report's release, apparently rubber-stamping it as an innocuous academic paper. (One of the authors, Barth, was a visiting scholar at the agency. He eventually was named its chief economist by Gray's successor.) But the authors knew the 1985 report would not be innocuous if it fell into the hands of someone who could understand its implications. They didn't know who that would be.

By chance, *Washington Post* editorial writer John Anderson received a copy of the report after being referred to the authors by the bank board's Press Office. Anderson saw right away that he had on his desk the first formal analysis establishing that the Reagan administration's policy of allowing insolvent institutions to stay open was increasing the scope and cost of the thrift industry's problem.

"The cause is no longer high interest rates," Anderson wrote in a July 3, 1985, editorial about the study, "but high-risk loans going sour. . . . It's Congress that is going to have to answer the basic questions. Should the regulations be enforced, and should the weakest S&Ls be forced to fold? The right answer is yes, but it will cost $10 billion more than the regulators have in the insurance fund."

The editorial ignited fireworks within the thrift industry and the bank board.

Gray was furious. When the Senate Banking Committee asked about the $16 billion figure two weeks later, Gray denounced the accuracy of the bank board's own work, saying it painted a worst-case scenario that was unlikely to occur. According to Brumbaugh and Barth, Gray was so angry with public reaction to the report that he tried to fire Brumbaugh, a junior economist at the agency, for giving it to the newspapers.

"I personally resent that he's rewritten history that he alerted the nation to the size of the problem when he attempted to fire me for doing that very thing," Brumbaugh says today of the credit Gray now receives for trying to alert the government to the problem. "Now he wants to say he saw the problem early and tried to stop it. In fact, he had to be dragged kicking and screaming to the realization of how bad it was. We lost a precious two years waiting for him."

But one of Gray's top aides, Eric Hemel, the director of the bank board's Office of Policy and Economic Research, thought that even the 1985 report wildly understated the problem. Before he left government at the end of that year to join a Wall Street investment banking firm, Hemel felt he had to visit various departments around Washington—the OMB, White House, Congress—to set the record straight: Despite what was being said privately and publicly, the actual lost of closing insolvent thrifts was closer to $50 billion to $100 billion.

Several officials at other agencies remember Hemel's warning. Gray does not.

Eickhoff went back to the OMB with the information gleaned that summer at the bank board, only to lose an important intellectual battle that fall with her bosses. She argued that the thrift problem was a policy issue, a political question as much as an economic one. As such it belonged on the "management" side of the Office of Management and Budget. That side of the agency looked at the big picture. If the thrift crisis had been handled as a management problem, OMB officials might have started to discuss the wisdom of leaving insolvent institutions open, perhaps the need for a separate thrift industry at all.

But James Miller, OMB's boss when Stockman left for Wall Street in October 1985, decided the thrift problem was a budget issue as far as his office was concerned. The question was how to minimize its impact on the deficit, not to find a lasting solution.

Still, Eickhoff's effort was not entirely in vain. The OMB and Treasury were awake now. Unlike Regan, Baker understood that the problem was both deep and enduring. It would not, as Regan had predicted, go away when interest rates came down. At the end of 1985 internal Treasury documents showed that only $2.7 billion of the FSLIC fund was uncommitted, while thrifts held almost $1 trillion in insured deposits.

On September 30, 1985, at 10:00 A.M., Gray walked into the West Wing of the White House to see presidential aide Rollins, the Californian whom Gray had known from the days in Sacramento but who was leaving the administration after nine months on the job because of differences with Regan.

Rollins warned Gray that the chief of staff had renewed his efforts to get Gray fired. And Regan, he said, "runs about eighty percent of this place now.

"You do whatever you want to do, Ed," Rollins said, "but Don Regan wants you out. And I'm sure if he wants you out, he gets you out eventually. Regan was going to haul you over to the White House himself, but I told him, 'You don't do this to Ed Gray. He's worked for the President for a long time. He's an old friend. A personal friend.' "

Gray asked why Regan wanted him out.

"He thinks things are in turmoil over there," Rollins said.

"You mean at the bank board? Or the industry?" Gray asked.

"Both," Rollins said.

Gray steamed. He had promised his wife that he would quit Washington and come home in two years, a deadline already missed by several months. But he didn't want to appear to have been run out of town by anyone, especially Regan. Gray called his friend Meese and asked what he should do. Meese said he would talk to Regan.

Several days later Meese called Gray. "I talked to Regan, and he says if you resign, only three people will know about it: me, Regan, and you." The meaning was clear. Regan would let Gray leave the government on Gray's own terms, in a manner that could be billed as his own decision.

Gray said fine. But a few days later he got a call from a *Wall Street Journal* reporter who said she understood "on the highest authority" that Gray was going to resign. Gray asked if the "authority" was the president, fearing it might be. The reporter said no.

Gray knew it was Regan.

He decided he could not go, not like this. He denied the story. Regretting that the situation compelled him to break his word to his wife, he called the *New York Times* and leaked his own story: Ed Gray was staying at the bank board. Within days the White House had issued a statement saying Gray could stay as long as he liked.

Still, rumors persisted.

On November 5, 1985, as Gray stood before a lectern in Dallas at the annual convention of the league and looked across an audience of the thrift industry's top executives, he felt their expectation. Many thought he was going to announce his resignation. Many crossed their fingers hoping he would.

"I'm the one whose resignation you've been reading about," Gray said, glad to disappoint the crowd. "I hope none of you hold your breath. It may be deleterious to your health." Then he gave his umpteenth speech warning the industry about its problems. For the umpteenth time he got a response that ranged from cool to hostile.

Executives buttonholed Gray after the speech. "Ed, everything's gonna be all right. Relax. Things have always worked out before, and they will always work out in the future," Gray recalls them saying.

"But that's not necessarily true," Gray answered. "You in the industry and I as a regulator have to come to grips with this problem because Congress is not going to act unless there is sufficient support."

But in typical fashion, even while Gray castigated the industry in his speech, he handed it an enormous plum. Following a script that had been written by McKenna, O'Connell, and the league's top brass, Gray used the league's convention to unveil a plan that raised the incestuousness of the bank board with industry to new heights. Its name was the Federal Asset Disposition Association (FADA).

24

The Government Competes with the Private Sector

C hartered with $25 million from the FSLIC and owned by the federal government, FADA was set up as a quasi-private, quasi-government company. The arrangement further blurred the distinction between the regulated and the regulators—a fuzziness that the industry intended to use to its advantage, just as it did in the district banks. As conceived by the industry, FADA provided all the benefits of government and none of the checks and balances. Its purpose was to sell the mounting pile of property and other assets the government inherited from failed thrifts. By controlling it, the industry sought to control the rate at which real estate was sold and thus control the price of property in various sections of the country. If a purely government group ran the show, the industry argued, it would "dump" the repossessed properties and further depress prices in areas like Dallas.

As a quasi-private company FADA wasn't subject to the federal pay cap. It paid its chief executive, Roslyn Payne, $250,000 a year in salary plus $75,000 in bonuses. She made more than the president of the United States or the Federal Reserve Board chairman. The justification for such a salary was that FADA would bring private-sector efficiency to the bank board's task of disposing of repossessed real estate, so it needed to pay private-sector salaries to hire the best talent.

Gray named McKenna, who had hatched the idea of FADA, chairman of the unit's board of directors. McKenna retained his positions as head of the

San Francisco bank and chairman of the Federal Savings and Loan Advisory Council, a group of industry officials who advised the bank board on regulatory policy. The rest of FADA's board read like a who's who of the league: Gerald Levy from Milwaukee, Thomas Bomar from Miami, Richard Diehl of Los Angeles (chairman of nation's largest thrift organization, H. F. Ahmanson), Barney R. Beeksma of Washington, W. W. ("Bo") McAllister of San Antonio, and Donald Shackelford of Columbus (the thrift executive who was with Governor Celeste of Ohio the night the governor decided to call a bank holiday, but who Celeste says never offered to help reach bank board Chairman Gray). All were active league members with wide influence over setting the trade group's policies and lobbying strategies. Also on the board was the president of the Federal Home Loan Bank of Chicago, Leo Blaber, a man whom officials in the Treasury and Congress regarded as largely controlled by league President O'Connell.

In October 1985 the league wrote the draft of a question and answer pamphlet about FADA for the regional banks to distribute to their boards of directors at a special meeting to be organized by O'Connell and held during the league's annual convention a few weeks later.

From the start FADA posed a contradiction. An administration dedicated to free enterprise created it to compete head to head with private-sector companies that managed and sold assets inherited by the government from failed banks and thrifts.

Not surprisingly, instead of streamlining the process, FADA added to the cost. It subcontracted out the duties of managing and selling the assets rather than perform them itself. Worse, some subcontractors were inexperienced firms with political ties to the Republican party. FADA thus added a layer of fees to a process that the FSLIC could have done directly with more established firms.

FADA saw itself as free of government-in-sunshine laws and therefore thought it could set policy and dispose of government assets without oversight from the public. From the start, accusations of conflicts of interest and cronyism arose. Within eighteen months of its formation, its chief counsel, Robert Axley, resigned when it was revealed that he and his longtime business partner, Richard Strauss, were intimately involved in several real estate transactions at failed S&Ls in Texas. The transactions were possible targets of the Justice Department.

Richard Strauss was the son of Robert Strauss, former chairman of the Democratic party and a lead partner in the Dallas law firm of Akin, Gump, Strauss, Hauer & Field. While Axley was still its chief counsel, FADA hired Akin, Gump to help it deflect criticism in Congress. Shortly before Axley resigned, Akin Gump received national attention when congressional investigators learned that the law firm had hired private detectives to probe a New Jersey man who had been publicly critical of FADA, charging in particular that the government corporation played favorites when awarding property management contracts.

Congressional investigators also discovered that FADA officials had awarded a major property management contract to a company owned by two men who also owned the recruiting firm Korn/Ferry International. Korn/Ferry had recommended Payne to head FADA. Lester Korn and Richard Ferry were major investors in the San Diego-based ConAm Corporation, which FADA hired for $650,000, "the most paid to any one FADA ... subcontractor," congressional investigators said. This at a time when scores of real estate management firms across the country complained to Congress that they couldn't get a return telephone call from FADA offices to find out how to go about bidding for work.

Korn/Ferry and Payne insisted that the recruitment of Payne and their contract award were unrelated. Even so, the perception didn't help FADA, the bank board, or Ed Gray. Ironically, the industry that backed FADA soon found that it could also use FADA's missteps to embarrass Gray and undermine the bank board's oversight of the industry.

Payne's exasperation with the media came to a head when she walked off a CBS set after a reporter on a show being taped asked about a Florida real estate developer's allegation that FADA officials bribed him in an effort to silence his criticism of the agency. Even some supporters began to wonder if she was right for the job. Payne resigned in 1987.

The blunders didn't stop. FADA gave the Florida Republican party eighteen months of free rent in an office building the government inherited from a bankrupt S&L. In another case it allowed a Florida businessman who had defaulted on property worth $18 million and had thus contributed to the failure of a savings and loan to buy the real estate back from the government for only $6.3 million.

FADA eventually was merged out of existence in 1990, a failed experiment that critics doubt ever justified the $35 million-plus that the FSLIC expended on it. FADA was supposed to wring every cent from the sale of government real estate and pump the proceeds back into the FSLIC. Instead FADA itself had gone broke.

25

The Fix

To shore up the ailing FSLIC fund, Gray sought to propose a one-time 1 percent surtax on thrift deposits. He was to explain the proposal to the House Banking Committee on October 17, 1985. But when O'Connell read an advance copy of the prepared testimony the night before, he stormed into Gray's office to protest.

"I told him he ought to know up front before he started his testimony," O'Connell explained to the *Wall Street Journal* months later.

Gray toned down his proposal. He eliminated the 1 percent surcharge proposal from his oral statement before the committee—though he preserved it in the written statement submitted to the record—and instead told Congress it had to find "alternatives" to restore the FSLIC fund to health.

Gray insists he didn't buckle, but some on his staff say they felt betrayed by the watered-down proposal. "We had everyone on the Hill convinced we should get 1 percent, but he [Gray] got pushed around very hard from the league," said Stearns, the FSLIC director. "At the hearing, in the first row sitting two seats down was O'Connell. You could feel him."

Gray also waffled at the hearing when asked the size of the total S&L problem, even as he hammered away on his pet theme that the FSLIC fund was in danger of going broke. "The consequence . . . wrought more often than not on the thrift deposit insurance system by high flyers and dare-devils who have chosen to play fast and loose on the system with a mentality that can best be described as 'heads I win, tails the FSLIC loses,' is incredible losses strewn with bad assets. As a result, the losses we have sustained and can look forward to at the FSLIC are far more expensive to deal with than the comparatively minor costs associated with the earnings spread problems encountered by institutions in 1981 and 1982," Gray said.

Yet under intense questioning from his old nemesis Representative Barnard about the actual size of the problem, Gray proved more timid. He conceded to Barnard that three hundred thrifts were insolvent, or soon would be. Assets of those thrift totaled about $90 billion.

"How much do you think you would recover from those institutions? In other words, what would be your estimated losses from that amount?" Barnard asked.

"It's very difficult, congressman," Gray said.

"10%?" Barnard asked.

"It would probably cost more than that over time."

"15%?"

"It would be somewhere in that range, 10 to 15 percent."

"So in other words we are talking about—if it is $90 billion—we are talking around about something like $14 or $15 billion."

"Could be. Might not," Gray responded.

Barnard's staff concluded in a report on the thrift crisis that "while [Gray's] attempts to calm concerns about the stability of the S&L industry and the solvency of the FSLIC fund are understandable, providing . . . erroneous and incomplete data denies to the Congress and the public information essential to their understanding of the problem."

Mushy estimates also infuriated other members of Congress such as Stan Parris (R-Va.), who a few months later called for Gray's resignation. If Gray could not give straightforward answers about the cost of the problem, Parris argued, he was not competent to run the bank board.

Other incidents belied Gray's claim to be a hard-nosed regulator. One night in early 1986 Gray called O'Connell in England to read aloud part of the testimony Gray intended to deliver the following day.

"How does that sound to you?" Gray asked.

O'Connell said it sounded fine. Gray delivered it as planned.

Critics of the surcharge found that mismanagement of the FSLIC made for effective ammunition. In November 1985 the Senate Banking Committee chairman, Jake Garn, asked Brent Beesley, FSLIC director under Pratt and now a thrift owner himself, if the FSLIC should be recapitalized by assessing the special fee on deposits. Beesley answered, "There is no evidence in the public domain that giving the FSLIC more money is required at this time or that such an infusion would solve the problems facing the FSLIC. I consider the problems of the FSLIC to be to a large extent the problems associated with management.

"The FSLIC's organizational and management problems must be resolved before . . . precious capital of the S&L industry is subjected to a potential loss at the hands of the FSLIC," Beesley added. "There has been much discusion and testimony on how to recapitalize the FSLIC. I am aware of very little candid discussion on the issue of how the FSLIC is managing its current resources." This became the crux of the argument used by the industry—honest and dishonest executives alike—to forestall plans to make it pay more: Why should anyone trust Ed Gray with more money when he was wasting what he had?

The surcharge idea was quietly dropped.

In late 1985 Treasury Secretary Baker named George Gould undersecretary for finance. Gould was Baker's answer to the thrift crisis. His principal mission was to devise a solution to the mess, one that, if not permanent, at least would tide the administration through the next presidential election in 1988. For Gray, Gould was a godsend.

Gould had all the right paper credentials. Yale. Harvard Business School. A cofounder and former chairman of Donaldson, Lufkin & Jenrette, one of Wall Street's old-line investment banking firms. But dozens of people had similar résumés. What set Gould apart was his negotiating skill, both on Wall Street and in Washington.

The new undersecretary commanded wide respect as one of Wall Street's elder statesmen. He had served as chairman of the committee set up to bail out New York City in the mid-1970s. He championed free markets but, unlike Regan, didn't let personal feelings dull his common sense or cloud his vision of government's role. Gould could be counted on to add credibility to any thrift bailout plan the government devised, no matter how tortured the effort to keep it off the budget. Certainly one of his main tasks was to sell the plan to the markets.

Gould's patrician yet gentlemanly manner was an invaluable asset to the White House. In Gould and his competent staff—Charles Sethness, Gregory Wilson, Robert Zoellick—Gray found friends, people who would listen as intently as Volcker but who, unlike Volcker, could forge legislation and enlist White House and congressional support for it.

With Gould's arrival, the search began in earnest for ways to replenish, or recapitalize, the FSLIC. Gould's mission: Find a solution that didn't need tax dollars; then sell it to the nation's politicians and investment bankers.

He asked Gray to dinner. He could hardly believe what he heard. Gray poured out his heart for hours, retelling in relentless detail not only the problems in the industry but also the snubs at the hands of Regan, how hurt he was, how loyal to the president, how concerned about the future of the thrift industry. Puffing on his pipe, Gould listened and let the dinner serve as a therapy session for Gray, a chance to cry on a shoulder rather than devise strategy. Gray could easily become more hindrance than help, Gould saw.

Gould was no fan of Regan's. But now Gould understood Gray's ineffectiveness, why he had put off many of the key players in the administration, why his style had closed so many doors. Gray was clearly a man obsessed. But Gould also realized that Gray was right and Regan was wrong. Gray may have lacked management and ambassadorial skills, but the thrift industry's problems were not his fault. He hadn't, perhaps, shown effective leadership or judgment in trying to get his message across, but that didn't make him wrong on everything.

As Baker had foreseen, Gould's mission would be to reopen channels Gray had closed. Gould began by charming Gray, listening to him complain, agreeing that he had been wronged. He had to win Gray's confidence and coax him into supporting a Treasury-led plan to plug the problem—at least for a time—even as he allowed Gray to indulge himself in the belief that the plan was mostly a bank board initiative. Gould would have to cater to Gray's view of himself as a manager, a leader. And Gould had a soft spot for Gray. He felt sorry for someone he considered essentially good-hearted.

Gould and his staff, particularly Zoellick, became Gray's life-support system to the rest of the government and, in many ways, to the press. Gray the public relations man was fighting a losing battle with the nation's newspapers. Where Gray lacked credibility regarding a government plan to recapitalize the FSLIC fund, Gould and his staff would step in to supply it.

By now the Treasury, the White House, and many in the bank board (though Gray was not among them) feared that closing all of the nation's insolvent thrifts easily could cost, as Hemel had estimated, in the range of $50 billion, possibly more. That amount had come down significantly from the $100 billion or so that such action would have cost when interest rates were at their peak a few years back—though the number was still big enough to bust the budget and, possibly, ruin a few political careers. The White House decided the mess still was too big to tackle head-on.

The known problem thrifts—the 400 or so the government knew it had to take over—could be closed or sold within five years with only $15 billion in new funding for the FSLIC, as Barth and Brumbaugh had concluded. Treasury officials knew that such a plan—with funds to be raised primarily by borrowing from the Federal Home Loan Banks and, therefore, from the industry—was a Band-Aid; $15 billion could not buy a permanent solution. There were, after all, 850 weak but as yet undeclared problem thrifts waiting in the wings.

But $15 billion would prop up the thrift deposit insurance fund until after the 1988 elections. And $15 billion for an industry-funded bailout was the most that the Treasury Department thought could be pushed past the league and its friends in Congress, who opposed tapping any additional industry funds for a bailout.

There is some controversy over who should be credited with the $15 billion bailout plan: George Barclay, then vice-president of the Dallas bank, and Gray; or Richard Syron, president of the Boston bank, and Gould. Both groups contributed, but many involved in the process give Syron and Gould the lion's share of the credit.

Although nominated to his Treasury post in July 1985, Gould did not win Senate confirmation until November. By then Gray already had asked the regional bank presidents to try to come up with a new plan. The special assessment, the transfer of examiners out from under the pay cap, creative ways of keeping ailing thrifts open, the creation of FADA—none of these was sufficient, Gray thought.

In mid-October, at a joint meeting of the Dallas and Atlanta district banks, Gray asked for ideas to recapitalize the FSLIC. The meeting, as usual, was a lavish affair, held at Bishop's Lodge in New Mexico. Barclay, then a vice-president at the Dallas bank, proposed a $15 billion plan that involved borrowing money from the industry.

A month later Barclay and the Dallas bank president, Roy Green, flew to Milwaukee to pitch the idea to a league subcommittee. The response was predictable. League officials said the bank board was exaggerating the problems, that federal regulators, not the industry, were responsible for the problems that did exist, that a government bailout, not an industry-financed one, was appropriate.

The California thrifts were against any plan that asked them to pay anything on top of the special insurance premium assessment to bail out the highfliers. Levy, the Wisconsin thrift executive who a few weeks earlier had become chairman of the league and who, as its vice-chairman, had testified against Gray's enforcement rules, vowed to "drive a stake into the heart" of the plan.

Several Federal Home Loan Bank presidents, including Syron, a former assistant to Volcker, began to work on a variation of the Barclay plan, one that called for the regional banks to buy Treasury bonds that could be pledged for yet another layer of bonds. The complex web would raise $15 billion in fresh cash for the FSLIC. Although Syron would not officially assume his new job at the Boston regional bank until January, he began to confront the task.

Syron liked the idea of using the reserves of the regional banks to fund the bailout. It was a complicated scheme that called for $3 billion in bank funds to be used to buy government securities. The securities would be pooled and sold as thirty-year instruments called zero-coupon bonds to investors at a deep discount that would yield $15 billion.

In December 1985 Syron ran the idea past Gould, who liked it. The key to the arrangement was that the revenue stream to repay the $15 billion could be separated from the federal government's regular budget. It was a self-funded financing plan. It would not, in Gould's opinion, add to the federal budget deficit. The mechanism was similar to the strategy used years earlier to avert the bankruptcies of Lockheed and then of New York City.

In early 1986 Syron and several other bank presidents worked well into the night in a Cincinnati hotel to revise the plan to everyone's satisfaction. The next day they officially presented their work to Gould, who had flown in for twenty-four hours. He liked the outline. Now they had to sell the plan to the other bank presidents. Credibility required approval by all twelve.

Gray therefore summoned the twelve to his conference room to meet with Gould and his staff. With varying degrees of resistance, the presidents signed on. The exceptions were Chicago's Blaber, who was especially close to O'Connell, and San Francisco's Cirona. Cirona's reluctance was easy to understand. McKenna was chairman of his bank's board of directors, which was heavily influenced by executives from the largest California thrifts, thrifts that were among the most powerful in the country. They didn't want to pay a dime for the bailout. The Treasury ultimately had to strong-arm the Californians to come on board, threatening them with even harsher measures, such as proposals to merge the thrifts into the banking industry. Halfheartedly they agreed. The Treasury also succeeded in getting Blaber's reluctant endorsement.

On May 6, 1986, Gould leaked news of the proposal and the bailout to the *Washington Post,* and the behind-the-scenes fight over the plan became public. On one side was the Treasury, the bank board, and most of the bank presidents. On the other was the league.

"You're going to cut your own throats if you don't go along with this," Gould kept warning the reluctant league leaders. If the industry's problems grew too big and a government bailout was necessary, the bank board and even the banks might be dismantled in the process. It was in the industry's interest to find a quick, if not permanent, solution.

One oddity emerged: Gray remained loyal to McKenna throughout, apparently never realizing that McKenna was working feverishly behind the scenes on behalf of the California thrifts to thwart any industry-financed plan.

Critics of Gray's performance at the time say he failed to use his most powerful weapon: a headline-grabbing estimate of the true rescue cost. Gray says that pinning down a number was impossible because the estimates were changing every day. And, he says, using that weapon would have made him seem even wackier to his critics, who already accused him of exaggerating the problem. "If I'd said fifty billion, no one would have believed me. They would have said I was crazy."

But lack of firm numbers caused Gray to lose control of the situation. By the time Gray understood that Hemel's estimates were accurate, he couldn't say so. He was lobbying Congress for the Treasury's $15 billion plan. To concede that the money would be insufficient would have played into the league's hands; members of Congress would have been very reluctant to support such a controversial bill if they'd thought it was not a real solution to the problem.

Thus in 1985 and early 1986 Gray publicly objected even to the $16 to $22 billion in outlays that the General Accounting Office, the auditing branch of Congress, estimated the FSLIC fund faced, as well as the GAO's estimate that roughly thirteen hundred of the industry's thirty-two hundred remaining thrifts were weak and might need federal aid. The thirteen hundred represented 40 percent of thrifts in the country and held 43 percent of the industry's assets. Though the industry considered Gray too glum in his assessment, he seemed downright cheery next to the consensus building in the Treasury, OMB, and GAO.

"I am concerned that the [GAO] report . . . overstates the problems facing the FSLIC," Gray wrote on January 27, 1986, to Craig Simmons, the GAO's associate director. "To imply that over 42 percent of the industry is likely to require some form of FSLIC assistance seriously distorts the magnitude of the problem."

Gray, despite his own harsh warnings to Congress on the plight of the FSLIC, further argued that the GAO's public pronouncements could engender a self-fulfilling prophecy. "I fear that if such an overstatement were to become public it could seriously worsen the actual situation," Gray said in the same letter.

Even as he rebuked the GAO, Gray implemented a plan that amounted to a tacit recognition that problems had overwhelmed the FSLIC's means. Gray created the Management Consignment Program, in which the bank board paid healthy S&Ls fees to manage insolvent institutions it could not afford to close. MCPs—as the unhealthy thrifts in the program came to be called— soon became the biggest abusers of brokered funds, fueling the cutthroat competition for deposits and raising interest rates.

"When it comes to thrift matters in the U.S. Congress, the U.S. league and many of its affiliates were the de facto government," Gray now says. "What the league wanted, it got. What it did not want from Congress, it got killed."

O'Connell put it another way. "We worked with the Bank Board, and everything we tried to do we were successful at," he boasted of Gray's tenure.

But many of Gray's colleagues say he fueled the league's influence as much as anyone. Stearns, for example, finally quit in disgust at the end of 1985, charging that the league's stranglehold on regulators made it impossible for the government to do its job.

At the bank board's 1985 Christmas party, the legal department put on a skit parodying the music industry's efforts to raise money to feed the hungry. It was called "Live/Aid for the FSLIC Fund" and was copyrighted by "I. Seymour Failures." In one scene, a staffer who was a ventriloquist played O'Connell. The dummy on his knee represented Gray.

Gray: Hi! Eddie's the name and regulating thrifts is my game.

O'Connell: Tell the people just how closely the league and the bank board work, Eddie.

Gray: Sure thing, Bill. One of the nicest things about our relationship is that no matter whether the statement comes out of my mouth. . . .

O'Connell: Or mine. . . .

Gray: The thought's the same. In fact, there are some people who think we are the same person! But that's not true. . . .

O'Connell: Not at all, we don't even look alike.

Gray: We just think alike. And even though my head's wooden . . .

O'Connell: You're no dummy.

Gray: Why, thank you, Bill.

O'Connell: And thank you, Eddie. Why don't you tell the folks why FSLIC aid is so important?

Gray (in a loud whisper): Bill, that's my line.

O'Connell: Does it matter?

Gray: But I'm the chairman. I get to ask the questions. It says so in the script. I always ask the questions in public meetings.

O'Connell: But Eddie, this isn't a public meeting, this is a fund raiser for FSLIC. . . .

26

Lincoln Continued . . .
Keating Takes On Gray

On a late summer afternoon in 1983 the telephone on Lincoln owner Don Crocker's desk rang. "Can I come over and talk to you?" an investment banker asked. "I've got a buyer for your stock at sixteen dollars a share."

Lincoln's stock traded at $8, so the offer was quite generous, but Crocker said he wasn't interested.

"You won't even talk to them?" the banker asked.

"We're really not interested in selling," Crocker said, quickly hanging up.

Two weeks later Crocker received a call from a prominent Los Angeles lawyer who asked if they could talk in person. "What about?" Crocker asked. "Are you trying to talk me into selling the company?"

"Just let me come over and talk to you. I won't take more than half an hour."

Crocker agreed.

The lawyer told Crocker he had a client that wanted to pay sixteen dollars a share—or $40 million in all—for Lincoln. After a few minutes the lawyer revealed the buyer's identity: Charles Keating of the American Continental Corporation of Phoenix.

Crocker was leaving the next day for a management conference of California savings and loan executives in Scottsdale, a suburb of Phoenix. He would skip the golf game during the day and instead fly in for the evening reception and two days' worth of meetings.

"Will you please just see the guy?" Crocker recalls Keating's lawyer pleading.

"Why doesn't he go look at Southern California Savings or Santa Barbara Savings? They're both on the market for sale," Crocker said.

"He's already gone up and looked at Santa Barbara and looked at Southern California. He wants a superclean association. He doesn't want to buy somebody else's problems," he recalls the lawyer saying.

Knowing that American Continental was based in Phoenix, Crocker agreed to call Keating during the conference. "Maybe there is some kind of business we can do," he said.

Crocker already had met Keating in the 1960s, when Keating had worked with Carl Lindner at American Financial. Keating had been involved with American Financial's thrift holding company, and Crocker, while doing some thrift lobbying work, bumped into him occasionally. Crocker also remembered reading about Keating in the *Wall Street Journal* a few years earlier when Keating had a run-in with the SEC. Crocker wondered about the incident and planned to ask about it.

Crocker knew Keating expected him to call as soon as he arrived in Phoenix, but he waited until noon on the last day of the conference to telephone. He told Keating he could spend only an hour or two with him because he had a plane to catch back to Los Angeles.

"I've been expecting your call," Keating said. "I'd hoped you'd call so we could have dinner at my family's house and entertain you, but I'll have somebody pick you up at two P.M."

A Mercedes arrived at the hotel promptly at two and whisked Crocker off to Keating's office a few miles away.

"I'll pay between forty million and fifty million dollars for your institution," Keating said right off the bat. Keating's price had risen to $20 a share for Lincoln's stock, up $4 from a few days earlier.

Crocker asked about the SEC problem. Keating said that he had not been guilty, that he had agreed to sign the consent decree to avoid legal fees, that he didn't think the incident would affect his ability to enter the thrift business.

Keating went on to discuss American Continental and his successes as a developer in Colorado and Arizona. His company's business had two insurance affiliates, so the deal with Lincoln, which also had an insurance subsidiary, would "be a good fit." Keating had just raised several tens of millions of dollars in cash through Michael Milken, the junk bond king at Drexel Burnham Lambert, in connection with some very sophisticated mortgage securities Keating was offering, and said that he could raise another $50 million through Drexel to buy Lincoln.

Crocker said that even though he was the controlling shareholder, he would have to discuss the deal with the other shareholders. Keating took him around to meet his staff, whose nearly uniform good looks seemed a little too perfect. "They're all Ken and Barbie doll types," Crocker thought.

After meeting with Lincoln officials and shareholders through the weekend, however, Crocker decided the deal might work; $50 million in cash was more than twice Lincoln's market value.

"How will personnel work?" he asked Keating out of concern for his employees.

"We're all a big family, and everybody who wants to stay on will be able to stay on since we're like a big family," Crocker recalls Keating said. He also promised to run the company pretty much as it had been, a traditional thrift, one that, for the most part, specialized in home lending.

Crocker decided to go ahead. He hired Norman Raiden, then still at McKenna, Conner & Cuneo, to represent him in the sale. Raiden had negotiated for Anthony Frank when National Steel paid cash for the latter's San Francisco-based thrift.

Crocker wanted his deal to be structured similarly. Crocker and Keating traded a flurry of paper over the next several days, avoiding leaks to the press by disguising the exchanges as a loan application. At the end of September 1983, one week after the Phoenix meeting, Keating flew in his company jet to Burbank. He and Crocker signed a definitive agreement at the airport.

Three months later, on December 31, 1983, Raiden joined the bank board as chief counsel under Gray. In February 1984 the board approved the sale of Lincoln to Keating. California state regulator Taggart also approved it.

In granting their approval, board regulators hadn't ferreted out Keating's problems with the SEC, though they easily could have. Crocker had known, and certainly Raiden knew, too. Crocker had mentioned it because it was an element that might have soured the deal for the regulators.

Lincoln's residential lending just about stopped cold shortly after Keating took over. In 1985 and early 1986 the thrift originated only eleven home loans, including four to employees and several others on property owned by Lincoln. In 1983 residential loans had been more than 30 percent of Lincoln's assets. By 1988 the percentage had fallen to less than 2.

In five years Keating steered Lincoln from a company with $1.1 billion in assets to one with $6 billion, mostly through investments in land development and junk bonds, including $11.8 million in junk bonds of a Las Vegas gambling casino, Circus Circus, and a six-hundred-room luxury resort in Phoenix built at what regulators believe is a record cost of $500,000 per room. All these investments were being funded by federally insured deposits.

Much of Lincoln's spectacular growth was fueled by brokered funds. In 1983, 2.6 percent of Lincoln's liabilities—its sources of funding from deposits and borrowing—came from brokered deposits. By 1988 the figure stood at 35 percent.

Just about everything was transformed at Crocker's old company. As soon as Keating took over, he fired many of the top lending officials, despite his promise to Crocker. He named his son, Charles Keating III, a twenty-eight-year-old Indiana University dropout who only a few years earlier had worked as a country club busboy, as chairman of the thrift, at an annual salary of well over $1 million between his posts at the thrift and its parent company, American Continental.

Clearly, Gray's direct investment rule, scheduled to take effect on March 18, 1985, was a threat to Keating's game plan, watered down though Gray's proposal had become. Keating didn't want to limit his direct ownership in real estate. A 10 percent cap was out of the question. He had bought Lincoln in large part because California's 1983 Nolan Law permitted thrifts to invest without limit in real estate.

In early 1985 Keating, now owner of Lincoln for a year, turned to Alan Greenspan, then a private economist, for help. In January and February Greenspan wrote letters at Keating's request to key members of Congress on the House and Senate Banking Committees and to the bank board opposing Gray's direct investment proposal as one that could exacerbate rather than ease losses in the industry. Greenspan also wrote a letter explicitly endorsing Lincoln, citing Keating and his management team as "seasoned and expert," with a "record of outstanding success in making sound and profitable direct investments."

The bank board wouldn't budge. Its chief counsel, Raiden, stated that Lincoln used inadequate appraisals that overvalued property and cited the practice as one that had "led to some of the worst failures in FSLIC's history."

Keating next turned for help to Frank Annunzio, third-ranking Democrat on the House Banking Committee, and his aide, Curt Prins.

Prins is a good example of the power wielded by what has been called the unelected Congress. When they work on an important committee, congressional staffers often have more clout than junior members of Congress. Their hands are strengthened even more when their bosses rank high in seniority but are uninvolved in the details of a committee's operations.

Prins had close ties to the thrift industry. He and his wife accepted three free trips to England from 1987 to 1989 and two December trips to Florida in 1985 and 1988, all for "legislative seminars" paid for by the Beneficial Management Corporation, which operates a federally insured thrift.

Prins also knew Keating and his army of legal advisers from their frequent visits to Annunzio's office to confer with the congressman and with Prins on Gray's direct investment rules. In 1987 Prins traveled to Arizona at Keating's expense to meet the developer and review his properties. He was wined and dined during that visit at Keating's home and took in a little golf. The visit included a side trip to Las Vegas paid for by a Keating lobbyist.

Annunzio's ties to the thrift industry also ran deep. According to the *Pulitzer-Lerner Newspaper,* one of the few Chicago publications that covered Annunzio's role in the thrift debacle, one Annunzio son-in-law, Kevin Tynan, was a paid consultant to Skokie Federal until federal regulators closed it in 1988. (The estimated cost to taxpayers is about $170 million.) The chairman of the thrift was John O'Connell, Sr., brother of the league president, William O'Connell. Tynan's firm also provided consulting services to the league, for which it was paid more than $1,000 a month from 1985 through 1988. (Tynan managed Annunzio's election campaign in the fall of 1990, when the congressman billed himself as someone who fought the thrift industry. Annunzio sported a big button on his lapel touting his campaign slogan, "Put the S&L Crooks in Jail.")

Bill O'Connell, meanwhile, hired Annunzio's other son-in-law, Sal Lato, married to Annunzio's daughter Jacqueline, for $70,000 a year as a staff member of the league from 1987 to 1989. Annunzio told the *Pulitzer-Lerner Newspaper,* "In my heart of hearts, I knew some day there would be a bad interpretation" if his family ties to the league became public. Nonetheless, he told the paper, "I am very proud of both boys. I didn't tell them who to work for."

Annunzio's close association with the thrift industry wasn't the first time he'd been embroiled in controversy over his affiliations. Annunzio's early political career in Chicago in the 1950s and 1960s was marked by newspaper headlines about his close ties to figures allegedly involved in organized crime. When he was the Illinois director of labor, Annunzio launched an insurance company in association with suspected mobster, John D'Arco, a man described by one Chicago newspaper as "a prominent leader in the west side political bloc which has been an agency for hoodlum interests in the state legislature and in the city council." Also associated with the company was Benjamin ("Buddy") Jacobson, who "has a record dating back to 1923 and who has been arrested many times," according to a 1952 account in the *Chicago Tribune.*

D'Arco was a friend of Sam ("Momo") Giancana, the alleged chief of a Chicago crime syndicate, whom one Chicago newspaper described as "the top-shot syndicate boss," another as a convicted "gangster," and a third as "Chicago's No. 1 hoodlum."

211

Two years after Annunzio took office in Congress, his administrative assistant, Anthony Tisci, Giancana's thirty-six-year-old son-in-law, resigned, citing orders from his doctor, according to a *New York Times* article in 1965. The resignation came amid a political uproar in Chicago over whether Tisci should be removed from the Illinois bar after he invoked his Fifth Amendment right against self-incrimination and refused three times to answer questions about his father-in-law before a federal grand jury investigating organized crime in the state.

Annunzio and Prins brushed off those incidents by saying that any hint of alleged Mafia ties comes from unfounded prejudices associated with anyone with an Italian surname.

Annunzio had other image problems in Washington, however. Representatives and congressional aides who have worked with Annunzio over the years say that he is not an intellectual powerhouse. Al Hunt, Washington bureau chief for the *Wall Street Journal,* was a reporter for the newspaper in the mid-1970s covering the House Banking Committee's deliberations on legislation to impose wage and price controls. One day Annunzio successfully pushed his colleagues on the committee to approve an amendment that would not only freeze meat prices but roll them back to levels of the year before. "It's a victory for the American people," Hunt recalls Annunzio proclaiming.

The next day, however, Annunzio's colleagues convinced him to propose rescinding the amendment, which would have made the larger bill impossible to enact once it got to the floor of the full House. Annunzio reluctantly relented and dutifully undid his work from the previous day. Hunt bumped into him afterward and asked, "Well, what do you think now, Congressman? What can I tell my readers?"

"You can tell them the American people just got fucked," Hunt recalls Annunzio saying.

"But, Congressman, how can I say that? I write for a family newspaper," Hunt said.

"All right, tell them the American family just got fucked," the congressman snapped. Hunt says the comment was in dead earnest.

Annunzio, though he had always been considered a puppet politician, had been an active one. In the 1980s, though, he came to defer to Prins on most matters. By then Annunzio had been experiencing heart trouble for years. He appeared sickly, weak, and often unaware of the details of matters before the House Banking Committee. When he attended hearings, he sat on Chairman St Germain's right, motionless, wearing thick black glasses and a suit that seemed too big for him. He asked questions fed to him, either in written form or through whispers in his ear, by Prins. Even then he often bungled questions.

Time and again "Congressman Prins," as representatives on the Banking Committee disdainfully refer to him, would, via Annunzio, point out on behalf of the thrift community that commercial banks also had their share of problems. The point was to soften the severity of the thrift crisis in the eyes of fellow members of Congress by pointing out that if commercial banks also had problems, then—or so the reasoning seemed to go—external factors, such as an economic downturn or bungled federal supervision, not internal failings, such as bad management and fraud, were to blame.

A dramatic physical contrast with the frail Annunzio, Prinz has a hulking frame, a beer belly, and a style notoriously crude and bullying to go with it. He jokes about Jews, women, blacks, gays. One day he told a reporter from the *Washington Post* that he didn't want to talk to the newspaper unless it mentioned Annunzio more often. He said he thought the *Post* was "run by Jews" who thought all Italians were in the Mafia; that was why Jewish members of Congress were quoted so often and Annunzio so infrequently. After the incident was brought to Annunzio's attention, Prins denied making the remarks and offered this explanation of what he had been trying to say: "If a paper is run by left-handed people and only people who are left-handed get quoted, is that right?"

Members of Congress often leave it to their aides to work out the details of legislative compromises. In practice that duty translates into tremendous power to shade meaning. During one such negotiating session, while working out details of a provision to preempt state usury laws, Prins suggested language that Robert Feinberg, at the time the minority counsel to the Banking Committee, thought exceeded the provision approved by the members. Feinberg, slight of build, objected, asking, "Who are you to bring something like this up? Where's your certificate of election? Who elected you?"

According to eyewitnesses of the event, Prins responded by saying words to this effect: "I could ignore that remark, if I wanted to be a nice guy, or I could throw you out the window." After a moment of stunned silence among the dozen or so aides present, work resumed.

In another famous episode Prins was arguing with an attorney on St Germain's staff, Richard Still. According to eyewitnesses, each accused the other of having a boss that toadied to the savings and loan industry. Seeking to settle the matter, Prins grabbed Still by the collar and punched him in the face.

In January 1985, Annunzio, through Prins, circulated a resolution signed by 220 members of the House—more than half the 50-person House Banking Committee had signed—asking that the bank board delay implementation of the direct investment regulation. Annunzio insists that state regulators from around the country pushed the measure because they thought Gray was undermining the authority of the states and, in the process, the dual banking system. Members of Congress and aides on the Banking Committee say Keating was the force behind the project.

The resolution did not carry the weight of law, but it put pressure on Gray to back down. At hearings before a subcommittee of the House Banking Committee a week after the regulation went into force, Annunzio, presenting Gray with the 220 signatures, said, "We ask that the agency postpone the effective date of this rule."

Gray said that was impossible. The rule had taken effect. And without it the FSLIC would be exposed to billions of dollars in additional losses. Annunzio stormed out of the hearing in protest.

Keating persisted. On October 3, 1985, an attorney named Ray Gustini contacted bank board member Grigsby to say he had a client who wanted to offer Gray a job. Grigsby relayed the message, and Gray asked Shannon Fairbanks to find out who—and what—was behind the offer.

Fairbanks informed Gustini that she would discuss the offer only with the person making it. He soon called her back to say she should expect a call from the office of Charles Keating. On November 22, 1985, Fairbanks met Keating and his associates for breakfast at the Four Seasons Hotel in Georgetown.

"Mr. Keating told me that he wanted Mr. Gray to come with his organization in a job capacity which he described as 'using Mr. Gray's contacts and skills to further the corporate interests and activities of Lincoln Savings,'" Fairbanks later testified to Congress. "Mr. Keating explained his motivation by noting that 'there seems to be a problem in our ability to have our message heard' by the regulators and that he needed someone to help 'get our corporate initiatives past the existing regulatory roadblocks.'

"Mr. Keating said the regulators had 'changed signals in midstream.' Mr. Keating believed he should be able to operate unhindered by intrusive 'regulatory constraints.'

"I told Mr. Keating and his associates why the Board and Mr. Gray's regulatory philosophy was so distinctly different from their own and that I would not entertain any further discussions on Mr. Gray's behalf."

Fairbanks said she left the hotel and Gray never heard another word about joining Keating's staff, except for newspaper stories that said Keating would have been willing to offer Gray a salary of $300,000 a year.

Part V

A WOULD-BE HERO, PART II

—

He ain't pretty.

> —*Slogan on campaign poster for*
> *Representative Jim Wright*
> *(D-Texas) showing two side-by-*
> *side close-ups, one of a bulldog,*
> *the other of Wright*

27

Dancing in the Dark

In May 1986 Ed Gray was depressed. His assistant, Shannon Fairbanks, decided to cheer him up with a party. She telephoned officials at Freddie Mac, the bank board corporation that bought home loans from thrifts, and asked them to throw a gala dinner in Gray's honor. When they protested that might not be an appropriate use of the corporation's money, she suggested they honor both Gray and homeownership.

Freddie Mac agreed. Fairbanks got the regional bank presidents to chip in.

On Monday night, May 19, 1986, the Federal Home Loan Bank Board System sponsored a $60,000 dinner for fifty or so guests, most of them from the thrift agency, a few from other banking agencies and the league. Fed Chairman Volcker attended. So did Comptroller of the Currency Robert L. Clarke and FDIC Chairman Seidman. The dinner was held in the Pension Building, a beautiful red-brick structure in downtown Washington. Ironically, the building once housed the General Accounting Office, the auditing arm of Congress and, for several years, the only government agency that consistently challenged the bank board's low estimates of the thrift industry's problems. Ridgewell's, a posh Washington caterer, supplied the food and drink.

Gray, clearly battle-fatigued but apparently unaware that many of the "friends" gathered by Fairbanks resented his efforts as a regulator, was touched by the turnout. He gave a short speech noting the troubling trend that had put homeownership out of reach of more and more potential first-time buyers. Between 1980 and 1985 the percentage of people under the age of twenty-five who owned a home slipped 34.5 percent, the percentage between the ages of twenty-five and thirty-four fell by 15.8 percent, and that between the ages of thirty-five and forty-four dropped 8.5 percent. Gray warned that the industry had to work hard to reverse the trend.

After the speech diners watched a four-minute video prepared by Freddie Mac saluting homeownership. Several dozen shots of houses around the country were flashed on the screen to the accompaniment of soothing background music. There also was a photo of the cover of an industry trade publication, *Real Estate Quarterly,* with an article entitled "Housing More Affordable." And there were shots of several newspaper headlines predicting good times ahead for the thrift industry, including a nine-month-old clipping from the *New York Times,* NEW PROSPERITY FOR THE THRIFT INDUSTRY.

It had been no easy task finding optimistic headlines in the midst of the industry's worst period. Just a few weeks before the gala Gray had doubled the bank board's estimate of the cost of resolving the industry's problems to $16 billion. Freddie Mac officials spent days rifling through hundreds of clips to find the rare few carrying good news. The staff privately grumbled at having spent all that time and hundreds of dollars preparing a video to boost Gray's morale. And of course, many of the guests understood the absurdity of throwing an expensive bash just as the administration was going to Congress to plead for $15 billion to bail out the industry.

The penultimate frame of the video showed a shot of the bank board's offices in Washington and a league-sponsored ad featuring the FSLIC logo and the words "For 50 years this had been one of the most stabilizing signs of the economy." The film concluded with the American flag, waving first before a beautiful house and then in front of the Capitol dome. As the video's music grew louder and more upbeat, the image faded to a close-up of a bed of red and yellow tulips, then to the words "Don't let the sun set on the American Dream." The film ended with a dramatic picture of a sunset.

The audience, gorged on gourmet food and wine, applauded wildly. Then, to the tunes of a live band, the nation's thrift regulators danced the night away.

28

The Good Life

G ray had good reason to be depressed in the spring of 1986. By the time of the dinner, nearly three years into Gray's four-year term, his attempts to restore the industry to profitability clearly weren't working. S&Ls earned $3.7 billion in 1985, three and a half times more than the $1 billion earned in 1984. But bank board data showed the gains were illusory, the product of bogus accounting and the government's forbearance policy.

Interest rates had fallen. But thrift failures, and the cost to the government of each failure, were rising with alarming steepness. The FSLIC's notes and other obligations—totaling $3 billion—nearly equaled its reserves of $3.78 billion.

And worst of all, almost everyone seemed to have it in for Ed Gray.

To some, Gray talked too much about the industry's problems, breeding headlines that made the public nervous. To others, he was wrongheaded in his approach; they thought more freedom, more deregulation, not less, was needed. To still others, Gray was simply in way over his head; his inability to manage his agency or its relations on Capitol Hill was helping spread chaos in the industry and throughout the regulatory apparatus that he was supposed to be watching. He was called Mr. Ed, after the talking horse on the TV show, the reregulator, Mr. Gloom and Doom. The criticism and animosity stung.

Gray was not entirely without supporters; he kept close to his desk several letters offering proof. "With regard to the greased rail that some folks in the administration, and elsewhere, are tying to build under you, please know that I remain among your very strong supporters," wrote Representative Gonzalez, the Texas Democrat. (It was a brave move coming from a politician whose home state produced some of Gray's most fervent critics.)

Wrote Volcker in another: "I realize your regulatory and supervisory initiatives don't necessarily win popularity contests ... but I also know that a lot of people join me in great respect for the job you are trying to do in most difficult circumstances."

The FDIC's Seidman and his predecessor at the agency, William Isaac, also praised Gray's efforts. Senate Banking Committee Chairman Proxmire, himself a penny pincher who did not like Gray's propensity for frequent, expensive travel, nevertheless commended Gray's willingness to stand up against the industry's highfliers.

Privately, though, even Gray's supporters realized his style was not winning support for the Treasury's efforts to replenish the FSLIC.

Gray decided in early 1986 to strike at what regulators had begun to characterize as the Southwest problem by instituting a massive examination of the five hundred or so thrifts in the states under the Dallas regional bank's charge—Arkansas, Louisiana, Mississippi, New Mexico, and Texas. Although his term was more than half over, Gray had just learned that many of the institutions had not been examined by regulators for years. The review he now envisioned was so large it required the help of most of the other eleven regional banks, which donated personnel for weeks at a stretch.

To run the examination, Gray and the Dallas regional bank president, Roy Green, hired Joe Selby from the Comptroller of the Currency's Office. Selby joined the Federal Home Loan Bank of Dallas on May 1, leaving his Washington job of thirty-two years to return to his native Texas. "I want to send a message to Texas that we mean business," Gray told his staff about Selby.

Selby was lured not only by the salary—$165,000—and the chance to return home but by the prospect of running a massive cleanup of the industry in the Southwest. A demure, white-haired, soft-spoken man of fifty-five, Selby didn't look like the Hammer, a nickname he gave himself when it came to his style of bank regulation, or Rambo or the Angel of Death, as his critics in the industry soon called him, or "the most feared man in the state of Texas," as Representative Jim Wright referred to him.

When Selby walked through the front doors of the Dallas bank's headquarters, he was astonished at what he found. Most obvious was the physical disorder caused by construction workers who tramped through the corridors and offices to complete a $12 million renovation that included the addition of a five-story garage, a child care center, and a health club.

But the surface disarray turned out to be symptomatic of the examination force's disorganization. Despite the Dallas regional bank's $30 million annual budget for regulatory activities, the massive audit that Gray had ordered was being conducted by inexperienced staffers who didn't have typewriters, let alone computers, to help them in the hundreds of exams they now were undertaking. The thrift examinations were being done by hand, in pencil, and then handed over to a typing pool, just as they had been for thirty-five years. Selby, coming from the relatively state-of-the-art offices of the Comptroller of the Currency, couldn't believe what he saw. Who was running the show here? he asked. Who was in charge?

Selby's shock at the archaic examination tools was nothing compared with his outrage over the coziness he found between the regulators and the regulated. Supervisors accepted loans from institutions they supervised. Thrift executives of insolvent institutions sat on the board of the Dallas regional bank. S&L executives spoke of "our FSLIC." Bankers, Selby pointed out, would never say "our FDIC." He had always known that thrifts were worlds apart culturally from commercial banks, but now he began to understand how wide the gulf really was.

"The industry didn't want supervision and didn't receive supervision," he recalls of that period. Often during his tenure in Texas it seemed to him as though the bank board actually worked for the league, a relationship that makes him steam when he hears thrift executives claim they wanted better regulation. "My God, the thrift industry has fought and fought and fought regulation," he says.

Among the first institutions to draw Selby's attention in 1986 was Vernon Savings and Loan (soon to be nicknamed Vermin by regulators) and its owner, Don Dixon. Selby found that 96 percent of Vernon's loan portfolio was in default, a ratio so high thrift executives joked Dixon had worked hard to make it that bad. Vernon loan officers secured one $24 million loan, for example, with a ninety-nine-acre tract of land—a third of which was underwater. About 70 percent of the institution's profits had been artificially generated through loan kickbacks and other schemes that allowed the thrift to pay itself. Selby and his team began to question other practices, such as Vernon's purchase of a $2 million beach mansion in Del Mar, California, where Dixon and his wife lived for eighteen months and ran up entertainment and expense costs of $761,000—all charged to the thrift.

On one occasion Dixon, his wife, and an entourage of guests went on an eating tour of Europe that took them from one three-star restaurant to another. Later Dixon described the trip as research. "We were going to invest in restaurants and we needed a chef as a consultant. You think it's easy eating in three-star restaurants twice a day, six days a week?" he asked a reporter for the *Chicago Tribune*. The trip, entitled "Gastronomique-Fantastique!" by Vernon officials in a seventeen-page office narrative of the event, cost the thrift $22,000.

Another $6 million went for Vernon's fleet of corporate aircraft, and yet another $5.5 million for artwork to decorate S&L executives' offices. Employees, caught up in the spirit of the spending spree, printed up $3 bills with Dixon's picture on them and the slogan "In Don We Trust."

Vernon executives also charged the thrift for thousands of dollars in illegal campaign contributions to Representative Wright and Senators Garn and Cranston. (There was no evidence the lawmakers knew the contributions were illegal.)

And then there were the prostitutes.

Vernon President Patrick G. King, a former Texas thrift regulator, paid the eponymous Joy Love, a topless dancer at the Million Dollar Saloon in Dallas, $100 a night for her work during a 1986 pheasant-shooting party Dixon and King arranged in Kansas for Texas thrift regulator Bowman and Vernon clients. (During his trial on bank fraud a few years later King offered a novel defense. He claimed Bowman was impotent and therefore never actually received the gift of "female companionship." Bowman conceded he was impotent, but the jury didn't buy the defense, electing instead to convict King in September 1989 on all counts.)

King and Bowman had other ties that, when they came to light in 1986, underscored for Selby the close relationship Vernon and the industry as a whole enjoyed with its regulators. During Bowman's tenure as chief savings and loan regulator for Texas he co-owned a small real estate institution with King that the two had set up in 1980, when King still worked with Bowman as a regulator. When King left to go to Vernon, a state-chartered, federally insured thrift, the two maintained a business association.

Selby also found curious goings-on at Sunbelt Savings in Dallas, an institution that had been formed by Edwin T. McBirney III through the merger of a handful of tiny Texas S&Ls in the early 1980s. Sunbelt's assets ballooned more than 5000 percent in the four years between 1981 and 1985. Fellow businessmen dubbed the thirty-three-year-old McBirney Fast Eddy for his willingness to forgo the usual research that conservative real estate developers apply before making a deal. At Dallas restaurants like Jason's, popular with the go-go thrift crowd, McBirney could be seen drawing up deals for Sunbelt on the back of a tablecloth. He did it so often that Jason's owner made sure the table was covered in paper.

(Bowman also had connections to McBirney. Shortly after Bowman became the state's thrift commissioner in early 1983, he sold McBirney his holdings in a Greenville, Texas, thrift. Bowman and his family made $144,000 on the sale. The thrift became part of the Sunbelt empire.)

McBirney often lunched with other S&L executives known as big spenders, big risk takers, and far from conventional lenders—executives such as Vernon's Dixon and Thomas Gaubert of Independent American Savings and Loan. McBirney's Wild West business style soon earned his thrift a nickname, too: Gunbelt.

Once described by the *Los Angeles Times* as "high strung and jet fueled," McBirney had a reputation as a gambler in his social life as well, making frequent trips to the casinos of Las Vegas, often with an entourage of executives and Sunbelt clients.

Sunbelt operated a fleet of seven airplanes. It paid tens of thousands of dollars for McBirney's limousine bills. The industry still talks about the parties he threw, like the one in 1984 for Halloween, when McBirney dressed up like a king and served lion and antelope meat to hundreds of guests in his palatial home. Two disco singers known as Two Tons of Fun provided the entertainment. Sunbelt picked up the tab.

In 1985 real estate prices began their gradually accelerating fall. And in early 1986 oil prices, already sliding, fell below $20 a barrel, a psychological floor price that the market had established as rock bottom. A free fall ensued, with oil prices hitting single digits in the years ahead, a low unthinkable in the early 1980s, when some predicted oil would go to $100 a barrel. Compounding matters was the Tax Reform Act of 1986, signed into law in October of that year. It abruptly ended the many investment incentives the 1981 tax law had bequeathed to the real estate industry. The sudden halt imposed by 1986 law helped push land prices down further, and thrifts felt the pinch as would be tax shelter hunters grew scarcer and scarcer.

But for some in Texas in early 1986, economic reality hadn't yet registered. The downturn in prices certainly didn't crimp McBirney's style. In March 1986, shortly before Selby arrived in Dallas, McBirney flew several dozen executives and other guests to Las Vegas for a weekend at the Dunes. Recounted in lurid detail in the *Texas Monthly* magazine a year later—to the horror and embarrassment of Gray and state regulator Bowman—the party's entertainment on Saturday night began when "four women came into the room and began a strip-tease act. Once disrobed, they proceeded to perform sexual acts on some of the businessmen," Byron Harris wrote in the article. Except for the cost of the prostitutes, which McBirney's lawyer, Paul Coggins, insists was paid from McBirney's and others' own pockets, the tab for the outing was billed to Sunbelt.

But as McBirney rolled the dice and otherwise indulged himself that weekend, federal regulators back in Texas had started to scrutinize Sunbelt's spending. In June 1986, after a two-month audit under Selby's supervision, Sunbelt was transformed from one of Texas's fastest-growing S&Ls into one of several giant institutions vying for the dubious distinction of requiring the costliest federal bailout.

McBirney resigned as chairman of Sunbelt, but regulators permitted him to stay on as a director for eighteen months and to pick his successor, Thomas Wageman, a banker with experience at troubled financial institutions. That, McBirney's lawyer later insisted when the government sued McBirney, demonstrates that regulators at the bank board had confidence in McBirney.

"Sunbelt was run like a real S&L," Coggins would say. "It had good assets. It still has good assets. It wasn't like Vernon. Even Ed's critics will say he worked dang hard."

(In fact, some observers in Texas believe Selby went easy on Sunbelt. Although the bank board effectively took control of the thrift in 1986, behind the scenes Selby allowed McBirney to run it for months. The board merged several insolvent thrifts into Sunbelt in 1988 and allowed it to stay open. The government officially declared it insolvent in April 1991 and took possession of it. Wageman ran it, earning a six-figure salary—well into the $300,000s, according to congressional investigators—until September 1991, when federal thrift regulators say he resigned. He and the government officially refused to disclose the salary, arguing that Wageman was not directly employed by thrift regulators but was under contract and therefore not subject to such disclosures; congressional staffers, however, were eager to release the information.)

Selby's blitzkrieg shocked the industry. Selby compounded the effect with his demand for arm's length regulation and tough enforcement of the rules. He quickly became so hated that one contractor he hired to help manage failed thrifts made him a gift of a Rambo doll, spray-painted gold and mounted like a trophy. It became one of Selby's most treasured office objects.

But increasingly the rancor coming from the industry was hard to slough off with humor. One examiner found an electronic bug on his phone. Rumors of a plot to kidnap Selby began to make its way to regulators' ears. Selby began to wonder if his $165,000 salary was worth it.

The largely Democratic Texas thrift community, meanwhile, began asking why no similar mass audit had been ordered by regional bank of San Francisco, which was charged with overseeing thrifts in California, Nevada, and Arizona; the thrifts in these states were equally troubled, but most of the thrift executives there were Republicans. This was not a frivolous question. The San Francisco regional bank had no better an enforcement record than the one in Dallas. In 1986, for example, while Selby was striking terror into corrupt Texas operators, the California S&L commissioner, William Crawford, who took over from Taggart, had to make seventeen calls over eight days to the FBI, the regional bank in San Francisco, and finally a U.S. senator before he could interest the law enforcement officials in investigating allegations of corruption at North American Savings and Loan in California. (Even so, the S&L wasn't closed until mid-1988, two years later, when regulators had to pay depositors $209 million.)

Congressional investigators for the House Committee on Government Operations found that FBI reports on the status of S&L criminal probes routinely were sent to the Federal Home Loan Bank of San Francisco. Although the reports contained information that might have been useful in preventing abuses, senior officials at the bank never saw the reports. They "were filed away in a back office, with only one person knowing of their existence," according to a memo prepared by the committee's staff.

Gray insists that there was no political favoritism and that the decision to target Texas had nothing to do with his old friends in California. But the charge didn't help his reputation on Capitol Hill.

While Selby struggled to clean up Texas, a larger battle loomed in Washington, the fight over Syron's plan to save the industry by pumping $15 billion into the FSLIC. The political importance of hiding the plan's impact on the budget gave the scheme a Rube Goldberg appearance. It called for the twelve regional Federal Home Loan Banks to donate $3 billion from their profits. The government would use the $3 billion to buy twenty- and thirty-year Treasury bonds that, when they matured, would be worth $15 billion. Then the government, through a newly created federal entity constructed so that its obligations would not appear on the budget, would use the Treasury bonds as collateral to borrow $15 billion from the private sector over five years. (Interest on the borrowing would be paid from the regular fees the FSLIC charged the S&Ls it insured.) It would pump this money into the FSLIC by purchasing FSLIC stock. In this way the Treasury essentially would launder the money by making it look like an investment in the FSLIC rather than what it was: borrowing by the government. The professional OMB staffers who wanted the borrowing to count on the budget were overruled by the political policy makers, whose rationalization was that distinctions could be drawn between a direct government obligation—one made by the Treasury—and an indirect government obligation—one made by the Treasury through an intermediary government entity, such as the FSLIC.

Under this Byzantine arrangement, federal spending would go up only as the FSLIC spent the $15 billion, offsetting income registered by the fund when it received the money and thus having a net effect on the deficit of zero. In addition, the FSLIC would collect $10 billion to $15 billion more during the five-year borrowing period from premiums charged to thrifts and from the sale of property inherited from failed thrifts. All told, the government estimated that the fund would have $25 to $30 billion to handle a caseload of several hundred problem S&Ls over several years. The Treasury knew the problem might be much bigger than $30 billion, possibly twice or three times that, but Gould and his staff decided that $15 billion was the most the administration could expect to win from Congress and, at the very least, would suffice until after the presidential election of 1988.

As veteran banking lobbyists knew, 1986, a congressional election year, would be used to lay the groundwork for the plan, for political strategies to be worked out and tested. No matter what politicians said to the public, privately no one, not even the Treasury, expected the legislation to pass that year. If legislation were to come, it would be in 1987. But the plan's proponents used 1986 to begin lining up support to counter the anticipated opposition from the league.

The Texas and California chapters of the league fought the plan because many of their members did not want the government to have sufficient funds to close them down. For its part, the national league didn't necessarily oppose closing the highfliers, but it didn't want its members to pay for it. The league also knew that giving the FSLIC more money would mean that the government would close more sick thrifts of all types, including those run by incompetents as well as crooks. That would put scores of top thrift officials out of work. The league would lose members, dues, and, eventually, clout in Congress.

And the league had another problem with the plan. As the industry viewed it, taking money from the regional Federal Home Loan Banks meant taking money from the industry. Thrifts counted the stock they owned in the regional banks as an asset. Although $3 billion—the amount the banks would contribute under the recapitalization plan—was a small percentage of the bank system's collective $131 billion in assets in 1986, league and industry officials reasoned that if the Treasury raided the Federal Home Loan Banks for even a relatively tiny sum, there was no telling where it would end. If the banks' assets were constantly tapped to bail out the industry, the value of the banks, and of the thrift industry's stock in them, would fall.

Gould, the administration's point man on the plan, understood that the league would play hard ball in fighting recapitalization. In early 1986 he spoke at a league conference in Bermuda for the industry's largest thrifts.

Republican league lobbyist Rick Hohlt, driving Gould from the airport, asked the undersecretary to have breakfast the next day with Gordon Luce, Gray's mentor at Great American and President Reagan's friend.

Luce's demeanor astounded Gould. Throughout breakfast Luce seemed to have one point to make: The league held more clout with President Reagan than the Treasury did. "This is like ward politics," Gould thought, "very crass. Very bush-league." Angry and insulted by what he saw as an attempt at intimidation, he flew back to Washington early.

When the league, as expected, came out against the plan—testifying in early 1986 to Congress that only a third of what the Treasury asked for was really needed—many anticipated that St Germain would take the league's side. But the congressman also had a special vulnerability. In 1985 the *Wall Street Journal* ran a front-page story by reporter Brooks Jackson showing that St Germain had become a millionaire while in office through real estate deals financed by thrifts that were affected by legislation before his committee. The story prompted an investigation in early 1986 by the House Committee on Standards of Official Conduct, commonly known as the House Ethics Committee, that eventually was broadened to look into whether St Germain had properly reported gifts from the league and other lobby groups or had improperly used his office to obtain such favors. With all the campaign contributions the league had made to him over the years, not to mention the thousands of dollars in meal and entertainment expenses, throwing his weight behind anything less than the $15 billion sought by the administration could look suspicious. St Germain therefore had powerful political reasons to avoid doing the league any obvious favors, although many in the administration suspected that he might try to derail the plan in private.

Most Senate Banking Committee members were in a similar, though less politically acute, situation. Many, including Cranston and Riegle, had received large campaign contributions from the league. Treasury officials suspected that like St Germain, they were looking for a way to support the administration's plan publicly even as they devised a way to kill it, at least for 1986.

As the debate over recapitalization dragged on through the spring and summer, even some close to the White House began to question the political wisdom of the plan—and of Gray's blunt style of lobbying for it. President Reagan had prevented Regan from running Gray out of town, but that was the limit of White House support. Neither the president nor Vice President Bush, whose area of expertise was financial service deregulation, spoke publicly in Gray's favor. After all, the White House, like Congress, had money to think of: Closed thrifts would mean lost campaign contributions.

Lawrence Taggart, the former California thrift regulator who resigned at the end of 1984 to become a consultant to thrift executives such as Charles Keating and Don Dixon, wrote a letter to Don Regan late in the summer of 1986 stating that Gray's regulatory policy was "likely to have a very adverse impact on the ability of our Party to raise needed campaign funds in the upcoming elections. Many who have been very supportive of the Administration are involved with savings and loan associations which are either being closed by the [bank board] or threatened with closure."

Indeed, league Republican lobbyist Hohlt was a major GOP fund raiser, one who boasted of being a close friend of Vice President Bush's chief of staff, Craig Fuller, and of GOP political adviser and former White House aide Ed Rollins.

Despite these political imperatives, it was increasingly clear that something had to be done. Treasury statistics showed that as of September 30, 1986, at least 30 California thrifts were insolvent under traditional accounting procedures. In Texas the number was at least 65. In terms of asset size, and thus potential cost to taxpayers, the two states were running neck and neck. The 30 California thrifts had assets of nearly $14 billion, while the 65 in Texas had $16.3 billion. Third on the list of trouble states was Illinois, home of the league and Representative Annunzio, where fifty-seven thrifts with assets of nearly $10 billion were insolvent under GAAP.

Next came Florida, where 19 institutions with assets of $7.5 billion were insolvent. After that, assets at insolvent institutions ranked by state dropped into the $4 billion and $3 billion range. The figures showed that the thrift crisis had reached across the country, out of the economically depressed Southwest and into robust areas like the West. Bad management, not economic factors, was clearly emerging as the leading cause of failure. And the cost was escalating. The top four problem states—Texas, California, Illinois, and Florida—housed insolvent thrifts with assets totaling $48 billion. If the government recovered 75 cents on the dollar of those assets—a generous return—the cost of cleanup in those states alone would be $12 billion. That didn't begin to cover the additional 274 insolvent thrifts in other states holding another $66 billion in assets. A generous recovery on these assets still would leave $16.5 billion to be paid by taxpayers, for a grand total in the fall of 1986 of $28.5 billion, far in excess of the $16 billion Gray predicted.

Ominously, the thrift crisis had even begun to affect commercial banks. Already in early 1986 the side effects of five years of the administration's deficit-driven thrift policy had led to complaints of unfair competition as the fight for deposits escalated nationwide.

Seminole, an Oklahoma town with a population of nine thousand, provided an example of the problem that had begun to rankle banks and bank regulators alike. Standing at opposite ends of the town's main shopping center, a seventy-seven-year-old bank, First National Bank of Seminole, faced a daily showdown with a four-year-old thrift, Territory Savings & Loan. First National, healthy, though struggling, like every other business in the area now that oil prices had slumped, could offer 6.10 percent interest on six-month CDs, while Territory offered 7.14 percent. Territory, which had a negative net worth of $15 million, had gambled away its money on high-risk, high-loss investments that included playing the futures markets. Now it essentially was run by the government. "If I were allowed to run my bank at a negative net worth, I could offer higher rates, too," said Phil O. Rigney, chief executive of First National. "But the regulators won't let me. Evidently you don't have to run an S&L well as long as you have it [federally] insured."

Hundreds of unhealthy S&Ls created what bankers likened to a cancer. Bankers argued that sick thrifts undermined the strength of healthy financial institutions on two fronts. Ailing S&Ls eroded public confidence in all financial institutions, healthy or not, and they sparked unfair, cutthroat competition by offering higher than market rates to lure deposits that they could sink into risky but potentially high-yielding investments they hoped would let them outgrow their problems.

29

The Wright Cause

C raig Hall was one of the largest real estate developers in Texas. In 1986 his borrowings from banks and thrifts totaled as much as $1 billion, including $200 million from a troubled thrift in Los Angeles, Westwood Savings and Loan.

The bank board had taken over Westwood in March 1986. Because the agency lacked the funds to close the S&L, however, it appointed Scott Schultz, a supervisory agent from the Federal Home Loan Bank of San Francisco, to run the institution until a buyer could be found or the FSLIC could pay off the depositors.

In late 1985 and early 1986 Hall began to realize that because of the collapsing price of real estate, income from his holdings would not cover the payment obligations on his $1 billion in debt and that he would have to renegotiate the loans on his properties, asking that lenders reduce his interest charges and give him a longer time to repay. For the restructuring to work, all the lenders had to agree to it. If one did not, the entire process would unravel, forcing him into default.

After months of negotiation, all of Hall's creditors but one agreed to a debt restructuring. Westwood, on advice Schultz received from outside counsel, notified Hall it would foreclose on his loan rather than restructure it. Hall was furious.

He turned for help to Texas Congressman Wright, then the majority leader and, as everyone knew, soon to be Speaker of the House. Hall met the congressman in Wright's Fort Worth office on Tuesday, September 2, 1986. The meeting, set up by a common friend, was supposed to last fifteen minutes. Instead it went for an hour and a half, with Hall describing the bank board under Gray as "an agency that was run amok, that had been out of control" and the situation as "a potential and impending financial disaster that would have extreme ramifications not only to the Dallas and Texas communities, but nationally as well."

Hall said he had written Gray seven letters but had received only one response, in which Gray said board policy precluded the two from meeting. If Westwood refused to cooperate, Hall would file for bankruptcy on October 5, a development he estimated would push many otherwise healthy thrifts over the brink and cost the FSLIC as much as $724 million.

Wright, visibly upset by what he heard, made two telephone calls while Hall remained in the room. One was to St Germain. "This just doesn't seem right. Something has got to be done," Hall heard Wright tell the House Banking Committee chairman. Wright then had a similar conversation with Representative Tony Coelho, House majority whip and head of the Democratic Congressional Campaign Committee, the organization that raises money to help elect Democrats to the House. In that position Coelho had raised millions of dollars in contributions from thrifts in Texas.

Shortly afterward, on September 15, Wright summoned Gray to his Washington office, where he had assembled several other representatives from Texas: Republican Steve Bartlett and Democrats John Bryant and Martin Frost. Hall was not the main topic of conversation. The discussion centered on general reports that the bank board mistreated thrifts in Texas. The meeting lasted more than one and a half hours, although Wright left after twenty minutes.

A few days later Wright called Gray to complain specifically about Schultz's treatment of Hall, saying that Schultz was not as "flexible or understanding" as Wright thought he should be.

"Isn't there anything you can do about this?" Wright asked.

"I'll look into it," Gray said.

On Wednesday, September 24, Gray's chief of staff, Shannon Fairbanks, met with Hall. Afterward, the board issued a statement urging thrifts holding Hall's loans to meet with him "at the earliest practical time to renew efforts to reach an agreement acceptable to all parties." Two days later Fairbanks accompanied Hall to Los Angeles for a meeting with Hall's California creditors.

That same day Wright postponed the House vote on the $15 billion recapitalization bill, which had been set for September 29. His reasons were clear to his colleagues. As Republican Stan Parris of Virginia explained it on the floor of the House at the time, "our distinguished Majority Leader is concerned about the independent regulatory actions taken by the Bank Board in his home state of Texas."

To Gray and Fairbanks, Wright's action meant one thing: The board had better help Craig Hall or Wright would hold the emergency recapitalization bill hostage. They felt this pressure acutely. The Banking Committee had approved the entire Treasury package, along with some unrelated and controversial housing amendments, on September 23. Without the new funding, the bank board was paralyzed. It didn't have enough money to do its job.

Gray and Fairbanks, desperate to get Wright to let the House vote on the measure, decided to placate the Speaker, even if it meant breaking bank board policy. So they fired Schultz and replaced him with another employee, Angelo Vigna, giving the new negotiator instructions not to listen to the outside counsel that had advised Schultz to foreclose on Hall.

"I was given a formal order from . . . Washington dismissing me," Schultz later recalled. "It came as quite a shock."

The decision was a slap in the face to the bank board regulatory staff, and Gray and Fairbanks knew it. Schultz had been doing his job when he decided it was in the troubled thrift's best interest to foreclose on Hall's loans. Several top staff members complained privately that Gray made the wrong decision by buckling to pressure from Wright and compromising the agency's standards, giving the congressman the incentive to continue to put pressure on the board. Some of Gray's closest advisers, even those who helped make the decision to replace Schultz, came to the same conclusion.

"We tormented, we didn't like what we did. . . . We felt terrible about the choices posed for us and I personally took a great deal of time to torment over the fact that from our perspective . . . we [thought] we crossed a line between what we felt was permissible or not," Fairbanks later told a House Ethics panel investigating Wright's actions. "I made a judgment that I did not like doing this, but I was committed to get the bill and willing to violate what I felt was . . . right in order to get the bill. . . . I had spent a lot of years growing up talking theoretically about means and ends . . . but the means was a perversion of the system and that is precisely the way we looked at it."

On October 3, after Schultz had been fired, Gray requested a meeting with Wright and spent thirty minutes explaining his agency's policies and duties. Gray pleaded with Wright to help secure passage of the $15 billion bill. At the end of the meeting Wright thanked Gray for coming. Neither brought up specific thrift institutions.

A few days later Wright rescheduled the vote, and the House passed the bill.

The plan's course in the Senate was not quite as checkered. Garn had introduced the administration plan in June 1986 but appended it to a broad, controversial financial deregulation bill. Garn eventually was pursuaded to drop most of the controversial items. But the Republican-controlled Senate failed to approve the package until October 18, the last day of the session before Congress adjourned for the year. By that time it was too late for the House and Senate to reconcile their respective bills, which accordingly died. Everyone, however, could claim that he or she had tried to do something about the S&L mess, all the while blaming someone else for the failure of Congress to pass the Treasury plan. Senators charged that the House version contained housing amendments that were too controversial; that was true. (Administration officials believed friends of the league on the House Banking Committee had purposely attached the amendments to kill the legislation.) For their part, representatives could charge that the Senate acted too late for any final bill to pass; that also was true.

For its part the league chose this moment—when it was entirely clear that legislation could not be enacted—to endorse the Treasury plan publicly. On October 16, league President O'Connell issued a statement declaring the plan "must legislation" before the Ninety-ninth Congress adjourned.

This was an act of remarkable shamelessness, as league lobbyists Hohlt and Freeman had been—and still were—working behind the scenes to kill the Treasury plan.

"Bob, No one is more frustrated than me," Hohlt scrawled on a copy of O'Connell's statement for the league that was delivered to Robert Zoellick, the top aide to Treasury Undersecretary Gould. "Who know [*sic*] if this will help?"

On October 21, 1986, a few weeks after Wright met with Gray to complain about the bank board's treatment of Craig Hall, the congressman arrived at the Ridglea Country Club in Fort Worth. After his success in getting the board to go easy in Hall's case, word had spread through Texas that Wright was willing to help. The phone in Wright's office had rung off the hook. But Wright felt he didn't know enough "to become the referee of S&Ls," so he had his staff set up a meeting in Fort Worth, in what he called S&L country.

"I expected thirty people," Wright says. "I got one hundred sixty-five."

In thirty-three years in government Wright had never seen anything like it. He listened to story after story about unfair and arbitrary thrift regulators, about the bank board's failure to respond to inquiries about suspected reprisals for public criticism of the board or of Gray. "I have never known people, business people, being afraid to criticize the government. If the government

233

had them so intimidated, maybe there's something to their claims," Wright thought.

Two days later Wright met in San Antonio with Bo McAllister, a third-generation thrift owner from a prominent and staunchly Republican Texas family who in 1986 also was president of the Texas Savings and Loan League. McAllister was an inside player in the national league. Gray had named him to be on the board of directors of FADA, the quasi-government company set up to handle problem real estate; Gray also picked McAllister's thrift, San Antonio Savings, to earn a fee from the bank board to run troubled thrifts the government couldn't afford to close. But that didn't stop McAllister from lambasting Gray's regulators.

"I am convinced," McAllister wrote in the league's magazine after the meeting, "that Congressman Wright is taking this issue very much to heart and is dead serious about insuring that Texas financial institutions are given every opportunity for survival."

It didn't hurt the Texas thrifts' cause that two major thrifts, First Texas and Gibraltar, were owned in part by the former Democratic party chairman Robert Strauss and his son Richard. (The government closed the thrifts in December 1988, although both had been insolvent for years, at a combined cost to taxpayers of over $4 billion.) Nor did it hurt that one of Wright's top aides, Phil Duncan, was a close friend of Thomas Gaubert, the owner of a Texas S&L, Independent American Savings, and a prominent Democratic fund raiser who in 1986 was treasurer of the Democratic Congressional Campaign Committee and a contender for the chairmanship of the Democratic National Committee.

Gaubert was a college dropout turned home builder who, after his company was forced into involuntary bankruptcy in 1969, became what he called a "junk dealer," specializing in the rehabilitation of hard-to-sell real estate.

In January 1983 cigar-smoking Gaubert paid $1 million to buy a controlling share of Citizens Savings & Loan, an institution whose owner had died, leaving its seven employees and $40 million in assets with an uncertain future. He rechristened the thrift Independent American and embarked on a growth frenzy that doubled assets every few months until, three years later, the thrift had ballooned to a $1.08 billion company.

Gaubert looked down on many traditional thrift operators, once comparing them to "a Rotary Club luncheon in Hamtramck, Mich." He preferred the company of executives like Don Dixon and Patrick King at Vernon or Edwin McBirney at Sunbelt. In fact, Vernon, Sunbelt, and Independent American often lent one another millions of dollars, swapping loans and other holdings in an arrangement that Gaubert once described to the *Wall Street Journal* as "correspondent banking" but that government regulators told the newspaper they considered "backscratching," a process where "one thrift refinances or purchases a bad loan to scrub the books prior to a federal examination or to avoid loan write-offs and losses."

Gaubert knew Wright and Coelho well from campaign activities; Gaubert had raised tens of thousands of dollars for Democratic causes, much of it going to the House Democrats' fund-raising committee. He had donated $2,000 to the Wright Appreciation Committee in 1985. In November of that year Wright had held a fund raiser in his hometown of Fort Worth that raised $1 million for his campaign and political action committees. Gaubert's sons contributed $15,000; Texas lobbyist Curlee, $7,000.

"I don't know why you're not involved in their [politicians'] business. They're involved in our fucking business every day," Gaubert would tell colleagues. The donations give you access, he would say; "they give you a chance to have a forum when you have a problem."

"There's no way you can get around the fact that people who come forward with money have access," he once told the *Washington Post*. "I mean that's the real world. But I'll tell you, I don't have any more access to Jim Wright than the precinct chairman that supported him since 1954."

Gaubert knew Wright and Coehlo well, but he was best of friends with Phil Duncan, Wright's aide, in whose house he occasionally stayed and whose car he often borrowed when he visited Washington. More often he stayed on the *High Spirits,* Don Dixon's yacht and the sister ship to the presidential yacht, the *Sequoia*. Gaubert entertained Coelho, St Germain, and other congressmen there. The *High Spirits* became a regular sight on the Potomac, where Coelho and Wright used it for fund raisers.

Gaubert's run-in with the bank board started when he tried to buy a group of unfinished apartments that had been started by Empire, the Mesquite, Texas, thrift that collapsed with such a thud in 1984. Regulators killed the plan, and Gaubert, smarting from the rejection, agreed to share information about Empire with the congressional committee that was probing the thrift's failure, to Gray's embarrassment.

Two months later Gaubert discovered he was the target of a bank board investigation of $65 million in loans that a thrift in Mount Pleasant, Iowa, Capitol Savings & Loan, had made to him or to entities under his control. As of April 1984, all the loans were in default, and regulators suspected that Gaubert had engaged in a major land flip involving the thrift.

In December 1984 Gaubert and the bank board signed an agreement removing him as chairman of Independent American until the Iowa situation could be sorted out. After further investigation of the troubled Iowa thrift, the board's chief of enforcement, Rosemary Stewart, determined that Gaubert should be barred from the thrift business forever. "This is a man who has been so deeply the cause of loss at another institution, he needs to be barred from going back to his own institution," officials in the enforcement division concluded.

The two faced off in August 1985, when Stewart accused Gaubert of being "a crook." After a shouting match, the portly, usually undaunted Gaubert left in tears. In the men's room an official from the Federal Home Loan Bank of Dallas, Louis Roy, tired to console him. Just a few months earlier Roy and the regional bank had convinced Gaubert to have Independent American take a failing thrift off their hands, saving the government $50 million. Now the regulators were saying he wasn't fit to be in the business at all.

In January 1986 Gaubert and the bank board signed a second agreement, this time banning Gaubert from the thrift business unless he had approval from federal thrift regulators.

The board replaced Gaubert with Thomas E. Hendricks, a senior vice-president at the Federal Home Loan Bank of Dallas. Hendricks, with bank board backing, immediately awarded himself a $109,000 bonus to compensate him for leaving his secure job at the Dallas bank for one of uncertain duration. This was on top of a salary of $135,000 a year. Adverse publicity caused the Sunbelt board of directors to lower the bonus to $67,500 and spread it over six months.

Within a few months, however, Gaubert had begun to have second thoughts, charging that he had been illegally forced by Stewart into giving up Independent American. And when he went to Wright for help in November 1986, he presented the congressman with industrywide grievances, not his alone. "I have forty-four savings and loan institutions here, I and other investors. These guys have come and kicked me out. They said one day, 'Pick up your things and leave. You're no longer managing this savings and loan institution.' It is my money and the money of my investors, put together, but they made me leave," he complained.

Wright responded by telephoning Gray. At the time the liabilities of Gaubert's Independent American exceeded the thrift's assets by nearly half a billion dollars. Gaubert contended the government's mismanagement of his institution had caused the losses. The bank board said that it had simply adjusted the thrift's balance sheets to reflect accurately the damage done by Gaubert.

"Ed Gray, Tom Gaubert," Wright opened the conversation with Gray.

"Yes, I know of him," Gray said.

My "friend Tom Gaubert" has complained about being "mistreated" by the board, Wright told Gray. "Do you know the circumstances surrounding his situation?"

"No."

"He claims what legal counsel has advised him, what has been done to him is unlawful, usurped power that wasn't rightfully that of the bank board, and taken over his property. That's what he claims. I don't know the answer to it. He claims the people who took it over are running it in the ground, losing money. Would you hear him? Would you let him come talk to you?"

"Yes."

The bank board had a rigid rule that the chairman would not meet with parties engaged in a dispute with the agency; the chairman, as one of three board members, often had to vote on such disputes. But Gray agreed to break the rules for Wright. Come January, Congress would revisit the Treasury's $15 billion recapitalization plan for the FSLIC. Wright, as the new Speaker of the House, could again control the fate of the legislation.

To calm Wright, Gray and Fairbanks met with Gaubert for two and one-half hours, even though they knew that such a meeting signaled, in Fairbanks's words, "to our own Enforcement Division, all of our enforcement attorneys, that [although] a process had been worked through very carefully for [resolving enforcement matters], someone was going outside the process and coming directly to the chairman. And the Enforcement Division could not even be present to counter what was being said."

After the meeting Gray considered three options. He thought of turning the Gaubert case over to the bank board's general counsel for review but decided Wright would not regard the judge as impartial. Gray next weighed the possibility of asking an inspector general from one of the banking agencies to review the case, but the other agencies refused to cooperate.

Gray settled on a course of action believed to be the first of its kind in banking regulation. He appointed an independent lawyer acceptable to Gaubert to review the board's actions. Gray went so far as to pick an attorney from a list supplied by Gaubert, Nashville lawyer Aubrey Harwell. To the astonishment of fellow banking regulators, Gray was permitting a regulated institution to review and challenge the actions of its regulators outside the existing channels available to everyone else—administrative procedures within the bank board and the court system. Even one of Gray's chief legal advisers, FSLIC Deputy Director William Black, worried that the appointment of a special counsel would open Gray up to charges he made "special deals." In Gaubert's case, that was exactly what he had done.

Gaubert's arrangement with the bank board was especially irksome to individuals who were in good standing with thrift regulators but could not get a timely response from anyone at the agency, let alone an audience with Gray or his top staff. Gray stubbornly insisted, for example, on awarding the sale of an ailing Washington, D.C., thrift, National Permanent, to Citicorp over a rival bidder, oil billionaire Gordon Getty—in part, some board staffers believe, because Getty's lawyer was Roger Mehle, former assistant at the Treasury to Gray's enemy Don Regan.

Gray insisted on awarding the bid to Citicorp even after it was disclosed that the banking giant had made tens of thousands of dollars in questionable payments to the longtime social companion of D.C. City Councilwoman Charlene Drew Jarvis, who chaired a committee whose recommendation the bank board had to consider in making its decision. The payments sparked a Justice Department investigation (no charges were ever brought) and caused Citicorp to fire the vice-president who provided the money to Jarvis's companion, Woodrow Boggs, by funneling it via a "consulting contract" arranged through a law firm.

As for Tom Gaubert, in January 1987 Gray's staff recommended shutting Independent American. Gray held off, however, awaiting Harwell's report. In the meantime, Independent American's shareholders, many of whom were still closely tied to Gaubert, voted out the FSLIC-appointed board of directors.

But Gaubert's recontrol over the thrift didn't last long.

On April 21, 1987, Harwell issued his findings, concluding that the bank board had in some instances acted unfairly or improperly but that "there was not any illegal conduct, insofar as illegal means any clear and convincing violation of statute or regulation . . . [T]here is no basis for Gaubert's claim that the [bank board] improperly took over [Independent American] or purposefully or negligently caused the net worth of [it] to decline." A month later the bank board officially declared Independent American insolvent. The following year the bank board effectively nationalized Independent American by combining it with six other ailing thrifts into a newly reorganized Sunbelt, one that required an infusion of $5.5 billion in federal assistance to stay open. Gaubert, meanwhile, filed suit against the bank board claiming that it had ruined his institution and seeking $550 million in restitution. The suit was ultimately thrown out by the U.S. Supreme Court.

Shortly after Wright called Gray in November 1986 about Gaubert, he made another call to the nation's top thrift regulator.

Fairbanks walked into Gray's office and announced Wright was on the phone. As Gray picked up the receiver, Fairbanks settled in, as was her custom on such occasions, to listen to Gray's end of the conversation.

Gray was prepared for another complaint about the agency's handling of the Texas thrifts, perhaps with particular comments about Hall or Gaubert.

But soon his habitual nodding stopped.

"No," he said. "I was the one who recruited him. I think very highly of him. He is doing what I want him to do. He is being a tough regulator."

When he hung up the phone ten minutes later, he muttered, "No way! No way!" as he assembled staff members to hear his version of what Wright had just told him. Wright had said he understood that the Dallas regional bank's chief regulator, Joe Selby, was a homosexual and was referring all the government's regulatory business to a "ring of homosexual lawyers."

"Isn't there anything you can do to get rid of Selby or ask him to leave or something?" Gray recalls Wright saying. Wright says he never suggested Selby was a homosexual and denies that he tried to get Selby fired.

Although Gray defended Selby to Wright, after he hung up, Gray called the Comptroller of the Currency's Office, where Selby had worked for thirty-two years, to see if officials there had heard anything about homosexuality or about Selby giving special treatment to homosexuals. They had not.

At this inopportune moment, as the future of the recapitalization plan floated unresolved and the bank board came under increasing political pressure, Gray's travels on the industry's dollar became public.

In the summer and fall of 1986 Gray's travel and entertainment expenses were disclosed in front-page stories in the *Wall Street Journal* and *Washington Post*. (One story included a drawing that showed all of Gray's air trips plotted on a map of the United States; there were so many lines that some bank board employees dubbed it the airlines' routing map.) Many of these stories had been leaked by S&L executives in an attempt to destroy Gray's already fragile credibility.

The stories recalled the gaffe committed in early 1986 by Gray's chief of staff, Fairbanks, who had ordered her secretary, on agency time, to send out mailgrams seeking a $500,000-plus home loan for a house she and her husband had recently purchased. The mailgrams were signed "Warmest personal regards, Shannon Fairbanks, chief of staff, Federal Home Loan Bank Board." When the incident came to light, Fairbanks sent handwritten notes to the recipients saying, "Inadvertently, my title and place of work were added at the end."

The news stories prompted the Office of Government Ethics to launch an investigation into Gray's travel practices. The investigation eventually was turned over to the Justice Department to determine whether Gray had committed a criminal offense by accepting money from the industry and, in the process, spending hundreds of thousands of dollars a year beyond that approved by Congress during its annual review of the bank board's budget.

Gray's indiscretions were especially noticeable in contrast with the buttoned-down conduct of his counterpart at the Federal Reserve, Paul Volcker. The cigar-chomping Volcker was so cheap that the entertainment budget he permitted the Fed became a running joke among visitors to the central bank's grand marble headquarters, called the Temple. At one dinner members of the board of directors of the Federal Reserve Bank of Richmond were told they could have a salad or a vegetable but not both. One of the directors, Hanne Merriman, turned to Volcker and said, "This is like coming to Tiffany's and getting K Mart jewelry."

Gray hired Leonard Garment, former White House counsel to Richard Nixon, to represent him in the investigation into his spending practices. At Garment's suggestion, Gray paid back at least $28,000 to the regional banks and, shortly before the end of the year, apologized to Congress for his "flawed judgment." The Ethics Office ordered all bank board officials immediately to "cease from accepting official travel expenses for themselves or accompanying family members from any source except the Board itself," a ban followed by an order from Gray's office.

Gray suffered personally as well as professionally. To pay Garment and continue on at the bank board without the perks he had been accepting, Gray had to borrow $75,000. He even had to raid his daughters' college funds and ask his mother for money. Eventually the General Accounting Office, the audit arm of Congress, and the Ethics Office ruled that Gray had accepted improper travel and entertainment money from the industry but that no legal action would be taken if the practice stopped.

The Justice Department never acted, presumably because Gray's apology came at the end of 1986, just a half year from the date his tenure was to end, June 30, 1987.

Weakened by those personal embarrassments, Gray couldn't seem to get anyone's attention when he loudly complained about the White House's failure to fill the two bank board seats that became vacant upon the resignations of Mary Grigsby and Donald Hovde in the fall of 1986. The vacancies were left open in the weeks prior to the November election, leaving the agency without the quorum of at least two presidential appointees needed to make any decision requiring a board vote. Gray was still chairman, but he was powerless to close the doors of badly managed or failed S&Ls or to perform countless other duties. The inaction was perceived on Capitol Hill as a signal from the White House that it wanted Gray to resign before his term expired. In response, Gray characteristically dug in his heels, declaring his refusal to step down and continuing to complain about the vacancies.

But when the White House finally answered Gray's complaints, he was horrified. On November 7, just three days after the election, President Reagan nominated Lawrence White, a Democrat and a finance professor from New York University's Stern School of Business with a reputation as a free marketer for Grigsby's seat. To replace Houde, he nominated Lee Henkel, who had been an Internal Revenue Service lawyer during the Nixon administration and then became an Atlanta businessman with strong ties to thrift executive Charles Keating. (White House officials couldn't figure out why Senator Dennis DeConcini, a Democrat from Arizona, was pushing for Henkel's nomination. Representative Doug Barnard was a Democrat from Georgia, Henkel's home state, so his endorsement of the nomination made sense. But a senator from Arizona? Later the association became clear between Henkel and Keating, whose parent S&L company was based in Phoenix.)

According to a league official, the White House had told league leaders that, for Houde's seat, the lobby group could in effect quash the nomination either of Henkel or of another White House choice, George J. Benston, a professor at the University of Rochester who had often written that the thrift industry was obsolete, but not both. The league chose to oppose Benston publicly and remain officially neutral on the nomination of Henkel, though the lobby group's officials worked behind the scenes to poison Henkel's chances of remaining at the agency.

The nominations, Henkel's included, were no small item on the league's agenda. In a memo to league members in the fall of 1986, O'Connell warned that "we must continue to be extremely vigilant about such things as Bank Board appointments and the philosophy behind key legislative and regulatory decisions that affect us. . . .

"The strong recovery now being enjoyed by our business as a whole and the majority of the institutions in it must not allow us to become complacent about this issue. *What is still as much at stake as much as ever is our future as a separate, identifiable system of financial institutions.*"

O'Connell wrote Senator Garn and Robert Tuttle, the director of White House personnel, attacking the proposed nomination of Benston. O'Connell argued the professor could prove "potentially embarrassing to the administration" because of his aggressive criticism of Gray's efforts to impose stricter direct investment rules.

The White House killed Benston's nomination in favor of Henkel, but the league's triumph was illusory: NYU Professor White was by reputation just as radical as Benston when it came to questioning the need for a separate thrift industry.

Gray, Henkel, and White were an odd trio, personifying three regulatory philosophies. Gray, despite his run-ins with the league, was most sympathetic to its desire to maintain a distinct industry. At the same time he favored a return to the old-time religion, focused mainly on home lending, even though many economists believed such a return to the "good old days" would reexpose the thrifts to interest rate risks.

White represented new thinking, the free marketers who questioned the need for a separate thrift industry in an age of computer technology and sophisticated financial institutions. Why, he asked, should the Ford Motor Company be allowed to own a thrift that could do everything Citicorp could do—and more—at the same time that Ford was banned by law from owning Citicorp or vice versa? Further deregulation, not less, was needed.

Henkel, through his business association with Keating, was thought by many to represent the growing presence of highfliers in the S&L industry, men who claimed to favor deregulation but who really were drawn by the prospect of making easy money in the absence of supervision.

Gray could hardly sit in the same room with Henkel and be civil; he suspected Henkel's business partner, Keating, of being a crook and, worse, of leaking the stories about Gray's travel extravaganzas to the press.

Arguing that deregulation was the only way to save the industry, Henkel at his first bank board meeting proposed a liberalization of the direct investment rule that the agency had adopted in 1985 over Keating's objections. A quick survey by board staff found that 109 thrifts might have benefited from Henkel's proposal—which was defeated—but that Lincoln would have been the major beneficiary: Of Lincoln's $3.9 billion in assets, 20 percent, or twice the percentage allowed by the bank board, were in real estate investments owned directly by the thrift rather than indirectly through loans to borrowers.

Board officials loyal to Gray immediately leaked to the press that a business partly owned by Henkel had borrowed $62 million from Lincoln. Henkel countered that he had put all his holdings in a blind trust and that his financial ties to Lincoln had nothing to do with his support for regulations that Keating favored. That he and Keating agreed on business policy, specifically on the need to deregulate the thrift industry even further, was coincidence.

Senator Proxmire, who regained the chairmanship of the Senate Banking Committee when the Democrats took control of the Senate in the 1986 elections, called on the Justice Department to determine if Henkel had a conflict of interest and had violated the law by proposing a rule that would benefit one of his business associates. But the White House stood firm behind Henkel.

In early January 1987, however, Henkel agreed to have lunch with the author of this book. Henkel suggested they meet at the posh Willard Hotel dining room. When they arrived, the maître d' announced no one could be seated without a reservation. Henkel was undeterred, especially when he saw that the dining room was virtually empty. He asked the reporter to stand back while he spoke to the maître d'. Soon Henkel and the reporter were seated.

"How'd you do it?" the reporter asked.

"I waved cash under his nose like a fan," Henkel said. "If I can handle the Willard, don't you think I can handle this bank board business?"

When the episode was published a few days later at the end of a newspaper story profiling Henkel, the White House withdrew its support. "We were afraid we had another Bert Lance on our hands," said one White House staffer. Henkel soon resigned and returned to Atlanta.

30

Vermin

A round Christmas 1986 Wright's chief aide, John Mack, convinced the congressman to hear the complaints of Don Dixon, owner of Vernon Savings, the thrift nicknamed Vermin by regulators. It was urgent, Mack told Wright. The bank board was about to shut down Vernon, and unless the congressman intervened now, all would be lost.

The appeal for help had come to Mack not directly from Dixon but from Representative Tony Coehlo, who wrote a memo noting Dixon's criticism of the bank board: "A Joe Selby, with the Dallas Trouble [*sic*] Home Loan Bank Board, was specifically mentioned as desiring that [Vernon and Sunbelt Savings] be shut down."

"Look, they are getting ready to put me out of business," Wright recalls Dixon pleading. "They are going to put me and all the stockholders completely out of business. They are going to take our business away from us. If I can be given a week, I have located a source of income, a source of loans, financing in Louisiana . . . a person who will take over all the nonperforming notes and provide capital to continue and redo our operation here, if they will just give me that time."

A few days after Christmas, as Gray stewed over Henkel's appointment and tried to relax with his wife and family at their seaside home in San Diego, the telephone rang.

"Ed, I don't know anything about Vernon Savings and Loan," Wright recalls saying. "I don't know if it's valid or not. I don't know if it's meritorious." But, Wright said, Dixon claimed he was about to be taken over by the bank board. "He's being kicked out of business. He's got a week or three or four days that he can save it and avoid foreclosure. Why don't you look into it?" Wright said that Dixon was particularly upset because he had found a potential buyer for the thrift.

Gray was baffled. Vernon had been under state supervision since September 1986. It was at least $600 million in the red and was losing an estimated $10 million every month. Gray couldn't understand Wright's seeming gullibility in crediting Dixon's account.

Gray told Wright that Vernon could not be closed without a vote of the bank board. No such vote had been taken. Gray said, however, that he would check on Vernon's status. Wright told Gray to call John Mack with the information.

After calling Dallas Home Loan Bank President Green, Gray informed Mack that the bank board was seeking a "consent-to-merger" agreement from Vernon's board of directors; technically that was an attempt not to close the institution but to find a way to sell it or merge it into another thrift. It did represent, however, an effort to remove Dixon from control of the institution. Within an hour an angry Mack called Gray back. "I talked to some people about this, and they say that this is in fact closing down the institution," Gray recalls Mack saying. Gray assured him that he was wrong and that if Dixon had a buyer for Vernon, the bank board would be happy to consider the offer.

On December 31 Vernon's board signed the consent to merger agreement. The bank board didn't shut the institution down, though it was hopelessly insolvent. The inaction had less to do with pressure from Wright than with the FSLIC's own insolvency. But the board did the next closest thing. On the morning of March 20, 1987, more than two hundred of Gray's regulators closed Vernon Savings and Loan, a state-chartered, federally insured thrift that they said ended 1986 with a negative net worth of $349 million. But instead of liquidating the institution, they transferred its deposits and assets to a newly created S&L called Vernon Savings and Loan Association FSA, a federally chartered, federally insured thrift that was run by the government.

Some in Congress interpreted the timing of the take-over as a way to embarrass Wright and other Vernon allies to prevent them from blocking passage of the recapitalization plan. "If this is an attempt to embarrass Wright, then Mr. Gray is lucky that the Speaker is an advocate of the homeless, because after June, when Mr. Gray is out of a job, he may be sleeping on a grate," Annunzio aide Curt Prins told the *Washington Post.*

(Many viewed that as the second public attempt by politicians to threaten Gray. In early March 1987 Texas Attorney General James Mattox, who had profited from at least one I-30 transaction involving Empire's Faulkner, announced he had launched an investigation into how the bank board decided to close ailing S&Ls. He said the probe came in response to complaints by Texas thrifts.

Wright's press secretary, seeking to head off accusations that the congressman had tried to exert improper influence on Vernon's behalf, issued this statement: "The Speaker has no personal knowledge one way or another of this or any other individual savings and loan. If an institution is failing, the depositors must be protected.

"The Speaker's aim from the beginning has been to make sure that depositors are protected and that sound and salvageable private businesses are not forced into bankruptcy or foreclosure whenever that can be avoided."

The government's take-over of Vernon stemmed but didn't stop its losses. The thrift continued to lose about $10 million a month until it was shut down for good in November 1987, at a cost to taxpayers of $1.3 billion, at the time the costliest bailout in thrift history.

31

Congress

The 100th Congress convened on January 6, 1987. As they had promised the White House, Representatives St Germain and Wylie introduced in the House the administration's plan to pump $15 billion into the FSLIC. As expected, and despite its eleventh-hour declaration the previous fall that the recapitalization bill was "must legislation," the league again geared up to oppose the plan.

St Germain held hearings on the proposal on January 21 and 22, 1987, when the league officially voiced its opposition. It offered an alternative $5 billion scheme, with "forbearance" provisions that would give "breathing space" to "well-managed institutions in trouble due to local economic conditions."

After a morning of testimony O'Connell, Texas league President McAllister, and Texas league executive Tom S. King met for lunch with Wright and other Texas congressmen. "Speaker Wright indicated to us that he was considering 'slowing up' the FSLIC recap until he was satisfied with efforts toward forbearance," McAllister wrote in the Texas league's magazine two months later. "We encouraged him to take this action and that is exactly what happened."

On January 29 Wright had lunch with St Germain and several other members of Congress to discuss the growing complaints from Texas thrift executives who were accusing Gray of "high-handedness" and of using "Gestapo-like" tactics. "Why did Hitler go into Russia?" was the way Durward Curlee, lobbyist for Vernon, Independent American, and a dozen other Texas thrifts, liked to put his gripes about the bank board chairman (even though the precise nature of the analogy was fuzzy). Wright brought up the idea of "forbearance" and emphasized its importance to any legislation being considered. After all, he argued, the Texas economy would recover someday, and so would the region's troubled thrifts.

St Germain agreed to hold hearings on the allegations of mistreatment and, when lunch ended, ordered two of his staff, Gary Bowser and James Deveney, both former auditors for the General Accounting Office, to Texas to investigate the charges. There the two investigators looked into five troubled thrifts, including Vernon and Independent American, and examined the Federal Home Loan Bank of Dallas's records on the S&Ls. Bowser concluded that while there was some evidence Selby and his team of Rambos might have committed minor, technical violations, he could find nothing inappropriate in their decisions. His biggest complaint concerned the "previous ineptitude of that District Bank in not getting these problems under control a lot quicker than they did."

Notwithstanding this favorable report, Selby and Dallas bank President Green decided to try to convince Wright face-to-face that the thrifts' charges were unfounded. At their request the Speaker met with the two regulators on February 10 in his office in the Capitol. Selby and Green had brought along a batch of confidential information, normally available only to regulators, on the condition of some of the thrifts Wright had asked about. They thought they could show Wright just how shaky these institutions were.

They were in for a surprise. Sitting with Wright was his Texas business partner, Fort Worth developer George Mallick, and Mallick's son. Mallick, who had participated in the Fort Worth meeting with Wright the previous fall, had written a report to the Speaker concluding that Dallas thrift regulators were being too harsh. That was especially so, he wrote, in contrast with the treatment regulators gave banks in New York, which were allowed to weather the problems they suffered from bad foreign loans.

Mallick had hit on a favorite theme of Texans. Even Senator Phil Gramm (R-Texas), who generally backed the administration's FSLIC bailout plan, harped on the purported disparity in treatment accorded New York banks and Texas thrifts. On occasion Gramm set the audience laughing as he leaned over the table during Senate Banking Committee hearings to grill banking regulators. Using the thickest Texas twang possible, he would ask those testifying whether they thought the Texas economy was as likely to rebound as the economy of Mexico. Why, he would ask them, shouldn't Texas institutions be shown the same leeway that regulators gave banks holding worthless foreign loans?

The same argument was the backbone of Mallick's report. Like league officials, Mallick insisted that economic bad luck, not fraud or mismanagement, was troubling Texas thrifts. With Mallick and other unelected officials in the room, Selby and Green could not show Wright the information that would prove the Mallick report wrong. Worse, from the regulators' point of view, was the presence of a journalist, John Barry, who was writing a book about Wright. There was no way they could offer confidential information that would explain the crackdown in Texas.

From Wright's point of view, Selby and Green had brought along their own surprise: Gray's assistants in Washington, the bank board director of supervision, William Robertson, and FSLIC lawyer William Black. Black, by all accounts an idealistic, intelligent attorney, shared one unfortunate trait with Gray: He was too emotional and blunt in his criticism. The consensus at the bank board was that Gray and Black saw the world in black and white; anyone who disagreed with them was accused of being on the crooks' side.

Standing beside the Speaker, Mallick described the Texas situation as a "systematic thread of horror stories that involve unfair, unjust, intimidating, unduly expensive and illegal tactics" that has been "the modus operandi of the regulatory agents in District 9," the Dallas bank district. He appealed to Wright as a champion of the underdog, "people who are the single-family homeowners, the developers, the appraisers and the thrift owners themselves."

Wright himself then agreed that the regulators had mishandled some Texas thrifts and that he thought Gray misled him about the status of Vernon. "When I talk to the head of a federal agency and he tells me something, you know, I believe him. And I asked Gray when they were going to shut down Vernon Savings and Loan, and he personally assured me that they were not going to do that, and then I discover that you did just exactly that, and the very [same] day," Black recalls Wright saying.

Black couldn't let that pass. He tried to explain, as Gray had, the difference between liquidating a thrift and pressuring managers to sign what the bank board calls a "voluntary agreement" placing it under federal control. In fact, the difference was one of almost insignificant degree, having more to do with the FSLIC's lack of funds to close an institution than with any real-life distinction between a thrift taken over or closed by the government.

Black was making a distinction without a difference, the Speaker said. He went on to say that the bank board was using words like "conservator" and "consent to merger" to draw distinctions when there were none, that these terms were just words. Though Black denies it, others in the room say that he kept interrupting Wright, at one point saying, "I am not from Washington. These aren't just words."

According to Black, Wright accused him of being "less than truthful," to which Black took exception, saying, among other things, that he was a mid-westerner and that wasn't how midwesterners operate.

The Speaker, his face red and his trademark bushy eyebrows working up and down, exploded. "Wait just a Goddamned minute," he yelled. "I waited patiently for you and heard you represent your case, now you listen to me."

Twenty seconds of silence followed. At that the meeting ended. To Green, Selby, Black, and Robertson, the session was a disaster. In the cab back to the bank board, Robertson became frantic. "What are we going to do now?" he said. "The Speaker hates us! Recap [of the FSLIC] is shot! We'll all get fired."

To Gray and his fellow top staff members, the bank board's attempts to have a cordial relationship with Wright were over. From now on it was war.

On February 24, 1987, the Independent Bankers Association of America, a lobby group representing community banks, held a reception at the Sheraton Grande Hotel near the Capitol to honor Jim Wright and his new position as Speaker. House Banking Committee Chairman St Germain also attended.

The two congressmen gave informal, short speeches full of mutual praise. They draped their arms around each other and shook hands for the camera. But for those in the know that chilly wintry evening, the sweet words dripped with hidden meaning.

Wright's remarks were taken by several people in the room as a subtle threat that St Germain had better recraft the Treasury's $15 billion recapitalization bill to the Speaker's liking—namely, to one providing only $5 billion. St Germain was painfully aware that Wright, as Speaker, held great sway over the timing of the release of the House Ethics Committee report on St Germain's finances and maybe even on the report's content.

St Germain's kind words were taken as a plea for Wright to understand his predicament: He had been doing the league's bidding for years, and now he was being investigated for it. There were even hints that the Justice Department might conduct its own investigation into St Germain's relationship with league lobbyist Snake Freeman (which it did months later), and St Germain, those in the audience knew, had to be sure to seem independent. To capitulate to the league and push for a $5 billion bailout plan could hurt his argument that the league's contributions to his campaigns (to say nothing of his dinner and evening entertainment) did not affect his voting record.

Wright had St Germain in the hot seat. The Rhode Island Democrat's dilemma was simple: With an ethics investigation going on, how could he acquiesce to the Speaker when the numbers surrounding the thrift industry appeared so bad? Yet how could he ignore pressure from the Speaker, the leader of his party in the House and a man who could be ruthless politically?

Despite the growing angst on all sides about FSLIC recapitalization, February 1987 ended with good news for someone. Gray's nemesis, the White House chief of staff Don Regan, was fired at the end of the month, a casualty of a run-in with Nancy Reagan. When Gray heard the news, he gathered his staff and celebrated with three bottles of champagne.

The celebration was short-lived. Two congressional reports issued in 1987 suggested that it might not after all be a good idea to entrust the FSLIC with additional funds.

One report leaked to the press in March by Representative Dingell's House Energy and Commerce Committee documented gross mismanagement by the FSLIC of property inherited from failed thrifts. At a resort at Lake Placid in upstate New York that the FSLIC took over in 1985 from a failed Mississippi S&L, for example, congressional investigators found that regulators awarded a property management contract paying $97,000 a year to a man who had no property management experience and who subsequently was investigated by the IRS and the Labor Department. Dingell's staff also found that basic repairs were left undone. In one main room of the resort, potential buyers passed by a bucket catching water that dripped from the ceiling on rainy days.

The report added that FSLIC officials spared no expense on themselves when they inspected the property. After flying to Albany, instead of renting a car for the two-hour drive to the resort, they spent $769.50 to rent a plane and limousine to take them there. When they left, they took property from the historic resort. The items were small tokens, such as china, but enough to put the officials in violation of government rules. Dingell's staff concluded that "it became obvious that FSLIC has virtually no internal controls that would identify waste, fraud and abuse in the handling of their properties."

Even more embarrassing to Gray was the simultaneous leak of a report he himself had requested in the fall of 1986 from the management consulting firm of Booz, Allen & Hamilton Inc., which concluded that the FSLIC had no proper auditing system to handle the money it managed in the deposit insurance fund, that it had no uniform policy for selling or closing thrifts, and that it had mishandled the sale of property it repossessed from failed thrifts.

The report noted that a key reason the bank board was in such turmoil and so ineffective was that Gray left key jobs open for months. Gray blamed the vacancies on the federal pay scale, which he said was too low to attract workers. But critics said Gray and his lack of leadership were the problem: Few wanted to join his staff.

This criticism, added to the constant sniping by Wright and the Texas thrifts, had an effect on public attitudes. Even Senator Proxmire, not one to side with the league or other special interests, nonetheless was convinced by the drumbeat of criticism that the bank board needed to be kept on a "leash" by giving the FSLIC far less than $15 billion.

The league thus had a ready audience when, as a subcommittee of the House Banking Committee opened hearings on the administration's $15 billion FSLIC recapitalization plan in early March 1987, the lobby group accused the Treasury of trying to "frighten" Congress into passing a "bloated" measure.

A few days later Representative Annunzio—evidently acting at the behest both of the league and of Speaker Wright—drafted legislation calling for a FSLIC recapitalization of no more than $5 billion over two years, or $10 billion less than the administration sought. It also called for regulators to use forbearance on troubled thrifts. The bill was to be offered as a substitute for any legislation proposed by St Germain.

St Germain liked to have the votes of the House Banking Committee lined up before the committee actually met to put legislation into final form. Committee meetings, as the chair usually ran them, were well-rehearsed reenactments of what already had been agreed to behind closed doors. With Wright pressing on behalf of Annunzio's (and the league's) plan, St Germain feared he lacked the votes to carry the $15 billion proposal he had introduced and to defeat Annunzio's challenge. Hoping to avoid a public confrontation, St Germain canceled a scheduled session of the Banking Committee until the key players could reach an agreement.

After much back room discussion, St Germain came to believe that the votes lay with the league, or perhaps he had intended to push its cause all along. In either case, he himself introduced the league's plan on March 31, making Annunzio's contingency bill unnecessary. Committee investigator Deveney, astonished at St Germain's reversal, turned to his colleague Gary Bowser one day and said he was "amazed at how things are accomplished up here on the Hill."

St Germain's startling move left the committee temporarily nonplussed. Thomas R. Carper (D-Del.) introduced, and the committee adopted, an amendment raising the recapitalization to the full $15 billion. But on April Fool's Day the committee reversed itself, adopting by a vote of 25–24 an amendment, backed by the league and introduced by Stephen L. Neal (D-N.C.), that reduced the amount back to $5 billion.

The key votes sustaining the Neal amendment were cast by St Germain and by District of Columbia Delegate Walter Fauntroy, who voted by proxy. He had pledged to Carper that his vote would be cast in favor of $15 billion, but at the last minute St Germain cast Fauntroy's vote in favor of the $5 billion plan, apparently having been given permission to do so.

Several members of the Banking Committee credited Wright's lobbying efforts with swaying the vote. The Speaker had appeared before a March 17 caucus of Banking Committee Democrats to push for the $5 billion league plan, citing the many "horror stories" about Gray's regulators. After the committee's vote on April 1, Carper described Wright's tactics by saying, "I'll let today's vote and the broken arms speak for themselves." Barney Frank (D-Mass.) called the victory Wright's attempt to "retake the Alamo."

"The Speaker is absolutely right on this issue," Annunzio's aide, Curt Prins, said at the time. "He is not protecting people in Texas unfairly. These are businessmen who deserve to run their businesses without the vendetta atmosphere of the Federal Home Loan Bank Board."

The league's vigorous campaign against the $15 billion recapitalization produced a similar payoff on March 10, when the Senate Banking Committee voted to provide only $7.5 billion to replenish the FSLIC. An amendment by Senator Gramm to increase the funding to $15 billion was defeated 13–5, with votes against cast, among others, by Democrats Proxmire, Cranston, and Riegle and Republican Garn. Senator Garn's attempt to raise the amount to $10 billion was defeated on a tie vote of 9–9, split nearly on party lines. The sole Republican to vote against the Garn proposal was William Armstrong of Colorado. By unrecorded voice vote, the committee then adopted Gramm's amendment to include the forebearance provision sought by the league, which instructed regulators to go easy on thrifts that were in trouble because of an economic downturn.

The league was aided in the Senate by a debate between Proxmire and Garn over whether the thrift bailout should be considered within a broader banking bill dealing with all aspects of financial services deregulation. That turned the focus away from the thrifts, allowing league lobbyists to press their cause without much public scrutiny.

The House and Senate Banking Committee votes set off a round of frantic lobbying. Treasury Undersecretary Gould and his aides made the rounds, talking one-on-one with various members of Congress to underscore privately the gravity of the industry's troubles. On several occasions, for example, Gould met with Riegle, third-ranking Democrat on the Senate Banking Committee. Gould and his aides implored Riegle, who had sided with the league, to back the $15 billion plan, even though the Treasury official conceded that the bank board was a poorly run agency that, even in the best of circumstances, could spend efficiently no more than $3 to $5 billion a year to close thrifts. Even an inefficient expenditure of $15 billion over several years, Gould and his staff told members of Congress like Riegle, would ameliorate the problem. At the same time $15 billion was the minimum amount required to convince Wall Street investors that the complex funding mechanisms concocted by the Treasury to keep the amount off the budget was indeed legitimate.

But it was Gould's admissions about the bank board's yearly spending limitations that Riegle used to support his decision to back the league.

"The [$7.5 billion] bonding authority agreed to by the committee are reduced from what the Treasury and the Bank Board had sought," Riegle said on the floor of the Senate on March 27, 1987. "There are good reasons for this, not the least of them being the admission by Treasury Undersecretary Gould in testimony before the House Banking Committee that: 'Given FSLIC's organizational constraints, this infusion probably represents the maximum level of resources that FSLIC can efficiently use to resolve problem cases.' "

Some of Gould's lack of success may have stemmed from misrepresentations of his position by league lobbyist Hohlt, who often had conversations with Gould and his aides that they thought he then inaccurately repeated to House and Senate staffs. At the same time they thought that Hohlt made misrepresentations to them. Once he stood in the Treasury promising Gould league support for the $15 billion plan even as the league's top officials were meeting in a hotel down the street from the Treasury Building voting to push for their alternative $5 billion proposal. The behavior so infuriated Gould that he banned Hohlt from his office.

Gray himself got into the act, telling Congress on April 23, 1987, just two months before his term expired, that the league wanted Congress to adopt a "plan that will allow the FSLIC to exist for two years, albeit in a state of continuing crisis. After two years of inadequate funding, problems would have increased to a magnitude that no recapitalization will be possible without taxpayer support."

Gray later added that: "The league's consuming strategy was to buy time and buy time and buy time, and, if enough time was bought, if the disaster was permitted to get big enough, so that only the taxpayers could pay the bill, its members would have been well served. . . . The folks at the league told me this not once but on a number of occasions." Gould too says he heard league officials acknowledge this as their aim, and some league officials, though they deny it publicly, will say so in private.

The most influential person in the parade of lobbyists was Treasury Secretary Baker, who met with Wright in Fort Worth just after the House Banking Committee's April Fool's Day vote. Whether or not Wright understood finance and banking, Baker knew that the Speaker would appreciate political armtwisting. So Baker turned Wright's technique around: He threatened a presidential veto of the recapitalization bill if it contained only $5 billion, which was enough for one year. Wall Street, Baker told Wright, needed the reassurance of more money over a longer period of time. Otherwise, the investment banking community would neither take seriously nor trust the unusual financing mechanism of the recapitalization plan.

With a presidential veto, Baker explained, Wright and the Democrats would bear the blame for holding up the emergency bailout of the thrift industry and, possibly, for causing a meltdown of consumer confidence. Runs, perhaps a full-scale financial crisis, could ensue. And all this would occur just eighteen months before the presidential election of 1988.

Baker knew his man. On April 28, 1987, Wright and St Germain issued a joint statement supporting the $15 billion plan the White House wanted. Perhaps the switch was sincere. Or perhaps they thought the proposal had no chance of passing, with or without their approval. If so, they were right. Baker's arguments didn't sway the league, and Majority Whip Coelho—the man most involved in raising campaign funds for the Democratic majority— spoke on the floor of the House in support of the league's $5 billion plan. St Germain's amendment on the House floor raising the amount to $15 billion failed by a vote of 153–258. The House then passed the $5 billion plan by a vote of 402–6.

On May 14 the full Senate passed the slightly different $7.5 billion plan previously approved by the Senate Banking Committee.

While debate raged in Congress, in the real world the condition of thrifts continued to deteriorate. In January 1987 Gray had raised the estimated cost of closing insolvent thrifts to as much as $23.5 billion, a 50 percent increase from the $16 billion estimate of a year earlier; at the same time the GAO declared the FSLIC insolvent by at least $3.8 billion. The industry's profits in 1986, meanwhile, had fallen to $32 million, a steep drop from the $3.7 billion of a year before.

In the first three months of 1987 depositors withdrew a record $14 billion from S&Ls—primarily in the Sun Belt states—in what regulators were nervously calling a silent run. The industry's losses mounted so fast they reached a record $7.8 billion in 1987, more than $3 billion higher than the previous record yearly loss of $4.6 billion in 1981. State-chartered, federally insured institutions such as Vernon and Sunbelt in Texas and American Savings in California (the largest troubled S&L in the country) alone accounted for $5.8 billion of the loss.

On May 7 the General Accounting Office released a report explaining why the numbers were so dismal: The Reagan administration's six-year-old policy of allowing thrifts to use relaxed accounting rules and government notes to tide themselves over the bad times had failed, with 70 percent of the thrifts that had taken advantage of these forbearance provisions failing to improve or getting worse. A third of the industry was still stubbornly insolvent, another third in serious financial difficulty, and only a third healthy by standard measures.

Just two days earlier the bank board had voted to make the industry return to generally accepted accounting principles. Typically, though, the board, in a bow to the industry, delayed implementation of the new rule until January 1, 1988.

Against this alarming backdrop, the House and Senate Banking Committee conferees met between June 23 and June 30 to reconcile the differences between their respective recapitalization bills. The industry's deteriorating condition prompted most to agree that the level of federal expenditure should be increased. League lobbying, however, kept anyone from suggesting a return to the original $15 billion; instead, House and Senate representatives agreed to raise the recapitalization to $8.5 billion, though this, of course, meant once again voting for more money during conference than proposed in either of the original bills.

But the White House wasn't satisfied. To increase the outlay even further, Baker intervened personally to offer a deal. As approved by the conferees, the recapitalization bill contained a controversial provision only distantly related to the thrift crisis that would have closed a loophole in federal banking law concerning so-called nonbank banks. These institutions looked to consumers like regular banks, but they were operated in such a way that they didn't meet the technical definition of a "bank" in the Bank Holding Company Act. As a result, nonbank banks—unlike regular banks—could be acquired by nonbanking businesses and could operate across state lines. The administration, which approved of the loophole as a way of promoting deregulation, had threatened to veto any bill that plugged it. But Baker now said that the president would withdraw his veto threat and would live with a plugged loophole if the conferees anted up more money for the FSLIC.

The conferees, led by St Germain and Annunzio on the House side and Proxmire, Cranston, Garn, and Riegle on the Senate side, agreed, but with one condition: They would raise the funding to about $11 billion, but the White House had to pay $800 million of that money directly to healthy thrifts as a refund of some of the premiums they had paid to the FSLIC.

Treasury officials were furious but finally accepted the deal, viewing it as the best they could get. They insisted, however, that the amount approved be stated exactly as $10.8 billion, rather than as a round $11 billion, to remind all involved that the industry, largely through the league, had once again worked its will in Congress and extracted a subsidy for itself—in this case exactly 0.8 billion. The unusual number was meant to draw, and succeeded in drawing, questions from the press. The irony was apparent: A bailout package aimed at making the industry shoulder the cost of closing mismanaged institutions also gave thrifts an $800 million refund check.

To enact the deal with the White House, conference leaders St Germain and Proxmire, in a highly unusual move, reopened the conference after it had adjourned. As scripted, the conferees approved the $10.8 billion package. But there was dissent, most of it from league loyalists Riegle and Neal.

For his part, Speaker Wright pressed hard for forbearance provisions through the final conference meeting. He was so ubiquitous that Senator Gramm referred to him as the "phantom conferee." His provisions were included in the final package.

In the end, despite all the compromises, skeptics abounded. "Confronted with an industry that is undercapitalized, underregulated and overextended, I fear the [FSLIC] bill is too little, too lax, too late," said Representative Jim Leach (R-Iowa).

"Never have I seen Congress do anything short of accepting every prescription that the [S&L] industry prescribed to us," said Representative Gonzalez. "We accepted it and we followed it and look where it has gotten us."

In the fervor over funding, another key provision went largely unnoticed. The bill exempted the FSLIC from the obligation to obtain OMB approval for expenditures involved in closing down and selling ailing thrifts, a provision that significantly lessened White House influence over the Bank Board, which went from having a tight leash to having virtually no leash at all.

The House voted to adopt the measure on August 3, 1987, with the Senate following on August 4. President Reagan signed it into law on August 10.

A notable subtext of the congressional considerations of recapitalization had been the ethical—or criminal—elements of the thrift mess. In the spring of 1987 the House Ethics Committee released its report on St Germain, saying it had found no evidence after a fourteen-month probe that the Rhode Island congressman had enriched himself by abusing his office. The committee did conclude that he had violated House rules by accepting two free flights to Florida in 1980 on planes owned by Florida Federal Savings & Loan, but it called the violation minor, "a singular occurrence not part of an overall pattern of improper acceptance."

St Germain wasn't off the hook, however. The Ethics Committee, widely regarded as a toothless watchdog, had studiously avoided any examination of St Germain's relationship with league lobbyist Snake Freeman, from whom the congressman reportedly had received lavish entertainment gifts. The

Justice Department wasn't satisfied with the committee findings. In July the department began its own probe into St Germain's finances, expanding the inquiry to include an examination of the congressman's relationship with various lobby groups, including the league.

How did the league fare so well when the dimensions of the crisis were becoming clear? For many the answer is easy: money. Contributors to political action committees, better known as PACs, give money not so much to influence the outcome of elections as to influence elected officials once they are in office. Most financial service industry PACs give to both parties and often to both candidates in a single race. The same motivation often accompanies payment of honoraria, the money members of Congress get for giving speeches.

Thrift PACs, those formed either by individual corporations or by lobby groups such as the league and its state affiliates, contributed $4.5 million to House and Senate candidates in the six years from 1983 to 1988. On the basis of information compiled in the *Wall Street Journal* and the *Washington Post,* the members of the Senate Banking Committee who received the most PAC money and honoraria were Cranston and Riegle, followed by Garn, D'Amato, Heinz, and Bob Graham (D-Fla.).

The top ten list of members of the House Banking Committee who received the most money from these sources included St Germain, Annunzio, Neal, and Carroll Hubbard (D-Ky.).

Still, these donations couldn't stem the steady stream of bad headlines that accompanied the growing crisis in the summer of 1987. Consumers were withdrawing more from thrifts than they deposited, a disparity that reached $1.8 billion by year's end. And news of St Germain's ethics problems and Wright's intervention on behalf of the Texas highfliers began to hit the newspapers.

Indeed, that summer the Justice Department created a major white-collar crime task force in Texas, issuing subpoenas to hundreds of thrift executives and politicians, many of them associates of Wright and other high-ranking politicians.

About the same time Coelho's use of the *High Spirits* yacht became public. Acknowledging that the Democratic Congressional Campaign Committee had broken federal election laws by using Dixon's private yacht, as well as his private airplanes, for political events, Coelho publicly apologized on July 2, 1987, and reimbursed Vernon $25,168.

32

Lincoln Continued . . .
The Keating Five

During much of the debate in Congress about the Treasury plan to refinance the FSLIC, examiners in the San Francisco district had been poring over and criticizing the books of Keating's thrift, Lincoln. Gray said that the exam, started just a year after Keating bought Lincoln—and just after Gray and Keating had begun sparring over direct investments—was spurred by concerns about the S&L's fast growth and headlong jump into risky ventures.

Keating and his staff met with San Francisco regulators in July 1986, but the meeting deteriorated into a shouting match, with each side accusing the other of bad faith. Soon the battle turned public. In September 1986 details appeared on the front page of the *Washington Post* and the *American Banker*. Keating's lawyer, Margery Waxman of the national law firm of Sidley & Austin, accused the bank board of leaking negative information about the S&L to the press—a violation of law—and of having a "vendetta" against Lincoln.

According to Keating, grounds for suspecting a "vendetta" had surfaced the year before. Gray and Keating found themselves dining a few tables from each other at a posh Honolulu restaurant while attending that year's convention of the California League of Savings Institutions. The two had never met, but Gray knew of Keating because of Keating's wholesale attack on Gray's direct investment limitation. Keating insists that Gray looked over at his table and with a wave of his hand said something to the effect of "See that guy? I'm going to run him out of business." Gray denies he ever said such a thing.

There's no dispute, however, that former bank board member Hovde told Keating that "Keating was on Gray's shit list." Hovde, saying "there's a big difference between a shit list and a hit list," denies he intended to imply that Gray was out to "get" Lincoln or had a vendetta against its owner. But a former Keating lobbyist said in sworn testimony to Congress that Keating interpreted Hovde's remarks as evidence that the bank board chairman was personally involved in directing actions against Lincoln.

Keating says he found further evidence of a vendetta in the length of the bank board examination of Lincoln, which by late September 1986 had lasted seven months, or about five and a half months longer than was normal for a review involving an institution of Lincoln's size. Making the exam even more unusual was that it was being directed not from the San Francisco regional office but from headquarters in Washington, Keating's aides say he was told. Lincoln officials suspected Gray was fishing for dirt with which to retaliate for Keating's outspoken criticism of Gray's regulatory policies. Waxman, on Keating's behalf, complained about the exam to the press.

Gray felt compelled to snipe back. Through his own lawyer, Leonard Garment, Gray accused Keating of leaking details of Gray's expense account abuses to the press. Bank board officials also leaked confidential information about Lincoln's exam reports.

Although many thrift executives had reservations about Keating's integrity, they also found plausible his claim of unfair treatment. Many of Gray's friends at the league and in the California industry urged him to close Lincoln; it was easy to believe California thrift executives such as Anthony Frank and Herbert Sandler wanted to quash competition from gung ho entrepreneurs like Keating. Lincoln wasn't even a member of the league; the Honolulu convention was the first and last league outing Keating attended. Instead Keating was active in—and for a time dominated—the rival National Council of Savings Institutions, which, for more than the league, favored deregulation.

After 1986, however, even members of the national council began to question the wisdom of being so closely associated with a man like Keating, whose business practices were so controversial.

On March 6, 1987, Gray and his assistant Mary Ellen Taylor sat in the office of Senator Riegle, urging the Michigan Democrat to support the $15 billion FSLIC recapitalization plan. The Senate Banking Committee was to vote on the plan in a few days (when Riegle would side with the league). Coincidentally, just a week earlier Gray and Bank Board member Lawrence White—the third seat, briefly filled by Henkel, was empty—had renewed the regulation limiting direct investments. That was the rule Keating claimed would cripple his thrift.

After Gray and Taylor had made their pitch, they rose to leave. But as Gray walked out the door of Riegle's office, the senator tugged on Gray's sleeve, pulling him back inside the doorway. Riegle doesn't recall the incident but concedes that it could have occurred. As Gray recollects it, they had the following conversation:

"Some senators out west are deeply concerned and quite unhappy about the bank board's regulation of Lincoln, and they've made their concerns known to me," Riegle said. "You ought to talk with them."

"It's the same old feud, the same old vendetta," Gray protested. "It's an invention of Charlie Keating's. I'm very happy with the people we have out there [at the Federal Home Loan Bank of San Francisco]. I don't see why I should meet with the senators."

"You'll be getting a call," Riegle said.

"What do you mean?" Gray asked.

"You'll be getting a call," the senator repeated.

Gray knew about Lincoln's ties to former California thrift regulator Taggart. But unbeknownst to Gray as he sat pleading with Riegle, Keating had established strong ties to the senator as well, as Riegle's suggestion suddenly made clear.

Riegle had first met Keating a year earlier, on March 1, 1986, at a dinner in downtown Detroit to celebrate the opening of the Pontchartrain Hotel, which Keating had recently purchased and refurbished. Senator John Glenn (D-Ohio) had approached Riegle about attending. In addition, Riegle had known Keating's brother William, a former member of Congress and a high-ranking newspaper executive at the Gannett Company, Inc.

Keating says that late in 1986 or early in 1987 he was approached by Riegle's assistant and campaign manager, Kevin Gottlieb, who asked for a campaign contribution. Gottlieb says that Keating offered the money directly to the senator. In any case, a Riegle fund-raiser dinner was scheduled for March 23 at the Pontchartrain. Tens of thousands of dollars were expected to be raised. Shortly after the dinner arrangements were set, Riegle met with Jack D. Atchison, manager of the Phoenix office of the accounting firm of Arthur Young and the chief outside accountant for Lincoln. Atchison told Riegle that he thought regulators were unfairly hounding Lincoln's management and that their conclusions regarding Lincoln's health were unduly harsh.

A week later, when Riegle told Gray to expect a phone call about Lincoln,

261

the senator was well aware of the Keating-Gray feud, both from press accounts and from Keating's accountant. He also knew, of course, that in two weeks Keating and his associates at American Continental and Lincoln were going to raise a large sum at the dinner for his own 1988 reelection campaign.

The day after his March 6 meeting with Gray, Riegle and Gottlieb became further acquainted with Keating's real estate empire. While in Phoenix on March 7 and 8 to address a group of New England Life Insurance salesmen, Riegle and Gottlieb went on a side trip to meet with Keating and take a helicopter tour of properties built by American Continental with funding from Lincoln. According to the *American Banker,* one Lincoln executive recalls Riegle remarking during the helicopter ride, "I like what I see here. I can reason with Ed Gray."

(Just in case Riegle couldn't, Keating filed suit against the bank board challenging the direct investment rule, arguing that it represented a change in policy that unfairly hurt American Continental and Lincoln. He also moved in federal court to disqualify Gray from acting on the pending Lincoln examination report, charging bias. The federal courts eventually upheld the direct investment rule, and Gray left office a few months later, making the bias case moot.)

When Riegle returned to Washington, he received a $10,000 contribution from Keating and his associates. The money was given to Riegle via Arizona Senator DeConcini, who forwarded it shortly after the trip.

The March fund-raising dinner garnered another $66,000 for Riegle.

Meanwhile, Keating called other senators—Cranston, DeConcini, and the only Republican among the group, John McCain, also of Arizona—and asked them to meet with Gray. Keating also sent the senators copies of letters from Atchison and from economist Alan Greenspan. Greenspan's letter praised Lincoln, repeating past claims that it was a "strong institution that poses no foreseeable risk to the FSLIC."

Keating, of course, paid Atchison and Greenspan. And he didn't skimp with the senators.

Cranston received $39,000 for his 1986 campaign, $850,000 for three voter education projects in which he and his son, Kim, were involved, and $85,000 for a California Democratic party voter drive. The voter education projects, though ostensibly nonpartisan, were widely believed to be beneficial to Cranston's campaign.

Glenn received $34,000 in campaign contributions, and a now-defunct PAC associated with Glenn received $200,000. McCain received $112,000 in campaign contributions and nine private plane trips worth $13,433 to the Bahamas for him and his family from 1984 through 1986. DeConcini received $48,100.

(Keating's free-spending way with politicians was not limited to Washington officials. Phoenix Mayor Terry Goddard once remarked that Keating usually got what he wanted from local politicians in part because of the $500,000 he spent on campaign contributions during the 1980s. Goddard said Keating's involvement in politics was "a little like a bulldozer. It was an involvement that was too prominent to ignore.")

Keating, when asked later whether his $1.3 million in financial contributions to Senators Riegle, Cranston, McCain, DeConcini, and Glenn—who became known as the Keating Five—influenced the politicians to take up his cause, said, "I want to say in the most forceful way I can, I certainly hope so."

Gray does not remember details of the call promised by Riegle, only that he or an aide received it. "The next thing I heard was that I was to come to Senator Dennis DeConcini's office in the Senate office building at six P.M. on April 2, 1987. I do not recall who issued the invitation and how it came to the bank board. I do remember, however, that I was to come alone," he says.

When he arrived at the appointed time and place, Cranston, DeConcini, McCain, and Glenn were there alone, without staffers, an unusual occurrence in and of itself, since senators seldom meet outsiders without aides present. Riegle did not attend. (His absence irked some of the other senators' staffers, who felt Riegle had set up the meeting and should have attended.)

Gray felt uncomfortable without witnesses of his own. "A meeting with four senators and no staff whatsoever boggled my mind," he says.

There was no small talk. DeConcini sat across from Gray. To his right was McCain, then Cranston. To Gray's right was Glenn.

"We don't want to do anything improper here," Gray recalls McCain saying.

"Well, it is not improper for senators to ask questions, for you to ask questions," Gray said. "No, as long as you are asking me questions as a regulator, I can answer questions." The implication Gray says he was trying to make is that it would be improper to ask about specific negotiations with Lincoln or about any arrangement the senators were trying to promote between the bank board and Lincoln.

"We're here on behalf of our friend at Lincoln Savings and are concerned that a regulation the bank board adopted is unconstitutional," DeConcini responded, according to Gray.

DeConcini then offered what appeared to Gray to be a deal, a quid pro quo: If Gray rescinded the direct investment rule, Lincoln would agree to make more home loans. The senators have vigorously denied making such an offer, even though some recall the subject of direct investments did arise. A staff memo from DeConcini's aide Laurie Sedlmayr, titled "What American Continental Wants from Gray for Concessions," prepared prior to the meeting, seems to some to back up Gray's version of the meeting. DeConcini denies that is so and calls the memo "routine."

The meeting lasted an hour. At the end Gray says he told the senators that he could not answer specific questions about the Lincoln exam report and that "if they wanted to know about Lincoln, they would have to talk with our top regulators in San Francisco."

The four senators took Gray up on the offer to meet with the San Francisco regulators a week later, on April 9. The evening session, also in DeConcini's office, lasted two hours. This time Riegle attended. (The senators later disagreed about who invited the others to the meeting, engaging in a vigorous bout of finger pointing.)

Attending the meeting from the bank board were San Francisco Federal Home Loan Bank President James Cirona; Cirona's top regulator, Michael Patriarca; and FSLIC Deputy Director William Black.

Black, who takes shorthand, made copious notes at the meeting, which he recorded in a memorandum circulated to the other bank board officials in attendance, all of whom agree to its accuracy.

According to the notes, DeConcini again suggested that Lincoln would increase its investment in home loans if the bank board adopted some "forbearance" toward the thrift. The meeting broke up after the regulators revealed to the senators that the board intended to make several criminal referrals to the Justice Department regarding Lincoln. (In fact, it was only hours earlier, while brainstorming about what strategy to use at the meeting with the senators, that Black and the other regulators decided to make criminal referrals.)

The high profile of the San Francisco regulators prompted renewed claims by Keating and others that the major California S&Ls used the Federal Home Loan Bank of San Francisco to set loan rates, run competitors out of town, apply inconsistent regulatory standards to S&Ls, and otherwise try to control market share in the western United States.

Black believes the theory survives because of the secrecy surrounding most of the San Francisco bank's activities. Its meetings are closed to outsiders, and documents relating to examinations or other matters, such as how the bank spends its money, are not made public. "Inherently when you don't know why people do things, you breed conspiracy theories," Black says.

In 1986 a U.S. court of appeals threw out for lack of evidence a suit by a small California S&L that claimed the San Francisco bank acted to run it into insolvency. Black says the case shows the lack of justification for the conspiracy theory. It is "crooks" like Keating who try to use the theory, he says.

But the allegations persisted. In 1987 nearly a dozen major California S&Ls and the California league paid $1 million to settle a lawsuit by two developers who charged the thrifts and the lobby group with conspiring to set prices on loans. The lobby group and all but two of the thrifts involved in the suit were represented by the McKenna firm. Under the settlement, neither side can discuss the case.

In May 1987, as the end of Ed Gray's term of office drew near, field examiners in San Francisco had completed their lengthy examination of Lincoln Savings. They found that Keating's thrift had almost wholly abandoned the home mortgage market.

But Lincoln's record worried Gray's staff members for reasons that went beyond a belief that the industry was bound ethically to focus on home lending. They had a much more immediate concern: The thrift's risky investments were soaring while its record keeping and loan practices were sloppy and incomplete. Indeed, earlier in the year Gray's staff had found evidence that Keating's companies were selling securities using misleading financial statements. That had prompted the bank board in early 1987 to send the Securities and Exchange Commission a referral regarding American Continental.

In other words, Lincoln was out of control. The examiners' 285-page report made a simple recommendation: Close Lincoln. But much as Gray would have liked to do that, he couldn't. On January 1, 1987, six months before his term ended, a provision of the Garn-St Germain Act that had authorized him to close state-chartered thrifts had expired. Now in May, with just two months to go before he left office, Gray was powerless. The only available sanction was to pull Lincoln's deposit insurance. But that was almost unthinkable. While it might stop Keating's risky practices, it also would ignite runs at hundreds of institutions in the fragile industry.

Gray decided that his only course was to recommend that his successor, already known to be Garn aide M. Danny Wall, shut the thrift as soon as the bank board's authority was restored, as it would be when the bailout legislation then wending its way through Congress finally became law (as it did on August 10). Gray correctly guessed that the bill would pass after he left.

So, as one of their final acts, Gray and his chief of staff, Shannon Fairbanks, put a summary of the Lincoln exam report on what was to become Wall's desk, underscoring the importance of Wall's dealing with the case as soon as possible after President Reagan signed the new legislation.

Gray couldn't find a job as his term neared its end on June 30. He realized the one goal he had aimed for, the full recapitalization of the FSLIC, would not happen during his tenure. Even so, he kept up his fight for the $15 billion, although the bank board's internal estimates of the problem now put it at least at $50 billion.

He also campaigned up to the last minute to vindicate his tenure, using an endless round of telephone calls to fellow regulators, congressional staffers, and sympathetic Treasury officials. Consistency was not the hallmark of Gray's thinking at this point: While he acknowledged his mistake in accepting travel money from the industry, for example, he complained bitterly about the industry's disclosure of the practice to the press, sounding, as one close aide admitted, "wacko . . . off the deep end."

Such reactions served only to redouble Gray's efforts. They brought out the old reporter in him. He kept a copy of every speech he made, organizing them into a twelve-volume, blue-bound chronology that he still keeps at his desk. He took notes at nearly every meeting he attended or made sure to tell Fairbanks and other key staffers the contents of conversations he had with Wright, Riegle, Cranston, or others. "History will prove us right," he would tell Selby during their darkest moments. "History will vindicate us."

On the eve of his departure from office Gray pecked away at his typewriter, pounding out history as he saw it. Fairbanks had to drag him away to the second-floor amphitheater, where hundreds of employees had gathered to throw their controversial boss a farewell party.

The *Washington Post* described the scene this way: "As Ed Gray, his clothes rumpled, his soul tormented, walked through the throng, Kenny Rogers' 'The Gambler' pounded through a set of giant stereo speakers: 'You got to know when to hold 'em, know when to fold 'em, know when to walk away. And know when to run.' "

For weeks after he was out of government, Gray used the bank board's typewriters and telephones as he searched for a job. All his predecessors had gone on to lucrative careers in the industry or on Wall Street, choosing from among many offers. For Gray, weeks went by with nothing. There was talk that the California league, some of whose members felt sorry for him, would offer him a consulting contract to help tide him over, but it never happened.

Finally, Chase Federal Bank in Miami offered him a job, the only thrift of the nation's three thousand to do so. "The rest of them hate me," he said.

Part VI

STONEWALLING

Historically it's fair to say that the Federal Home Loan
Bank System has . . . been . . . insufficiently independent
from the industry it regulates. While you can do a lot of
regulation, or deregulation, that seems very favorable to
the industry in the short run . . . the net result is to drive
the industry on the rocks.

*—Former Federal Reserve Board
Chairman Paul Volcker*

33

Rose-Colored Glasses

A ugust 6, 1987: The murmur of conversations died down, leaving only the occasional cough and clink of stainless steel against china as luncheon guests at the National Press Club settled in to hear the first public statement by M. Danny Wall, newly sworn-in as chairman of the Federal Home Loan Bank Board.

Wall approached the lectern, wearing his signature attire: striped shirt with white collar and cuffs, a three-piece suit with buttoned vest, and, incongruously, shiny brown zip-up ankle-high boots.

As he stood looking out over the crowd and into the cameras of C-Span, Gray's successor made it clear that his would be a very different bank board. Restoring order to the agency, confidence to the public, and health to the industry—these were his goals, he told the audience. Many in the crowd left feeling upbeat. The Gray era had been a disaster. Even O'Connell and Keating, sworn enemies on savings and loan policies, could agree on that. Wall seemed to promise something better.

At the Press Club, after the speech, reporters crowded around the new chairman. Wall vowed that S&L executives were going to have less control than in the past over the bank board. "It's going to be ... hard for the agency to continue to be perceived to be too close to the industry it regulates," he said.

Bank board policy, thrift cases, the fate of programs Gray had imple-mented at the behest of the league—all would be reviewed and judged ac-cording to merit, not industry pressure, Wall promised.

Down the street that hot, muggy afternoon, President Reagan prepared to sign the $10.8 billion bailout bill into law. It would give Wall the money and authority to act as Gray could not in his final months.

Despite its inadequacies—everyone knew that $10.8 billion could not solve the S&L crisis—the legislation amounted to a tacit political peace treaty between Democrats and Republicans facing the upcoming election year. Both sides had plenty to be embarrassed about. But the law was expected to provide sufficient funding so that Wall could keep the problem under control, at least until after the elections of 1988.

The new law, called the Competitive Equality Banking Act (CEBA), did more than strike political peace. With the stroke of a pen, President Reagan eliminated OMB oversight of how the bank board could spend the govern-ment's money. In fact, the law's title was a misnomer. It didn't place banks and thrifts under similar operating rules; thrifts still could venture into many more businesses than banks and still could cross state lines to do business more easily.

Wall had been majority staff director of the Senate Banking Committee for Jake Garn from 1981 to 1986, when a Republican majority controlled the Senate. According to his résumé, Wall was "actively engaged in all legislation under" the committee's jurisdiction, including the 1982 Garn-St Germain Act. Wall had earned an undergraduate degree in architecture, "with an emphasis in planning," from North Dakota State University, also according to his ré-sumé. But his principal claim to fame was his service to Garn.

Like Garn, Wall was forceful but aloof, one few felt truly close to. Wall got along well enough with his co-workers, but he wasn't one to go drinking with the boys after work. Even people on the Senate and House Banking Commit-tees who had worked with him for years say he rarely opened up. He was, however, thin-skinned. Like his boss, Wall was apt to blow up at even slight criticism.

When, in late 1986 and early 1987, the White House turned to choosing Gray's successor, Wall made his availability known. Garn says he warned Wall not to take the job, that it was a thankless, no-win task. But Wall was determined.

His efforts weren't lost on the bank board staffers, who in their 1986 Christ-mas skit parodied him with a song entitled "If I Were a Chairman," sung to the tune of "If I Were a Rich Man."

Although outwardly Wall and Gray seemed like opposites, one cool and the other a tormented glad-hander, many saw a similarity they didn't like: Wall, like Gray, had an inflated view of his own ability. Just as Gray had been keen to prove himself by running his own show, so Wall seemed bent on establishing his record out from under Garn's shadow.

Wall would snap at reporters who relayed White House reservations about his ability to run an agency, retorting that Washington was full of people with an unwarranted prejudice against congressional staffers. "My title is not 'congressional aide,' " he once said. "I am chief of staff of the Senate Banking Committee."

Many key senators on the committee, including Democrats Cranston and Riegle, liked Wall. But in seeking the bank board chairmanship, Wall had only one real credential, one real piece of leverage, that anyone at the White House noticed or cared about: his tie to Garn.

Keating and others in the industry, notably many belonging to the league's rival lobby group, the national council, pushed to secure the chairmanship for Philip Winn, a former assistant secretary of housing and urban development who, in the words of a *Washington Post* story, "has been accused of using his political connections to profit from HUD housing programs." But they weren't actively opposed to Wall. He was as good a second choice as any.

Wall faced one other obstacle. In early 1987 the White House chief of staff, Don Regan, came close to securing the president's nomination of Roger Mehle to replace Gray. The league, however, pushed for Wall. The president, the league knew, would give in to Garn on this one, and it was right. A battle-weary Regan saw the writing on the wall and threw his support behind Garn's aide.

As Wall spoke to the Press Club in August, Rick Hohlt, the hyperactive Republican fund raiser and chief GOP lobbyist for the league, sat in the audience listening.

Just a month earlier, as Wall prepared for his swearing in with friends and family, Hohlt had telephoned the bank board and, according to one press account, reduced a secretary to tears by demanding that she interrupt the occasion and get Wall to take his call. "I don't give a goddamn who in the hell he's talking to. I want him right now," *Regardie's* magazine quoted Hohlt as telling the reluctant secretary. Wall reportedly took the call.

In giving orders like this, Hohlt had come a long way from Millikin University in Illinois, where he was graduated in 1970 with a degree in accounting. According to his résumé, he worked in a department store in Indianapolis before joining the staff of Richard Lugar, the Republican mayor of Indianapolis. When Lugar was elected to the Senate in 1976, Hohlt moved with him to

Washington. But Hohlt's reputation for being rude to clerical staff and his inability to operate as a team player eventually cost him his job, according to people close to the situation. Lugar reportedly eased Hohlt off his staff in 1980 by helping him obtain a job with the league, at the time considered a powerful lobby for a sleepy, noncontroversial industry.

Hohlt soon gained a reputation at the league for being long on gossip, short on substance. He was thought to be someone who was not above making threats to get what he wanted or making up information. Many found Hohlt insufferable. Bank board Chairman Pratt banned Hohlt from his agency, as did George Gould at Treasury. Ed Rollins says that he is close enough to Hohlt to have invited him to a birthday party for Mrs. Rollins, but Rollins acknowledges that many Washingtonians can't stand to sit at the same table with the lobbyist.

Gray says that while he was chairman of the bank board, he stopped talking to Hohlt after Hohlt threatened to make McKenna persona non grata at the league. (Hohlt apparently was angry that Gray had named McKenna to head McKenna's brainchild, the Federal Asset Disposition Corporation. Hohlt reportedly had promised the job to Thomas Bomar, the Florida thrift executive and a former bank board chairman.)

Even many top league officials found Hohlt difficult. They say he was hard to work with, a fact reflected in a high turnover rate among his secretaries.

But in one of those peculiarities of official Washington, Hohlt, while widely disliked even among fellow Republicans, enjoyed at least intermittent access to the highest levels at the White House and Congress. He was friendly with Craig Fuller, Vice President Bush's chief of staff. And he was close to Rollins (from whom he sought advice on how to answer questions for this book).

Hohlt's willingness to pick up the tab for big dinners or other entertainment made him a frequent guest at GOP gatherings, Rollins says. Others say Hohlt's access stemmed from his habit of pestering a host for days if he wasn't invited to a function. "He's a pain in the ass," said one GOP operative. "It's easier just to invite him." Hohlt also could provide valuable political services: He often did volunteer work for the Republican party and could be counted on to advance for Nancy Reagan or to raise money.

Whatever his personal shortcomings, Hohlt was extremely effective at his principal role at the league: lobbying Garn. Hohlt concentrated his efforts not on the senator, however, but on Wall. Hohlt and Wall, an incongruous pair, became close friends. Wall came to rely on Hohlt's advice, and for his part, the lobbyist came to spend so much time in Garn's office that fellow league officials say he seemed like part of the senator's staff.

"When it comes to Danny Wall, he doesn't take a piss unless I give him permission," Hohlt once told his colleagues at the lobby group, according to *Regardie's* magazine. Hohlt denies he ever made such a comment, describing it as "sick" and probably the handiwork of colleagues who did not like him. (And there were many of them.) But several thrift industry and league executives say they often heard him make such boasts. Besides, they point out, such a comment would be in keeping with his style.

It is not surprising, then, that Hohlt and the league pushed for Wall's appointment at the bank board. And once Wall became chairman, he and Hohlt stayed close, sometimes conferring several times a day. They would have much to talk about.

A week after the Press Club luncheon Wall's promise to bring order and leadership to the industry met its first major challenge. Texas Governor William P. Clements, Jr., told a reporter for the *Amarillo Daily News* that federally insured depositors would recover only thirty cents for every dollar of insured money at insolvent S&Ls in Texas and around the country. The governor accused the bank board of committing "fraud on the general public" by keeping hundreds of insolvent institutions open. (No doubt the governor meant that the government might only recover thirty cents on the dollar once sick thrifts were closed and their wildly inflated assets sold, not that Congress would break its promise to guarantee deposits.) The comments sparked a run at thrifts in Amarillo, with crowds in the lobbies of many institutions. In Washington officials worried about what to do. Wall and his top staff feared, as all regulators did, that their reaction might fuel the problem. Rebutting the governor in public could aggravate a bad situation by drawing attention to it, but saying nothing could prove worse.

Wall decided to be bold. He held a press conference in the bank board amphitheater, calling in television crews as well as newspaper reporters. He denounced Clements's remarks. "The governor is wrong," he said. "All insured deposits are good and will be honored." Congress would pledge tax dollars as a last resort if need be, he said.

It was a dramatic step. As the meeting broke up and reporters rushed to file their stories, board officials began a long, long twenty-four-hour wait, watching nervously for signs of full-scale runs. But panicked depositors didn't materialize. Wall's comments seemed to restore consumer confidence.

This, many people thought, was going to be a very different bank board from the one it had been under Ed Gray.

Wall's dynamism, however, was short-lived.

In 1986 and in 1987 Representative Barnard had chaired hearings on fraud and abuse by insiders, borrowers, and appraisers in the California thrift

273

industry. One reason for the focus on California was that it was where the national industry's wealth was concentrated. Another was that an economic boom was in full swing in California, making it impossible to assert that adverse economic conditions were to blame for the local failures of S&Ls there.

Barnard's subcommittee concluded that lack of standards in real estate appraisals was a key facilitator of fraud. The bank board examination staff had reached the same conclusion and planned to make use of authority granted the agency under the 1987 bailout bill to stiffen appraisal standards. The aim was to make it harder for dishonest thrift executives and developers to get appraisals that overstated the value of a parcel of land, thus enabling the thrift to make excessively risky loans and book bogus profits.

But in early October 1987 Wall abandoned the plan to tighten and unify appraisal standards. Instead, according to an internal congressional memo, he and his new chief of supervision and oversight, Darrel Dochow, decided to permit *"each"* thrift institution to decide for itself what appraisal standards it will require in connection with real estate loans and investments."

It was a decision that the thrift industry applauded but that Barnard's staff concluded would lead to chaos in thrift regulation because government examiners would "have to decide, on a case-by-case basis and without the benefit of specific guiding principles, whether a particular thrift institution's appraisal policies and procedures are adequate."

Considering the complexity of real estate transactions, especially where fraud was involved, the idea that examiners could ferret out abuse without guidelines seemed ridiculous to congressional staffers who had spent years studying the role played by bad appraisals in the thrift crisis. "I believe the [bank] Board's position to be indefensible in view of the continuing evidence of appraiser misconduct throughout the financial institutions industry," a staffer concluded in the memo to Barnard.

On Sunday, October 18, 1987, Wall and several of his top staff conferred anxiously in his sixth-floor office. Treasury Undersecretary Gould was there, smoking his pipe and trying to build a consensus between a representative from the Federal Reserve Board, Manley Johnson, and officials from the Ford Motor Company.

The problem was a big one. California's Financial Corporation of America, the largest troubled thrift in the country, was on the verge of collapse. In keeping FCA open, Gray had implemented a risky plan to restore the company's profits by investing heavily in mortgage-backed securities, which are highly interest rate-sensitive. But Gray lost his bet. Interest rates had been going up, depressing the value of the securities and pushing FCA toward insolvency, even under the thrift industry's generous accounting rules. A jittery stock market the previous Friday put nerves even more on edge.

The Fed urged Wall to do something. FCA was too big and too sick to be allowed to stay open. It was destabilizing the system. It faced a cash crunch that could spark runs in California, a major banking market, and no one knew where that would lead.

Wall had two choices: Sell FCA, or close it. The problem that afternoon was that Ford wanted to buy the thrift but couldn't get the government to offer the financial incentives that would make the deal attractive. (Ford already was one of the nation's top ten thrift operators by virtue of its subsidiary, First Nationwide of San Francisco, headed by Anthony Frank.)

In structuring a deal, Wall thought that his hands were tied by the FSLIC's shaky financial condition. The $10.8 billion authorized by the recapitalization bill would be collected only over several years. And the FSLIC was about to end 1987 $14 billion in the red, more than twice the $6.3 billion deficit it was now known it had run in 1986. Even these numbers were conservative. They included known problem cases but not shaky institutions yet to be included on the list of sure-to-fail thrifts. For that reason, the financial subsidies Wall could offer had to include as little cash as possible.

The best he could do was offer Ford FSLIC notes in lieu of cash. Ford officials said they would accept the deal on one condition: The government had to guarantee that the notes carried the full faith and credit of the U.S. Treasury. Because the FSLIC was itself insolvent, Ford's auditors would deem the notes worthless unless assured that the Treasury—that is, taxpayers—stood behind them.

That was the rub.

The government long had insisted that FSLIC notes should not be counted as part of the federal budget; making them explicit Treasury obligations would change that policy. And considering the number of notes the FSLIC had issued over the years, that was a step Gould was unprepared to take despite Wall's pleas to do so.

Wall then turned to the Fed, asking it to provide cash or other backing to solve the problem. Johnson refused. The Fed was a pinch hitter in time of crisis, but it had to draw the line. It could not lend money to a thrift with worthless collateral unless there was a threat to the entire financial system. And Wall had another option available before that would happen: He could close FCA and pay off depositors.

The meeting broke up late in the afternoon. Gould and Johnson spent a restless night worrying that Wall might not act swiftly enough to prevent FCA's troubles from contaminating the banking system.

For his part, Wall dispatched bank board employees to California to be ready to shut FCA's thrift subsidiary, American Savings, at a moment's notice, probably early the next day. It was not a restful night for bank board personnel either.

But fate intervened. On Monday, October 19, the stock market crashed. While an enormous headache for the Federal Reserve and Treasury, the collapse was a godsend for Wall and thrift policy makers in the White House. The crash pushed down interest rates. Overnight the value of FCA's securities portfolio was restored. FCA sold much of its mortgage-backed security inventory for a tidy profit. The company's looming insolvency abated for the time being, and with it, the need for immediate bank board action.

For Wall, and possibly for the country's banking system, the crash brought surprisingly good news. Not only was the collapse of the nation's largest troubled thrift (and third-largest thrift, healthy or unhealthy) averted, but depositors, frightened by the crash and seeking a safe haven in federally insured accounts, abandoned the stock market in large numbers, placing their savings in banks and thrifts instead. For thrifts, a welcome but short-lived respite ensued, providing a few months when deposit outflows from the industry slowed.

In November 1987 the league held its annual convention in New Orleans. The mood at the meeting was festive, and not just because of the Bourbon Street atmosphere that pervaded the city's giant convention complex on the Mississippi River.

The recapitalization plan was law, giving hope that the daily headlines about the FSLIC's insolvency would cease. Gray was out, giving hope that reporters would no longer find his tirades on the industry's woes newsworthy. And Wall was in, raising hope that the industry finally would be overseen by an upbeat regulator, one who could be as much cheerleader as chief cop. Wall did not disappoint.

He used the convention to announce the bank board's intention to formulate a special plan for troubled thrifts in Texas and other hard-hit states in the energy belt. He called it the Southwest Plan. Most of the thrift industry was healthy, Wall told the conventiongoers, and he intended to pay as much attention to helping robust S&Ls as he would to shutting the insolvent sector that was dragging down the industry. The falling dollar and the decline in stock prices since the Wall Street collapse a month earlier made the prospect of investing in S&Ls, including those in Texas, very attractive to bidders in Europe and Asia, Wall said. Foreigners were, in fact, "at least 10 percent" of all potential buyers of sick thrifts, he added. This was what the industry wanted to hear.

Wall also sounded three themes at the convention that he often repeated in the months ahead:

- No one can estimate the cost of the bailout.
- Blame for the disaster is so widespread, why bother trying to assign it?
- After eight years of incremental deregulation of the thrift industry, including the role played by the Garn-St Germain Act, the thrift charter was the best bank charter around because it allowed thrifts to sell a broader array of products than commercial banks.

"Hold your heads high because you continue to have the best charter going," Wall told conventioneers. In what many interpreted as a hint of a taxpayer bailout, he urged them to remember that the FSLIC, set up in the 1930s, had not been intended to pay for a mountain of failures such as those that had bankrupted the fund and threatened the existence of the industry.

Gray did not attend the convention. But partying along with the crowd was his former chief of staff, Shannon Fairbanks, now a consultant to the housing industry. McKenna also wined and dined with league leaders. And the parties were lavish. Black ties. Evening gowns. Limousine service.

Of course, this was a working convention. In the mornings the league held panel discussions that chewed over issues facing the industry. Companies closely tied to thrifts also sponsored special working get-togethers. One such session was a breakfast hosted by the investment banking house of Drexel Burnham Lambert, admired at the time for nearly single-handedly creating the market for the high-risk, potentially high-yield (or, as it turned out, high-loss) securities known as junk bonds, which several large troubled thrifts used heavily.

Guests at a breakfast hosted by Drexel included Gerald Levy, president of Guaranty Savings and Loan Association of Milwaukee, a former chairman of the league and one of its most active members, and Dan Brumbaugh, the economist who several years earlier, while at the bank board, had angered Gray by coauthoring the paper that estimated the thrifts' problems had already bankrupted the FSLIC. Brumbaugh, now a consultant, counted Drexel among his major clients.

Also present was Debra Cope, a reporter for *National Thrift News,* a weekly publication geared toward S&L insiders, whose editor and publisher, Stan Strachan, was friendly with industry leaders such as O'Connell and McKenna. For the issue of *National Thrift News* coming out the next day, Cope filed a story on the breakfast that began: "As recapitalization dollars begin to flow into the Federal Savings and Loan Insurance Corp., some thrift industry leaders are preparing to ask Congress to authorize the use of taxpayer revenues to complete the rescue of the beleaguered fund."

Cope quoted Levy as saying, "We're going to pay our fair share, but it's impossible for us to pay the whole tab," and paraphrased him as saying that "the next two years will be a crucial time for the thrift industry to lobby for use of taxpayer funds once FSLIC recapitalization dollars dry up."

Cope then said Levy "expressed confidence that the thrift industry has an important ally in [bank board] Chairman M. Danny Wall. Throughout his tenure as staff director of the Senate Banking Committee, Mr. Wall was 'constant in his position that he could not see how the industry could fund itself.' "

She quoted Brumbaugh as agreeing with Levy that the $10.8 billion recently allotted by Congress would not suffice to clean up the mess.

The story jolted the industry, which rushed to try to discredit it. Levy's comments, if accurately reported, contradicted everything the league, Wall, and Levy himself had been saying publicly for months—namely, that the size of the problem had been overblown and that tax dollars wouldn't be needed to solve the crisis. The story seemed to confirm Gray's contention that the league planned to let the problem get so big only taxpayers had enough money to bail out the industry.

Brumbaugh confirmed Cope's version of the breakfast, including her account of Levy's remarks. But Levy and the league's incoming chairman, Theo Pitt of North Carolina, told a different story. Pitt, though not at the breakfast, insisted that neither the league nor its top officials believed a taxpayer bailout was necessary, adding that he could not believe Levy would ever say such a thing. Levy, for his part, denied having made the remarks. The two men reiterated the view they and O'Connell had expressed publicly so often in the past: The cost of the cleanup was anyone's guess, so why try to pinpoint a number? But even though in their view an accurate estimate of the cost was impossible to make, they and the league believed no tax dollars would be needed for the job. Later in the day Wall also denied that he thought the use of tax dollars inevitable.

Strachan, buckling to pressure from Levy and Drexel, a major advertiser in *National Thrift News,* ran a "clarification" stating that Levy's comments "were intended to describe a number of possible developments, rather than to outline Mr. Levy's own position." The clarification also noted Levy's suggestion that the comments about Wall that were attributed to him really had been made by Brumbaugh.

To Cope, new to the staff of *National Thrift News,* Strachan's willingness to allow industry leaders to challenge her stories in such a manner amounted to a slap in the face. Sure she had described the dialogue accurately, she checked and rechecked her notes.

Eighteen months later, in the spring of 1989, Levy acknowledged to Cope and another reporter that he had made the quoted remarks. He'd had to deny it at the time, he explained, because "it was not the official league position."

Though Wall had vowed to curtail the league's role in bank board affairs, his enthusiastic reception at the convention underscored his continuing close relationship with Hohlt and other industry officials. Several FSLIC aides felt that Hohlt's influence with Wall was far greater than Wall let on. During Wall's tenure, for example, Hohlt was known to call up field officials at the FSLIC and berate them on behalf of contractors (usually contributors to the GOP) doing business with the agency who weren't being treated as well as they thought they should be. Contractors are supposed to lodge such complaints with bank board officials, either in Washington or in the field offices. When asked about such calls, Hohlt said he occasionally called FSLIC staff members on behalf of friends to try to cut through red tape. He said he was calling to friends as a friend, not a league official. But everyone in the industry and within the bank board knew who Hohlt was and that he was close to Wall.

Indeed, in early 1988 Wall, at Hohlt's suggestion, named Gerald Carmen to run FADA. Carmen had headed President Reagan's campaign in New Hampshire in 1980, had run the transition team for HUD for the newly elected president, and then headed the General Services Administration from 1981 to 1985. At the GSA he had gained a reputation for cronyism, hiring relatives and political pals and appointing an official later convicted of bank fraud.

Carmen also chaired Citizens for America, a conservative lobby group whose members described themselves as working for President Reagan's political agenda. In September 1987 the group designated 49 senators and 183 representatives as members of its "Pork Barrel Hall of Shame." Carmen said the group's thirty-five-page publication *The Pork Book: A Guide to Congressional Excess* "will show the American taxpayer who is responsible for the runaway spending on Capitol Hill and who is trying to curb federal spending."

House Democrats found it peculiar that Wall had picked a man with such a record to run FADA, a money-losing venture that had been plagued since its creation in late 1985 by charges of conflicts of interest, favoritism, and mismanagement. In a letter to Wall, St Germain and other Democrats cited newspaper stories from 1982 reporting allegations that Carmen had created more than thirty-five political patronage jobs with salaries totaling $1.5 million while he was at the GSA. The reports said the "beneficiaries of these high paying jobs included his daughter and her boyfriend, political cronies, and former employees of his automotive business in New Hampshire." The Democrats also questioned whether Carmen had sold properties competitively and fairly when he headed the GSA.

Carmen responded by saying, "Sure I hired people I had confidence in and who I knew. As far as cronyism is concerned, maybe [Congress] ought to take a good look at itself." He added that each allegation in the letter was "old news" that had been investigated by "appropriate committees of the Senate and I've passed two Senate confirmations."

The letter also brought up Carmen's appointment of Donald Ellison as director of the GSA's regional office in Boston, Ellison's indictment four months later, and his guilty plea to embezzlement and defrauding a bank. Carmen acknowledged the incident but said he had relied on Ellison's references. "The record speaks for itself. The newspaper clips speak for themselves," he said, adding that they would confirm his claim that he generally received high marks for his tenure at the GSA.

Wall, when asked about Hohlt's role in recommending Carmen, said only, "It doesn't make any difference who makes the introduction if the person is qualified."

Under Carmen, FADA continued to take business from private-sector firms specializing in the management and sale of repossessed property. Executives from those firms wasted no words in expressing their dismay that the Reagan administration, which claimed to favor free markets, not only created a government entity to compete with the private sector but, through Wall and Carmen, went out of its way to protect and guarantee profits for the government company. It also guaranteed jobs for FADA's cadre of high-paid executives, whose salaries had specifically been exempted from federal pay caps.

Under Carmen, as under his predecessor, Roslyn Payne, potential purchasers of FSLIC property complained to Congress that they often couldn't find out how to go about making bids to FADA. There seemed to be no set rules. Requests for information on how to do business with FADA languished for months or went unanswered altogether. And because FADA couldn't handle all of its work in-house, it had to subcontract out management work to the same companies that the FSLIC used to hire directly; now FADA acted as middleman, in the process adding another layer of fees and expense to the government's task of handling its mounting load of bad assets.

"FADA is a socialized, inefficient monopoly created by the Reagan administration," Representative James Florio (D-N.J.) said at the time. "It doesn't make sense. You've got these private companies out there and you've got this failed agency [the FSLIC] and you decide to give more money to FADA rather than to the more efficient private sector."

Critics of FADA, and of Carmen, found Carmen's endorsement of *The Pork Book* ironic. Some joked that the book should be expanded to include many of the Reagan administration's efforts to deal with the S&L mess, starting with Carmen himself. FADA's foibles, they argued, symbolized a systemic problem infecting the entire bank board.

Carmen himself remained active in Republican politics while he headed FADA. He did not resign from Citizens for America until May 1988, four months after he joined the government. At a staff meeting at the bank board in September 1988, employees were told that if they needed to talk to FADA, they should not try to reach Carmen until "after the November 8th election," but instead should talk to his assistant Jerald Fox. Carmen remained a member of the Republican National Committee during most of his tenure at FADA (which ended in early 1989), and he gave a speech at the GOP National Convention in August 1988, urging minorities to vote Republican.

"I consider myself an active Republican," Carmen said in defense of his activities. Saying he took the job at FADA only because it had been exempted from federal laws limiting political activity by government employees, he said he felt "free" to pursue any political activities he had time for. In an interview with the *Washington Post,* he said the board of directors of FADA, nearly all of them thrift executives and active league members, knew about and had not objected to his political activities. (Months later John Zellars, a thrift executive from Georgia who was on the league's legislative policy committee and was vice-chairman of FADA while Carmen was there, said he does not recall ever being informed by Carmen or anyone else of Carmen's political activities. He said he would have objected if he had known about them.)

But Carmen was not alone in his political activity. The General Accounting Office released a report saying the bank board had illegally exempted scores of its employees from federal laws limiting the pay and political campaign activities of federal workers. In addition to FADA employees, the report's criticism took aim at high-paid, and possibly politically active, workers in the bank board's Office of Regulatory Policy, Oversight and Supervision, which employed 146 people to oversee hundreds of field workers who examined the nation's thrifts. The report also pointed to the Office of Finance, a bank board unit employing 52 people, which raised money at federally subsidized rates for the regional Federal Home Loan Banks.

Wall countered with a legal opinion of his own that challenged the GAO's finding. And he found no fault with Carmen's performance. Congress took no action, most of its members being too busy with their own campaigns to push the issue. Besides, next year a new president would be in office and—who knew?—he might even do away with the bank board altogether, rendering the dispute moot.

Choosing Carmen was not Wall's only personnel action to raise eyebrows. To head the insolvent deposit insurance fund, Wall named Stuart Root, a controversial industry insider.

When bank regulators from the FDIC had examined the books of New

York's Bowery Savings Bank in 1984, they found that its chairman, Ellis T. ("Bud") Gravette, Jr., had led the company into a number of questionable investments, including several in the relatively risky area of commercial real estate. (The FDIC usually regulated commercial banks but, for historical reasons, also regulated a few FSLIC-insured thrifts, most of them in the Northeast.)

The regulators forced Bowery executives to sign contracts agreeing to stop making such investments. They also required Gravette to submit a signed, undated letter of resignation that the government could accept at any time should he steer the company away from the path regulators thought prudent. But the FDIC's intervention didn't solve the Bowery's problems, and in 1985 the agency was forced to sell the thrift to avert its collapse. (After the FDIC sold it, the Bowery's new owners had better luck than former management: They sold the thrift for $200 million to the Home Savings of America, a California thrift that is the nation's largest.) As usual in such cases, the FDIC demanded that top executives resign, Gravette among them.

Gravette, however, did not stray far from the industry. In 1988 the bank board paid him $200,000 to develop the Southwest Plan that Wall had broadly outlined at the league's New Orleans convention in the fall of 1987. The consulting contract was awarded to Gravette by Root when Wall named him head of the FSLIC.

Root, it turned out, also was a former Bowery official. From 1980 until the Bowery was sold—the same period in which the thrift made the investments regulators found so risky—he played a key role at the company. He was the Bowery's chief outside lawyer for many years until 1981, when Gravette brought him in as president. In 1982 Root was promoted to vice-chairman; on January 1, 1983, he returned to private practice and his role as outside counsel. In the Bowery's 1983 financial statement Gravette praised Root as a man "in the forefront of the [Bowery's] efforts to achieve deregulation" and said that Root would remain on the company's board of trustees.

This all led to some expressions of surprise when Wall hired Root, who in turn hired Gravette. Wall's chief press officer and congressional liaison, Karl Hoyle, defended the decisions. He said that Wall and other agency officials knew about the FDIC's problems with the Bowery and the FDIC's assessment of the roles played by Gravette and Root in the thrift's failed rescue effort. "We knew there were some people in the FDIC who weren't pleased by our choices," Hoyle said. "But we have the highest confidence in both men."

The Southwest Plan was officially unveiled to the public on January 15, 1988. Smaller, ailing thrifts would be merged together to tap economies of scale and weed out redundancy and inefficiency and then be sold to the highest bidder.

It all sounded very positive. But Gravette's estimate of the cost of implementing the plan proved wildly inaccurate from the start. Wall initially told Congress he could clean up Texas for $7 billion. But he soon had to double that estimate, though many industry executives familiar with the situation thought even the revised figure far too low.

And across the country losses at hundreds of insolvent thrifts were costing the deposit insurance fund an additional $10 million a day, up from $6 million a day eighteen months earlier, when the White House first had unveiled its $15 billion recapitalization proposal. The $10.8 billion in new funding actually approved didn't cover even the nearly $14 billion deficit that the FSLIC rang up by the end of 1987.

In the face of these problems, Wall's "optimism for the business outstripped even the industry itself," said Tom King, head of the Texas league. When Wall became bank board chairman, the Texas league presented the balding thrift regulator with a foot-long yellow comb, a symbol of Wall's optimism. Wall hung the gift on his office wall.

But some suggested another metaphor for Wall's tenure. The chairman wore tinted eyeglasses that seemed to have a reddish hue. When the cost of the Southwest Plan doubled, reporters asked Hoyle if the chairman's spectacles could really be rose-colored glasses. Hoyle, duly noting Wall's irritation at the question, assured everyone that the glasses were tinted brown, not red.

As part of his campaign to accentuate the positive, Wall traveled across the country in 1988, holding daylong conferences to lure investors with what seemed to be the pitch of a car salesman. Easy credit terms, a small down payment, cash back—that was the bait Wall used to lure prospective buyers. He praised the benefits of owning an S&L over a commercial bank, while agency officials handed out a bank board brochure listing the real estate, securities, and insurance activities that S&Ls could engage in but that federal law prohibited to banks, as well as the tax advantages thrifts had over banks. Wall's performance at one daylong conference in San Francisco, held at a posh hotel, amounted to promises of a "benevolent regulator," according to bankers and others who attended the meeting, with assurances that buyers of S&Ls could count on the government to uphold its end of the bargain regarding any generous terms.

Those in the audience at the San Francisco seminar were less sanguine. Some attendees worried aloud that if Congress were forced to go to the taxpayers to solve the industry crisis, it likely would merge the S&L and commercial banking industries. That would mean folding the bank board into the federal agencies that regulate banks—agencies that were viewed as much tougher than S&L regulators. "What happens to the idea of the 'benevolent regulator' then?' " asked Jeffrey M. Bucher, a banking lawyer from Los Angeles, who was among hundreds of luncheon guests attending the conference. "That's really what they're trying to sell us on here today, the idea of the benevolent regulator."

The thought sickened officials at the Federal Reserve Board, who increasingly resented having to step in because of lax thrift regulation. To tout that laxity as a benefit . . . well, some Fed officials were incensed, to say the least.

Publicly the league was as optimistic as Wall. "I want to make clear that we do not predict a need for further resources to deal with the federal deposit insurance funds' responsibilities," O'Connell wrote to the *Washington Post* in March 1988. The $10.8 billion bailout bill of the previous summer was more than sufficient, he said.

But to industry executives, O'Connell had a different—and far more realistic—message. "For some months, the leadership of the League has been concerned that the problems facing savings institutions and commercial banks in some economically depressed areas are beyond the financial resources of the FSLIC and the FDIC," he wrote in a letter to league members that same month. The government, he told members, should recognize its duty to bolster the fund—a policy that administration officials interpreted as meaning the league wanted taxpayers, not the healthy portion of the industry, to foot the bill for the cleanup.

That same month top league officials prepared a secret fifty-page document detailing plans for a massive federal rescue of the industry. The plan called for four new federal agencies to spend billions of taxpayer dollars.

As the league envisioned it, the agencies would use notes guaranteed by the Treasury to buy and warehouse bad loans from failing thrifts, essentially a resurrection of the plan the league had pushed in the early days of the Reagan administration. The plan also suggested the imposition of an oil import fee as a way to subsidize the economy of the oil-producing states, where thrifts were particularly hard hit. And it called for the reinstatement of tax breaks that had been provided by the Reagan administration in 1981 but taken away in 1986. "Clearly this proposed Mini-Marshall Plan involves a massive federal effort," the report said, referring to the plan, named for Secretary of State George C. Marshall, to rebuild Europe after World War II.

Within hours of a league meeting in Washington to discuss the plan, word of the proposal leaked to the Treasury officials. They steamed.

"The League should be marched off Capitol Hill in shackles for attempted theft from American taxpayers," said Charles O. Sethness, an assistant treasury secretary and a key figure in the administration's effort to contain the thrift problem.

But whatever its defects, the league's plan recognized the realities in the industry. Shortly after the "mini-Marshall Plan" leaked, bank board calculations established that in 1987 the industry had suffered its largest loss ever. Losses at a thousand S&Ls offset the profits of the remaining two thousand to give the industry a yearly loss of $6.8 billion. Worse still, of the two thousand profitable thrifts, as many as a thousand were considered weak and candidates to slip into the unprofitable category, according to administration and private industry estimates.

The bad news, however, did not change Wall's regulatory style. By the time Wall took office, it was widely believed that the bank board's field examination and supervision were often arbitrary—in particular, that thrifts with executives who sat on the boards of directors of the regional Federal Home Loan Banks were able to win lenient treatment from regulators. The bank board accordingly set up an internal review system in which officials from the regional banks would evaluate the procedures of each other's operations. In early 1988 the review by Cincinnati officials of the Dallas bank was dismal; the review panel was flabbergasted by the decision of officials at the Dallas regional bank to underreport the losses at ailing thrifts in Texas.

The reviewers issued a report in April 1988, which was made available immediately to Wall, warning that Texas thrifts were losing $27 million a day, or about $10 billion a year. Lamar Savings, the thrift whose owner had applied to open a branch on the moon, had in the past been permitted to underreport known losses by $400 million. It turned out that one of Lamar's directors was on the board of the Dallas regional bank. Similarly, Dallas regulators gave the San Antonio Savings Association a high rating even through the thrift was on the verge of collapse (it eventually failed). The thrift was owned by a prominent Texas Republican family named McAllister, and its president also sat on the Dallas bank's board. (The thrift's chairman, Bo McAllister, sat on FADA's board of directors.)

Similarly, an investigation by the House Banking Committee noted the example of Dallas bank President George Barclay, who was elected by bank directors in November 1987 in a close race. At the time he had been acting president for three months.

C. Todd Miller, chairman of the troubled Southwest Savings Association of Dallas, was among the bank directors who voted for Barclay. Despite Southwest's troubles, regulators at the Dallas bank permitted the thrift to stay open in 1988, when it was sold (with massive federal subsidies) to Caroline Hunt, sister of bankrupt ex-billionaires Herbert and Bunker Hunt. Barclay permitted Miller to remain at the helm of the institution and, while he ran it, allowed the S&L to buy four troubled thrifts in the Texas region with $2 billion in federal assistance. During congressional hearings in 1989 Barclay denied that his decisions concerning Southwest were made in return for Miller's vote. The thrift failed a second time, being seized by the government in May 1990, nearly two years to the day since it had been purchased by Hunt. Miller resigned within a few weeks, federal regulators say. Until he left, Miller ran the institution on behalf of the government. (He did not return telephone calls, and thrift regulators refused to disclose what he was being paid. Congressional sources, however, said they learned that, before he left, Miller was being paid more than $300,000 as a base salary, not including bonuses or other extras.) The thrift was closed and liquidated in July 1991.

Despite the Cincinnati bank's report, the bank board allowed officials at insolvent thrifts to continue sitting on the boards of the regional banks until the situation was reported by the press. Then it stopped the practice. But even then the ban was temporary and applied only to new directors joining the boards.

This is not to say, however, that Wall was entirely passive. Also in April 1988, about the time he received the report on the sorry state of the thrifts in Texas, Wall fired Joe Selby, the self-styled Rambo of the regulators.

The news was delivered to Selby by Dallas bank President Barclay over breakfast in the coffee shop of a Washington, D.C., hotel. Barclay accepted 30 percent of the responsibility for the decision and gave the remaining 70 percent to Wall. Barclay explained to Selby that times had simply changed. Under Wall, an optimism pervaded the industry, and Selby was a reminder of the pessimism rampant under Ed Gray.

Other effective (and therefore gloomy) regulators suffered similar fates under Wall. During his tenure, for example, there were at least two instances in which whistle-blowers were fired when they refused to keep quiet about multimillion-dollar abuses.

One was Lisa Walleri, an examiner with the Federal Home Loan Bank of Seattle, which regulated S&Ls in Alaska, Guam, Hawaii, Idaho, Montana, Utah, Washington, Wyoming, and Oregon. She had responsibility for overseeing Far West Savings, one of Oregon's largest thrifts. Far West, needing an infusion of money, sought investors with the help of a $1.5 billion line of credit from the regional bank. At the end of 1987, when the investors were about to complete the purchase of the ailing institution, Walleri balked at the values Far West management placed on the thrift's assets and questioned the wisdom of lending $1.5 billion to such a shaky operation.

Seattle bank President James Faulstich refused to review the matter, even though bank board policy seemed to require it. The deal went through. The thrift got new owners, though most of the top management kept their jobs. In

Walleri's mind, the deal attested to an inherent conflict of interest: The Seattle regional bank stood to earn sizable interest and fees on the $1.5 billion line of credit it would extend to the newly purchased institution.

Walleri was then made chief examiner of Far West. In early 1988, in her first exam of the institution since it was placed under new management, her supervisor tried to "suppress exam findings [and] permitted the public reporting of higher than actual profit earnings," Walleri later testified to Congress. Among the practices at Far West that she challenged was the payment of hundreds of thousands of dollars in fees to top managers, purportedly for arranging the sale of the thrift to the new investors. Walleri pointed out that the fees were illegal, the management having been specifically barred by regulators from paying itself such bonuses. According to Walleri, however, Far West managers, many of whom were good friends with top Seattle bank regulators, circumvented the prohibition by backdating the bonuses to make it appear they were paid before regulators imposed the ban. Walleri says she was told by superiors at the Seattle bank to "forget" the bonus issue, that it was "water under the bridge."

Walleri's superiors then altered her report without her consent. Her attempts to protest to Washington were futile. She was told she had to sign the altered report. When she refused, she was harassed and eventually fired.

Thrift regulators now acknowledge that changes to the Far West exam report by Walleri's supervisors were improper and, in the words of Representative Charles Schumer (D-N.Y.), "severely compromised the integrity of [Walleri's] findings."

Far West, meanwhile, ranks among the largest insolvent thrifts in the country. Walleri's superiors who changed her report have since been promoted in the thrift regulatory system.

John Geddes, who worked for the Federal Home Loan Bank of Chicago, had a similar experience. In 1988 and 1989 Geddes discovered that interest charges on as many as 50 percent of all outstanding adjustable rate home loans—the instruments the California thrift industry had fought so hard for—were being miscalculated, sometimes in the customer's favor, sometime in the thrift's. Worse, he found, when the bank board took over and ran a thrift, it had often *knowingly* sold improperly calculated loans to other thrifts and even to other government entities, such as Fannie Mae.

"I personally know of [bank board] employees who were advised not to fix any known errors unless the borrower complained or were told not to investigate for possible errors because 'it was [the bank board's] job to sell loans, not to fix them,'" Geddes subsequently testified to Congress.

Consumers may demand a rebate if they have been overcharged, but institutions cannot force consumers to make up lost interest that the thrift mistakenly didn't charge. In either case, Geddes warned, small errors in calculations can grow into sizable errors over time. In one extreme case, for example, Geddes discovered that a borrower in Oklahoma had been overcharged $10,000 on a $25,000 loan. More often the errors involved smaller amounts in the range of hundreds of dollars. Still, Geddes concluded, consumers stood to lose a great deal by the bank board's decision to do nothing to rectify the situation.

By late 1990, Geddes estimated, consumers had been overcharged by as much as $8 billion. Left uncorrected, the amount could grow exponentially to $65 billion within several years. If thrifts suddenly were called on to refund such an enormous sum, it could bankrupt the industry.

The bank board took one action in response to Geddes's calculations in August 1989: It presented him with a confidentiality agreement that would have obligated him to stop talking about the problem. He refused to sign. He was fired four days later.

Geddes's findings were later confirmed by outside consultants and government banking regulators.

34

Wall Paper

Having disposed of Selby, Wall turned to another thorn in the bank board's side: the General Accounting Office, which in the spring of 1988 was completing its audit of the FSLIC's 1987 operations. The review would disclose losses of nearly $14 billion. Wall and Root traveled to GAO headquarters to challenge the $14 billion figure, arguing that the auditing agency was using invalid accounting methods.

The GAO had heard the same arguments a year earlier, in March 1987, when league President O'Connell wrote to its head, Comptroller General Charles A. Bowsher, protesting the accounting agency's then-recent estimate that the FSLIC's liabilities exceeded its assets by more than $6 billion. "The GAO has unwittingly aided and abetted the Treasury and the Federal Home Loan Bank Board in their efforts to frighten the Congress of the United States into passing the bloated [$15 billion] FSLIC recapitalization plan they have proposed," O'Connell wrote. He argued that thrift losses stemmed from unfairly harsh loan write-off requirements imposed by Gray's bank board. He also questioned the GAO's professionalism, arguing the agency used raw data obtained from FSLIC rather than collected them directly, a method he argued deviated from the practice of private accounting firms.

As the auditing and investigative arm of Congress the GAO ranks as one of Washington's most influential bean counters. When Wall and Root came to call, GAO officials were livid. They had no sooner brought Gray around to face reality than he was gone, replaced by another Pollyanna. Wall and Root were wrong, GAO officials responded. To prove it, they would submit the GAO's methods for review by a private firm of Wall's and Root's choosing.

The firm selected by the bank board officials sided with the GAO, and on May 17, 1988, the agency published an audit placing the FSLIC's deficit at $13.7 billion. Further, the GAO said the deficit "is not a projection of the cost to resolve all known problems in the industry. Instead . . . it is primarily the estimated cost to resolve the problems of those insolvent institutions for which the [FSLIC] had assumed responsibility." The report added that there were at least three hundred additional thrifts with assets totaling $88 billion that were both insolvent (that is, lacking any capital cushion to absorb losses) and losing money. Worse, GAO auditors said, hundreds of additional thrifts likely would fall into the "worst-case" category.

"We believe that further congressional action, beyond that already taken under the Competitive Equality Banking Act of 1987 to recapitalize the [FSLIC], may well be needed to enable the [FSLIC] to continue to meet its obligations and provide the deposit insurance it is mandated to provide," Bowsher concluded in the 1987 audit, which officially was released on May 17, 1988.

A few days after Bowsher signed the audit, Wall testified before the Senate Banking Committee that the estimated cost of the problem over ten years would be $22.7 billion and that the FSLIC's resources to deal with the problem would be $30.2 billion. This estimate of the cleanup cost was actually a decrease from Gray's last public prediction in January 1987, when he put the figure at as much as $23.5 billion. Privately, since early 1987 Gray had been using a $50 billion estimate.

The bank board's position was that "the nature of the present problems in the thrift industry are manageable with the resources that will be available to the FSLIC over the next few years," Wall told the committee. The implication was that the fund had about $8 billion more than it needed to solve its problems.

Wall's former boss, Senator Garn, defended the bank board's assertions, railing against suggestions by the GAO and others that the crisis was out of control and tax dollars would be needed. "There is no doubt in my mind that it is possible to manage this problem without a taxpayer bailout," he said. ". . . I am adamant that taxpayer money should not be used to bail out losses caused by fraud and abuse."

As if to mock Wall's optimistic predictions, however, in early June regulators had to undertake the largest cash payoff of depositors to date. The payout followed a decision to close two California thrifts whose branch office systems were the corner mailbox.

The thrifts, both based in Orange County, south of Los Angeles, and regulated at the federal level by the San Francisco regional bank were the North American Savings and Loan Association and American Diversified Savings Bank. Despite Wall's preference for keeping thrifts open by selling them to new owners, the absence of a branch network gave the institutions little franchise value and made them impossible to sell. The two simply had no brick-and-mortar offices or steady, loyal local customers who could be turned over to a new owner. Instead the thrifts used telephone and mail solicitations to gather deposits from around the country, investing the cash they netted in high-risk ventures such as commercial real estate. North American had lacked net worth for nearly two years; American Diversified, for two and a half years. Yet the San Francisco examiners, along with California regulators, had allowed the state-chartered, federally insured thrifts to grow unbounded. Their collapse cost taxpayers $1.4 billion.

The next month, on July 7, 1988, Wall appeared before the House Banking Committee with a new set of numbers: Resources available to the bank board over ten years had increased to $42.5 billion, while the cost of the problem had increased to $30.9 billion, he said. Most of the increased cost stemmed from the doubling of the Southwest Plan's cost estimate. According to two bank board officials, Wall and his staff had decided that they had to raise the cost figures to preserve their credibility; after all, many economists were now bandying about cost estimates of $50 billion to $100 billion. Even so, the revised numbers suggested that the bank board had roughly $12 billion more than it needed to resolve the problem.

But the $12 billion in increased bank board reserves was a fiction. Wall had calculated the cost of the problem in 1988 dollars, excluding interest expense from the total, a method that depresses the aggregate figure. But he calculated the bank board's resources using a cash flow method that included interest and other expenses over time and had the effect of inflating the amount of money available to pay off depositors. Either of the two methods of calculation is proper—as long as both costs and resources are calculated by the same method. But calculating costs in one way and revenues in another yielded a meaningless jumble that compared apples with oranges.

When questioned about the inconsistency, Wall's assistant Karl Hoyle defended it, saying, "That may not be the way to do it, but that's the way we do it." But Wall never used the method again once the issue was raised publicly.

Bank board member White was more forthcoming, admitting there had been much confusion and misunderstanding over the issue in Congress and the press. He confirmed that Wall should have stated in July, for example, that the board's estimated costs and revenues just about matched—making each $30.9 billion in current dollars, or $42.5 billion over ten years. The impression that a cushion of $12 billion existed was regrettable, White said.

Though some high-ranking bank board officials say Wall simply didn't appreciate the problem with his numbers, others, including officials he appointed, say they believe he purposely used inconsistent numbers in his presentation to Congress to hide the size of the problem.

Two officials who served under Wall say that at meetings of top bank board staff or in smaller one-on-one meetings Wall's aides often would ask the agency's widely respected chief economist James Barth if he could endorse the methods they were considering. Barth often had to decline. Usually that's where the matter rested. Wall didn't punish Barth. He simply didn't let Barth speak about the size or cost of the problem in public.

According to these officials, Wall and his aides asked Barth if he thought the bank board could substantially reduce the agency's estimate of the cost of cleaning up Texas on the assumption that the state's economy eventually would recover, and with it the price of real estate and the fortunes of scores of thrifts. Barth said no. When Barth and others pointed out the incompatibility of the cost and revenue figures Wall was preparing to give Congress in his July testimony, James Boylan, one of Wall's aides, is said to have snapped, "If you don't like our numbers, don't come to our meetings."

"Wall knew what he was doing because he chose who he listened to," said one top staff aide involved in the preparation of the numbers. "Danny Wall was a very good soldier."

The official said he did not know of any direct orders from the White House to Wall asking him to keep the cost estimates down until after the election. But, he said, "Sometimes soldiers do what they are expected to do, and sometimes they do what they think people want them to do. It's hard to say which Danny was."

Soon Wall came to be known on Capitol Hill as M. Danny Isuzu, after the chronic liar on the television commercial, or as M. Danny Off-the-Wall.

As Wall sparred with Congress, the Federal Home Loan Bank System found itself with an unanticipated problem. For years the regional Federal Home Loan Banks had been accepting FSLIC notes from ailing thrifts in return for cash advances. In its effort to keep thrift expenditures off the budget, the OMB had said that the notes were not guaranteed by the federal government. In the past that hadn't mattered to the regional banks (although it had troubled Ford when it considered buying FCA's thrift subsidiary). But as the FSLIC's funds became depleted, the regional banks' accountants were concluding that the FSLIC notes they held would be worthless unless the deposit insurance fund could find enough cash to return to solvency. Without tax dollars, that was unthinkable. But allowing the value of notes held by the Federal Home Loan Banks to drop also was unthinkable, as was any attempt to turn off the cash spigot that the regional banks provided to cash-strapped, insolvent thrifts.

Even the league, though publicly stating that the $10.8 billion allocated in 1987 was sufficient to handle the industry's problems, thought the FSLIC's problems so great that the fund's notes were essentially worthless. The lobby had adopted a policy in March 1988 advocating that the regional banks no longer accept the notes as collateral for advances to sick S&Ls.

Treasury Undersecretary Gould, frustrated by what he saw as increasingly inconsistent treatment of FSLIC notes by the administration, decided to tackle a seemingly obvious question: Was the OMB correct in saying the notes were not backed by the federal government? And if the notes were backed by the United States, did that automatically require that they be put on the budget?

After consultation with experts at the Treasury and OMB, Gould reversed the OMB's decree, concluding that the government did back FSLIC notes and that, to take the logical next step, any instrument backed by the full faith and credit of the government had to be included in the deficit.

This decision to recognize the obvious, coupled with the provision in the 1987 bailout legislation exempting Wall from OMB control over his issuance of notes, had a remarkable result. By issuing notes, Wall now could draw directly from the U.S. Treasury without limit or interference or permission from anyone.

Though no one from the Republican ranks tried to stop Wall, many expressed horror at the prospect that the chairman of the bank board now had unlimited access to taxpayer dollars.

"Danny Wall had a printing press out of control," remarked one high-ranking Treasury official.

"What the Federal Home Loan Bank Board has come to symbolize is the corruption of our constitutional process," said Representative Leach.

Not surprisingly, Wall found this power enormously helpful in inducing people to acquire failing institutions. From January to September 1, 1988, the bank board closed, merged, or sold 101 thrifts, with half the actions taken in the last three weeks of August. Cement for the deals included nearly $10 billion in notes handed over to people who acquired sick S&Ls, with half the notes issued as part of the August transactions. By issuing most of the notes after mid-August but before October 1, the board helped the administration comply with the Gramm-Rudman-Hollings Deficit Reduction Act, which required automatic spending cuts if the federal deficit exceeded a stated target; a quirk in federal law meant that notes issued after August 15 would not be counted as part of the 1988 deficit for Gramm-Rudman purposes.

And keeping down the deficit could only be helpful to Republicans in the upcoming election. In fact, despite public outrage over Wall's so-called print-ing press, the administration worked closely with Wall to time the 1988 deals to minimize their effect on the deficit.

In late September 1988 Senate Banking Committee Chairman Proxmire be-came the first elected official in Washington to admit publicly that a massive infusion of taxpayer dollars would be needed to clean up the S&L mess. In a speech on the Senate floor, Proxmire said, in a direct challenge to Wall, that at least $20 billion in public money would be required to close or merge nearly a third of the nation's three thousand thrifts.

Also in September, the GAO estimated that closing the nation's 514 sickest thrifts—roughly 15 to 20 percent of the industry—would cost about $50 billion at a minimum. Even this estimate, though, excluded hundreds more institutions that nearly everyone agreed would have to be added to the sick list in the next few years.

Wall made a final attempt to stem this avalanche of bad news. In early October 1988 the executive director of the bank board's Office of Regulatory Activities, Darrel Dochow, renewed the agency's challenge to GAO cost esti-mates. Dochow said new data showed that 40 percent of insolvent thrifts between 1984 and 1988 had been rehabilitated without cost to the FSLIC. GAO officials, like most other experts, were unconvinced. They said they were unaware of any such recovery rate. (Since then, of course, Dochow's claim has been proved wildly incorrect.)

In the meantime, while few senators other than the maverick Proxmire were willing to criticize Wall too harshly in public out of respect (and fear) of Garn, members of the House didn't labor under similar constraints. Repre-sentatives Leach and Gonzalez, and even Banking Committee Chairman St Germain, were becoming increasingly angry at Wall's shifting estimates, not least because each change added billions of dollars to an already stagger-ing debt.

Adding to the pressure on Wall were a myriad of estimates coming from private-sector economists and fellow regulators, all challenging his figures. FDIC Chairman Seidman put the cost at a minimum of $50 billion. Consultant and economist Bert Ely put it at $60 billion. Other independent estimates put the cost as high as $100 billion.

In Wall's defense, Garn (and the league) sought to belittle these estimates, sniffing that making guesses about the size of the problem had become a silly Washington pastime. Garn even told Seidman to mind his own business, suggesting that FDIC-insured banks had enough problems to keep Seidman occupied; he needn't venture into the thrift arena. (Seidman, for his part, thought he had to. Insolvent thrifts that were allowed to remain in operation were causing a mounting strain on the nation's commercial banking system.)

But despite Garn's help, Wall couldn't hold out forever. Even Wall's fellow board member Roger Martin (who had replaced Henkel) rebelled, announcing to reporters in September that he reckoned the cost of resolving the mess to be as high as $62 billion.

Wall finally surrendered in October, upping the agency's official estimate of the bailout cost to $50 billion, $20 billion more than he had offered three months earlier. The bank board, Wall said, could cover the cost of this new estimate only if it were allowed to continue a special levy on the thrift industry for thirty years. The idea of assessing the special fee for decades, which thrift executives argued would kill even healthy thrifts by burying them in costs their commercial banking rivals didn't carry, was considered in Congress to be so unrealistic that it amounted to a tacit admission by the bank board that taxpayer dollars would be required for a bailout.

Estimates of the cleanup costs were not the only numbers going up. The salary of James Cirona, the principal supervisory agent in the San Francisco regional office, was $195,000 in 1985. Though his district rivaled only the Dallas region in numbers and costs of troubled thrifts, his salary increased until it hit at least $216,300 in 1988. Dallas Federal Home Loan Bank President Barclay earned $206,000 in 1988, a sizable increase over the $185,000 his predecessor had made in 1985. In Topeka, where regulators oversaw a four-state district that included Colorado, another region known for lax regulation and a large number of troubled thrifts, the salary of the regional president, Kermit Mowbray, increased from $170,000 in 1985 to $190,550 in 1988. By contrast, the salaries of the presidents of the twelve Federal Reserve Banks, who held far more demanding positions than did the Federal Home Loan Bank presidents, were much less, usually hovering in the $160,000-a-year range in 1988.

High salaries also were the norm at the bank board's office in Washington. The flack for the agency, William Fulwider, a man who often took his time about returning telephone calls from the press (and, when he did return there, often said he did not know the answers to questions), was paid $103,140. Others received even heftier salaries. Dochow, for example, got $185,000. Regulators at the better-managed, better-run agencies that regulated commercial banks watched with some resentment as the salaries of thrift regulators went up and up along with the size of the industry's problems.

Despite the increasingly dire state of the industry, Wall's strategy of obscuring the size of the problem achieved its short-term objective: The thrift mess did not become an issue in the 1988 presidential campaign. Democratic nominee Michael S. Dukakis brought up the subject only once, in late September, blaming the Reagan administration for letting S&Ls get into disastrous investments that cost the industry's insurance fund "at least $50 billion."

"George Bush could have headed off" the crisis when the vice president directed the White House task force on financial regulation, Dukakis said. But the task force "made no recommendations about the problem and the state of the FSLIC," he said. "Mr. Bush walked away from a ticking time bomb. Now four years later, Mr. Bush's inattention will cost tens of billions of dollars."

Dukakis broached the topic by endorsing a study released by Representative Schumer that predicted the thrift deposit insurance fund would be "broke through this century" and require at least $70 billion for a cleanup.

Wall responded by attacking Schumer's estimate as "rubbish." Garn defended Wall, too, and continued his vehement insistence that no tax money would be needed for the cleanup. Garn and other Republicans even took the offensive, pointing to the role Congress had played in delaying passage of the $15 billion bailout plan. (They did not mention that many Republicans in both chambers supported the league's rival $5 billion plan.)

Many congressional Democrats, meanwhile, urged Dukakis to drop the issue, fearing that Democrats like Wright and St Germain were vulnerable to criticism. And the political press, largely bored by and uninformed about the thrifts, failed to pursue the issue.

Indeed, the thrift fiasco was so far off the screen during the campaign that several weeks before the November election, league lobbyist Hohlt was among those honored at a dinner for major GOP fund raisers and donors. A banking consultant and former Federal Reserve Board official who attended the event said he was dumb struck when Hohlt was asked to rise and take a bow. "The spoon dropped from my hand. I couldn't believe it. Here was one of the key architects of the fiasco, one of key opponents of the White House recapitalization plan, being honored by the Republicans," he said.

Just before the election in early November 1988, the league held its annual convention, this time in Honolulu. The lobby group could not have picked a more beautiful and less appropriate place to discuss the industry's troubles.

Aware of the potential public relations nightmare, league officials barred television news cameras and reporters from the luau where thrift executives and federal regulators feasted on roast pig while they watched female hula dancers. But TV crews rented a hotel room overlooking the party and filmed it from above in time for the national evening news.

Trying to contain the damage, Wall and other bank board officials had told executives of troubled thrifts that they couldn't attend the convention. But the board itself sent seventeen employees to Honolulu, explaining that the industry most needs to hear from its regulators face-to-face when it is in deepest trouble. Wall himself wore his signature suit and vest whenever he appeared in public at the convention, evidently concerned that casual attire might give reporters the impression that he was living it up.

The convention marked one important turning point: League leader O'Connell stepped down after decades of service. His replacement was Fred Webber, a lobbyist for the soft drink industry.

The league membership had been divided over Webber. Some wanted a leader with more knowledge of the thrift industry and someone who, like O'Connell, would lobby with no holds barred. But others realized that the league had been damaged by its sleazy reputation, and they liked Webber's promise to have an "arm's length" relationship with the regulators. Image, this faction argued, now was everything to the industry. O'Connell's tactics had sliced the Reagan administration's proposed bailout of $15 billion to $10.8 billion, forestalling a large levy on S&Ls. But that approach ultimately cost the league's members more than it saved them because as the cost of the problem mounted monthly, it underscored to many in Congress the extent of the league's deception.

Webber started out as good as his word. Almost immediately upon taking office, he cut the league's ties to Snake Freeman, who had been on a consulting contract for the lobby group after recently retiring. But the new broom swept only so far. Webber didn't fire Rick Hohlt, though he said privately that he wanted to. Hohlt's Republican connections were simply too good. For the time being, Webber left him alone.

A primary topic of discussion at the Hawaii convention was the deficit and the cost of a thrift bailout. A league spokesman, Mark Clark, said over dinner with reporters that he didn't believe most taxpayers would really mind bailing out the industry. Mark Obrinsky, an economist for the league, wondered aloud during the same dinner if taxpayers even cared about the deficit. (A few conventiongoers noted the irony of league Chairman Pitt's telling a packed convention hall, "We'll all be asking ourselves what we can do to bring down the budget deficit.")

Officials also urged generous contributions to the league's political action committee so that the lobby group could support members of Congress sympathetic to the preservation of a separate thrift industry. Even as they did so, however, many prominent thrift executives were hastening the day when the distinction between thrifts and commercial banks would disappear. Incoming league Chairman Barney Beeksma, for example, who was taking over from Pitt and had just lectured on the need for thrifts, was taking steps to blur the distinction between his thrift and commercial banks in the minds of consumers: Beeksma's S&L changed its name from Island Savings and Loan Association to InterWest Savings Bank. As already noted, the move to get the word "bank" in the title—and to remove the words "savings and loan institution"—was widespread, especially among the larger California thrifts.

For his part, Wall, just after giving a speech in which he told thrift executives to hold their heads high, seemed to be paving the way for the use of tax dollars by giving a history lesson. Congress, he said, intended the deposit insurance system, funded as it was by the industry, to pay for "normal" problems, not the "abnormal or catastrophic" S&L failures troubling states like Texas, Illinois, California, and Maryland. But when asked who was responsible for causing the crisis, Wall responded by saying that history was not important. "There's plenty of blame to go around. The point isn't whose responsibility is it," he said. "That's all history."

This was all too much for the assembled reporters. A group of them, coming across a marquee indicating the location of a league reception, surreptitiously rearranged the letters so that the sign read THE U.S. LEAGUE PRESIDENT'S DECEPTION. Another group changed a sign for THE U.S. LEAGUE PRESS ROOM to read the U.S. MORGUE OF INSOLVENT INSTITUTIONS.

The reporters weren't the only comedians in Hawaii. Bob Hope, who has often traveled to cheer troops under fire, put on a show at the convention. "I know the savings and loans are in trouble," Hope told a packed audience of thrift executives and their wives. "My checks show a picture of my branch manager standing on a ledge." The crowd loved it. At the end of his performance Hope asked for a show of hands for those supporting Dukakis for president. He counted a dozen or so. He asked for show of hands for George Bush, and the room went wild. "Banking," said Hope. "That's Republican."

Most league members got their wish on election day. George Bush was elected president without once having said anything substantial about the thrift crisis. But there also was disappointment for the league in the election returns. Its staunchest ally in Congress, Representative St Germain, lost his bid for reelection after the Justice Department's criminal investigation of him found evidence of serious improprieties.

The Justice Department's inquiry was wider than the Ethics Committee's probe that had largely cleared St Germain. It called on league lobbyist Freeman and others to testify before a federal grand jury. When the *Washington Post* ran stories during the 1988 campaign about a department memo prepared for the grand jury that said the agency's criminal investigation of St Germain had found "substantial evidence of serious and sustained misconduct," it seemed likely that St Germain, the son of a dye factory foreman who had amassed a fortune as he climbed in seniority on the Banking Committee, was likely to lose.

Back in 1986, even as the Ethics Committee was investigating how he made his money and whether he had broken any House rules in the process, St Germain had run a television ad for his reelection campaign that claimed he donated $38,000 in speaking fees to charity. "Without him we'd all be a lot poorer," the ad concluded. In 1988, however, as it became clear that he was going to lose, St Germain canceled several television spots, allowing him to end the campaign with substantial campaign funds unspent. Under the law then in effect, he was permitted to keep the money, and he did.

35

The Deals

A t the league conference in New Orleans in 1987, Wall had vowed to close or merge two hundred of the sickest thrifts by the end of 1988. By November 8, 1988, election day, Wall had barely met half his goal. And time was running out. Existing law allowed the bank board to offer tax breaks as well as subsidies to investors who assumed ownership of failed thrifts. But the authority to provide tax incentives was to expire on January 1, 1989.

With just a few weeks before year's end Wall and his staff set off on a frenzied campaign to find buyers for insolvent thrifts, conducting a flurry of negotiations with some of Wall Street's mightiest titans. In one sense Wall succeeded: Of the 179 thrift cases resolved—mostly through sales or mergers—in 1988, 75 were completed in this burst of activity. Between December 20 and the end of the year alone Wall agreed to sell nearly 60 institutions.

Skeptics, of whom there were many, believed Wall and his staff were out of their league when they bargained with Wall Street sophisticates. The bank board, after all, spent millions of dollars a year in outside legal fees—$110 million in the twelve months ended on October 1, 1988 alone—on the theory that the expertise provided by outsiders more than compensated the government for the cost of getting it. But Wall and his staff followed no such logic when it came to investment banking. His staff, including Stuart Root and Root's assistant, Thomas Lykos, formerly the banking aide to Republican Senator Alfonse D'Amato, thought they were up to the task of negotiating most of the deals themselves without the use of professional bargainers.

One of the biggest of the 1988 deals involved Ronald Perelman, the street-smart billionaire who went from being a poor kid in Philadelphia to one of the richest men on Wall Street.

When the bank board sold a bankrupt Texas S&L to Perelman in December 1988, it told the public that he would put $315 million into the thrift and that the federal government would provide $5.1 billion in assistance. But internal board documents describing the transactions show that it painted a public picture that was far too rosy.

Perelman, using funds from his Revlon cosmetics empire, actually put up only $160 million to buy 75 percent of First Gibraltar Bank, an S&L created from five bankrupt Texas thrifts (including those in which Robert Strauss and his son had once owned a stake). A First Gibraltar executive bought an additional 5 percent and the government 20 percent.

First Gibraltar itself borrowed the remaining $155 million in new capital from the investment firm of Shearson Lehman Hutton, making the transaction a leveraged buyout. At the time Perelman defended the use of borrowed money on the ground that if Shearson couldn't sell the $155 million in First Gibraltar bonds within ninety days, Perelman was obligated to buy them. But what he didn't say was in that case First Gibraltar would have been obligated to reimburse Perelman; the ailing thrift, propped up with millions of dollars in government subsidies, would have been obliged to pay the billionaire $155 million plus interest over the life of the bonds. (As it turned out, as of November 1989 Shearson could not refinance the loan, though regulators had tolerated the delay in finding permanent financing. Perelman and the government had to take over the loan, assuming responsibility for paying it off by 1994 through profits from the thrift. Because the thrift was profitable largely because of massive federal subsidies, taxpayers, not Perelman, have ended up effectively footing the bill for much of the S&L's recapitalization.)

When tax breaks are included, the government promised to give First Gibraltar not the $5 billion announced by the bank board to the public but $6 billion in federal aid. Adding interest costs over ten years boosted the total government outlay to $10.4 billion, according to board documents.

The board initially kept secret the details of the Gibraltar sale—and of the other year-end deals it arranged to dispose of insolvent S&Ls—by contending that their release would undermine negotiations with investors. It disclosed the terms of the transactions only to Congress, only after the contracts were signed, and only after lawmakers protested they were being left in the dark.

Even after the December 31, 1988, deal-making deadline expired, the bank board refused to make public details of the deals. But copies of its documents spelling out the costs were leaked to the *Washington Post*. They showed that the $10.4 billion granted Perelman broke down into $8.9 billion in cash payments and $1.5 billion in tax breaks over ten years. First Gibraltar also will pay several million dollars in fees that Perelman owes to the lawyers, accountants, and investment bankers who put the sale together.

The $8.9 billion will make up for the lost principal and interest on soured loans made by First Gibraltar's previous management. Through 1999, for example, First Gibraltar will receive $4.8 billion in cash from the government to compensate it for losses on the face value of the loans, and another $4.1 billion to cover lost interest payments on those loans.

The $8.9 billion in income will not be taxed, however. And the S&L reaps millions of dollars in additional tax advantages by claiming losses on the bad loans, even though the government has reimbursed it for the losses. These advantages flow directly up to Perelman's cosmetics empire. Perelman can use the breaks to lower taxes by $1.5 billion at MacAndrews & Forbes Holdings, Inc., his investment vehicle, which counts Revlon Group, Inc. and First Gibraltar among its subsidiaries.

The deal was a fantastic money-maker for Perelman. If he distributed the $1.5 billion in tax breaks over ten years, he saved enough in 1989 alone just about to cover his initial $160 million investment.

Estimates of the annual return on his investment ranged from 30 cents to possibly $3 on the dollar. At worst, then, it netted Perelman at least double the return he could have made in a private-sector investment. "Ronald Perelman makes money just by opening his mail to get his government check," quipped one thrift industry executive. It was, some noted, a kind of welfare for the very, very, very rich.

In 1990 Senate investigators concluded that Perelman's investment was so lucrative for a simple reason: Wall and his staff had overestimated the cost of cleaning up the thrift by $1.6 billion and, as a result, gave Perelman overly generous subsidies—$461 million in cash in 1989 alone. It would have been cheaper for taxpayers if the government had simply shut down First Gibraltar and paid off depositors, the investigators found.

In a December deal similar to Perelman's, S&L regulators said New York financier Lewis Ranieri put up $200 million in new capital to buy United Savings Association of Houston. Actually Ranieri invested only $90 million and Shearson Lehman agreed to lend United Savings $110 million "sometime in the future," according to an official at an investment firm familiar with the transaction.

(Ranieri, one of the kingpins of bond trading at the investment banking firm of Salomon Brothers until being ousted in 1987, helped Salomon single-handedly create a public trading market in mortgage-backed securities. A loophole in federal law enabled thrifts to earn big tax breaks by trading mortgages or mortgage-backed securities. The loophole, which appealed to cash-starved thrifts on the edge, enabled Salomon to earn millions of dollars in fees by serving the trading needs of sick S&Ls.)

And in another huge deal closed during the last minutes of 1988, Texas billionaire and financier Robert Bass gained possession of American Savings in California. While a bonanza for Bass, the American Savings deal became one of the most expensive bailouts of the S&L crisis, costing at least $4.8 billion in government subsidies, not the $1.7 billion Wall estimated at the time.

(That American Savings was kept open and sold rather than closed also was a bonanza for several other faces familiar to those who followed the thrift industry's problems. One was Shannon Fairbanks, who had become a consultant to American Savings after she left her job as chief of staff at the bank board under Gray. She helped orchestrate the sale of the institution to Bass and acted as a consultant to the thrift after he took it over. And the board's general counsel under Gray, Norman Raiden, now returned to the private sector, represented Bass in the purchase of American Savings.)

In 1989 Bass used the thrift to go on a Texas-size junk bond buying spree that at its peak reached nearly $500 million and put the institution on the top ten list of junk bond holders in the thrift industry. (When, months later, Congress banned junk bond ownership by S&Ls, the thrift had to sell its portfolio at an estimated loss of $100 million, possibly more.)

In yet another deal an Arizona insurance executive named James M. Fail was allowed to buy fifteen insolvent Texas thrifts with $1,000 of his own money, $70 million in borrowed funds and $1.82 billion in federal subsidies.

The bank board chose to pursue the deal with Fail ahead of another bid that would have been roughly $97 million cheaper for taxpayers. And it closed the deal with Fail after February 1989, even though President Bush had ordered a halt to any new board deals. This was seemingly the more peculiar because Fail had been indicted in 1976 by the state of Alabama on securities fraud; although the charges had been dropped, he had agreed not to do any new business in the state. A firm controlled by Fail, the United Security Holding Company, had pleaded guilty to the felony charge of securities fraud.

Dallas Federal Home Loan Bank President Barclay sent a letter to headquarters on December 22, 1988, informing Washington of Fail's indictment but not his company's plea to the felony charge. And an hour before the three-member bank board met to vote on whether to approve the deal, Barclay overruled his staff's objections to Fail, instead writing a letter to the board stating that Fail was an eligible buyer under its rules. The board needed that statement from Barclay before it could approve the deal, as it subsequently did.

Wall and Root deny that any political considerations were involved in the transaction. But Fail did contribute generously to Republican causes. And he had another strong factor weighing in his favor. Representing him before the board was Robert Thompson, a lobbyist whose key selling point was his prior role as congressional liaison for then Vice President Bush. Thompson wrote several letters to Wall on Fail's behalf. In one of the letters, written in early 1988, Thompson referred to his friendship with Wall, whom he had gotten to know when the bank board chairman worked for Garn.

Thompson borrowed $500,000, including a $350,000 mortgage on his Washington home, from two firms controlled by Fail. Thompson also won a 2 percent stake worth millions of dollars in the thrift deal.

Root says the lower bid was not pursued because the structure of the deal was too complicated for the bank board to evaluate effectively in the few remaining days of the year. Documents obtained by the House Judiciary Committee, however, show that Root's lawyers were about to review the lower bid when he told them to try to close a deal with Fail.

Wall, when questioned about the propriety of selling failed thrifts to a man with Fail's record, defended the bank board's action in part by pointing out that the FDIC had earlier allowed Fail to buy a troubled commercial bank in Oklahoma on generous terms. Chairman Seidman, however, at least had the good grace to describe the FDIC's sale of the bank to Fail as a mistake. "He slipped through," Seidman said. "He duped us."

Wall has issued no similar recantation. Barclay, however, has stated that if he knew then what he knows now about Fail, he would have objected to the sale. When asked during a congressional hearing why he failed to do a more thorough background check on Fail for the Washington office, Barclay said, "I have no acceptable answer to that."

Regulators gave different rationales for such deals. Wall argued repeatedly that the bank board lacked the money to close insolvent thrifts and pay off depositors, leaving the agency little choice but to sell them using deferred government subsidies. In contrast, board member White said that most of the sales would have been the cheapest solution even if the agency had the cash to shut the thrifts down.

The GAO disagreed with both assessments. Its auditors found after analyzing the deals that the government would have been better off waiting for Congress to supply the necessary funding to shut the 179 thrifts sold by the bank board in 1988, including those given to Perelman, Bass, and Ranieri. The S&Ls would have lost an additional $4 billion in 1989 had they been left open, awaiting a federal bailout, rather than the tens of billions deals cost. "I think the deals are more expensive than the alternatives," said Frederick D. Wolf, the GAO's chief S&L and bank analyst at the time.

Even a study commissioned by Wall questioned whether selling thrifts was cheaper than closing them. The Mid America Institute for Public Policy Research, a think tank, said the bank board's methods of estimating costs of both courses "is subject to considerable error." The board was obligated to dispose of insolvent S&Ls in the manner cheapest for the government. But when the agency calculated whether it was cheaper to close an institution and pay off depositors or sell the institution and provide aid to the buyer, its math failed to take into account the tax breaks given the buyers.

Many critics at the time questioned the transactions, dubbing them McDeals and arguing that they had been slapped together too quickly and at terms that were too generous to buyers. There was concern that many of the thrifts that Wall had "rescued" would fail again. "The new owners of these institutions in many cases don't have a lot of capital or a lot of experience, and many have business interests that raise the potential for conflicts of interest," warned William Haraf, banking analyst at the American Enterprise Institute, a conservative think tank. "There's a very serious probability of repeat failures."

Some in the league, unhappy that thrifts were being sold to Wall Street operators who were industry outsiders, also questioned who got what in Texas. Perelman and Bass, they pointed out, were among those who a few months before winning their contracts had become members of the Republican National Committee's Team 100 donors—a list of those who contributed $100,000 or more to the GOP.

The investors themselves seemed not to care. Nor did the administration. While officials in the Treasury bemoaned Wall's 1988 transactions to reporters, they never asked him to stop making the deals. And except to orchestrate the timing of the deals so they would not interfere with budget preparations under Gramm-Rudman, no one in authority from the White House ever picked up the telephone to voice concern.

In a few months Wall committed the government to pay what he estimated to be $40 billion worth of subsidies to investors. The estimate was off. Even at the time, government auditors knew that the amount was closer to $60 billion; now they put the cost at $95 billion. In addition to ignoring the cost of tax breaks, Wall's estimates used what congressional auditors termed unrealistic interest rate calculations. The *Wall Street Journal* expressed the view bluntly: "A review of the 1988 cases suggests that Mr. Wall's public accounting of the deals was based on a series of miscalculations and on financial legerdemain."

Wall maintained throughout that the bank board would have enough income from deposit insurance premiums and the sale of repossessed property and other assets to pay for the subsidies without using taxpayer funds. Few in government believed that, however. Many of the rank-and-file staff at the

OMB viewed the deals as if Wall were printing money. The notes and other paper promises amounting to many tens of billions of dollars that he issued to complete the transactions became derisively known around Washington as Wall Paper.

On Capitol Hill concern also rose. A memo to Senate Budget Committee Chairman Lawton M. Chiles (D-Fla.) from his staff came to these conclusions about Wall's policies:

> FSLIC has not released sufficient data on a regular basis to independently verify its cash flow. . . . While FSLIC is incurring these massive expenses and exposing the taxpayers to a massive contingent liability, it is doubtful that much of its rescue action constitutes permanent case resolution.
>
> Perhaps most troubling, there is absolutely no control over the issuance of these non-cash commitments. FSLIC's broad grant of statutory authority which allows them to issue these credit instruments was intended to allow the agency the flexibility to meet its statutory mandate to structure the least expensive case resolutions. However, FSLIC refuses to release sufficient information to independently verify that this statutory mandate is being fulfilled.
>
> Instead, in creating and using these instruments, FSLIC appears to be the only agency which has an unlimited draw on the Treasury.

Representative Gonzalez questioned the legality of the arrangement. "How can it be that an individual or an agency would have the power to commit the Treasury to [tens of billions of] dollars without going through the authorization and appropriation process, which even the President can't do?" he asked.

36

The Politics

A s the transition between the Reagan and Bush administrations began, officials in the Treasury were hard at work on plans for the thrift industry.

The secretary of the treasury now was Nicholas Brady, named by President Reagan at Vice President Bush's request on the assumption that Bush would win the election. James Baker had gone on to run the Bush campaign, his sights set on becoming secretary of state in the new administration.

After Baker's departure from the Treasury, most of the team he had assembled to deal with thrifts remained behind to help Brady. Gould and his aides busily, and very secretly, prepared an emergency plan to raise tens of billions of dollars should the creaking thrift system collapse entirely and massive runs begin. The plan was coordinated with the Federal Reserve Board. It was so hush-hush that it was printed on plain white paper rather than Treasury Department stationery. If the plan leaked to the press, the Treasury could disavow it and claim that it was only one of many being considered.

To act as point men on the thrift crisis, Gould and Brady—ironically, considering Bush's bashing of Harvard University and Massachusetts as hotbeds of mushy-headed liberalism during the campaign—hired two Harvard professors. Robert Glauber and David Mullins, who came to be known as the Brady Boys, began work in Washington, first as consultants and then full-time, months before Bush actually took office. The two unabashed academic elitists were notorious for lacking political sense. As a consequence, they began developing a bailout package largely on what they thought best, without regard to what would or would not play in Congress.

Glauber, forty-nine, and Mullins, forty-two, had met the treasury secretary when he was chairman of the investment banking firm of Dillon, Read & Company. Brady, a good friend of Bush's, had been asked by President Reagan to head a commission to study the stock market crash of 1987. Glauber and Mullins wrote the commission's report, gaining a reputation for being able to assemble and analyze complex information quickly.

Coordinating the S&L efforts of the Treasury and the other banking agencies was Richard Breeden. A graduate of Stanford University and Harvard Law School, Breeden had been a Wall Street securities lawyer at the white-shoe firm of Cravath, Swain & Moore. As a top aide to Vice President Bush he had written Bush's report on financial service reform. Now, at thirty-nine, on the eve of Bush's presidency, he was considered by many regulators and many in Bush's inner circle to be among the most knowledgeable officials in Washington on the thrift crisis, as well as a politician who was savvy beyond his years. Although Breeden was a great believer in free markets, his approach was more sophisticated than that of many he had served in the Reagan administration. He understood that so long as there was deposit insurance, with its implied guarantee of tax dollars, the government had to have a hand in overseeing the financial system. That role, as Breeden saw it, was to make sure banks operated fairly and safely and that the gamblers who ran them risked their own money before tapping taxpayers.

In the view of people like Breeden, the old-boy network that had been regulating the thrifts was disgraceful. He was outraged, for example, to learn that the president of the Federal Home Loan Bank of San Francisco, James Cirona, and five bank colleagues flew to Italy in September 1988 to pick out granite for the bank's new headquarters. That sort of reaction was becoming commonplace. Increasing numbers of people on Capitol Hill, even those who had been longtime allies of the league, expressed anger at the snowballing size of the thrift problem and the league's past practice of lowballing the numbers. As the prospect of a taxpayer-funded bailout became more substantial, a "bake sale" mentality began to emerge: Every unnecessary expenditure had to be slashed, every penny possible saved, even if that meant, to paraphrase one aide to a top Senate Banking Committee member, holding a bake sale on the Senate lawn. Spending several thousand dollars for a junket to Italy was not keeping with that spirit.

One of the first tasks that Mullins and Glauber set for themselves was getting an accurate estimate of the cost of cleaning up the thrifts, one that didn't depend on figures peddled by the bank board or Danny Wall, whom they didn't trust. They spent months working on the problem, finally concluding in early 1989 that it would cost $90 billion to close all the insolvent institutions—if, that is, the government could write a check at that moment for the entire amount. But of course, that was impossible. The deficit was hovering midway between $100 billion and $200 billion annually, depending on who calculated it, and the prospect of adding some $90 billion or more to that was highly unattractive.

Instead the money would have to be borrowed and spent over time, an approach that would add substantial interest costs. Glauber and Mullins estimated that the total cost of borrowing the money over ten years would be $159 billion. Over thirty years, perhaps $300 billion.

With this in mind, the two went to work with William Seidman, the FDIC chairman. Seidman was everything Wall was not. He was Ivy League—Dartmouth undergrad and Harvard Law School. And he was polished, from his bald head to his facility with the press. His relaxed uniform of tan preppy pants and dark blue blazers contrasted sharply with Wall's stiff suit and buttoned vest. He wore loafers to Wall's shiny boots. He bicycled to work from Georgetown; on weekends he was apt to be riding horses on his ranch in New Mexico or taking it easy at his homes in Hawaii or Nantucket. Seidman and Wall, it seemed, had only one thing in common: Both were friends with league lobbyist Hohlt.

Early on Seidman was held in the highest regard by the new administration. At one point Breeden said he was so impressed with Seidman that he wished he could "clone him" and put him in charge of the other banking agencies, including the bank board.

And in effect, unbeknownst to Wall, that's just about what Glauber and Mullins were planning. At first they contemplated having Seidman run the FSLIC, effectively easing Wall out of that position. Some Treasury staff wanted to go farther and actually oust Wall from the bank board. But Brady, counseled by wiser heads at the Treasury, reportedly blocked the move, recognizing that it would mean hell to pay with Jake Garn, an ally the administration needed in the Senate.

So Glauber and Mullins set out to accomplish the same result less directly. They devised a plan that would have the FDIC and Seidman take over hundreds of the worst-case thrifts immediately and close, sell, or operate them until a solution could be found. It would be an interim measure until the president got a larger bailout and restructuring package through Congress. It also would be a slap in the face to Wall, who, after all, had been the good soldier through the election. But that couldn't be helped. Wall didn't project the confidence, nor did his agency have the staff and skills, to handle efficiently a new caseload of hundreds of institutions.

The move would be the more painful to Wall because Seidman had been speaking openly about the thrift industry's desperate situation. Wall, attempting to paint a rosy picture, had resented Seidman's interference and had come to harbor a strong dislike for the FDIC chairman. Wall seemed especially to resent the praise Seidman enjoyed on Capitol Hill and in the press, whereas he himself was berated almost daily. While Seidman didn't reciprocate the strong personal feelings—he didn't have to, holding the stronger hand—he clearly had low regard for Wall.

It fell to Glauber and Mullins to inform Wall that many of his agency's key oversight responsibilities were to be parceled out to his archrival. On an evening a few days before Bush was sworn in, the two men called Wall to the Treasury Building. They sat in Glauber's office on the building's south front. It was a surreal setting. The dusk outside was pierced every few minutes by fireworks, a display undertaken in anticipation of inauguration day.

For Wall, the explosion was taking place indoors. Glauber and Mullins informed him that in a few weeks, immediately after the president unveiled the administration's new S&L plan, Wall would no longer be responsible for handling failed thrifts. Wall was stunned. He protested, enumerating what he thought were his agency's strengths and what he thought were the weaknesses of the FDIC. The decision had been made, Mullins and Glauber told him.

Soon the threesome met with Breeden and Seidman at the White House to discuss the details of the plan. Wall spent an hour venting his spleen about Seidman. The other four listened until according to several participants, Wall began to repeat himself. Then Breeden shut him off, saying, "Enough."

The meeting ended after several hours. The deal was done. Wall not only had to live with it but was told he had to assist the FDIC and help make the transition as smooth as possible.

Mullins, Glauber, and Breeden were agreed that the president's bailout package had to include a structural overhaul of the thrift regulatory system to eliminate its many conflicts of interest. In addition, they agreed that tougher capital standards had to be imposed on the industry in exchange for what was now regarded as the inevitable taxpayer bailout.

But even as they put the finishing touches on the plan for the FDIC's new role in the thrift crisis, the three advisers were far from decided on other key components of the new bailout package. There were many odds and ends to resolve, and some of these points would not be decided until a few hours before the president unveiled the plan. Until then many different possibilities were considered live options.

One in particular had a lasting effect on how the plan played out in Congress. It was the idea, variously ascribed to Darman, the incoming director of the OMB, to Glauber, and to Mullins, of forcing customers of banks and thrifts to pay a large part of the multibillion-dollar rescue through a tax on deposits.

Darman was suspected of originating the idea because he had often boasted that the Reagan administration had raised taxes several times (mostly through fees) and gotten away with it. During the Reagan years taxes had been increased, for example, on Social Security and long-distance telephone calls, hikes that offset the overall tax rate reduction in 1986. But once again it fell to Glauber and Mullins to do the dirty work.

They had to sell the idea to Congress.

Intellectually the proposal made sense. Tax the people who were using the service—namely, deposit insurance—and who had, given the extent of thrift and bank failures, been underpaying for decades.

Politically the suggestion was the kiss of death.

Word leaked out within hours of Mullins's describing the proposal behind closed doors on Capitol Hill. A story on the front page of the *Washington Post* on January 25, 1989, proved to be the first major embarrassment for the new administration.

Seidman was quoted by the *Post* as opposing the fee on deposit idea. "It's the reverse toaster theory," he said. "Instead of the bank giving you a toaster when you make a deposit, you give them one."

Soon the proposal became known as the reverse toaster idea, a tax disguised as a fee. The White House chief of staff, John Sununu, tried to argue that the fee was not a tax, that Bush was not violating his no-new-tax pledge, but the fallout came swift and furious.

"Taxing bank customers to bail out the savings and loan industry would be a gross injustice," said Donald G. Ogilvie of the American Bankers Association.

"I think it is ironic that in the first week of the new administration, they came up with a new tax," said Ross Towne, president of the Perpetual Financial Corporation, then the largest thrift in the Washington, D.C., area. "I don't care what they call it, it's a tax. Whatever happened to all that 'Read my lips' stuff?"

Within weeks the proposal was dead politically, though Brady and Sununu bravely tried to defend it for a time. The issue did, however, sour Seidman's relationship with Sununu. (Shortly after the *Post* story appeared, Sununu told a group of White House staffers where Seidman should "stick" his toaster.)

More important, the fire storm for the first time drew the public's eye to the certainty that one way or another, the average working person would have to pay for the bailout. The day before the story broke, the mention of the S&L debacle put the average citizen to sleep. After the story broke, "Saturday

Night Live" did a skit on the S&L mess, and within weeks Phil Donahue devoted an entire show to it.

(The Donahue show provided a disturbing glimpse into some citizens' understanding of government. One man, outraged that taxpayers might have to foot the bill for fraud and mismanagement, was cheered when he asked, "Why can't the government pay for these debts instead of taxpayers?")

Four out of five of the nation's thrifts experienced net withdrawals in January, a phenomenon the bank board's chief economist, James Barth, attributed entirely to the fee on deposits proposal.

The affair dealt a setback to the new administration. But it also carried a silver lining. The raised public consciousness—and indignation—could be harnessed in lobbying Congress and taking on the league should it oppose the Bush bailout. Members of Congress normally willing to do the league's bidding would have to risk facing angry voters back home.

"It was great," Glauber said a few months after the controversy. "It was great because it got teed up what turned out to be the president's first major success. As it turned out, the publicity was helpful." Brady eventually gave Glauber and Mullins each a toaster to commemorate the occasion. Glauber kept his in his office. Mullins kept his at home, boasting that it was the first home appliance he had ever owned.

On a hot, sunny morning in the spring of 1989 crews of reporters were ushered from the press office in the West Wing of the White House into elevators and down corridors to an auditorium in the Old Executive Office Building. There President Bush stood before the television cameras to announce to the public what many in the Reagan and Bush administrations had known for years: A massive, multibillion-dollar problem existed in the thrift industry, and tax dollars would be needed to solve it. The president estimated that taxpayers would have to pay $40 billion, a number even his aides knew was probably woefully low.

If the government could write a check today, Bush said, the cost would be $90 billion. About $50 billion of the money would come from the sale of assets from failed thrifts and from premiums and other fees charged to S&Ls. The rest would have to come from the Treasury. But, Bush insisted, the maximum taxpayer exposure would be $40 billion.

"Nothing is without pain," Bush said of the plan, referring reporters' technical questions about how the plan would work to Brady, Glauber, and others at the Treasury, who were to make details available after the press conference. (In fact, few accurate details on how the financing would work were released. The Treasury referred many questions to the OMB, whose officials punted them back, and so on.)

312

As unveiled by the president, the plan included a complicated financing mechanism that funded the portion of the cleanup not paid for with tax dollars by using thirty-year notes, the principal of which would in theory be repaid by the thrift industry. Taxpayers would pay the interest on the notes. The plan also called for a revamping of the Federal Home Loan Bank System that would split the supervisory functions of the regional Federal Home Loan Banks from their credit function and place the FSLIC under the jurisdiction of the FDIC, whose chairman would then oversee two deposit insurance funds, one for banks and one for thrifts. The bank board would be abolished. A new unit of the Treasury would oversee the day-to-day regulation of the thrift industry.

In addition, thrifts no longer would be able to use bogus accounting; the industry would have to adhere to more standard bookkeeping rules. Most important of all, within three years thrifts would have to boost their net worth—their cushion against losses—to levels no less strict than those required of commercial banks.

Finally, President Bush said, his plan would call for tough law enforcement to put the crooks who had looted S&Ls in jail.

The president underscored his hope that Congress would put passage of the proposed cleanup package on a fast track so that it could be completed and signed into law within months. In the meantime, the two hundred sickest thrifts would would be taken over by the FDIC, which would manage and run the institutions until Congress provided more money to shut or sell them.

Questioned whether he shared some of the blame for the actions taken during the Reagan administration to deregulate the thrift industry, President Bush said, "I'm not inclined to go into any personal blame, simply to say that we've got to solve this problem and we're on the path to doing that."

As the president stood talking at a lectern, seated behind him and to his left was a cadre of government officials that were to assist in implementing the plan. Seidman was among them. So were Brady and Attorney General Richard Thornburgh. And so was Wall.

As Bush talked on, several Treasury officials noted that Wall appeared ill at ease. He squirmed in his seat and appeared flushed. The officials thought they knew why. The president ended the press conference without ever mentioning Wall, let alone thanking him. A spokesman for Wall denied it at the time, but Treasury officials insist that Wall had expected—indeed, may have been promised by White House officials—that Bush would commend him for the job he had done.

But Wall was too controversial for Bush to do any such thing. The president left the room without a word for the bank board chairman. According to Treasury officials, Wall fumed. So Treasury Secretary Brady sent Wall a

313

letter several days later (it was actually written by Glauber and Mullins) thanking Wall "for all of your assistance to put the President's comprehensive FSLIC reform package in place in a timely and forthright fashion.

"The men and women of the Bank Board and the FSLIC deserve our thanks for their tireless efforts for the work they have done to bring some order to the S&L industry," it said.

"Under your continued leadership, I know we can move ahead together to put in place the most sweeping regulatory overhaul of the S&L system in fifty years with a single focus in mind: to better serve the American people. I thank you again for all your past efforts and look forward to working with you in the future to enact the President's program."

It was signed "Sincerely, Nick."

The faint praise irked Wall. It was taken as intended: a lukewarm tip of the hat. If Wall hadn't known before how far outside the inner circle he was, surely the letter told him. But according to Treasury officials, Wall, undaunted, penciled in how he thought the letter could be improved and sent it back to the Treasury. Brady never responded. A spokesman for Wall acknowledged that "some had hoped" the president would personally thank Wall. But he denies Wall "edited" Brady's letter and returned it.

There was a serious vulnerability in the administration's plan. A chorus of private-sector economists and leaders in Congress warned President Bush that he was underestimating the size of the thrift problem, an error that could have significant political consequences down the road. If the cost of the problem rose, so would the taxpayers' share of it. That could force the administration to revisit the thrift problem, an outcome that would keep the issue in the public eye.

Officials at the league's rival lobby group, the National Council of Savings Institutions, warned President Bush's aides that the thrift problem, in the words of one council official, "would come back to bite the president in the ass" if he didn't present a more realistic assessment of the total cost and the taxpayers' share of it. Better to get all the bad news out now rather than close to the next election, this group argued. Besides, honesty would work to the industry's advantage by making it obvious (if any doubt remained) that thrifts could not afford to pay the tab themselves.

Treasury officials held firm. They said the administration's numbers were as good a guess as anyone's. And they insisted that higher insurance premiums and higher capital standards—standards that promised to put many thrifts out of business—were the pound of flesh required before the industry would get any more of what it had been trying for a decade to get its hands on: tax dollars.

Within days, however, it became clear that President Bush, while exhibiting a great deal more frankness about the thrift crisis than he or President Reagan had in the past, still was painting a rosy picture indeed. In the immediate hours after the president's press conference his aides began filling in the plan's many details. Because the total cost of the bailout could not be added to the budget immediately and most of the money would have to be borrowed in future years, they explained, the plan would entail interest costs over the first ten years alone that would tack $36 billion onto the $90 billion tab. But even the projected $126 billion needed over ten years was based on extremely optimistic assumptions, including a prediction that interest rates would drop sharply, with three-month Treasury bills yielding 4.7 percent in 1991, compared with about 8.8 percent at the time the bailout was announced—a projection that few private-sector economists could endorse. (Rates did fall by the end of 1991 to the 4 percent range, but the drop was caused in large part by the severest recession in decades, one that raised the cost of the thrift cleanup by depressing real estate prices and pushing borderline institutions into insolvency.) The projected recovery from sales of repossessed property also seemed unrealistic. Indeed, Treasury officials simply refused to make public most of the economic assumptions they had used to arrive at the $126 billion figure.

Two weeks later Treasury Secretary Brady, in testimony before the Senate Banking Committee, again raised the administration's estimated cost of the cleanup, saying $157 billion, including interest, would be needed over the next ten years. Brady repeated his pledge that taxpayers would pay no more than $40 billion of the cost, with the rest of the money coming from the sale of repossessed assets or fees charged to the industry.

The Treasury refused to make public its thirty-year forecast of the bailout cost, even though the financing plan called for much of the money to be raised through long-term government-sponsored bonds. Thirty-year estimates from Republican and Democratic lawmakers put the figure at $300 billion or more.

A few days later OMB director Darman upped the estimated cost yet again, this time to $166 billion over ten years. But he also tacked ten extra years onto the time the government would take to repay the money borrowed for the cleanup, making it forty years instead of thirty and, in the process, adding billions of dollars in interest payments to the original plan. So much for the accuracy of the Harvard professors' painstaking forecast system.

There was much about President Bush's plan that the league opposed. Fearing the industry would lose its clout with regulators, it didn't want the existing regulatory mechanism dismantled. Nor did it favor the timetable mandated by the Bush plan for increasing net worth. Many borderline thrifts wouldn't make the three-year deadline, and that would lead to more failures and further erode the industry's clout.

Even before congressional debate on the plan began, the president's proposal caused the league grief. As the FDIC took over from the bank board in the management of ailing thrifts, Seidman issued a novel but obviously sensible order: When the government stepped in, a thrift could no longer spend tens of thousands of dollars on league membership fees. Wall and Gray had allowed sick thrifts to pay such fees, effectively contributing government funds to the league's struggle against efforts to impose greater discipline on the industry.

At first the league came out swinging. "Rather than staunch the bleeding, the administration proposal appears to open the wound even wider," league President Webber said.

And many of the league's objections to the Bush plan were shared by some old friends in Congress: Senator Riegle expressed a strong commitment to preserving a separate thrift industry dedicated to housing; Senator Garn opposed splitting the regulatory side of the bank board into a unit of the Treasury; Representative Annunzio argued for permitting thrifts to count goodwill as part of net worth.

But the league had lost perhaps its most reliable ally in Congress, Representative St Germain. He was to be replaced as chairman of the House Banking Committee by the next ranking Democrat, Representative Gonzalez, a populist by inclination and, in the eyes of some of his peers, an eccentric rambler by temperament under whose control, it was feared, the political discipline of the Banking Committee would disintegrate.

Gonzalez was a protégé of Wright Patman, the great Texas crusader who had himself chaired the House Banking Committee until unseated (with St Germain's help) by Henry Reuss. Almost immediately upon becoming chairman in January 1989, Gonzalez moved the oil painting of Patman from the back of the House Banking Committee hearing room (itself named for Patman) to the front wall, where Patman could look out and down over the crowd. The other portrait hanging in the front of the room, a window away, was of St Germain.

Gonzalez, unlike St Germain, believed both in the tradition of the House committee seniority system and in openness in government. He talks freely, sometimes endlessly, with reporters. Once, during a typical session with a reporter, before getting to the business of the thrift crisis, he took forty-five minutes to explain the circumstances surrounding one of the many pictures that sit among the political memorabilia cramming his office—a photo of a younger Gonzalez laughing in the Oval Office with President John F.

316

Kennedy and Vice President Lyndon B. Johnson. Gonzalez talked about his years of friendship with the two men, of Kennedy's assassination in Dallas, of a private moment he spent with a bloodstained Jackie Kennedy in the hospital afterward.

Gonzalez had waited twenty-seven years to rise to the top of the Banking Committee. Now the seventy-three-year-old legislator had a chance not just to voice his opinions but to be listened to. He was a promoter of housing, but not a friend of the thrift lobby. Gonzalez had opposed the 1982 Garn-St Germain Act, one of the few legislators to do so. He warned at the time that no good would come of allowing the industry to stray from its original purpose of providing housing.

Now he would run the committee. For Annunzio aide Prins, Gonzalez's ascendancy would be a nightmare—an honest man running the show, one who thought elected officials, not their staffs, should craft legislation. "Staffers should be on tap, not on top," was a favorite aphorism of Gonzalez.

Others simply feared that Gonzalez lacked the political wherewithal to keep the Banking Committee's fifty members from becoming factionalized and unruly. "Too often it seems that Henry has been more interested in making speeches quoting Cicero and Homer than in twisting arms and passing legislation," a congressional aide quipped. Gonzalez did indeed have a vast store of knowledge. The lawyer and former math teacher could, it seems, find connections among a host of seemingly unrelated subjects; sometimes a conversation with him could sound like James Joyce engaging in free association. As a GAO official noted, one could never be quite sure whether "Henry B." or "Gonzie," as the congressman is often called, is a genius or simply a touch crazed, or both.

And there was, some congressional aides thought, more than a tinge of prejudice toward people of Hispanic ancestry among those who opposed Gonzalez's ascendency.

On the Senate side the unknowns were equally great. In the House St Germain, widely considered among the sleaziest members of Congress, had been replaced by a man (for all his idiosyncrasies) of unquestioned rectitude. By contrast, in the Senate, William Proxmire, widely acknowledged to be among the straightest of shooters, was replaced as head of the Banking Committee by Senator Riegle, a former Republican who turned Democrat in 1973 while serving in the House. In the eyes of many lobbyists, Riegle's chairmanship shifted the sleaze factor to the Senate. The senator was, with D'Amato and Cranston (and to a lesser extent Garn), considered a best friend to the securities industry and other big financial company special interests. An intensely ambitious politician with eyes on the White House, he was widely thought to be driven by political expediency and his interest in campaign contributions.

In 1976, during Riegle's run for the Senate, he became mired in controversy over transcripts of taped conversations between him and a staff member with whom he became romantically involved. The *Detroit News* published the transcript of what it called "a torrid and tape-recorded extra-marital affair," prompting Riegle to complain that the newspaper was engaged in a smear campaign.

After the stock market crash of 1987, reporters for the *Detroit News* decided to see if the securities industry increased its political contributions to Riegle, who was up for reelection in the fall of 1988. A search of Riegle's records didn't turn up any increase, but it did disclose something curious: nearly $80,000 in contributions from Arizonans. The reporters were puzzled. Why was a Michigan senator getting so much money from Arizona? What was the connection?

At first, said one of the reporters, Michael Clements, "We didn't know what we had."

It turned out the dozens of names were tied together by one man: Charles Keating. Most were Keating employees or otherwise closely associated with him.

There was more. Thrift executives showed the *Detroit News* reporters an article in a thrift industry trade publication, *National Thrift News,* describing the two meetings between a group of senators and Ed Gray in early 1987 concerning regulators' handling of Keating's Lincoln Savings. Riegle had attended the second meeting.

During a two-hour interview in Riegle's office in early 1988, Riegle told the reporters he had no knowledge of the first meeting; he didn't mention his suggestion to Gray that the bank board chairman meet with the other senators. A few days later the *Detroit News* ran a story on the front page of its Sunday edition detailing the contributions from Keating and his associates, and the meetings the senators conducted on Keating's behalf. A week later, on March 7, 1988, Riegle returned Keating's contributions.

News of the potentially explosive meetings made the rounds of the thrift industry. But none of the nation's major newspapers followed up on the story. To Riegle's relief, the Keating story did not become a major issue.

Meanwhile, Riegle named the man who had run his campaign, Kevin Gottlieb, to be staff director of the Banking Committee. Gottlieb set the tone of Riegle's tenure in the eyes of many aides who worked with him. In contrast with the more open style favored by Proxmire and his staff, Riegle and Gottlieb thrived on control and secrecy. They ordered that no staff member but Gottlieb talk to reporters. Riegle's handling of the rescue package became a private event that left out Republican staffers—and, of course, the public. But Gottlieb had no control over the minority staffers, and many were more than happy to complain to reporters about the style of the committee's new chairman.

It wasn't just the change in heads of committees that worried the league. Many members of the Senate and House Banking Committees understood that the thrift mess could become an enormous political liability and resented the misinformation they had been spoon-fed over the years from the lobby group.

One month after President Bush's speech league Chairman Beeksma sat before the Senate Banking Committee to spell out the industry's objections to the president's plan. But instead of a hearing, the league got its ears slapped.

"If anyone has been irresponsible on this issue, it's been the U.S. league," said Senator Gramm. "I'm sure you all have lots of friends here, but less than you used to."

Richard Shelby (D-Ala.) was even more direct. "You have no credibility here today," he said.

Against that background, league President Webber realized that the lobbying styles of Hohlt and Freeman no longer would be effective. But many of the league's members still hadn't caught on, and they opposed Webber's strategy of keeping a low profile and lobbying on a grass-roots level through the state leagues and, less visibly, by hiring law firm lobbyists in Washington.

In the end the league tried to cover all its bases. Shortly after President Bush proposed his cleanup plan, Webber and a half dozen other league officials and S&L executives visited Representative Annunzio and his aide Prins. The league representatives assumed that Annunzio and Prins would be instrumental in shaping the legislation, according to a top-level league official who attended the meeting.

Annunzio and Prins evidently shared that assumption, telling their visitors not to worry. "They would control the legislative process in the House. They were adamant they would take control," according to the participant. Annunzio "said don't overreact to the Bush plan. Remember 'the President sends up a bill and we rewrite it.' He said not to overreact to the negatives. He said, 'We will take care of these issues.' He told us not to worry."

(Annunzio called that account "a rotten lie," contending he told the league officials that he was just one vote and that "they better get their act together. I told them they were in deep trouble.")

In the meantime, Webber decided to come out in favor of the Bush plan in general, while pushing to modify key parts of it, especially the provisions on goodwill and other capital questions. But, Webber vowed, the league would speak with one voice and no longer say one thing in public and another in private. Hadn't the league admitted just prior to Bush's February announcement, despite the lobby group's years of denial, that tax dollars would be necessary?

But even as Webber spoke, league lobbyist Hohlt was shopping around a plan that several top league officials had commissioned privately from the investment banking firm of Shearson Lehman Hutton. The plan was similar to Bush's in its dependency on tax dollars for the big fix, but as might be expected, it kept the existing thrift regulatory structure in place.

Specifically it called for keeping the bank board's day-to-day oversight functions out of the Treasury. Hohlt and several other league officials pushed the alternative plan hard, though quietly, behind the scenes. In the end the pressure for real reform proved too great, and the Shearson plan died a quiet death. (Months later Webber acknowledged that he had known about the Shearson plan and Hohlt's role in lobbying for it. He said, however, that the president's proposal had not been compromised. Hohlt and the others were acting privately, Webber explained, not as official league spokesmen.)

The Senate acted first, considering a version of the legislation drafted by Riegle that closely matched the Bush bill. On April 19, 1989, just a little over two months after President Bush spoke to the public about the crisis, the Senate passed its thrift rescue package by a vote of 91–8. (Most of the negative votes came from senators such as Bill Bradley [D-N.J.] who said they opposed forcing taxpayers to pay for such a large chunk of the cleanup.)

The measure included tougher net worth, or capital, standards than even the White House had asked for. They were the brainchild of Howard Metzenbaum (D-Ohio), a millionaire liberal, former Cleveland businessman, and now moral gadfly of the Senate, who late on a Wednesday evening threatened to hold up a final vote on the bailout package until Friday unless stricter net worth rules were adopted. The postponement would have delayed an eleven-day Senate vacation that was supposed to start at sundown Wednesday.

Metzenbaum single-handedly succeeded in pressuring the chamber to require that thrifts have at least 1.5 percent of their assets in cash or near-cash investments—so-called tangible net worth—by 1991. His success was a significant blow to the thrift industry. Under the original Bush plan, thrifts could have counted what many regarded as bogus capital—the "supervisory goodwill" that had been concocted by the Pratt bank board early in the decade—toward the tougher net worth requirement.

The White House hailed Metzenbaum's action, though it was no small embarrassment that a Democratic liberal had one-upped the president in imposing safer business standards on S&Ls.

But Riegle and Bob Graham were unsuccessful in pushing another reform, which would have put the entire bailout tab on the budget, as opposed to a part-on/part-off scheme the White House favored.

In addition to the reforms President Bush had requested during his news conference earlier in the year, the Senate bill contained a key provision that the White House pushed but didn't talk much about: making Danny Wall the new chairman of the Treasury unit that would replace the bank board and doing so without requiring that he be reconfirmed by the Senate. The White House's support for the provision reportedly was an attempt to appease Jake Garn.

The political dynamic was different in the House, where the Democratic leaders labored under an ethics cloud because of their widely publicized ties to the S&L industry. By late spring both the Speaker of the House, Jim Wright of Texas, and the majority whip, Tony Coehlo of California, were forced to resign while the president's proposal was pending.

For months the House Ethics Committee had been investigating Wright, in large part because of his intervention on behalf of the Texas thrift industry. The committee took up the investigation halfheartedly, dragooned into it by Newt Gingrich (R-Ga.). Gingrich constantly sniped at the Democrats' record on thrifts despite warnings by GOP consultants such as Ed Rollins that doing so would backfire because Republicans also had plenty of S&L skeletons in their closet.

But Gingrich persisted, sending reporters packets of newspaper clippings that he entitled "The Ethics Mess in the House: Editorials from around the United States."

His campaign ultimately paid off. The Ethics Committee's outside counsel, Richard Phelan, concluded that Wright had broken House rules in his dealings on behalf of thrift executives.

Coincidentally, on May 4, the *Washington Post* ran an extraordinary story about Wright aide John Mack. The story chronicled how Mack, at age nineteen, while working in a discount import store in Virginia, attacked a twenty-year-old college student named Pamela Small in the store. He grabbed a hammer that he slammed repeatedly into her skull, exposing it in five places, and he stabbed her five times in the chest with a steak knife and then slashed her several times across the throat. "Bundling her limp body into the car she had left parked out front, he drove around for a while, then left the vehicle in an alley behind the store, the keys in the ignition. Then he went to the movies," the *Post* story read.

Miraculously Small regained consciousness eight hours later and somehow drove herself to a gas station, where an attendant called for help. Mack was arrested. He pleaded guilty to malicious wounding and was sentenced to fifteen years in the Virginia State Penitentiary, though seven years of the sentence were suspended. But he never spent any time at the penitentiary. Instead he served less than twenty-seven months in what the *Post* called "the more civilized confines" of the Fairfax County Jail.

Mack attributed the attack to his having been under unusual stress from long workweeks and a failing marriage. He told a psychiatrist who examined him a year after the attack that he felt he had "reacted in a way in which any man would perhaps react under similar circumstances."

When Mack got out, Wright, whose daughter was married to Mack's brother, gave Mack a job in his congressional office. Wright had offered Mack the position before he was sentenced, a fact Mack's attorney "pointed out repeatedly to the sentencing judge," according to the *Post*. The letters Wright wrote at the time on Mack's behalf are, in accordance with Virginia law, sealed from the public.

By May 1989, when the story broke in the *Post* (the *Fort Worth Star-Telegram* had printed Small's story in 1987 but without using her name), Mack was executive director of the congressional Democratic Steering and Policy Committee. He also had become Wright's right-hand man, a role that gained in influence when Wright became Speaker.

Small had recovered and become an executive in the Washington office of a major corporation. Increasingly her job required she spend time on Capitol Hill, in hearings and attending receptions. Increasingly she found excuses not to go, telling the *Post* she had no wish to bump into Mack.

Shortly after the story ran in the *Post,* Mack resigned.

But the story was an enormous embarrassment for Wright. It gave added prominence and, because of its gory details, greater circulation to Wright's battle with the House Ethics Committee. By the end of May, with the Speaker's political support eroding steadily, Wright gave a teary-eyed speach announcing he would step down from the House.

Coelho's ethical problems ended more swiftly—and more gracefully. Shortly after revelations were published in the *Washington Post* concerning Coelho's close ties with the junk bond and thrift industries, he announced he would resign on June 15, after twenty-four years on Capitol Hill, first as an aide and then as a young congressman who quickly rose to power and prominence.

His departure defused calls for an investigation into an unusual $100,000 high-risk, high-yield junk bond investment he had made in 1986 with the help of Thomas Spiegel, a thrift executive in Beverly Hills whose S&L was one of the largest dealers in junk bonds through Drexel Burnham Lambert and Michael Milken. Drexel, which went bankrupt in 1990, and Milken, who that same year pleaded guilty in the largest Wall Street securities fraud case ever brought against a trader, both made large contributions to the Democratic Congressional Campaign Committee in 1985 and 1986.

Spiegel lent Coelho $50,000 to buy the bonds, which Coelho failed to disclose on his finance forms. After holding the bonds for less than six months, Coelho made a profit of $6,882.

It didn't help him politically that Coelho was close to Wright's aide John Mack. Coelho is godfather to Mack's children, the two men are partners in a software business in California, and Coelho arranged for Mack to receive speaking fees from special-interest groups in California. When the story of Mack's attack on Pamela Small was reported in the *Post,* Coelho defended Mack, saying he had paid his debt to society.

Thanks in part to these political disasters, Democrats in the House became firm backers of reform as the thrift industry tried to modify the president's proposed legislation. Republicans labored under no such constraints and, to the embarrassment of the White House, were the principal source of resistance in the House to the president's rescue plan—and the principal sponsors of the league's agenda.

In April, as Wright's ethical problems were coming to a head, a House Banking Committee subcommittee chaired by Annunzio, which had first crack at modifying the Bush bill, voted to require the same net worth requirements as had the Senate—1.5 percent of assets in cash or near-cash holdings. At the same time, however, the subcommittee loosened rules governing the use of goodwill for other net worth requirements, generally watering down the new standards. But this change met with opposition in the full committee, where Gonzalez led the charge to toughen standards even further than the Senate had.

Annunzio and Prins tried to head off the attack by circulating a letter to members listing the thrifts in their states that would be hurt by the tougher rules. The atmosphere became tense. Fellow Democrats on the committee accused Prins of staging a meeting at which he tried to make it appear that Gonzalez had blessed a compromise when the chairman had not. At the same time Prins told members that they could be on the conference committee if they voted his way—a promise it was not his to make.

A compromise eventually was reached, thanks to Representative Bruce Vento (D-Minn.), who proposed toughening the capital standards and eliminating the use of goodwill by the end of 1994—far shorter than the twenty-five or thirty years the thrift industry favored. But the Vento amendment would make it slightly harder for regulators to shut a thrift just because it didn't meet net worth rules.

The committee voted 36–15 for the Vento package, with only four Democrats opposing it (Annunzio among them), and Republicans split 9–11.

But as it emerged from the committee, the bill was not an exercise in pure reform. Walter Fauntroy, the delegate from the District of Columbia and an ordained minister, at one point had asked the committee to pray with him for the "strength to resist special interests." The prayers went unheeded. Chemical Bank, First Interstate, and other likely suspects succeeded in getting special provisions benefiting themselves placed in the bill. Even Gonzalez succumbed, putting in language to help a bank in his hometown of San Antonio.

And on the question of how to treat the accounting device of goodwill, the league wasn't finished yet. Because the bill contained provisions affecting the federal budget and the Justice Department, it had to go through several other House committees, and in each the league had lined up allies to undo the tougher capital rules.

The issue was a crucial one to the league. Goodwill amounted to more than half—$22 billion—of the thrift industry's $43 billion in net worth. Another $20 billion of net worth came from government aid, most of it provided by bank board Chairman Wall in 1988. In short, thrifts as a group had only $1 billion in private capital to back the industry's $1 trillion in deposits.

Financier Warren E. Buffett, a widely respected billionaire and investor from Nebraska, was so offended at the league's lobbying efforts against tougher capital and other standards that at the end of May he withdrew his thrift, the Mutual Savings and Loan Association of Pasadena, from the league, calling the group "disgraceful."

Charles T. Munger, Mutual's chairman, said in a letter explaining the withdrawal that "the League responds to the savings and loan mess as Exxon would have responded to the oil spill from the *Valdez* if it had insisted thereafter on liberal use of whiskey by tanker captains." Munger blamed the league for "constant and successful" lobbying over many years that prevented government regulators from cracking down on S&Ls run by "crooks and fools" and that persuaded regulators to use "Mickey Mouse" accounting. "It is not unfair to liken the situation now facing Congress to cancer and to liken the League to a significant carcinogenic agent," he said.

Largely on the strength of the reputations of Buffett and Munger and their use of colorful language, every major newspaper ran the story of Mutual's withdrawal. It was one more blow to the league's lobbying efforts. Lawmakers were becoming worried. Could a vote for the league come back to haunt them?

But the league still had friends in high places.

In the Rules Committee, which would decide if the net worth issue could be decided on the floor of the House, that was obvious. Dozens of lobbyists stood outside the committee's tiny hearing room when the procedural question came to a head. As most were being told they couldn't get in, two lobbyists were ushered through a side door and offered a pair of the thirty-eight seats in the room. The two were from the league and from the largest commercial banking lobby, the American Bankers Association. The seat for league lobbyist Coleman O'Brien was provided by Republicans on the committee. The ABA's seat came compliments of John Joseph ("Joe") Moakley (D-Mass.), who had just taken over as Rules Committee chairman. (In more bad timing for the league, the former chairman, Representative Claude Pepper [D-Fla.], widely expected to be sympathetic to the league, had died.)

And behind the desks where the thirteen elected officials on the committee sat, in the small space reserved in theory only for their staffs, sat Theodore H. Roberts, head of Talman Savings, the largest thrift in Chicago and a significant holder of goodwill. His seat also came compliments of the Republicans, according to staff.

Meanwhile, aides to several legislators, including Chalmers Wylie, the ranking Republican on the House Banking Committee, were forced to stand. And an aide to Toby Roth (R-Wis.) was ordered out of the hearing room altogether because of crowding.

At issue was whether a Republican-led initiative, spearheaded by Henry Hyde (R-Ill.), to weaken capital rules could be offered as an amendment when the full House voted on the Bush bailout package. The league was sure it could win on the floor what it had lost in the Banking Committee. The Rules Committee voted to allow the proposal of fifteen select amendments on the floor, and Hyde's was among them.

The White House cringed. Here its reform package was being sabotaged by members of its own party.

To avoid an embarrassing defeat, President Bush personally summoned Hyde, House Minority Leader Robert Michel of Illinois, and other Republican leaders to the White House for some arm twisting. The administration could not ask taxpayers to pay for the bailout without imposing discipline on the industry, Bush told them.

Reluctantly the Republican leadership gave in. Michel and Gingrich, Wright's nemesis, agreed to take up the cause. On June 15, as the House considered the bailout bill, Hyde's amendment was defeated, with many of his former Republican allies speaking in favor of weaker rules but then voting for the tougher standards, arguing they had to stick with the president. Hyde described the approach as "the perfumed ice-pick" and shook his head in disgust at his defeat.

To the industry, it was the public attention paid to the net worth issue that spelled defeat. "The press destroyed us. We were treated like fast-talking Texas cowboys," said Washington lawyer Douglas Faucette, the industry's chief lobbyist on the goodwill issue. "We got killed."

And there was more bad news for the industry, this time delivered (to the White House's relief) by a Republican, Jim Leach, though with the aggressive backing of Gonzalez. Leach offered an amendment to delete most of the special-interest provisions from the legislation. Even he was stunned when it passed by an overwhelming 412–7 vote. Only one special-interest provision remained untouched: Lobbyists for oil billionaire Robert Bass, who had purchased the nation's largest troubled thrift in one of Wall's 1988 deals, helped defeat a provision that might have opened for reconsideration the generous terms the bank board had given Bass and others when they bought S&Ls, in 1988.

There were several big differences between the House bill and its counterpart in the Senate. The House bill banned thrift investments in junk bonds. The Senate version—at the insistence of traditional securities backers Riegle and Garn—permitted such investments if limited to 11 percent of a thrift's portfolio. It also allowed Wall automatically to remain as the nation's chief thrift regulator, no matter what the bank board's successor agency would be called. The House bill required that Wall be reappointed by the president and reconfirmed by the Senate.

And the House bill contained one provision that likely would elicit a veto threat from President Bush: It put the entire cost of the bailout on the budget but exempted it from the Gramm-Rudman budget limits. The White House wanted to keep S&L spending largely off the budget and not fiddle with Gramm-Rudman.

All in all, however, the administration got much that it wanted from the House and, in the case of capital requirements, even more than it originally pushed for. And all because of an improbable alliance between a patrician Republican, George Bush, and a populist Democrat, Henry Gonzalez. About the only thing the two men had in common before the thrift crisis was that both call Texas home. Now they were allies against many in Bush's own party. But, as usual on banking legislation, everyone knew where the final deals would be worked out: the conference committee.

Meanwhile, according to staff at the bank board, as the House and Senate debated the Bush plan, the agency's efforts became concentrated on one goal: preserving Wall's job. To that end the board had issued a press release in late March 1989, stating that the industry's net worth had risen to a record high of $46.2 billion. But the number included at least $20 billion in federal subsidies, and even the board's economist, James Barth, conceded a more accurate picture would be given by subtracting the government aid.

The ploy angered members of Congress. "The present bank board—particularly its chairman, Danny Wall—seems incapable of presenting a straightforward story to the American public," said Gonzalez. "The Congress and the public don't need sugarcoated news releases distorting the numbers. We need hard numbers—the truth."

Even with massive government aid, the industry continued to bleed. In the last three months of 1988 it lost $2.3 billion including the aid, $2.7 billion not including it. It was cold comfort that the red ink had declined from the $4 billion the industry had lost during the last three months of 1987. It was, as one thrift industry economist, Martin A. Regalia, put it, "good news of a very modest sort." Very modest.

In 1981 and 1982 the thrift industry's losses were operating losses, essentially the difference between the low rates of return it was earning on mortgage loans and the higher rates it had to pay depositors during a period of rising prices. By 1988, when the industry lost a record $12 billion, the losses stemmed from soured loans. This was bad loan underwriting, not interest rate risk. In 1980 thrifts' assets were 67 percent in home loans. In 1988 mortgages had declined to 39 percent of the industry's portfolio.

At the beginning of the decade the industry had assets of roughly $600 billion. By the time Wall was sworn in, the assets had nearly doubled to more than $1 trillion. But so did the problems. What might have cost $40 billion to solve in the early 1980s had now grown to three or four times that amount.

Wall appeared to accelerate his campaign in the days before the conference committee convened. In June he told reporters that he thought it would be unwise to change the nation's chief S&L regulator in the middle of a crisis. A week later—as Gonzalez was preparing a highly critical report for the conference committee on Wall's performance since becoming chairman in mid-1987—Wall called a press conference at which he declared that he thought he should be allowed to retain his job automatically.

37

Junk, Wall, and More Accounting Tricks

As the conference committee convened in early July, Gonzalez wanted to deal with all the issues in public. He also sought the widest possible participation from his fellow representatives. He therefore selected ninety-four of them to sit at the bargaining table, including all fifty-one members of the House Banking Committee and representatives of several other committees whose jurisdictions would be touched by the legislation, including Ways and Means, Government Operations, Judiciary, and Rules.

Riegle favored doing as little as possible in public. To the chagrin of several of the twenty-one members of the Senate Banking Committee, Riegle decided that only the committee's top three Democrats—Riegle, Cranston, and Paul S. Sarbanes (Md.)—and top two Republicans—Garn and Heinz—would square off with the crowd from the House. Also representing the Senate would be three members of the Finance Committee.

On the first day of the conference, conferees agreed to break up the bank board, give its regulatory duties to an agency inside the Treasury to be called the Office of Thrift Supervision, and transfer its insurance functions to the FDIC. (The FDIC would manage two deposit insurance funds whose money would in theory be kept separate: the Bank Insurance Fund [BIF] for commercial banks and the Savings Association Insurance Fund [SAIF].) The conferees also agreed to create a new agency, the Resolution Trust Corporation, to manage and sell assets the government inherited from failed thrifts—assets that by some estimates would total as much as $400 billion. FADA, the quasi-government agency that had done so poorly in disposing of assets, would be folded into the RTC.

The Federal Home Loan Banks, it was decided, would remain, but they would be separated from the regulatory field operations of the new thrift supervision agency. The regional banks would serve only to raise money at cheap government rates and lend it to institutions making home loans; now, however, commercial banks as well as thrifts would have access to the funds, as long as the money was put into mortgages.

The conferees also agreed to toughen penalties for those who defraud financial institutions, raising to $1 million the maximum fine that could be imposed per person, per day, per violation. And they decided to curb the use of brokered funds by giving federal regulators the right to bar any troubled thrift from using such funding.

Finally, the conferees agreed to strike out the myriad special-interest provisions that had been tucked into the Senate bill to benefit a host of companies, including the Ford Motor Company, Citicorp, Sears, and Merrill Lynch.

One of these provisions, pushed by the American International Group, an insurance company that is the largest provider of liability insurance to officers and directors of thrifts, would have limited the government's ability to collect on the insurance when officers and directors are held responsible for causing S&Ls to fail. Another, pushed by Senator D'Amato, would have exempted two giant bank holding companies, Chemical of New York and First Interstate of Los Angeles, from having to come to the financial aid of the subsidiaries of troubled banks the two had purchased in Texas. Yet another, sponsored by Senator Tim Wirth (D-Colo.), would have made it easier for state-chartered thrifts to continue to invest in junk bonds. The provisions seemed absurd when they were opened to public examination, as happened when congressional aides leaked a list of the special interest items.

When the conferees next convened, Riegle dropped a bomb.

Although in Gonzalez's mind the two sides had agreed to tackle each item of contention one by one, no matter how cumbersome and lengthy the process, Riegle presented the House with a package listing the issues on which the senators would accept the House version and those issues on which they demanded that the House accede to the Senate.

In the package the senators suggested the conferees combine the toughest capital standards of both bills. But they also proposed that the bailout financing be kept off the budget, that Wall be allowed to run the new thrift agency without having to be reconfirmed, and that a compromise be struck on thrift investment in junk bonds, which the House bill banned but which the senators believed should be permitted, though on a limited scale.

At first Gonzalez balked, angry at the change in approach. But after sleeping on it, he set the House staff to drafting a response to the senators' proposals. At this point, in a major victory for Riegle, the conference negotiations moved behind closed doors and stayed there until a final compromise was reached two weeks later.

It went without saying that the tougher capital standards would be adopted. For weeks the House and Senate had been falling over each other to see who could adopt the stricter measures. The other bones of contention were far harder to resolve: junk bonds, Wall's job, and whether the multi-billion-dollar cleanup would be on budget.

The fight for junk bonds was led by Senator Garn, who argued the point as a true free marketer. No one has lost any money in junk bonds, he said, so why are we restricting investment in something that hasn't caused harm?

The counterargument was pushed in the House by a fellow Republican, Jim Leach, who pointed out that it is better to stop risky practices before they cost taxpayers money.

Garn argued his position with his usual vigor and appeal to ideals of fairness and logic. But observers from Wall Street familiar with the junk bond industry thought that his judgment may have been clouded by that industry's heavy financial support of the Garn Institute of Finance at the senator's alma mater, the University of Utah.

In 1986, three years after stepping down as bank board chairman to join Merrill Lynch, Dick Pratt had created the Garn Institute, where he subsequently served as chairman. He hatched the idea, got Garn's approval, and then began to solicit funds for a tax-free "institute of financial studies." There were four membership categories, broken down by contribution, starting with a minimum of $1,000 and going up to the highest one, "Founding Member," for those who gave $100,000 or more. Among other benefits, members would be able to "take part in one-on-one discussions with government policy-makers," including, of course, Garn himself. Many lobbyists said they thought that the Garn Institute was a "shakedown" for money to build a shrine to the senator, whose ego was known to be robust. Many gave anyway, though reluctantly, figuring they should do everything possible to keep on Garn's good side.

The names of major contributors to the institute became a who's who of the troubled thrift and junk bond industries, as well as those lawyers and securities firms that benefited from S&L woes. In 1988, at the height of the unfolding thrift fiasco, among the more than a dozen institutions that donated $100,000 or more to the tax-exempt organization were:

- CenTrust Savings Bank of Miami, which failed in 1990 at a cost to taxpayers of an estimated $2 billion amid government allegations that its chief executive, David Paul, wasted depositor money on excesses that included $29 million for fine art, $1.4 million a year for a corporate jet, and $43,000 for limousines. (Paul paid himself $16 million a year in salary and bonuses, according to suits filed by federal thrift regulators. Among other things, he used CenTrust's insured deposits for a $7 million yacht, on which he installed gold nails and so much marble that some doubted it could stay afloat.) CenTrust was a major junk bond buyer, tied heavily to deals with Drexel Burnham Lambert.

- Columbia Savings of Beverly Hills and the Imperial Corporation of America in San Diego, both of which invested heavily in junk bonds and failed in 1989 and 1990 respectively. (In addition, Imperial was plagued by gross mismanagement, such as an executive decision to lend millions of dollars to a nonexistent car dealer, an arrangement that enabled con men to run off with the thrift's money.)

Columbia chief executive Thomas Spiegel, who had helped Representative Coelho buy his $100,000 junk bond, was forced out of the company by regulators in December 1989. In July 1990 thrift regulators filed a civil suit against Spiegel seeking to recover $24 million to replace depositor funds the government claims he misused for, among other things, corporate jets, three vacation condominiums, a $3 million bonus, wine-tasting classes, and Uzi submachine guns. In addition to contributions to the Garn Institute, Spiegel was a heavy donor to the Ronald Reagan Presidential Foundation.

- Merrill Lynch, a major dealer in junk bonds and, in addition, a major player in the mortgage-backed securities industry and in brokered deposits.

- Drexel Burnham Lambert. Government securities lawyers estimate that Michael Milken obtained at least 10 percent of the $300 billion he traded in junk bonds from thrifts such as CenTrust, Columbia, Imperial, and Lincoln.

- Fried, Frank, Harris, Shriver & Jacobson, the law firm where the bank board's chief counsel under Pratt, Tom Vartanian, was a partner. Vartanian was vice-chairman of the Garn Institute.

- Merabank, the largest savings institution in Arizona, which federal regulators seized in January 1990, at a cost to taxpayers of at least $388 million. At the end of 1988 under Wall's Southwest Plan, Merabank received $670 million in federal aid to take three troubled thrifts off the government's hands. When Merabank failed, the thrifts once again reverted to government control, meaning they had failed for a second time in a little over twelve months.

- Federal Home Loan Mortgage Corporation. The corporation's board of directors was the bank board, and its chairman Wall.

- Great Western Bank of Beverly Hills and Home Federal Savings and

Loan of San Diego, two of the biggest and most influential of the California thrifts.

There were eight contributors of $25,000 to $99,999, the second-highest level of sponsorship. They included:

- AmeriFirst Bank, one of Miami's largest thrifts, beset by troubled real estate loans that forced a federal take-over. Shareholders sued the thrift and its erstwhile chairman, Thomas Bomar, a former bank board chairman and a personal friend of Wall and of league lobbyist Hohlt, in 1989 as disclosures of loan losses at AmeriFirst grew. The shareholders charged that Bomar, as AmeriFirst's top executive, misled investors by hiding bad real estate loans and even, in one case, constructing a complex transaction to make a failed investment in a subsidiary of the thrift look like a loan to a third party.

  The institution lost $112 million in 1989. Its stock fell from $18.50 a share in January 1989 to less than $3 a share a year later. In January 1990 the thrift announced it would pay $4.5 million to settle four shareholder class actions filed against it and the former management. But one month after the announced settlement, AmeriFirst filed its own suit against Bomar, other top officials, and auditors, charging fraud and mismanagement and seeking $75 million in damages for allegedly unsafe and unsound lending practices. The thrift failed in 1991, and the government continued the civil suit against former management. Bomar denies any wrongdoing.
- Lincoln Savings and Loan, the California thrift owned by Charles Keating.
- Shearson Lehman Hutton, the investment banking unit of American Express, also a major trader in junk bonds.
- The U.S. League of Savings Institutions.

The list of those who contributed more than $1,000 but less than $5,000 includes the accounting firm of Arthur Young (since merged with Ernst and Whinney to become Ernst & Young) which gave clean audit opinions to several major thrifts—Vernon and Lincoln, for example—that then failed at significant cost to taxpayers. This category also includes Great American, the thrift run by President Reagan's friend Gordon Luce, which, largely because of bad real estate investments in Arizona, was seized by the government in 1991. Many other lobby groups gave $500 or so to the institute, just so they wouldn't be left out.

Garn knew that some donors expected to get something in return. Lawrence Miller, who ran Lyons Savings and Loan in Illinois until 1986, when federal regulators kicked him out but let his wife assume the reins, even approached Garn at a black-tie Garn Institute fund-raising dinner to remind the senator of his thrift's contribution, a reminder Garn says he interpreted as a plea for help in warding off regulators who had begun to bear down on the thrift. (A $6,000 contribution from Lyons was listed in the institute's records as coming from the FSLIC. The reason: The thrift's commitment for the contribution was fulfilled after the thrift was taken over by the government, which occurred shortly after Miller's wife took over. When asked about the appropriateness of a contribution from a failed thrift, Wall replied, "So?")

Gonzalez and other Democrats have wondered aloud if Wall might have handled Lincoln, Centrust, Columbia, and other heavy investors in junk bonds gingerly because, among other things, of their contributions to the Garn Institute.

The institute held symposia on banking, usually in posh, expensive settings, such as Key Largo, and often with gala dinners. (Goldman Sachs executive John Oros, who served on the institute's board of trustees, says that in advance of the institute's Florida meeting in the winter of 1989, he advised Wall not to attend, given the enormity of the S&L bailout's cost to taxpayers. The trip, Oros explained, might not generate good publicity for Wall. Wall did not attend.)

Garn had other ties to the junk bond industry. He publicly defended Pratt's interpretation of the 1982 Garn-St Germain Act as allowing federally chartered thrifts to invest as much as 11 percent of their holdings in junk bonds—although in late 1989, when the junk bond market soured and became a major factor in the demise of several thrifts, including several major contributors to the Garn Institute, the senator's staff quietly backed away from defending that interpretation.

But during the conference committee meeting in July 1989, Garn was among the staunchest supporters of allowing thrifts to continue investing in junk bonds. And he wasn't alone. Riegle, who had ties to Lincoln and other thrifts heavily involved with junk bonds, also defended the junk bond provision in the original version of the bill passed by the Senate.

From the first day of the conference Garn and Gonzalez locked horns over whether Wall deserved to keep his job. Wall should be allowed to complete the four-year term he had begun in mid-1987, Garn argued. After all, Wall didn't create the problem. He inherited it when he took over from Gray. Garn wasn't alone in this position. Riegle pushed against confirmation hearings for

Wall, but congressional and administration staffers said Cranston in particular didn't want Wall to have to be confirmed as head of the OTS because Senate hearings might focus attention on Lincoln, its problems, and actions by the Keating Five.

Gonzalez countered by arguing that Wall had bungled the job by consistently underestimating the size of the S&L problem and denying the need for taxpayer funds to clean up the industry. Wall inherited a mess, Gonzalez agreed, but he made it an even bigger, far costlier mess through his secret deal making and by failing to perform his single most important duty: keeping Congress informed. If the president wanted Wall, Gonzalez concluded, he should renominate the bank board chief and subject him to the confirmation process, in which his performance could be examined.

"President [Bush] says, 'I don't want anything like this to ever happen again. My bill's going to ensure it. I don't want anybody that had anything to do with this to be in there,' " said Gonzalez, paraphrasing the president's February remarks. "And yet, he grandfathers Danny Wall."

Gonzalez's position was expressed in the report accompanying the House Banking Committee's version of the bailout legislation, which declared, "In the opinion of the committee, the current chairman of the Bank Board has not effectively executed the responsibilities of the position and has failed to assist Congress in its effort to examine the current crisis in the savings and loan industry."

During the conference Senator Graham, the Democrat from Florida, took up the House position in a letter to Riegle dated June 28, 1989. Wall's "representations contributed to the atmosphere of passivity which pervaded the Administration in late '88," Graham wrote, adding a passage from a May 1, 1989, *Wall Street Journal* article that read: " 'We did not cry fire in a crowded theater, of that we're guilty,' Mr. Wall said. He added, however, that Congress and the White House weren't about to deal with the crisis in an election year. 'They gave us a Band-Aid and said take care of it until 1989. That's what we did.' " The quote from Wall is an apparent reference to the $10.8 billion bailout package passed in August 1987.

To Graham and to the majority on the House Banking Committee, the analogy to Justice Holmes's famous dictum on free speech was strikingly inappropriate. One shouldn't cry "fire" in a crowded threater unless there really is a fire. Wall failed to sound the alarm when the industry was being consumed.

But to others, Wall's explanation confirmed the obvious: He was a good soldier and thought he had no choice but to work with what the politicians at the White House and in Congress gave him.

During the conference committee's deliberations Garn said he would accept Wall's having to be reconfirmed if the FDIC's Seidman also had to be reconfirmed. Gonzalez called Garn's bluff; while pointing out that Seidman's agency was not being dissolved and re-created by legislation as Wall's was, Gonzalez nevertheless tentatively agreed to the compromise. Garn quickly backed away from the idea. The White House, meanwhile, sided with Garn in the dispute, though it made it clear it would not go so far as to veto the legislation if Garn didn't get his way.

The Bush administration wanted to keep the cost of the bailout off the budget. The Democrats wanted to put it on the budget but exempt it from the Gramm-Rudman spending cap.

Both sides agreed that neither remedy was perfect. Privately members of both parties admitted that the only honest accounting would have put the entire cost on the budget and subjected it to Gramm-Rudman. Such a move would have forced Congress and the president either to accept drastic cuts in all agencies or to raise taxes to cover the new expenses. But President Bush still was pledging no new taxes, and the Democrats were not about to take the initiative in solving a problem they believed the administration was largely responsible for creating.

So the administration and congressional Democrats fell to squabbling over which approach was the lesser of two evils. The Democrats argued that putting the bailout on the budget would at least level with the public. But the White House countered that allowing Congress to exempt a major item from Gramm-Rudman would undo what little budgetary discipline Congress had mustered in recent years. Let Congress do this for the thrift tab, Treasury official Mullins argued, and it would use the same method to fund every other project pushed by special interests.

The White House argument was highly hypocritical. Its method—simply putting expenditures off the budget entirely—also could be used to circumvent Gramm-Rudman. The only explanation for the administration's tactic was political. Perhaps, some suspected, budget calculators like Darman had already realized that deficit reduction negotiations would come to a head soon. And if the budget would have to be slashed in a few months, why add a colossal item to it now? But Darman played his hand close to the vest, as usual. Meanwhile, many Democrats (and some Republicans) thought that the administration's solution merely postponed what they saw as inevitable—a day of reckoning when the president would have to break his promise not to raise taxes.

In the middle of the conference Riegle had a change of heart on junk bonds, agreeing with the House conferees to ban the risky investments. Garn and the other senators went along. They also ultimately capitulated on the financing question, agreeing to place the bailout on the budget. In fact, by the end the senators had given in to the House on every major issue save one: Wall. Remarkably the Senate conferees gave up everything to win Wall the job of heading the agency that would regulate thrifts. The House conferees, having won every major point of substance, reluctantly agreed to keep Wall in, reasoning that they could have at him another day.

The conference adjourned. But as expected, President Bush threatened a veto over the budget treatment of the bailout. In response the conference was hastily reconvened in early August, and after intense negotiations among conferees and administration officials, including direct talks with Brady and Darman late into the night on August 3, a compromise was reached. In it $20 billion of the $50 billion that would have to be raised over five years would be put on the budget in 1989, with the remainder going off the budget in 1990 and 1991. On August 4 the conference was adjourned for good.

Both chambers approved the compromise legislation, and the bill was sent to the president.

At the league officials had little to celebrate, but they could claim a small victory of sorts. Thanks largely to lobbyist Hohlt, the trade group had successfully won a provision in the bill that allowed thrifts to put the FDIC sticker—rather than the tarnished thrift deposit emblem—on their doors. Thrift executives argued this was only fair now that the FDIC would oversee deposit insurance funds for both banks and S&Ls. Bankers considered the move an affront, a step toward the day when the thrifts would raid their deposit insurance fund to pay for thrift failures.

On a sunny morning, August 9, 1989, President Bush signed the bailout bill into law. Standing by him were Senator Riegle and Representative Gonzalez, Treasury Secretary Brady, and OMB director Darman. In characteristic fashion, Wall reportedly complained loudly when he discovered that his assigned seat to watch the signing was not in the front row. That was soon fixed, at his insistence, according to participants.

Otherwise the event was a relatively happy occasion. Even Ed Gray had been invited to witness the signing of a bill that just six months earlier many thought had no chance of overcoming stiff opposition, much of it from Republicans, in Congress.

The new law was easily the most comprehensive overhaul of the thrift regulatory system since the Great Depression. It also was the most expensive piece of legislation outside of war costs in the country's history.

The league had lost nearly every specific battle in the crafting of the new law. But after years of trying, it had won the war: It had obtained a taxpayer-financed bailout.

Gonzalez had won nearly every major battle with the Senate. But he had lost a fight that rankled him, the contest with Garn over Wall's future. Gonzalez had conceded defeat over that point to get the bill through. But for Gonzalez the question of who should be the nation's top thrift regulator was far from settled.

38

Lincoln Continued . . .
Keating's Demise

You don't put Michelangelo or Leonardo da Vinci in jail. To
lose that mind for even a day would be a tragedy.

> —*Charles Keating on former junk*
> *bond king Michael Milken's*
> *guilty plea*

A person who makes a contribution has a better chance to
get access than someone who does not. . . . I'm not going to
mislead them [the public] into the belief that every citizen
will have an equal opportunity to get at me, because it's not
true."

> —*Alan Cranston during a*
> *deposition taken in the Senate*
> *Ethics Committee's investigation*
> *of the Keating Five*

When Wall took office, he found Gray's recommendation that Lincoln
be shut. And just six weeks after Wall took office, the president
signed the recapitalization bill that restored the bank board's ability to close
state-chartered thrifts. But the new chairman didn't take advantage of the
opportunity to shut Lincoln. His top aides decided that because the battle
between Gray and Keating had devolved into a personal fight, the facts were
tough to sort out. Wall and his advisers, including his top aide on enforcement, Darrel Dochow, decided, in Wall's words, that "we did not have a solid
case" against Lincoln.

Within ten days of being sworn into office, Wall ordered a complete review of the case. It was, in effect, an exam of the exam Gray's staff had conducted.

In fact, the material Wall and his aides sifted through that August already contained a piece of information that, by itself, would have been enough to enable the bank board to take drastic action: American Continental and Lincoln were engaging in what Wall later termed an "illegal" tax practice.

The documents showed that Lincoln had passed up more than $90 million to its parent corporation to cover federal income taxes. The parent, however, didn't owe taxes, so the money amounted to an interest-free loan to Keating's company from federally insured depositors. Failing to detect the transaction as a sham, regulators had approved the arrangement in April 1986, during Gray's tenure and a year before they gave Gray the report recommending that Lincoln be closed. Wall and his staff also overlooked the material, which Wall later called the "smoking gun," that would have supplied the indisputable evidence needed before the government could move in.

Instead in September 1987 Wall and Dochow met with Keating. "I was asked at that meeting to have a new examination conducted of the San Francisco district's findings; in other words, asked to have my staff look at the San Francisco 1986 examination to see if we could support its findings," Dochow recalled. "I asked for that review to be done by two of the top staff members, Mr. Al Smuzynski and Mr. Kevin O'Connell. . . ."

Smuzynski conducted the review, and the following month he sent a memo to Dochow stating that the San Francisco examiners generally had been right in their findings. "I recommend," Smuzynski said in the memo, "that the [bank board] proceed with a consent cease and desist order which addresses the unsafe and unsound practices" at Lincoln and take other measures to restructure the organization of the thrift. Again Dochow didn't accept the recommendation.

He decided that while the examiners might have been correct in their fact-finding, they were not necessarily correct in concluding that Lincoln should be closed. Nor, apparently, did Dochow agree even that a cease and desist order—generally, a formal order by regulators that an institution stop unsafe practices—was necessary. Action was again delayed. Dochow's feeling, expressed in internal bank board communications, that "Lincoln's future need not be as bleak or hopeless as it is viewed by the San Francisco bank" was in keeping with Wall's desire to seek a "peaceful resolution" of the Lincoln dispute.

On December 23, 1987, Wall announced the formation of what he called the Enforcement Review Committee to deal with thorny cases such as Lincoln's. "The creation of this committee is another significant step taken by the board to emphasize the importance of prompt and effective enforcement actions against institutions that are unwilling or unable to comply with statutory and regulatory requirements," Wall said. But to the regulators in San Francisco, the committee appeared to provide a means for Wall to delay action against Lincoln indefinitely.

The committee consisted of a group of people close to Wall. They were Dochow; bank board chief counsel Jordan Luke; Federal Home Loan Bank of Dallas President George Barclay (the man who later fired Joe Selby); Rosemary Stewart, director of enforcement; and Karl Hoyle, who was in charge of congressional relations and functioned as a political adviser to Wall. Stewart was a career employee at the bank board. But Dochow, Luke, Barclay, and Hoyle had Wall to thank for their jobs.

Months of back-and-forth negotiating between Keating's and Wall's staffs ensued. In early 1988 Dochow, whom bank board employees derisively nicknamed the Pillsbury Doughboy, suggested—evidently in response to a request from Keating—that oversight of Lincoln be transferred from the San Francisco field office to the Federal Home Loan Bank of Seattle. Officials in Seattle opposed the idea. After reviewing Lincoln's record, they didn't like what they saw. They also recognized that such a transfer would set a bad precedent, allowing thrifts to shop for the regulator they liked best.

Selby agreed. He attended the meeting of the Enforcement Review Committee at which Keating's transfer request was discussed. Selby advised Barclay that allowing Lincoln to switch to another region would send the wrong signal to high-flying thrift operators who didn't like being reined in. Barclay responded by disinviting Selby from future meetings of the committee. A few weeks later Barclay told Selby to clean out his desk.

Shortly after Selby's departure, on May 5, 1988, Luke presented the bank board with the committee's options for handling Lincoln. None of the members of the Enforcement Review Committee opposed allowing Lincoln to switch regulators, though they disagreed on how and when such a transfer would take place. "It's my personal belief that Mr. Keating is probably a very fine real estate developer," Dochow said during the presentation to the board.

It agreed, voting 2–1 to allow Lincoln to transfer out of the San Francisco district and be supervised instead directly by bank board headquarters— directly, in fact, by Dochow himself. Before casting the sole dissenting vote, Lawrence White, the Democrat on the three-member board, expressed his concern about the appearance of such a transfer. The notion that a thrift could "shop" for a regulator "is a very, very serious problem," he said.

Wall and the third board member, Roger Martin, remained unconvinced and cast their votes accordingly.

———

The decision to transfer oversight of Lincoln humiliated the regulators in San Francisco, making their task of overseeing one of the most corrupt and mismanaged regions of the industry that much harder. Indeed, some industry insiders wondered whether Wall's mistreatment of the San Francisco staff might be traced to the hard feelings between league lobbyist Hohlt, Wall's close friend, and Federal Home Loan Bank of San Francisco Chairman McKenna. The decision also tripped off shock waves among Wall's fellow bank regulators at the Federal Reserve Board, the FDIC, and the Office of the Comptroller of the Currency.

"It undermines the integrity and the perception of the integrity of the supervisory process," complained an aide to one bank regulator. "It will encourage [banks and S&Ls] to say, 'Let's make big contributions to politicians, and maybe if we do, we can buy our way out of the grasp of a tough regulator.' " The comment was an obvious reference to Keating's contributions to senators with whom Wall had worked while an aide to Senator Garn.

"If the regulators [in San Francisco] erred, the persons responsible should be reprimanded or even fired," said another government aide, "but the regulatory jurisdiction of the S and L should not be changed. That just sends out the wrong signal."

That perception was cemented by the outcome of the transfer. Shortly after Wall reassigned oversight of Lincoln, enforcement director Stewart issued a memorandum of understanding to Lincoln promising that the agency would not seek criminal investigations of the thrift's activities. It was a document that many federal officials thought was so lenient that, in House Banking Committee Chairman Gonzalez's words, "it was the kind of enforcement action that Charlie Keating would probably have been willing to sign seven days a week."

As Wall and his staff dithered, Keating was keeping himself busy channeling federally insured money from Lincoln into its parent, the American Continental Corporation, through a variety of schemes. In addition to the tax arrangement that regulators had failed to detect, the two companies engaged in complex, highly questionable financial transactions that the government later charged amounted to ACC's lending itself money and booking phony profits.

Most questionable of all, Keating raised money for American Continental by selling the corporation's bonds in Lincoln's branch offices. It was an arrangement that led many buyers of the bonds to believe the instruments were federally insured.

Keating sold more than $250 million in American Continental debt in the lobbies of Lincoln's branches from late 1986 until late February 1989, just weeks before ACC's declaration of bankruptcy made the bonds virtually worthless. About twenty-two thousand customers, many of them Lincoln depositors who were talked into taking their money out of the thrift to buy the bonds, invested in the corporation. Even as President Bush unveiled his thrift cleanup plan, the bonds were being sold to unsophisticated investors.

As Wall since has taken pains to point out, it was Gray's bank board that first approved ACC's sale of securities. "We all must have been smoking dope," Smuzynski, a senior supervisory assistant first under Gray and then under Wall, said in a June 16, 1987, memo about the agency's decision several years earlier to allow Lincoln to sell the securities.

On April 14, 1989, two months after President Bush announced that the FDIC would be taking control of the worst thrifts in the country, the bank board moved in on Lincoln, declaring it insolvent. That was the procedure under Bush's plan: The bank board still had sole responsibility for finding thrifts insolvent, but as soon as it did, it handed responsibility for the institutions over to the FDIC. It was a makeshift procedure intended to manage the crisis while Congress debated the president's proposed legislation for permanent changes.

Months later Wall defended his delay in closing Lincoln by pointing out that the bank board finally took action against the thrift during his chairmanship. But Wall's critics argued that by April 1989 the board was being given marching orders by the White House via the FDIC and Treasury. Wall, some complained, closed Lincoln only because the FDIC was leaning on him to do it. And Wall still couldn't explain why it took him nearly two years to act on Gray's recommendation.

"In fact, nineteen months ago, the board's own Office of Regulatory Activities informed Wall that Lincoln 'currently presents an excessive risk to FSLIC and is operating in an unsafe and unsound manner,' " an angry Representative Gonzalez remarked when the government's seizure of Lincoln was announced that day in April.

"The Lincoln case is Exhibit Number One in the failures of and mismanagement of the [bank board] under Wall," Gonzalez continued. "The board has known from the day Danny Wall took office that Lincoln was sick. It took no action. In fact, its only action was to block regulatory moves by the San Francisco Federal Home Loan Bank. It is one of the saddest cases in a long, long list of regulatory disasters.

"The delays and the outright sabotage of regulatory actions will cost the Federal Savings and Loan Corporation and the taxpayers, ultimately, billions of dollars," Gonzalez concluded.

He asked President Bush to remove Wall from office. The White House didn't respond.

The day before Lincoln was seized, Keating moved to put American Continental into Chapter 11 bankruptcy, which protects a company from creditors but allows it to stay in business.

A key purpose was to keep the Phoenician, a luxury resort Keating had built using Lincoln's funds, out of the government's hands. The posh hotel boasted $25 million in marble floors as well as a lavish golf course and desert-defying gardens.

Outraged bondholders, whose investments were now virtually worthless, filed a lawsuit charging that employees in California's Department of Corporations had been aware that the bond sales were being made without proper warnings about their riskiness but that those objections had been overruled by officials who had ties to lawyers representing Keating and his company. Bondholders pointed out that the Department of Corporations, which approved the bond sales, "ignored violations" of its rules against conflicts of interest by its officials. Franklin Tom and Christine Bender served consecutively as California corporation commissioner during the period when the bond sales were okayed by the state. Bender came from a private law firm that hired Tom after he left the commissioner's post. Keating retained the firm to work on the bond matter. The firm was named as a defendant in the bondholder lawsuit but, according to a lawyer for the bondholders, eventually settled by agreeing to pay bondholders $4.5 million.

On April 17, 1989, the bank board sent the Justice Department criminal referrals on alleged fraudulent and insider transactions relating to Lincoln. On August 2, a few days before President Bush signed the newly passed thrift cleanup legislation into law, the FDIC, which had been running Lincoln, closed it. The estimated cost to taxpayers: more than $2 billion.

Later that month Keating sat in an office at the Phoenician, clearly shaken by the government's actions, describing the attitude displayed by federal and state regulators in 1983 when he decided to enter the thrift industry. The six-foot-five-inch Keating held himself ramrod straight, peering out of Coke-bottle thick glasses that magnified his blue eyes and set them off sharply against the sunburned red of his face and neck.

That same August day a local newspaper had broken the news that the government intended to file a $1.1 billion bank fraud and civil racketeering suit, the largest of its kind ever, against Keating and other Lincoln officials. "We've lost everything in this thing, my wife and I," Keating said. "It's devastating."

His office setting was surreal. Hummingbirds hovered outside the ground-floor window in the hundred-degree heat of the Arizona sun. Several miles away sat an even more expensive Keating monument: a man-made lake and sprawling lawn in the desert surrounding Phoenix. The lake was to be the center of a Keating-built town. There had been one snag. Keating planned the town, paving miles of streets and installing hundreds of streetlights, in the middle of a nationwide housing slump. No one wanted to live in the planned community. Instead of houses or schools or shopping centers, the roads in the development ran past empty desert, leading nowhere. Now taxpayers own the property.

(When the government's civil fraud suit was filed several weeks later, the story was almost ignored by the *Cincinnati Enquirer,* the same paper that broke the news of the Ohio thrift crisis in 1985. The story ran on page 4 of Section C. And when the business editor complained, he was fired for not being a "team player." *Enquirer* editor George Blake explained his paper's attitude by saying that "we don't consider this a local story. It's an Arizona story with local implications." But, according to the *Columbia Journalism Review,* there might be another explanation for the paper's approach to one of the biggest financial disasters in American history: Named in the suit was Charles Keating's brother and a director in Lincoln's parent company, William Keating, who also was chairman and is now publisher of the *Enquirer.* Since then the government has dropped William Keating from the suit, and, Blake said, in any case the charge that the paper downplayed the story is "ridiculous."

News of the impending lawsuit depressed Keating so much that he said he was unable to talk to reporters that day. But when canceling an interview arranged weeks earlier with a reporter, he did slip in the thought that day that while federally insured money probably should not go to such enterprises as junk bonds, that was not the issue. The point, he said, is the rules said you could invest in such things, and so he did.

The Lincoln fiasco threatened the reputations of Wall and the five senators who had interceded with Gray on Keating's behalf. Headlines on the subject briefly appeared but quickly disappeared, lost in a media frenzy as reporters struggled to understand the complex thrift legislation moving through Congress.

But shortly after the new thrift bill became law, Wall found himself in an unwanted spotlight. On August 28, 1989, an opinion piece about Wall appeared on the *Wall Street Journal*'s editorial page with the headline THE S&L LOOTERS' WATER-BOY. The article accused Wall of being a "political servant" to those in "Congress and the White House who controlled his career." It said that Garn, Riegle, and Cranston led the fight to preserve Wall's job without reconfirmation by the Senate to avoid directing "unwanted attention on Lincoln.

"Both Congress and the White House clearly want to preserve a separate S&L industry," the *Journal* went on to say, "even though the distinction between thrifts and other financial institutions makes little sense in today's economy. So rather than push for healthy banks to take over insolvent S&Ls, Mr. Wall has tried to force the ailing S&Ls into dubious mergers" through the 1988 deals, all of them at excessive expense to taxpayers.

In this atmosphere, with the conference committee over, Gonzalez saw his opportunity. He had acquiesced on the legislation appointing Wall head of OTS. Now Gonzalez again asked President Bush to fire Wall. The Banking Committee chairman joined the request with an announcement that he would hold hearings on Lincoln, hearings, as everyone knew, that would be embarrassing to Wall and to the administration. The White House, reportedly under pressure from Garn, again didn't respond. Gonzalez proceeded with the hearings. Gonzalez, his critics began to realize, might be crazy, but if so, he was crazy like a fox. He now set the stage to make Wall a catalyst for public debate on the thrift debacle.

Why did it take two years for Wall to seize Lincoln or to discover Keating's tax evasion or to realize that consumers would lose the $250 million they had sunk in American Continental's bonds? The hearings didn't provide new or satisfying answers to those questions, although there were a few never-before-told details brought to light, like the bugging equipment found on the supposedly secure telephones Lincoln had provided to examiners poring over its books. And though everyone knew Keating had hired an army of attorneys, the hearings revealed an exact count: He employed eighty law firms.

But the principal effect of the hearings was the transformation of Keating into a lightning rod that focused public attention on the thrift crisis. During more than fifty hours of testimony in October and November before the House Banking Committee, all the sordid details of Keating's influence machine were laid out, along with the story of Wall's squeamishness regarding Lincoln. Wall's top aides, it was revealed, had advised against closing the institution. Several senior regulators said they had been told by Wall to handle the Lincoln case amicably. Keating's failed attempt to hire Gray was aired, as was Keating's success in hiring the Arthur Young auditor Jack Atchison, who had written letters on Arthur Young letterhead to the Keating Five in early 1987 protesting the bank board's treatment of Lincoln.

With Keating the villain who hooked the public's interest, Gonzalez used the hearings to focus on a far wider review of thrift issues. The reputation of the regulatory system, not just Wall, was at stake.

Wall ordered the San Francisco field officials not to testify, but Gonzalez subpoenaed them. One after another, they challenged Wall's policies.

William Black, Gray's former assistant and then chief counsel for the San Francisco bank, called Wall's decision to transfer oversight of Lincoln a "shot in the back" to regulators. Senior San Francisco regulator Michael Patriarca said it "called into question the whole organization's willingness to function as a regulator."

Newly appointed SEC Chairman Richard Breeden (who won his appointment to the agency in part as reward for his role in helping forge President Bush's thrift policy) accused Wall's agency of impeding a separate SEC probe into Keating's company, including the sale of American Continental securities in Lincoln's branch offices. Breeden told Gonzalez that Stewart's memorandum of understanding with Lincoln, nicknamed Rosemary's Baby during the hearings, made it virtually impossible for the SEC to try to prove that the bonds issued by Lincoln's parent company had been based on false financial information. After all, the memo amounted to one arm of the government's giving Keating's operation a clean bill of health.

Breeden's comments were explosive. They were widely viewed as the final blow to Wall's effort to hang on. As a White House insider and the Bush aide who oversaw the creation of the president's thrift bailout plan, Breeden was thought to have been given administration approval to lay into Wall and, in the process, deliver the more subtle message that the president thought it was time for the thrift regulator to step down.

Finally, on November 21, 1989, it was Wall's turn to testify.

Only one member of the Banking Committee seemed openly warm, longtime Wall friend Carroll Hubbard, a Democrat. Republicans were among the most critical.

Wall has "some very powerful friends in the Senate because when the S&L bill was before us, the senators absolutely insisted that Mr. Wall stay on as part of their price for agreement to the S&L bill," Representative Roth said in an opening statement the day Wall testified. "Now, Mr. Wall holds the key to the central mystery of this investigation. Even Perry Mason would have to ask: Why did the bank board let Keating off the hook?"

Said Representative Leach: "While leader of a moralizing campaign in Arizona against pornography, Mr. Keating appears, by the record, to be an economic pornographer, defiling the value of the savings of the elderly and adulterating the safety and soundness of the American financial system. If the allegations the Committee has heard so far are true, Charles Keating is a financio-path of obscene proportions—the Reverend Jim Bakker of American finance—given license to steal by a bank board headed by the Neville Chamberlain of financial regulation, a cheerleader who saw little evil and thus spoke little truth.

"The bottom line is that at critical junctions the bank board provided misleading if not false numbers on the depth of the S and L problems to Congress and perhaps to the executive branch," Leach said. "And the bottom line is that the bank board refused on a timely basis to rein in the direct investment authorities which are at the heart of the problems at Lincoln and several other thrifts as well."

Wall saw things differently. "Washington regulators acted in a responsible and prudent manner in supervising Lincoln Savings, according to testimony today from the nation's top thrift regulator," stated the press release issued by the Office of Thrift Supervision even before Wall actually testified.

(A few weeks before Wall testified, his aide Karl Hoyle stood outside the hearing room and passed out to reporters a list of significant events in the supervisory history of Lincoln by federal thrift regulators, a list that made Wall appear to have taken firm action. As Wall testified, however, House Banking Committee staff plastered large placards on the hearing room walls with lettering big enough for the television cameras to pick up; the signs chronicled the several dozen "Known Calls and Meetings Between Bank Board Officials and Keating and Associates," all of which Hoyle had failed to include in his chronology.)

As Wall began his appearance before the committee, he flung accusations at Gonzalez. He asked why the chairman, who headed the Banking Committee's subcommittee that oversees the Department of Housing and Urban Development, had not detected the fraud, cronyism, and mismanagement that, it was becoming clear, were rampant in that agency. But Wall soon dropped that line of attack, and for good reason: He had been staff director (and then minority staff director when Republicans lost control of the Senate) of the Senate Banking Committee, which also oversees HUD and also failed to uncover the agency's misdeeds. (Indeed, Senator D'Amato was the fourth-ranking Republican on the committee and knee-deep in accusations that he was among the biggest abusers in Congress of HUD contacts.)

Wall also tried to blame the San Francisco regulatory staff for its failure to gather evidence permitting him to close Lincoln. Later in the hourslong session, however, Wall admitted he should—and legally could—have shut Lincoln in mid-1987 because of the fraudulent tax agreement between the thrift and American Continental. "The tax-sharing agreement is the Achilles' heel in this whole situation for all of us," Wall said. "We missed it."

As for American Continental bonds sold in Lincoln's branches, Wall blamed himself for the mess but said responsibility for the "human tragedy" lay as well with California regulators and the SEC. "None of us are clean on that one," he said. (During a break in the hearings Hoyle insisted that neither Wall nor anyone else at the bank board owed an apology to the bondholders. "You don't hear the SEC apologizing," he said. "Why should we?")

The hearings, broadcast to living rooms across the country thanks to C-Span, were devastating to the White House. Gonzalez began hinting that he would hold a new round of hearings into Wall's handling of the failed Silverado Banking, Savings and Loan of Denver, where President Bush's son Neil had been a director. And the chairman again wrote the president, asking that in light of information revealed in the hearings, he remove Wall. Others in Congress and on newspaper editorial boards echoed the request. Top Bush aides turned up their behind-the-scenes hints that the president wouldn't mind if Wall resigned.

In mid-November 1989, in the middle of the hearings, President Bush made his first comment on the Lincoln mess, saying he would consider removing Wall if it became evident that the crisis was caused in part by regulators who had not been sufficiently aggressive. The president was careful not to condemn Wall, but he praised Gonzalez for holding hearings into the Lincoln fiasco, a comment widely interpreted in the industry as a slap at Wall.

On December 4, just two weeks after he had appeared before Gonzalez's committee to give his side of the story and declare his honesty and competence, Wall obliged his critics. He resigned before a hastily called audience of reporters who packed the bank board's auditorium. To the end Wall insisted that his decision to take the Lincoln case from the San Francisco regional regulators was based solely on his feeling that they had failed to find the evidence the agency needed to shut down Lincoln. "Neither political influence nor Lincoln's Charles Keating affected my decision," Wall said. But he also conceded it was a mistake to have ordered the transfer.

In a letter to President Bush Wall said, "I am proud of my tenure both as chairman of the Federal Home Loan Bank Board and as director of the Office of Thrift Supervision." But, he said, the threat of continued hearings "with me as the primary target" would be too disruptive to the thrift agency and to the administration for him to stay on.

"Having failed to secure my departure legislatively, Mr. Gonzalez resorted to corruption of the truth and abandonment of our historical devotion to fair play and due process in his effort to remove me from office," Wall wrote. "I come from a small town on the plains of South Dakota, a shopkeeper's son. Service to God, country and community, personal integrity and not leaving undone a job once begun were just some of the virtues by which I was taught to live. And I still abide by them, Mr. President."

Several days later the president released a "Dear Danny" letter commending Wall for his hard work as thrift director. The less than robust endorsement angered Wall's patron, Senator Garn, who accused the administration of "not having any guts" and of failing to stand up for Wall, indeed, of allowing him to take the fall for a problem that was at least as much Bush's

348

fault. Garn, who routinely described Wall as the "kind of person you would want as a neighbor," blasted the administration for failing to stick up for the thrift regulator. "They certainly in no way came to his defense," he told the *Deseret News* in Salt Lake City.

Wall's departure did not stop him from embarrassing the Bush administration. In March 1990 the decision to let Wall remain in his job as director of the Office of Thrift Supervision came back to haunt the government. A federal judge barred regulators from seizing Olympic Federal Savings and Loan on the ground that regulations effectively making the thrift insolvent—regulations that had been promulgated when Wall and his successor, acting OTS director Salvatore Martoche, headed the agency—were illegal because both were named without confirmation by the Senate, in violation of the Constitution.

The White House had been warned that such challenges might arise if it let Wall assume the post without being confirmed, but it apparently hadn't taken the threat seriously. Concerned that an avalanche of suits might follow the Olympic decision, the White House quickly nominated T. Timothy Ryan, a Washington labor and pension lawyer who served as solicitor of the Labor Department in the early 1980s, to head the OTS. The Senate confirmed the nomination despite a halfhearted effort to discredit Ryan by critics who, dismayed at his lack of banking experience, leaked an FBI report that he had tried cocaine and smoked marijuana as a law student in the early 1970s.

But even that didn't end the embarrassment for Wall. In August 1990 U.S. District Court Judge Stanley Sporkin ruled against Keating's claim that the government had seized Lincoln improperly. But even as Sporkin did so, he chastised federal regulators for a sloppy job, specifically citing Wall's unusual decision to switch regulation of Lincoln from San Francisco to Washington as "inexplicable and clearly inappropriate."

In his ruling Sporkin said of the Lincoln case, "What has emerged is not a pretty picture. It is abundantly clear that [American Continental Corporation] officials abused their positions with respect to Lincoln. Bluntly speaking, their actions amounted to a looting of Lincoln. This was not done crudely. Indeed, it was done with a great deal of sophistication."

Sporkin also took the opportunity to turn the light on an element of the thrift fiasco that had not been much discussed: the role of private-sector professionals, Lincoln's outside lawyers and accountants, who failed to detect the apparently widespread abuses that led to the thrift's failure. Expressing a sentiment shared by many people familiar with the causes of the S&L debacle, Sporkin noted in his ruling that Lincoln symbolized the breakdown of private-sector safeguards. Keating had hired some of the best-known names in the legal profession—Sidley & Austin of Chicago, and Kaye, Scholer, Fierman, Hays & Handler of New York, for example—and in the accounting profession, most notably Arthur Young, one of the predecessor firms to Ernst & Young. Outside professionals played similar roles at many of the thrifts that ended up on the government's sick list. In addition to Lincoln, Arthur Young alone audited the books of some of the most infamous thrifts, including the Western Savings Association and Vernon Savings and Loan, both of Dallas. (A spokesman for Ernst & Young says that the firm "stands by the audits it did for Western, Vernon, and Lincoln.")

"What is difficult to understand is that with all the professional talent involved, why at least one professional would not have blown the whistle to stop the overreaching that took place in this case," Sporkin said in the Lincoln ruling. "Why didn't any of them speak up or disassociate themselves from the transactions? Where were these professionals . . . when these clearly improper transactions were being consummated?"

Representative Ron Wyden, who sponsored a bill to toughen auditors' obligations to report fraud, made the same point more colorfully: "Elephants were walking through the living room and the accountants missed them."

The GAO found in a 1989 study that auditors—all of them among the biggest of the nation's auditing firms—for six of eleven thrifts studied didn't really try to determine what was going on. "They didn't do enough work, period," said David L. Clark, author of the GAO report. The GAO referred the two predecessor firms that merged to form Ernst & Young, as well as Deloitte, Haskins & Sells, for possible disciplinary action from regulators and professional auditing groups.

Critics have charged that many auditors, who are supposed to uphold what the Supreme Court has described as their public duty to report an accurate financial picture, acted less like truth tellers and more like magicians, making losses disappear and profits materialize out of thin air. Misleading audits by some of the biggest accounting firms in the country significantly increased the cost to taxpayers in at least half a dozen of the two dozen costliest thrift failures, government regulators say. In too many cases thrifts merely had to shop around to find an accounting firm that did its bidding.

Keating hired at least two accounting firms in five years for Lincoln before he found one, Arthur Young, that was pliant enough. Atchison, the Arthur Young accountant in charge of Lincoln, issued two years of clean opinions, wrote letters to the Keating Five defending Lincoln's accounting practices, and then, in early 1988, shortly before Keating reached his much-criticized agreement with officials at Wall's bank board, went to work for Keating for roughly $950,000 a year. Later in 1988, Ernst & Young parted ways with Keating when the two sides disagreed over Lincoln's accounting, according to an Ernst & Young spokesman. Lincoln then hired Touche Ross (now Deloitte & Touche), its fourth accounting firm in five years. But Touche Ross resigned shortly before Lincoln was seized by the government in early 1989 without ever having issued an audit report on the institution.

Wall wasn't the only official whose ties to Keating proved fatal. A few months after President Bush signed the 1989 thrift bailout bill into law, it was revealed that Keven Gottlieb had taken a leave as a top aide to Senator Riegle to serve as a consultant to the American Bankers Association, whose issues he worked on when he returned to the senator's payroll and became chief of staff of the Senate Banking Committee under new Chairman Riegle in 1989. Gottlieb also, by his own account, had been one of Riegle's key contacts with Lincoln. Indeed, Keating says it was Gottlieb who suggested that Keating contribute to Riegle's campaign. Gottlieb and Riegle say Keating offered to make the contributions.

On October 6, 1989, a front-page article in the *Washington Post* chronicled the enormous amount of money that industries pay to top congressional aides through speaking and other fees. Among the largest recipients: Kevin Gottlieb. In 1988, for example, Gottlieb earned $132,650 while running Riegle's reelection campaign. But speaking and consulting boosted his income to $600,000 for the year. Some came from the bankers' lobby group. And $357,600 came from the billboard industry's trade association, the Outdoor Advertising Association of America. Gannett, the media and publishing giant where Charles Keating's brother was a top executive, was the largest outdoor advertiser in the country and a member of the association. Gottlieb says there was no Keating connection with the job.

After weeks of being asked whether he had any financial ties to Keating, and after weeks of refusing to say anything publicly, Gottlieb finally made this statement: "Kevin Gottlieb and members of his family never have had any personal or professional relationship with Mr. Charles Keating. Gottlieb's only contact with Mr. Keating was in the proper conduct of his duties as a Senate employee. At no time has Gottlieb or any member of his family had a financial relationship with Mr. Keating or any of his business enterprises either directly or indirectly; this includes the areas of salaries, fees, investments or any other financial dimension."

But the amount of time Gottlieb was spending on activities other than his job as Senate Banking committee chief of staff, in combination with an autocratic style that had made him unpopular with aides to other committee members, was taking its toll on Riegle's image. On January 10, 1990, Riegle's office announced that Gottlieb would return to the private sector effective March 1. Publicly Gottlieb insists his decision had nothing to do with Riegle's

Keating problems. But Senate aides insist Riegle had decided that Gottlieb was a political liability whose style and professional activities were setting the wrong image for the senator.

The Gottlieb affair was only a prelude of things to come for the Senate. The House had been publicly chastised with the Jim Wright affair, the regulators with the Gonzalez hearings on Keating. Now it was the Senate's turn to sit in the hot seat.

The Keating Five had accepted more than $1.3 million from Keating for their campaigns and other political causes during the mid-1980s. (After publicity surfaced about the payments, Riegle returned $76,100, and DeConcini $48,100. McCain repaid $13,433 for nine plane trips to the Bahamas related to Lincoln and Keating and said he would return $112,000 in campaign contributions if the money was found to have come from Lincoln.)

Four of the five had meet with then bank board Chairman Ed Gray in April 1987 to discuss Lincoln. Riegle did not attend that first meeting, though he had allegedly proposed the idea to Keating and asked a Keating aide to arrange for the other senators to attend. In addition, Riegle allegedly asked Keating's aide to arrange for DeConcini and McCain to invite him to the second meeting in writing, which appeared to many as though Riegle were seeking a cover for his attendance. The first meeting was followed up in a few days with one where all five senators met with top bank board regulators Bill Black and Michael Patriarca regarding Lincoln. Gray suggested the second meeting to the senators after they expressed dismay at Gray's professed ignorance about the details the Lincoln case, but because it grew out of the first meeting, which many thought Riegle had helped orchestrate, it too was widely regarded as largely Riegle's doing.

In October 1989 Common Cause, the nonprofit, self-appointed public interest lobby group, filed a complaint with the Senate Select Committee on Ethics, asking that an investigation be opened into whether Keating's efforts to influence senators violated federal election laws or Senate rules of conduct. It also asked the FBI to investigate the role played by the Keating Five in intervening with Gray during the two by-now famous April 1987 meetings.

The Ethics Committee appointed a special counsel, Robert S. Bennett, who began a monthslong process of collecting and sorting through thousands of documents and of talking to dozens of individuals connected with the Keating Five, with Lincoln, and with the regulators who oversaw the institution. In the fall of 1990 the committee held televised hearings.

As was true of the Lincoln hearings held by Gonzalez a year earlier, little that was new came out of the Senate Ethics Committee's investigation. But the hearings—with hundreds of hours of testimony broadcast nationwide on

C-Span during the Christmas season—had a galvanizing effect on the public by setting out all at once the details of Keating's political activities.

At the outset Bennett's preliminary report largely cleared Glenn and McCain, two military heroes, recommending that the committee take no action against them. But that stirred a partisan fight over letting off McCain, the only Republican in the Keating Five, just before the elections. So the six-member Ethics Committee of three Democrats and three Republicans decided to hold hearings concerning the actions of all five senators.

As the hearings began, Bennett registered his harsh judgment of the other three of the Keating Five. "It is clear," he said during his opening remarks, "that Senators Cranston and DeConcini were important players in Mr. Keating's strategy [and that] there is substantial evidence that Senator Riegle played a much greater role than he now recalls."

Shortly into the hearings, Cranston, the Senate's assistant majority leader, announced that he had prostate cancer and would not seek another term. With Glenn and McCain off the hook and Cranston on the way out, the hearings became crucial to the political futures of DeConcini and Riegle.

That was particularly bad news for Riegle, because the hearings cast him in a surprisingly bad light. The investigation suggested that his involvement with Keating, and in setting up the controversial April 1987 meetings, had been far greater than he or Gottlieb initially had insisted to reporters and investigators.

In 1989, as scrutiny of Keating's influence heated up, Riegle at first insisted that he had had nothing to do with arranging the two meetings. "With respect to the Lincoln matter, at no time did I seek any meeting with regulators in Lincoln's behalf or suggest any course of regulatory actions with respect to Lincoln," he said in a press release on October 13, 1989. "My attendance at a single meeting on April 9, 1987, was at the specific written request of Senators DeConcini and McCain because of my perspective as a member of the Senate Banking Committee." The senator repeated the claim in a March 1990 deposition to the Ethics Committee. Gottlieb had told reporters a similar version of events. Later, however, while still insisting he in no way set up the meetings, Riegle conceded that he might have suggested to Gray that he "consider meeting with" other "senators to hear their concerns" about the bank board's treatment of Lincoln.

At the Ethics Committee hearings, however, Keating's lobbyist, lawyer James Grogan—testifying under a limited grant of immunity from prosecution based on his statements—offered a very different version of events. According to Grogan, shortly before the April 1987 meetings, during the trip that Riegle and Gottlieb took to Phoenix, Keating discussed with Riegle his concerns about Gray. During the same trip Gottlieb and Grogan discussed the upcoming fund raiser that Keating was arranging in Detroit for the senator. When Riegle returned to Washington, Grogan continued, the senator also received campaign contributions that had been collected for him by Lincoln employees and given to DeConcini to pass on to Riegle.

According to Grogan, Riegle had suggested the meeting between Gray and the senators when he spoke with Keating in Phoenix. Grogan said that Riegle then told him to ask Arizona Senators McCain and DeConcini to the meeting and to have them send Riegle a written invitation. "It was clear to me that [Riegle] felt he would be much more comfortable attending the meeting if he were invited by the constituent Senators who were the most knowledgeable of Lincoln's problems," Grogan told the committee.

Grogan said that Riegle wanted to be invited to the meeting because "he knew as a politician that this was a potentially politically explosive situation because there was tremendous media at the time about Mr. Keating and Mr. Gray and the regulators and all the fighting" among them over Lincoln.

Riegle didn't help his own cause. Unlike the other senators, who either fought back by denying they did anything wrong or apologized to the public for the untoward appearance of their association with Keating, Riegle seemed to take on a siege mentality, one that those around him described as Nixonian. He stopped talking to the press. Eventually he began referring inquiries to a well-known criminal lawyer, Thomas C. Green, who sent letters to columnists Rowland Evans and Robert Novak and other journalists taking issue—and, in Evans and Novak's view, making threats—regarding questions the journalists raised about Riegle and Keating.

In the meantime, while the hearings were under way, the sixty-six-year-old Keating was charged in a forty-two-count criminal case in California and spent a month in jail until his bail was lowered to $300,000 from $5 million. His gangly figure, handcuffed and dressed in jailhouse blue, was pictured on the nightly news. His police mug shot for the L.A. County district attorney's office appeared on the front pages of newspapers across the country. It was quite a turnabout for a man who had been able to enlist five senators in his cause, who had been accustomed to flying in his own helicopter, importing hummingbirds to the desert, and offering six-figure salaries to anyone who stood in his way.

As the hearings dragged on, it became clear, as noted by journalist John Crawford in the *Congressional Quarterly,* that even though accounts of the two April 1987 meetings differed, "establishing the facts in the case would be substantially easier than deciding at what point a senator's conduct crosses ethical boundaries." There were troubling revelations on all sides.

Cranston's chief banking aide, Carolyn Jordan, revealed that without Cranston's explicit consent, she regularly inserted into the *Congressional Record* statements that appeared to have been made by Cranston on the floor of the Senate. Such statements are often cited in court as evidence of congressional intent on the meaning of legislation. That practice had not been lost on Keating's lawyers. They used a statement Jordan had inserted without Cranston's knowledge to bolster their case in a suit they had filed (but eventually lost) against federal regulators.

Jordan said she had not included the statement explicitly for Keating's benefit. But a Lincoln lobbyist contradicted her recollection, saying he had asked her to insert the remarks to counter a damaging statement made by Senator Proxmire, at the time chairman of the Senate Banking Committee.

In other testimony, regulators Black and Patriarca said that during their meeting with the senators, their disclosure that they were going to make a criminal referral on Lincoln was like throwing "holy water" on a "vampire," causing the senators to back off, at least for the time being. Yet, Black conceded under questioning, the decision to make the criminal referral had been reached just hours prior to the meeting.

Gray testified that the meetings didn't alter bank board policy and therefore didn't delay government action. Technically they couldn't have had that effect. The board's power to close state-chartered thrifts like Lincoln had expired three months before the April 1987 meetings took place. But not surprisingly, Gray failed to note that his own indecisiveness had played a role in delaying a move against Lincoln. His staff undertook years of investigation but failed to recommend enforcement action prior to the expiration of that authority.

Although Gray and Black were vehement in accusing the Keating Five of impropriety, neither could explain why it was not until May 1987, just a few weeks before Gray's tenure expired, that Gray's staff first formally recommended action against Lincoln.

But Gray did advise Wall to close Lincoln as soon as federal authority to shut state institutions was restored. And despite the warnings about a criminal referral in April, Cranston and DeConcini continued to call regulators on Keating's behalf when Wall took over. Black testified that the efforts by the senators held up Lincoln's closing and that he believed Washington regulators under Wall were influenced by the lobbying, though he could not give specific examples of how the senators accomplished this feat.

As for the April 1987 meetings themselves, Gray testified that the only real impropriety was what he interpreted as an offer by DeConcini to negotiate a settlement of Lincoln's dispute with the bank board. Gray said he was unclear whether or not DeConcini, who used the word "we" in offering the compromise, was speaking for the other four senators. Curiously, however, Gray had written McCain a letter saying he had no problem with that senator's conduct during the two April meetings. But Gray offered no reason to believe that DeConcini's "we" included McCain any less than the other four of the Keating Five. In many observers' minds, Gray never adequately explained why he had singled out McCain, the sole Republican, as being blameless.

Gray and Black also did not have much of an explanation about why they waited two years before going public about meetings they now said they thought were highly improper. Gray said that it was simply a matter of that much time going by before he was approached by a member of the press with details of the meetings, and it was then that he decided to confirm the reporter's information. Black said his delay can be ascribed his desire to avoid a fight with senators at a time when the bank board was pushing for a refunding of the bankrupt thrift deposit insurance fund.

Despite these inconsistencies, Gray's testimony was viewed by senators on the Ethics Committee as the most damaging to Congress as an institution. Gray repeatedly suggested that the system of making campaign contributions amounted to bribery, saying over and over into the TV cameras, "It's a case of too much money chasing too many politicians."

"It is the Senate as a whole, some fear, that is looking bad," commented *Congressional Quarterly*.

At the end of the hearings Bennett, the Ethics Committee's counsel, advised the committee to drop any further investigation of McCain and Glenn but to take formal action against Cranston, Riegle, and DeConcini, saying "the political heart and soul of this country is at stake." Defenders of the senators, however, said they had trouble understanding which rules they had violated: There is no rule against accepting campaign funds from people a senator helps although it is illegal to trade help for such contributions.

Because Cranston had announced his decision to retire, Riegle, even more than DeConcini, appeared to have the most to lose as the committee's deliberations began. Bennett accused Riegle of "obscuring his role" in the Keating affair, which, in the words of a story in the February 4, 1991, issue of *Business Week,* is "a euphemism for lying in testimony." Should the Ethics Committee agree that Riegle was dishonest, some Senate aides worried, the Senate might remove him as chairman of the Banking Committee.

Later that month, after a fourteen-month investigation, the Ethics Committee found "substantial credible evidence" of ethics violations by Cranston but concluded that the other four of the Keating Five had broken no rules or laws. The committee said, however, that it could not condone the conduct of DeConcini and Riegle, which "gave the appearance of being improper" and was marked by "insensitivity and poor judgment."

The Senate, the House, the regulators, the industry personified by Keating—all had been embarrassed publicly in turn as the magnitude of the thrift debacle came to light. Now attention turned to the White House. Ironically, the administration's greatest embarrassment came from someone who had never held public office: the president's son Neil.

Part VII

THE PRESIDENT'S SON

First of all, I don't know that much about financial institutions.

—*Neil Bush*

39

"I'm Always Happy"

Neil Bush first met Michael Wise, head of Silverado Banking, Savings and Loan, at a dinner party in the mid-1980s. They engaged in small talk, party chitchat. Bush didn't think much about Wise or his fast-growing Denver thrift afterward until, a few days later, Wise called Bush to ask him to join Silverado's board of directors.

The incongruous pair met over breakfast at a pancake restaurant. Bush, George and Barbara's third son, was naïve, gullible, not the brightest man in the world, but a very nice guy. At thirty, he was in the oil business, though none too successfully. Two years of drilling had yielded mostly dry holes and no profit for his company, which he had started with loans from two of Denver's richest developers. His experience in finance was minimal: He had filled out forms one summer in the trust department at a Dallas bank.

Being the nice guy was the way Neil, dyslexic, made up for poor grades. His three brothers went to the Phillips Academy. Neil struggled through St. Albans, a prestigious prep school in Washington. His parents were told he'd never get into college. But he did, graduating from Tulane University with a 3.2 grade point average and then with a master's degree in business.

"It may be weird, but I'm always happy," Bush once told a reporter. "I always found the bright side." Said brother Marvin: "He is the most optimistic guy I've ever met in my life."

Perhaps that's why Denver appealed to him so when he moved there in

1980 with his new wife, Sharon Smith, whom he met while knocking on doors for his father's campaign. Oil prices were booming. So was real estate. Banking wasn't far behind.

Wise, a glib go-getter in the world of banking, was a champion schmoozer, used to getting his way. He hobnobbed with top regulators from the Federal Home Loan Bank of Topeka who oversaw his and other thrifts in the Colorado region. The Topeka regional bank's president, Kermit Mowbray, often sent a limousine to pick Wise up at the airport when Wise paid the regulators a visit.

Wise had impressed league lobbyist Rick Hohlt, who recommended him for appointment to a Federal Reserve Board advisory panel. In addition to the Hohlt connection, Wise was a friend of bank board Chairman Danny Wall and of Craig Fuller, chief of staff for then Vice President Bush. Mowbray knew that. So did most of the regulators at the Topeka office. They also knew that Wise could gain the attention of senators such as Don Riegle, who once agreed to give a private talk to the Silverado board of directors. All in all, Wise was viewed as someone with important Washington connections, well respected, a man the regional regulators considered on the cutting edge of the thrift business through complex real estate transactions and other deals.

Now Wise wanted a more direct Bush connection as well. Neil, described by one senior White House official as a "classic babe in the woods," understood why he was being wooed. "I would be naïve to think that the Bush name didn't have something to do with it," he later said. But he didn't seem to be insulted. On August 22, 1985, Neil Bush joined Silverado's eleven-person board of directors.

Like a director at any corporation, Bush, whether he knew it or not, assumed a responsibility to avoid conflicts of interest and, more broadly, to try to ensure the long-term health of the company. Indeed, regulators, backed by court decisions over the decades, have held that directors of banks and thrifts must adhere to even higher standards than directors of other companies. Although the board of directors cannot run the day-to-day operations of an S&L, in theory it holds the key to protecting the institution's well-being. Along with auditors and regulators, it is supposed to guard against fraud and mismanagement by thrift employees. Boards usually are made up of six to a dozen people, half of them top management and the rest, like Bush, outsiders who deal with the company only at board meetings.

From the outset there was reason to doubt Neil's efficacy as fiscal watchdog. Regulators from the bank board's Topeka office identified unsafe practices at Silverado as early as 1986, when thrift supervisors undertook a lengthy examination. Because of the questions raised, regulators began an extensive investigation of the thrift in 1987.

Neil Bush remained on the Silverado board until a week before the Republican National Convention in the summer of 1988, when his father was nominated as the GOP's candidate for president. One reason he left when he did, officials in Congress and the S&L industry say, was that regulators knew the thrift was on the verge of collapse. George Bush would have to grapple with the national thrift mess in January if elected president. Having a son on the board of one of the costliest thrift failures would not be good public relations.

Silverado officially collapsed in November 1988, shut down by regulators just after the presidential election at a cost to taxpayers of at least $1 billion. It was sold to the Ford Motor Company at year-end in one of the scores of deals that Wall rushed through in December.

The thrift didn't make much news after that, though among thrift executives and regulators there was speculation on whether the institution and its history were a political time bomb. Then, in early 1990, Representative Gonzalez announced he would hold hearings that spring into Silverado's collapse. The announcement, coming on the heels of the Lincoln hearings, which had done so much to arouse public interest and anger, galvanized the White House.

In January the Office of Thrift Supervision, the successor agency to the bank board (still run by Danny Wall despite his decision weeks earlier to resign), quietly moved against Neil Bush in what some suspected was an attempt to head off Gonzalez. Without public announcement, the OTS informed Bush that it was planning to bring formal charges against him, alleging violations of conflict of interest rules and other regulations. OTS officials wanted Bush to sign an agreement barring him from banking. Bush, insisting he had done nothing wrong, refused.

On February 5 OTS officials publicly began an enforcement action against Bush. But this time their sights were lowered. They asked only that Bush agree to cease and desist from the alleged wrongdoing. Bush, no longer even associated with a bank or thrift, again refused. A hearing before an administrative law judge ensued. The judge's final ruling would be subject to review by OTS chief Ryan, appointed to replace Wall by Neil's father.

In the action regulators noted that Silverado's wild growth—from $250 million in assets in mid-1983 to $2 billion by 1988—was "unsafe and unsound," characterized by bad lending policies, faulty appraisals of property, speculative investments in real estate, risky business dealings among thrift officials, and "excessive" pay for top executives. In fact, regulators concluded, the thrift's growth was driven largely "by the desire to have a larger base to absorb compensation" for management.

As for Neil Bush in particular, regulators said that he engaged in "one of the worst kinds" of conflict of interest as a Silverado director.

One prominent example of such a conflict, according to the OTS, involved his request in 1986 that Silverado provide a $900,000 letter of credit to a company owned by his friend and financial backer Kenneth Good, for an oil and gas exploration venture in Argentina. (Bush and Good had very strong ties. In 1984 Good lent Bush $100,000 to invest in a high-risk enterprise. Under the terms of the loan, Bush didn't have to repay the money unless the investment was successful. It wasn't, so he didn't repay it. "I know it sounds a little fishy," Bush told the House Banking Committee in the spring of 1990 when grilled about the loan.)

Although Bush informed other Silverado directors that he and Good had a business relationship, and abstained from voting on the request, the OTS charged that he concealed the fact that he was Good's partner in the Argentina venture and stood to gain from its success. Bush therefore stood to benefit from the letter of credit, even though it turned out not to be needed and was never issued. Regulators concluded that Bush "did everything in his power to bring about a regulatory violation" of rules governing how thrifts make loans to their own directors and officials.

A second charge alleged that Bush failed to disclose Good's agreement to pay him $3.1 million for an 80 percent stake in Bush's company at the same time that Good was telling Silverado he could not repay $8 million of $11 million he had borrowed from the S&L.

The OTS also charged that Bush acted "in a manner likely to cause abnormal risk to Silverado" when he voted to approve loans to a major Denver developer who had been his business partner for two years and owned a bank that had extended $1.7 million in credit to his company. The developer, William Walters, eventually defaulted on $100 million in loans from Silverado. The government portrayed Walters as a key figure in Silverado's demise, a man who was one of the thrift's biggest borrowers at the same time he was acquiring "conclusive control" over the holding company that owned it.

At one time Walters estimated his net worth to be $200 million. But the downturn in the oil and real estate markets hurt. Two of his banks failed in 1987. A third, Cherry Creek National Bank, from which Neil Bush had borrowed $1.75 million, failed in October 1990, after he had sold it.

In November 1990 Walters filed for personal bankruptcy, reporting debts of $196 million. "There are a few assets available, possibly a few hundred thousand dollars," Walters's lawyer said. Meanwhile, pictures of the house where Walters lived—a $1.9 million estate in Newport Beach, California, listed in his wife's name—surfaced in the press.

Together, Walters and Good defaulted on more than $130 million in loans from Silverado and thus contributed substantially to its collapse.

40

Sportsmanship

G onzalez began his Silverado hearings in June 1990. Like his inquiry into Lincoln the year before, the second round of hearings brought out little that was dramatically new. But like the earlier hearings and the Senate's Keating Five probe, the new investigation refocused the public's attention on the S&L scandal. And the fortuitous involvement of the president's son in the mismanagement of a particularly costly failed thrift directed the spotlight to the administration's role.

Neil Bush, lampooned on late-night television and in living rooms across the country, personalized the S&L debacle for much of the public. He became the poster child for the S&L scandal when practitioners of guerrilla theater put his picture on a wanted poster and plastered copies of it all over downtown Washington. The poster demanded "Jail Neil Bush" and urged public protest of the thrift scandal, saying that "these crimes were committed by the rich, for the rich and they should pay."

Everyone agreed Neil was being given special treatment. Critics said he was getting off easy because he was the president's son. Administration loyalists responded that he was being targeted as a scapegoat for minor problems that would be ignored by regulators were it not for his family ties. But this latter complaint was not without risk for the administration. It did not say much for the system of S&L regulation if the incompetence and backscratching displayed by Bush at Silverado were so typical of the industry that regulators usually overlooked such violations.

The Gonzalez hearings did shed additional light on the issue noted by Judge Sporkin in his ruling on Lincoln: the failure of accountants to police thrift abuses. One of the key problems was a practice, also used by Keating's Lincoln, that regulators call opinion shopping.

When Silverado officials told federal examiners in 1986 that the thrift had switched auditing firms, the S&L executives explained the change was made because the new firm, Coopers & Lybrand, was cheaper. But regulators discovered eighteen months later, when the thrift failed, that Silverado executives hired Coopers & Lybrand only after the accounting firm had sent a letter describing what types of transactions it believed had to be counted as losses.

Wise and other Silverado officials apparently liked the description. In 1985 Silverado lost $20 million. In 1986, thanks to the outlook of the new auditors, the thrift posted $15 million in profits and few bad loans. Silverado executives pocketed $2.7 million in bonuses. Regulators were left scratching their heads. The downturn in the Colorado real estate market suggested that Silverado could not be doing as well as the books reported.

The government subsequently accused Coopers & Lybrand of underestimating the thrift's exposure to loss in 1986 by relying on property appraisals that were highly inflated compared with prevailing market prices. The accounting firm promised that it would revise its auditing procedures and refrain from future wrongdoing.

The Gonzalez hearings also shed light on the curious question of why Silverado was not closed until after the 1988 presidential election. Former Topeka regional director Mowbray testified under oath that bank board officials in Washington ordered him to wait until the election to shut the thrift, although field examiners had been recommending the action for months.

Mowbray informally told board headquarters in July 1988 that Silverado's health had deteriorated to the point where the government soon would have to take it over. In September Mowbray's office formally requested that the thrift be seized by the federal government. It got no response until mid-October, when Colorado's state thrift commissioner informed the regional Topeka regulators that he was going to shut down the state-chartered, federally insured thrift by month's end. Topeka officials passed on the news to Wall's staff in Washington, which then accepted Topeka's recommendation that Silverado be seized—but ordered the regional regulators to delay the action for two months.

They did. On November 9, 1988, the day after George Bush was elected president, Mowbray signed the letter officially ordering the seizure of Silverado. The letter set in motion a series of actions that culminated in federal regulators taking over the thrift on December 9, 1988.

Mowbray testified that he didn't remember who had placed the call requesting the delay or who on his staff had received it. Other bank board officials had equally hazy recollections. Wall could not remember who made the call. Neither could his aides Karl Hoyle and Mary Creedon. After two days of searching in June 1990, neither former nor present federal regulators were able to come up with the name of the person who placed the telephone call. Despite the lapse of memory on that point, Wall, Hoyle, and Creedon were positive on another: They said there was no political motivation behind the order to delay.

This left an embittered Mowbray. Shortly after Silverado was closed, and a few days before Christmas 1988, Wall had fired Mowbray from his job as regional thrift supervisor. It was an abrupt ending to more than two decades of service in the bank board system. Perhaps Mowbray had been cozy with those he regulated and blind to their faults, but so were many in Washington. "I was the fall guy," Mowbray said during his testimony. He in turn accused Wall and other officials in Washington of trying to pin the blame on the Topeka office for "misleading" them about Silverado, a charge Mowbray denied.

"My staff, at my direction, had prepared information which I presented to ... Wall indicating that my staff had fully informed" officials in Washington of the thrift's problems, Mowbray told the House Banking Committee in the spring of 1990. "We supply the information. They [in Washington] determine what will happen on what day."

"The truth is we never did anything political," Hoyle, one of Wall's political advisers, responded. "It happens to be the truth."

As for whether officials in Washington were aware that the president-elect's son had been a director of Silverado, Creedon said, "People were certainly aware of it, but I don't know of any political factors driving the timing of the case." She, Hoyle, and others insist the only criteria driving the timing of actions were how much money an institution was losing, how strong a case regulators could make for closing it, and whether the government fund that insures deposits had sufficient cash to undertake such a closure.

After several news stories appeared in mid-1990 about the failure of the government to determine who had placed the 1988 call, and why, OTS director Ryan asked the Treasury Department's inspector general to investigate the matter formally. The request came hours after President Bush defended Neil's integrity in a press conference and said he believed that the government would be able to investigate fairly his son's role in the Silverado failure. But as the months went by, none of the key individuals involved in the decision to delay the closing of Silverado was contacted, much less questioned, by Treasury investigators.

Clearly the investigators were dragging their feet. It would have taken only a few telephone calls to regulators involved in the Silverado case to determine, as reporters did, that Washington bank board official Jay Earle placed the call to Topeka regulator Lou Roy, who then passed the request on to other Topeka officials.

The real questions remain, however, who told Earle to request the delay and whether Neil Bush's connection to the thrift entered into the decision to postpone closing Silverado. Unfortunately Treasury Department officials forbid Earle or Roy to discuss the matter until the investigation was over, but those officials left government after the 1992 election without ever starting such an investigation.

There were other odd things about the handling of Silverado. Bank board officials who arrived in Denver in December 1988, when the government finally moved against the S&L, say it was clear to them that someone, in violation of federal law, had tipped off Silverado officials about the impending take-over. One official says regulators found a memo to the Silverado staff warning of the pending government seizure. It appeared that many desks had been cleaned off and files emptied. Clearly Silverado officials had time to prepare for the worst.

Some former bank board officials suspect Hohlt of leaking news about the government's plans, noting that he was close to Wise, to Wall, and to the White House. Others suspect Wall's chief of the FSLIC, Stuart Root. Wall's staff found the allegations against Root serious enough that they referred the matter to the Justice Department for possible criminal investigation. The outcome of that referral has never been made public. For his part, Root has insisted publicly that he knows of no Justice Department referral. A bank board memo of March 19, 1989, however, says that Root hired an attorney "to look into the recent allegations of misconduct by him related to the Silverado takeover." The memo says bank board officials informed Root's lawyer that the referral had gone "to the U.S. attorney's in Denver, Colorado, with a confirming call to the Fraud Section, Criminal Division of the Department of Justice." Meanwhile, the source of the leak remains undetermined.

In the summer of 1990, as the hearings proceeded, the cost of the thrift bailout began to mount, and the administration abandoned President Bush's original promise that taxpayers would pay no more than $40 billion, Democrats and Republicans strove for the first time in earnest to paint the other party as the more culpable. The prospect of admitting that the read-my-lips, no-new-taxes pledge was bogus made Republicans especially vulnerable.

Democrats predictably saw Neil Bush as way to simplify the thrift crisis, put a human face on it, and highlight the political role played by Republicans in the debacle.

That led to embarrassing moments for the president. When he made a swing through Colorado in support of Representative Hank Brown's ultimately successful campaign to succeed retiring Senator Armstrong, the president found himself sharing the head luncheon table at a fund raiser with Colorado developer Larry Mizel, who had organized the affair. Mizel owned MDC Holdings, Inc., a real estate company that was among several firms under federal investigation in connection with the failure of Silverado. President Bush referred to many of the guests at the luncheon but studiously avoided any mention of Mizel, who had raised $1 million for Ronald Reagan's 1984 reelection campaign. White House aides went out of their way to explain that the president had no control over Mizel's presence. It was an uncomfortable meal.

Republicans countered Democratic assaults by defending Neil as a scapegoat and pointing out the S&L-related misdeeds of former Representatives Wright and Coelho. But the White House had more to lose in the finger pointing. The Democrats had suffered political fallout from the crisis with the resignations of Wright and Coelho; the Republicans, arguably more responsible, so far had escaped unscathed.

The White House throughout defended Neil and downplayed his importance in the industry. At one press conference the president said that he had discussed Silverado with Neil only "in that broad parental way," adding that his son "would be the last to ask me in any way to get involved in any side or the other.

"I have . . . full confidence in the integrity and honor of my son," the president said. "And I will stay out of anything to do with the investigation, but this is a fine young man. . . . Yet, the system's got to go forward. And I am convinced . . . if he has done something wrong, the system will so state. And if he hasn't, I hope it's fair enough to say, 'Hey, the boy did nothing wrong.' "

But the White House was sufficiently sensitive to the fallout from Neil Bush's misadventures that it apparently timed several announcements about Silverado so as to divert public attention from the president's son.

The Treasury chose Wednesday, May 23, 1990, to release its new estimate of the thrift bailout cost—a number as much as $82 billion more than its estimate of eighteen months earlier, when President Bush first addressed the problem publicly. The startling figures bumped from the front pages of many newspapers the other thrift news of the day: the House Banking Committee hearing at which Neil Bush acknowledged that his deal with Good "sounds a little fishy."

Not long afterward, after months of less than aggressive action against white-collar thrift abuses, thrift regulators announced they were filing a $24 million civil action against Thomas Spiegel of Columbia Savings and Loan.

The news, with details of Spiegel's outlandish life-style—a bulletproof bath-room, for example—and huge appetite for Milken's junk bonds eclipsed the regulators' simultaneous announcement that after weeks of pressure from Congress, they would hold the administrative hearings involving Neil Bush in public rather than behind closed doors as first planned.

Similarly, on June 20, White House spokesman Marlin Fitzwater, after having been virtually silent on the S&L issue during President Bush's tenure, came out swinging against the Democrats, accusing them of pushing through the increase in deposit insurance to $100,000 "in the dead of the night" in 1980. The prospect that politicians might finally take their gloves off eclipsed the scene being played out down the street in Congress, where former thrift regulator Mowbray was testifying that he had been ordered by regulators in Washington to delay the closing of Silverado until after election day.

Fitzwater's comments came back to haunt Republicans in the days ahead. While the deposit insurance initiative had been led by Democrats St Germain and Cranston, high-profile Republicans such as Garn were among those who had supported the proposal.

Friends in high places did not wholly insulate Neil Bush. In September 1990, four days before he appeared in front of an administrative judge in the OTS enforcement action, the FDIC filed a civil suit seeking to recover $200 million from him and ten other Silverado directors. The regulators claimed that Sil-verado's board had inflated the thrift's balance sheets, approving highly speculative loans and investments, and otherwise engaging in lax manage-ment that contributed to the thrift's collapse.

The FDIC's suit included far more serious charges than the enforcement action by the OTS. In addition to conflict of interest allegations, it said that Bush played a key role in authorizing bad business practices that, in the end, helped run the thrift into insolvency.

A prime example was Bush's role on Silverado's compensation committee, which was supposed to set appropriate salaries for top management. Regula-tors found that the management salaries and bonuses—which for Silverado's president and chief executive, Michael Wise, totaled more than $1 million a year—could not be justified in light of the precarious nature of Silverado's balance sheet.

Bush also served on the thrift's audit committee, which was responsible for ensuring that the company's operating policies were sound. As early as 1986 examiners found they were not, observing that the thrift "does not have comprehensive commercial real estate lending policies and frequently grants exceptions to those guidelines that have been reduced to writing." They also said the accounting treatment of a large group of loans "significantly distorted the presentation of credit risk, problem assets, income," and other key measures of financial health in periodic reports to regulators.

After the examiners had presented their concerns to management in early 1987 (and presented them again repeatedly over the next two years), they demanded that practices at Silverado be changed, and thrift officials ostensibly agreed. But, regulators alleged in the suit, Silverado never really implemented the promised changes.

In addition, the FDIC action focused heavily on Silverado's transactions with Bush's former business partner, alleging that "Silverado provided Walters with a ready source of cash for his ill-conceived, speculative projects" while the thrift assumed much of the risk. Walters in turn helped Silverado's officers by buying stock or bad loans from the thrift, according to the FDIC. That made Silverado appear to be more profitable than it was, permitting it to stay open longer than it should have. In one three-part transaction, for example, a Silverado subsidiary paid Walters far above the market value for two properties, ignoring information that one of them "was contaminated by an adjacent landfill." Walters then used part of the money to buy stock in Silverado's holding company. The holding company used some of the money from Walters's stock purchase to make $4 million in favorable loans to Silverado's Wise and to the thrift's principal shareholder, W. James Metz.

Despite the seriousness of the charges in the government's civil suit, some regulators in Washington admit to the difficulty the government would have in bringing a criminal action against Silverado's officials. The case would be undermined by the fact that Topeka regulators approved Silverado's business plans all along. The rank-and-file regulators of Topeka may have found much to fault at Silverado, but top regulators like Mowbray usually were very sympathetic to the thrift's practices.

In December 1990 administrative law judge Daniel J. Davidson decided that Neil Bush had engaged in "significant" conflicts of interest while serving as a director at Silverado and put the thrift at "abnormal risk" when he failed to disclose his business relationships with Good and Walters. The judge recommended that thrift regulators issue a cease and desist order requiring Bush to avoid conflicts of interest if he ever again became a thrift or bank director.

In April 1991 OTS chief Ryan largely affirmed the judge's decision. Ryan ruled that Neil Bush had engaged in conflicts of interest as a Silverado director but that, so long as he refrained from such practices in the future, he could work in a bank or S&L. Despite the embarrassment to Neil Bush and his father, the censure was one of the mildest possible for a banking violation. Neil subsequently decided not to appeal the decision.

In mid-1991 Neil Bush and other former directors and officers of Silverado agreed to pay the government nearly $50 million to settle the FDIC's $200 million suit. Little of the $50 million will be paid by Bush or the others, however. Most of the money recovered by the government will be covered by the defunct thrift's insurance or will come from a $23 million legal defense fund (what regulators call a war chest) that Silverado management set up for itself in 1986—using depositors' funds.

In July 1991, the FDIC negotiated a separate $20 million settlement with Silverado's former accountants, Coopers & Lybrand.

On May 29, 1991, the day the government announced the settlement of its case against Neil Bush and other Silverado officials, Neil was in the headlines on another matter. Considered a good tennis player, the president's son was thrown out of an amateur tournament during the Memorial Day weekend for cheating. He and his doubles partner broke the rules by playing in a division far below Bush's rated playing ability. Harold Aarons, head of the Colorado Tennis Association, said that he thought Bush made an honest mistake even though he is a veteran tournament player.

"He was very nice about it, very understanding," Aarons told the Reuters news service. "I suspect he just didn't know. The bottom line is that it's the player's responsibility. He blew it, as far as that goes."

EPILOGUE

___

The best way to rob a bank is to own one.

> —*William Crawford, California
> thrift commissioner*

One of the most incredible developments I've ever seen is the extent to which our problems in Maryland became the problems of the nation. I am shocked at the extent to which the Maryland experience seems to have existed in a vacuum. Lessons were not learned from it. If the federal government had moved decisively on the lessons of Maryland [and] Ohio . . . the price tag for taxpayers would be far less."

> —*Maryland State Senator
> Howard A. Denis, June 1989*

In the spring of 1990 a little more than a year had passed since President Bush unveiled his bailout plan with promises that the price tag would not exceed $90 billion (excluding tens of billions of dollars in interest) and that taxpayers would shoulder no more than $40 billion of that sum. In that short time the administration's estimate of the cost (again, exclusive of interest) had more than doubled. With interest added, realistic estimates of the tab easily exceeded $500 billion in ten years, or more than $1 trillion over several decades, enough by some calculations to add $13 billion a year in interest—forever—to the national debt.

In 1990 and 1991, with estimates of the bailout's ultimate cost reaching into the trillions, the Bush administration abandoned any pretense of limiting taxpayer liability. It was generally accepted that the public would foot most, if not all, of the cost.

"We certainly are concerned about additional costs, and it seems clear there will be higher costs than originally estimated," White House spokesman Fitzwater said in early 1991, in a stroke of understatement. "We don't have agreement on how how much they will be."

The tide of red ink didn't stop John Robson, the Treasury official in charge of the cleanup under President Bush, from trying to convince reporters not to call the administration's program a bailout. He and his colleagues favored the term "cleanup." The money, Robson argued, was not going to bail out shareholders, who generally lost everything when thrifts failed, but to depositors.

375

In fact, the deposit insurance fund had been created on the promise that the industry would finance it. When the fund went under, taxpayers had to step in to bail it out. In part, taxpayers are paying for the years of salaries, bonuses, and other benefits that thrift executives and owners enjoyed as their institutions were kept open. While it's true shareholders are wiped out once a thrift fails, they and management also are, for the most part, relieved of their obligation to repay customers or taxpayers for the money lost. And shareholders get to keep the money earned in dividends over the years.

No one in the administration explained why by mid-1991 they were warning publicly that there would have to be a "taxpayer bailout" of the commercial banking industry unless Congress adopted the White House's bank deregulation bill but that the taxpayer bailout of thrifts was a "cleanup." Several times even Treasury Secretary Brady forgot the silly distinction urged by his office and, in testimony before the Senate, called the tax dollars going to the thrift mess a bailout.

Another fight on Robson's agenda involved convincing reporters not to use the word "deregulation" when describing the Bush administration's plan, officially unveiled in 1991, to strip controls from the bank and thrift industries. The ill-executed deregulation of thrifts in the 1980s had acquired such a bad image that some Treasury officials joked they were holding a contest to come up with a substitute for the dreaded D word. The winning entry: "reform."

In late 1990 the Bush administration asked Congress for $60 billion in new "working capital" for the Resolution Trust Corporation, the agency created by the president's 1989 bailout plan to handle failed thrifts. By mid-1991 the administration asked that the RTC's borrowing for working capital be increased to $160 billion. This borrowing, as its name implies, is used to fund day-to-day operations of the agency but is supposed to be repaid once thrift assets are sold. Many analysts, however, think such sales won't cover very much of the borrowing and that over time, the debt simply will be added to the total cost of the debacle. Treasury Secretary Brady also asked Congress for an additional $80 billion to pay for closing thrifts.

At the same time, however, the administration struggled heroically to disguise the true, and ever-growing, size of the bailout. Among other tricks, it deleted 208 shaky thrifts (which would cost $25 billion to close) from the RTC's list of institutions likely to be shut by the government. Critics charged that the administration, possibly with an eye on the 1992 election, now less than sixteen months away, was trying to make it impossible for the public to determine the size of the bailout. Among those who claimed the administration was trying to obfuscate the true cost until after the election: the government's senior auditor, Comptroller General Bowsher.

Congress was not amused. "I see a bottomless pit into which we could pour all the resources the Treasury would summon," Representative Gonzalez said.

The GAO's Bowsher testified in early 1991 that the RTC lacked sufficient controls to guard against fraud and mismanagement in the sale of assets that by some estimates would total more than $500 billion in the years to come.

The RTC already had become the largest owner of real estate and junk bonds in the country, with hundreds of billions of dollars of inventory on any given day. A third of the thrift industry was now, in essence, socialized, owned and run by the federal government.

As the operator of very sick thrifts, the RTC ironically came to depend on once-vilified brokered deposits from Wall Street, needing the funds to keep many of its S&Ls afloat. As a consequence, taxpayer dollars for the cleanup continue to flow to Merrill Lynch and other securities firms. According to the *Wall Street Journal,* the amount of "excess interest," amounts above market rates, paid to Wall Street money brokers and their customers as of November 1990 was "$20 billion and counting."

And Wall Street's influence wasn't limited to the supply of funds. Investment bankers were gearing up to make money in the 1990s by advising those who had fallen into hard times because they had listened to them in the 1980s and by advising those left holding the bag, government agencies.

Salomon Brothers, for example, which gave investment advice to several thrifts in the 1980s that subsequently ran into trouble, took out ads in business publications in 1991 boasting: "We've advised the Resolution Trust Corporation on over $10 billion in mortgage and high yield assets." The ads went on to say that Salomon also had "structured transactions to solve financing problems" with the funding mechanism the Reagan administration set up in 1987 to keep the stopgap $10.8 billion bailout package off the budget. "One of our biggest clients is a relative," the ad's headline proclaimed beneath a picture of Uncle Sam.

Meanwhile, the RTC's effort to sell property was bogged down by the recession and by a nationwide glut of commercial real estate. And its public image suffered, with incidents such as one in Kansas City, Kansas, where the head of the RTC regional division spent thousands of dollars on fancy office furniture, not to mention $26,000 on oil paintings, sculptures, and prints. All this even though the agency was struggling to sell a warehouseful of such objects it had acquired from failed thrifts.

The RTC also came in for criticism when it allowed executives at some failed thrifts to continue drawing six-figure salaries after the government had taken the S&Ls over. When the agency refused to make the details public, according to the *Washington Monthly,* Ralph Nader's Public Citizen interest group and Cox Newspapers filed a freedom of information request in September 1990 for information on the salaries. It will take years to get a response.

The RTC's effort to provide low-income housing from its stash of repossessed real estate also was criticized for what even Treasury Secretary Brady acknowledged was a slow start. At the same time, according to members of the House Banking Committee, the agency allowed real estate developers to make a profit buying low-income housing, with one critic calling it "socialism for the rich."

And there were other indications that government officials in charge of the bailout were not as careful with the public's money as they could be. For example, it was not until mid-1991 that the RTC and the FDIC, the nation's largest purchasers of legal services, decided to implement for the first time a standardized contracting procedure to eliminate wide fluctuations in what private law firms charge the government agencies for services related to the S&L cleanup.

By spring 1991 the RTC, under attack both by public interest groups and by the struggling real estate industry (which had spiraled into a recession in part because the 1989 bailout bill shut off the easy credit from thrifts that had been so plentiful in the 1980s) announced it would conduct an internal review of the bailout operation. Representative Annunzio, meanwhile, the thrift industry's old friend, asked an RTC task force, set up by Congress in 1989 to oversee the new agency, to consider abolishing the agency altogether by turning its functions over to the private sector.

By the end of 1990 only 2,342 thrifts remained out of government control; they lost $2.41 billion for the year. That was down from the $6.23 billion the industry lost in 1989, but only because the government had taken over more than 200 troubled institutions in the interim. The segment still in private hands saw problems rising. Withdrawals continued to outpace new deposits, and loan defaults were up as the national real estate downturn led to gloomy quarterly results even for some of the strongest thrifts. H. F. Ahmanson & Company of Los Angeles, for example, parent company of the nation's largest thrift, saw fourth-quarter profits fall 99 percent in 1990, to less than one cent a share.

The industry even saw a drop in its bread-and-butter lending area of home mortgages, sparking renewed outcries against the 1989 legislation that had mandated a return to thrifts' original focus on home loans.

At the end of March 1992 there were 2,064 S&Ls still in the private sector, not being run by the government. Of those, fewer than half were well capitalized and profitable. The rest ran the gamut from those that were doomed to fail to those facing some possibility of recovery, if the economy cooperated.

Lower interest rates helped thrifts, but bad loans and a real estate recession continued to drag down many S&Ls. One GAO official, quoted in the *Washington Post,* warned that many thrifts "may look healthier in the short term than they really are."

In 1990 and early 1991 the White House and FDIC Chairman Seidman publicly criticized estimates by former bank board economist Brumbaugh that the commercial bank insurance fund was broke and, like the thrift fund, would need a sizable cash infusion from taxpayers.

But by mid-1991 Seidman and Treasury Secretary Brady, despite past denials, conceded that the bank insurance fund would need "recapitalizing," though the administration insisted this could be done through borrowing from the Treasury that eventually would be repaid by the industry after the sale of assets from failed institutions. (If the money wasn't repaid, however, the arrangement would become a taxpayer bailout without all the hoopla that attended the 1989 thrift bailout legislation because the lifeline to tax dollars already would have been tapped.)

Meanwhile, when bankers lobbied Capitol Hill in 1991 in support of the White House's proposal to deregulate commercial banking, they had to work hard to keep from being tarred by the S&L fiasco. They ran an ad campaign proclaiming: "Thrifts and Banks: Different Industries—Different Goals." Lawmakers became paralyzed, worried that a vote in favor of change could make them responsible for the next crisis.

Many politicians who once coveted a seat on the House Banking Committee, knowing that it was a great spot from which to collect campaign contributions, began to shun the assignment. In January 1991, as the 102d Congress convened, nearly a third of the fifty-one members who were on the committee at the end of the 101st Congress did not return, some having lost reelection campaigns but most having chosen assignments on other committees.

By the end of 1991 Congress had killed the major provisions of Bush's bank deregulation package. But it did approve a $70 billion line of credit to the U.S. Treasury that the FDIC could "borrow" on to cope with a mounting list of bank failures, a problem the recession only compounded.

History repeated itself in other ways. In mid-1990 the nation's chief thrift regulator, Tim Ryan of the OTS, decided to take a path reminiscent of the policies his predecessors had tried throughout the 1980s. He announced he would allow some weak thrifts to resume dividend payments to shareholders, hoping to attract new equity owners to struggling institutions. And he said he was reconsidering the wisdom of forcing thrifts to pay higher insurance premiums than banks, even though that was one of the conditions for the industry's receipt of a taxpayer bailout.

In late 1990 and early 1991 Ryan and Seidman dusted off another old idea the Bush administration in 1989 and it had abandoned: forbearance, the policy of propping up sick thrifts with government aid or lower government standards. Ryan used the term to reporters, only to learn the administration had given the "F word" the same status as "bailout" and "deregulation." The phrase "open-thrift assistance" was used for a while instead, only to be abandoned, at last check, for "early intervention."

On one occasion Ryan proposed trying to prop up ten of the remaining sickest thrifts, most of them in California, which had combined assets of $80 billion. According to congressional aides, the list of forbearance candidates included Great American, the thrift headed for so long by President Reagan's old friend Gordon Luce—this despite President Bush's 1989 promise as he unveiled his bailout plan that "never again should we allow insolvent federally-insured deposit institutions to remain open and operate without sufficient private capital at risk." (Luce stepped down as chairman and chief executive of Great American in mid-1990, and shortly afterward the S&L sold its branch network in California to Wells Fargo in an effort to raise money. But its struggle to remain solvent failed. It was seized by federal regulators in August 1991.) Ryan had worked out the plan in private discussions with industry representatives, just as Pratt, Gray, and Wall had done before him.

For his part, Seidman described a much broader policy, in which the administration would apply a forbearance strategy to an estimated thousand banks and thrifts that could fail in the next few years. The plan raised eyebrows in Congress, where Senator Garn articulated the thoughts of many when he said Seidman's idea sounded like the forbearance policy applied so disastrously to S&Ls. Garn said that he would be "yelling and screaming" if the administration duplicated "the stupid experience we had in the past."

To try to deter a return to the old approach, the Congressional Budget Office released a study that concluded the policy of leaving insolvent thrifts open had added $66 billion to the cost of the bailout, not including the billions of dollars in additional interest and related costs. The study went even further than one released by the OTS in early 1990 by James Barth, the government's chief thrift economist under Wall and then briefly under Ryan at the OTS. Barth's study showed that the government's forbearance policy during the 1980s frequently allowed as many as seven years to pass before insolvent thrifts were closed, adding greatly to taxpayer costs. He found, for example, that 489 thrifts lost a total of $42 billion from 1980 to 1988 while operating after they had become insolvent.

Then, in the spring of 1992, in what many viewed as an election year ploy, the administration considered using direct taxpayer money to merge troubled S&Ls with healthy ones. The proposal called for shareholders to preserve some of the value of their investment. Republican Representative Jim Leach blasted the idea, calling it "corporate socialism" and charging it would mostly benefit large thrifts in California and Florida.

In early 1991 problems resembling those in the thrift industry began to come to light in the nation's credit unions. In a move that bore an eerie similarity to actions taken by Ohio and Maryland in the mid-1980s, Rhode Island closed forty-five state-chartered credit unions because of insufficient funding in the private insurance company backing the institutions.

In mid-1991 the Center for Study of Responsive Law, a group affiliated with consumer activist Nader, released a report showing that investors in Wall's 1988 deals contributed at least $2.8 million to presidential and congressional candidates while the deals were being put together.

The study followed one commissioned by the federal government conclud-ing that thrift regulators mishandled the disposal of scores of thrifts in 1988, when they sold the institutions with the promise of billions of dollars in federal aid. The transactions increased the cost of the bailout, the four-volume report concluded. "It appears on the basis of all the available facts that [thrift regulators] were less than successful in fulfilling their self-imposed competi-tive mandate," the report said. "The plan did not provide the same opportuni-ties for all potential bidders to compete on a fair and equitable basis." In several instances groups of thrifts appeared to have been specially created and the sale "negotiated with only a single bidder, with no notice of the availability of these new groupings to other bidders."

The report renewed talk in Congress that the deals should be pulled apart and redone. But as of late 1992 nothing had come of it.

Federal regulators did begin to renegotiate some terms of the 1988 deals, however, a step permitted by the original contracts. Among the thrifts in-volved are those owned by Robert Bass, Ronald Perelman, and Lewis Ranieri. All told, the renegotiations, which largely involve early payment of govern-ment subsidies, would save taxpayers $3 billion, according to government regulators, or less than 5 percent of the 1988 deals' total cost.

According to data collected by the Census Bureau in 1987 and released in 1991, fewer people now can afford a first-time home than could afford one fifteen years ago. At the time of the survey 91 percent of households paying rent could not afford a median-priced home.

The U.S. League of Savings Institutions, sensitive to the effect such ad-verse statistics have on its industry, launched a public relations campaign pushing low-income housing. At its convention in the fall of 1990 its leadership also called for a revamping of the 1989 bailout bill and for tax breaks to bolster the housing industry. But in April 1991, in a typically contradictory move, leading thrift executives renewed the industry's fight to curb Fannie Mae and Freddie Mac, complaining that the efficiency of the secondary mortgage market created by the two government-sponsored corporations lowers the cost of home loans for consumers and thus eats into the already meager profits of the S&L industry. The league also began to lobby the administration to reduce the industry's promised contribution to the bailout plan, which was to come from money invested by the industry in the Federal Home Loan Banks.

At the time *USA Today* ran a profile of book author and reporter Michael Robinson, who wrote a song about the industry's troubles:

> Turns out the best thing to own
> is something called a savings and loan
> where you can live off the public trough
> with all the politicians you bought off . . .
>
> though the truth may seem surreal
> the government gave them the license to steal
> well let me tell you something funny
> they're savings a special place in hell
> for the scoundrels of the S&L's. . . .*

The league complained vehemently to the newspaper.

Meanwhile, a close relationship between the league and government thrift agencies continues. One example: The RTC hired longtime league lawyer Randall H. McFarlane in the fall of 1990 to be the agency's liaison to and lobbyist in Congress.

In 1992, faced with a declining membership and a tarnished public image, the U.S. League of Savings Institutions merged with the National Council of Savings Institutions and adopted the new name Savings and Community Bankers of America.

In the spring of 1991, thrift managers won a judicial battle to preserve an accounting gimmick created during the Reagan years. The U.S. Supreme Court upheld a practice sanctioned by federal thrift regulators that permitted thrifts to swap money-losing loans with each other and reap tax benefits from those losses without having to declare the loans in default for purposes of federal regulations governing solvency.

*Copyright 1990 Robinson/Quiroz. Lyrics used by permission

Regulators have found numerous incidents in which accountants and law-yers allowed thrift losses to be booked as profits, worthless property to be counted as valuable assets, or fraudulent transactions to be conducted with-out question. Thus far, however, there has been relatively little action against such professionals by the government.

But there has been some activity, much of it surrounding professionals connected with Lincoln. In June 1990 the law firm of Kaye, Scholer, Fierman, Hays & Handler paid $20 million to settle two securities fraud and racketeer-ing suits brought by investors in Lincoln's parent company. In 1992 the firm paid $41 million to settle a civil case regarding Lincoln brought by federal thrift regulators.

California officials began proceedings in 1990 that might have revoked the state license of Ernst & Young for the firm's auditing of Lincoln, although few experts believed the state would actually go that far. Indeed, in July 1991 a judge threw out the $250 million suit the state's attorney general had filed that accused Ernst & Young of negligence in its auditing of Lincoln.

At about the same time, however, the firm settled an enforcement inquiry by the California State Board of Accountancy by agreeing, among other things, to pay a $1.5 million "contribution" to the board's "major case" en-forcement program and to require its auditors to take additional education courses.

Meanwhile, Ernst & Young agreed, without admitting or denying guilt, to pay the federal government $40 million for what regulators say was the faulty accounting work one of its predecessor firms, Arthur Young & Com-pany, performed for Lincoln. As a result, the auditing firm, one of the six largest in the country, says it will not be named as a defendant in the govern-ment's $1.7 billion civil fraud and racketeering lawsuit stemming from Lin-coln's failure. Ernst & Young says it still stands behind its audits of Lincoln, and it contends there was nothing improper or unusual about one of its auditors going to work for Keating. In 1992, however, saying it wanted to avoid the potential cost of a jury verdict, it agreed to pay $63 million to settle a suit by bondholders in Lincoln's parent.

In a separate settlement with federal banking regulators, Ernst & Young agreed in late 1992 to pay an additional $400 million to the government for work the auditor performed in the preceding ten years at 400 banks and S&Ls, including Vernon and Silverado. The firm settled without admitting or denying liability.

Laventhol & Horwath, the nation's seventh-largest accounting firm at the time, failed in 1990 in part because of lawsuits stemming from thrift audits.

In October 1990 the Cleveland-based law firm Jones, Day, Reavis & Pogue was sued by the FDIC for $72 million in a malpractice suit involving what the government said were bogus loans and real estate deals for directors at two Austin, Texas, thrifts that have now failed. The firm settled the suit in late 1992 for $16.5 million. (Coincidentally, Rosemary Stewart, author of the infamous "Rosemary's Baby" letter to Keating, joined Jones Day in 1989, shortly after the dissolution of the bank board.)

The suit put the FDIC in an awkward position because Jones Day is one of the private firms it uses the most. For example, the law firm represented the federal agency in a similar suit against directors and officers of a failed New Mexico banking chain.

In 1992 Jones Day agreed to pay $24 million to settle claims by bondholders in Keating's American Continental Corporation. Still pending is a $50 million lawsuit brought by federal thrift regulators that names Jones Day as a defendant and says the firm was partly responsible for Lincoln's failure.

The law firm of Sidley & Austin has settled a malpractice suit by federal thrift regulators for an undisclosed amount (said to be $7.5 million) in connection with the work one of its partners, Margery Waxman, performed on behalf of Charles Keating.

In mid-1991 the government began an investigation into KPMG Peat Marwick's audits of thrifts. The action was prompted in part by revelations that one of the accounting firm's partners borrowed $900,000 in a series of home loans from a California thrift that was a Peat client. In addition, in July 1991 the GAO concluded that KPMG Peat Marwick's 1988 audit of FADA did not follow generally accepted accounting principles and that the balance sheets of the organization gave a misleading picture—specifically, that FADA had earned $3.3 million that year when in fact it lost $9.9 million. (The firm, as well as Danny Wall and Stuart Root, disagreed with the GAO's conclusion.)

In 1991 the SEC filed a civil action against the Dallas office of what had been Arthur Young, claiming that representatives of the firm presented themselves as independent auditors of a major Texas bank, Republic Bank, when in fact, the firm's partners received more than $20 million in loans from the bank. Republic merged with InterFirst Corporation in 1987 to form First RepublicBank Corporation, which failed less than fourteen months later. Ernst & Young claims that the amount of the loans is closer to $4 or $5 million but that in any case, there was nothing improper about them. The suit is ongoing. Meanwhile, in a potentially far-reaching decision in late 1991, a federal judge ruled that Ernst & Young cannot be held responsible for the 1986 collapse of a Dallas-based thrift named Western Savings. The judge threw out the $560 million suit by the FDIC. The FDIC is appealing the ruling, which could severely hamper the agency's effort to seek damages from the auditors who reviewed the books of failed S&Ls.

———

In December 1990 the White House chief of staff, John Sununu, sought to block a second five-year term for Comptroller of the Currency Robert L. Clarke after complaining that Clarke's regulation of national banks was too tough and had helped produce a credit squeeze. But others in the administration, mindful that the lax oversight and freewheeling lending standards of the 1980s had been a major factor in the collapse of the thrift industry, won reappointment for Clarke.

The reappointment proved to be a mixed blessing when it was disclosed that Clarke had failed to place his investments, many involving banks, in a blind trust to prevent conflicts of interest. After the disclosure he did set up a blind trust. But it was too late. The Senate rejected Clarke's renomination as the nation's top bank regulator.

The comptroller wasn't the only commercial banking regulator to come under fire. The Federal Reserve Board, considered the most blemish-free of the bank regulatory agencies, found its image tarnished in early 1991 as reports came to light of scandals at two banks under its supervision, one involving more than $3 billion in illicit loans to Iraq from an American branch of an Italian bank, and another the illegal ownership by an Arab banking company, the Bank of Credit and Commerce International, of the District of Columbia's largest bank holding company, First American Bankshares.

Among the allegations about BCCI, known in banking and regulatory circles as the Bank of Crooks and Criminals, was that according to the Fed, it secretly and illegally bought up to a 25 percent stake in CenTrust, the failed Miami thrift, and that in 1988 it bought $25 million in junk bonds from CenTrust to make the S&L appear healthier to federal regulators than it was.

The government's track record in recovering funds from S&L looters—and in putting them behind bars—is mixed. Much of the slow start in prosecuting S&L criminals can be traced to the bank board's decision under Ed Gray to emphasize financial recovery through civil suits rather than punishment through the criminal process. In 1985, for example, when the problems in the industry were well known, Gray's board referred only 434 cases to the Justice Department for criminal action.

The policy had its critics. "In the long run, the most significant deterrent is criminal prosecution, conviction and a meaningful jail sentence," said U.S. Attorney Robert Bonner of Los Angeles in early 1989. Bank Board policy frustrated his efforts. For example, the Justice Department wanted to put several of the top officials at the failed San Marino Savings Corporation of California in jail for their part in the fraudulent conduct that helped doom the thrift at a cost to taxpayers of almost $200 million.

But Bonner couldn't even try. Without consulting the Justice Department, federal S&L regulators promised some San Marino officials that they wouldn't face criminal prosecution if they helped the government recover part of the money lost when the S&L collapsed in 1984. According to Bonner, thrift regulators also agreed to settle civil suits against other executives of the S&L without consulting his office, undermining possible criminal action. "It borders on obstruction of justice," Bonner said of bank board actions in the case. "It's mind-boggling."

In the San Marino case the government spent about $3 million to recover some $19 million from former directors, officials, and outside professionals such as accounting firms. But that was only a fraction of the $193 million the S&L failure cost the government, and not one person has gone to jail in connection with the affair.

After repeated criticism from Congress, regulators at the bank board dramatically increased criminal referrals to a total of six thousand in 1989 before the agency was replaced by the Office of Thrift Supervision. (Among the people referred by the agency for criminal investigation was one of the bank board's own employees.) But the board's initial tardiness in making criminal referrals has impaired the government's ability to prosecute wrongdoers in some of the biggest, costliest failures, according to investigators on the House Government Operations Committee, which for years has kept tabs on such information. Moreover, when it finally arrived, the bank board's pent-up flood of referrals buried Justice officials in a blizzard of paper work, making it difficult for prosecutors to pick the important complaints from the minor and repetitive ones, according to congressional investigators.

But the Justice Department itself has contributed to the slow pace of prosecutions. After setting up the Dallas-based special financial fraud task force amid great fanfare in mid-1987, Attorney General Meese a year later quietly diverted $1 million of the task force's travel funds to his pet project, one Congress had chosen not to fund: the Justice Department's antipornography programs. (It was Meese who, to a roomful of reporters and television cameras, expounded on the Justice Department's war on smut while standing in front of a bare-breasted statue of blind Justice.)

The problem at Justice has been compounded by chronic manpower shortages. "I don't think doubling my staff would be sufficient," Marvin Collins, a U.S. attorney in Texas, said in 1990.

Sometimes overworked U.S. attorneys let the statute of limitations run out. That's what happened in San Francisco in at least two cases involving the former managers of one of the biggest failed thrifts, American Savings. "We concluded that the U.S. attorney's inaction and delay made it impossible to pursue these two cases," said a congressional aide on the Government Operations Committee. "The FBI expressed some frustration. It put these cases together, and then nothing happened."

Even when they have been prosecuted, the government has found it difficult to establish criminal activity in thrift cases, which typically are complex, hard to untangle, and even harder to explain to a jury. In addition, most of the cases involve white-collar criminals who often attend church, are active in community affairs, and mingle in influential circles, making it hard to convince jurors that the accused acted with criminal intent.

In October 1988, for example, the government lost its first big criminal S&L case, the prosecution of Thomas Gaubert on charges of wire fraud and of lying to government bank regulators regarding an $8 million loan from an S&L. At Gaubert's jury trial the list of his character witnesses included a federal judge and Texas State Treasurer and future Governor Ann Richards, a sharp-tongued speaker who a few months later wowed audiences watching the Democratic National Convention. Officials of the S&L testified they would not have agreed to certain loans if they had known Gaubert was the recipient of the money. In the opinion of several observers, the government, despite a strong case, blew it by boring the jurors with too many unorganized details.

The jury acquitted Gaubert on October 29, 1988. At the news Gaubert tearfully embraced his son, leaving Justice Department prosecutors to ponder the consequences of losing the first big S&L fraud case they had brought to trial. They had hoped that a conviction of Gaubert would cause other indicted S&L executives to plead guilty rather than waste time and money on a trial.

Even so, in mid-1990 Attorney General Thornburgh boasted that the Justice Department was sifting through eighteen thousand referrals involving 310 failed thrifts to determine the role played by fraud in their collapse. "There's not a major savings and loan failure today that is not at one stage or another of investigation," he told the Senate Judiciary Committee. But, he said, "I would mislead you if I said any substantial portion of those assets will be recovered. They have been spent and squandered, some have been devalued, some have been spirited away overseas."

He was right. Much of the money is gone, paid to Wall Street in fees or given to borrowers who defaulted after spending it. Plenty, of course, also went to crooks. The league and the government, once loath to admit the presence of criminals, now blames them for many of the industry's woes. Regulators estimate that fraud played some role in 75 percent of the thrifts that failed. But economists argue that the role of crooks should not be exaggerated. They say that there was at least as much simple incompetence by thrift managers who plunged institutions into risky businesses they knew little about.

From October 1988 through May 31, 1991, the Justice Department charged 764 people in connection with "major" S&L prosecutions, with "major" defined as a case involving losses of at least $100,000; involving owners or top officials of an institution; or involving schemes by multiple borrowers from the same thrift. Losses at the S&Ls involved were a fraction of the overall cost to taxpayers: $7.72 billion. During that period, the money ordered to be paid in both penalties and restitution in these cases was substantially less than that—only $279 million.

Even when the government successfully prosecuted crooks, its record in getting them to make good on court-ordered restitution—which restores money taken, in contrast with a fine, which is imposed as punishment—has been poor. Of the $5.8 million in restitution payments ordered in 1988, only $21,000 had been recovered by mid-1990. Of $3.1 million ordered in 1989, only $2,700 had been recovered. In the first half of 1990, $2.5 million in restitution had been mandated by the courts, but only $50 had been paid. The GAO told Congress in early 1992 that a total of only $365,000 had been paid on $84 million in fines and restitution in fifty-five major S&L criminal convictions.

The record of recovery of money through civil suits hasn't been much better. In 1987 and 1988, for example, thrift regulators spent over $75 million in legal fees to recover $181 million from directors, officers, and consultants who ran thrifts into the ground. That worked out to $1 in legal fees for every $2.40 recovered, well below the $1 to $3 recovery ratio that is typical in liability suits against company directors and officers in general.

In 1990, with the government's attention fully focused on the debacle, court-mandated recoveries from civil suits against S&Ls, their managers, and professionals totaled $241 million. Much of that—$197 million—had been recovered as of August 1991.

Pointing to this spotty record, Democrats tried to make political hay by charging that the Bush administration had not done enough to catch the crooks. The House Government Operations Committee, in a report issued in November 1990 entitled *The U.S. Government War against Fraud, Abuse, and Misconduct in Financial Institutions: Winning Some Battles but Losing the War,* said that lack of proper cooperation continues between regulators pressing civil cases and Justice Department officials pursuing criminal prosecutions. "The FDIC and RTC and their fee counsel have not produced certain documentation to Federal prosecutors in response to grand jury subpoenas," the report noted, usually on the ground that the material is privileged or that its disclosure would hinder civil recovery efforts.

The committee also accused the White House and Justice Department of "playing catch up." As an example it cited a June 1990 press conference at which Thornburgh assembled ninety-three U.S. attorneys to announce a major attack on financial institutions fraud. The report noted that "with the exception of the appointment of a special counsel for these cases, most of the proposals made during that press conference had already been proposed" in congressional legislation. And the announcement came eighteen months into President Bush's tenure in the White House, despite the months, even years, of study his top aides had devoted to the S&L scandal.

The White House in turn has exaggerated its efforts, making extravagant claims that are undercut by persistent Justice Department complaints about the understaffing of FBI and U.S. attorney field offices. In 1990, after a study of fifty-nine field offices, the FBI concluded it needed 425 new agents to start work on more than two thousand unattended thrift cases. It received half that number of agents, and reports of backlogs abound.

Still others charge both sides with trying to focus on crooks rather than the joint political culpability of Congress and the White House. Hence the dog and pony show by Thornburgh and others in the Bush administration and by Congress. According to a *Wall Street Journal* story on September 10, 1990:

> For all the sound and fury, politicians are actually using the FBI in a subtle public-relations campaign that has historical roots dating as far back as 1919. The message, intended to reassure voters, is that a forbiddingly complicated problem—the possible collapse of the thrift industry—is really a simple matter of cops and robbers.
>
> Such attempts to use the FBI to transform an ominous political or social issue into a crime-busting crusade date back to the post-World War I Red scare and the bureau's formative anti-radical investigations under J. Edgar Hoover. During the Great Depression, Mr. Hoover, a genious image-crafter, countered the loss of national confidence with a dramatic demonstration of government power: the FBI's successful gangster cases against the likes of Machine Gun Kelly, John Dillinger and Pretty Boy Floyd.

As for the thrift executives themselves:

Don Dixon, the former owner of Vernon Savings and Loan—called "the highest of the high fliers among [S&L] crooks" by Thornburgh—was convicted in December 1990 on criminal fraud charges that could have put him in jail for 120 years and exposed him to $5.6 million in fines. But when he was sentenced by U.S. District Court Judge A. Joe Fish in early 1991, he received only 5 years in prison, with eligibility for parole in 1992; was ordered to pay restitution of only $600,000; and was required to provide 500 hours of community service. The modest sentence astonished those familiar with Dixon's life-style—the art collection, the lavish homes and parties, all at his thrift's expense.

Edwin T. McBirney III, the former head of Sunbelt Savings in Dallas, pleaded guilty to criminal fraud charges in early 1991 and agreed to repay $7.5 million. He faces up to fifteen years in prison and fines of up to $8.5 million but, as part of a plea bargain, was not expected to be sentenced for two years while he helped federal investigators unravel thrift transactions that could lead to other convictions.

In April 1992 the government sold Sunbelt to San Francisco-based Bank-America Corporation, parent of banking giant Bank of America.

In late 1990 Stanley Adams, best known for having applied to open a branch of his S&L on the moon, was indicted with several others on federal criminal fraud and conspiracy charges in connection with his now-failed Lamar Savings Association of Austin. In a plea bargain with the government, he pleaded guilty in 1991 to two counts of conspiracy, for which he could face up to ten years in jail and $500,000 in fines, and agreed to cooperate with Justice Department officials in their investigation of S&L fraud.

D. L. ("Danny") Faulkner, Spencer Blain, and two others were convicted in November 1991 of looting $165 million from five S&Ls through fraudulent land deals in the early 1980s. The deals were blamed for the 1984 collapse of Empire Savings and Loan of Mesquite, Texas, which, at a cost of $284 million, was the largest thrift failure at the time.

Despite a $200,000 reward for information leading to his arrest, a fugitive Maryland thrift millionaire named Tom J. Billman still eludes police, who believe he is living the good life in Europe, where he apparently hid $22 million in Swiss bank accounts following the 1985 collapse of his Community Savings and Loan Association. After leaving his wife and the country in 1988, using the name of a college roommate, and settling in the Costa del Sol region of Spain, he acquired a girl friend, rented a seaside condominium, and maintained two yachts. Authorities say that at one point he hired attorneys and began setting up a business, although he has since gone underground again. They say he has been spotted reading the *International Herald Tribune* and other English-language publications containing financial news.

Countless other convicted thrift executives have yet to see the poorhouse, thanks to a savvy use of bankruptcy laws, trusts, and foreign bank accounts to shield and hide assets. For example, one former executive served time in prison for conspiracy and wire fraud at a Denver thrift. He filed for bankruptcy, leaving a dozen thrifts holding most of his $59 million in debt, but the bankruptcy laws allow him to return from prison to his $325,000 home and his Mercedes in Lubbock, Texas.

Despite the S&L debacle, bank and thrift regulators still keep much information about ailing and failed financial institutions secret. "The public is spending billions of dollars but has no idea what those dollars are going to," complained Senator Wirth in June 1991 on the Senate floor as he prepared to introduce an amendment that would have forced regulators to make public the examinations of failed S&Ls bailed out with taxpayers' money.

Regulators, arguing that public confidence could be undermined—but some cynics suspect actually trying to hide their own histories of inadequate oversight—have largely opposed such a policy. Because of active opposition by many senators, many Republican, Wirth didn't introduce the measure.

Drexel Burnham Lambert Inc. filed for bankruptcy in February 1990, after pleading guilty to six criminal felony counts and agreeing to $650 million in criminal and civil fines. In April 1990 Michael Milken pleaded guilty to six felony charges of securities fraud and other business crimes and agreed to pay $600 million in fines and penalties. Seven months later he was sentenced to ten years in prison, although he can be paroled at any time.

But the lawsuits haven't ended. Although the government, as part of its plea agreement with Milken, agreed not to file more criminal actions against him, it can seek civil remedies without limit. The RTC and FDIC accordingly have filed a $12 billion suit against Milken and former Drexel officials for "deliberately and systematically" plundering the S&L industry. (One of those named, former Drexel chief executive Frederick Joseph, agreed in August 1991 to pay $3 million to settle with the agencies. He also agreed to cooperate with them in their claims against Milken and others.) The government also sued Drexel for $6.8 billion, although it agreed to settle for a much smaller sum in exchange for Drexel's promise to turn over confidential files that the government expects will prove invaluable in its civil case against Milken.

The suit against Milken and other former Drexel officials centers on Drexel's extensive dealings with at least forty-four failed S&Ls that bought some $28 billion in junk bonds. In essence, the government charges that Milken artificially inflated the price of securities. A handful of those thrifts received special attention from the government in the suit, including Lincoln, Columbia Savings in California, and CenTrust in Florida.

In mid-1991 bankrupt Drexel agreed to pay the Internal Revenue Service $290 million in back taxes and interest to settle an IRS claim against it that originally sought more than $5 billion. The agreement cleared the way for Drexel's creditors, including the FDIC, to reach a settlement with the firm on its bankruptcy reorganization plan. Even as the settlement was being reached, Milken was hiring Harvard Law School Professor Alan M. Dershowitz to fight the civil suits and to try to reduce his sentence in his criminal case. And Milken filed objections to the Drexel bankruptcy plan, objecting to the government's claim that he had controlled the junk bond market, that Drexel—and by implication Milken—were responsible for losses at S&Ls resulting from the collapse of that market, and that thrifts or other clients bought the instruments without being aware of the high risk involved.

Charles Keating was found guilty in December 1991 of seventeen counts of securities fraud by a California Superior Court jury and sentenced to ten years in prison and ordered to pay a fine of $250,000. Shortly after the verdict, a federal grand jury returned a seventy-seven-count indictment against Keating, his son, and three others, charging they engaged in a series of illegal financial schemes. They face up to $17 million in fines and could be forced to forfeit as much as $265 million in assets.

In July 1992 a jury awarded $2.1 billion to the investors who bought junk bonds at Keating's S&L. As of this writing, the bondholders also have regained, through settlements with accountants, lawyers, and other plaintiffs, roughly 34 cents for every $1 they lost.

Although the Senate Ethics Committee, widely criticized as a toothless self-regulatory body, questioned the wisdom of the actions of the Keating Five, it sought a formal "rebuke" by the Senate on the Senate floor only of Cranston. In November 1991, after his actions on behalf of Keating were described as "improper and repugnant," Cranston responded that his actions were no different from those his colleagues engaged in every day. "You are in jeopardy if you ever do anything at any time to help a contributor," he warned them.

There has been no word on the FBI probe of the Keating Five.

Neil Bush's lawyer claimed that Bush would have to pay his own attorney's fees stemming from the government suits regarding Silverado. In fact, in early 1990 Thomas ("Lud") Ashley—lobbyist for America's biggest banks, former congressman from Ohio, and longtime friend of the Bush family—set up a fund to collect private donations to pay Neil's legal costs. At the time Ashley was lobbying on behalf of the banking industry for many of the provisions that the Bush administration included in its 1991 bank deregulation bill (which eventually died in Congress).

Ashley will not say who has contributed to the fund, but said he believes Neil does not have to pay taxes on the money.

The Treasury, which in June 1990 said it had begun investigating who ordered a delay in the closing of Silverado, quietly referred the matter to the FBI five months later, a letter from October 1990 and made public under the Freedom of Information Act, shows. In 1992 a Treasury spokesman told the *Washington Post* that the Treasury never interviewed anyone in the case prior to turning the "investigation" over to the FBI. "Treasury never investigated this," the spokesman told the *Post*. By mid-1992, two years after OTS chief Ryan requested the investigation, the central men in the case said no federal agency had contacted them. In the meantime, the investigation technically remains alive, and so, too, does the gag order on those involved.

In mid-1991 the House Banking Committee released documents showing that the Federal Reserve Board took the unusual step of lending $98 million to Lincoln Savings and Loan in 1989. The loan was unusual because the Fed normally lends only to banks. And it was made well after the thrift had been taken over and was being run by the government, thus raising questions in the mind of Committee Chairman Gonzalez about whether the Fed's intent was to allow uninsured depositors, those with more than $100,000 in the thrift, to get their money out. Federal Reserve Chairman Greenspan—who was a paid consultant to Lincoln in the mid-1980s—was briefed about the loan before it was made, as were the other members of the Fed Board. They could have vetoed the loan but did not.

Representative Annunzio was reelected in the fall of 1990 despite revelations of his role in the thrift crisis. His Democratic colleagues in the 102d Congress were less kind than the voters. They ignored protocol and voted to oust him from his longtime post as chairman of the House Administration Committee, where he had wielded enormous power by controlling such mundane but crucial matters as office accounts, office assignments, and the delegation of computers and other office equipment. According to the *Congressional Quarterly,* Annunzio was ousted because he was considered weak and ineffective and because his staff was considered unresponsive and arrogant. In December 1991, Annunzio announced he would not seek reelection, thus avoiding a fight with House Ways and Means Chairman Dan Rostenkowski in the Democratic primary in Chicago's new Fifth Congressional District.

California Republican Assemblyman Pat Nolan, who led the fight to deregulate thrift activities in the state in the early 1980s, helping unleash a race to the bottom between federal and state lawmakers favoring thrift deregulation, resigned a GOP leadership post in December 1988. Several months earlier it had been reported that he and several other state legislators were under investigation for allegedly accepting money from undercover FBI agents investigating political corruption in the state. According to Common Cause, Nolan received $154,000 in campaign contributions from S&Ls in the 1980s, including several thousand from Keating's Lincoln Savings. By mid-1992 Nolan had not been charged with wrongdoing.

As of 1991, Danny Wall had joined the crowded Washington field of financial service advisers.

In 1990 Senator Jake Garn began a campaign to convince the public that he had been unfairly blamed in the media for helping cause the thrift mess. He defended the 1982 Garn-St Germain Act as a small step toward deregulation and published figures from the OTS showing that the cost of state-chartered thrift failures—those involving thrifts that were not affected by the Garn-St

Germain Act—so far had outpaced the cost to the government of federal thrift failures. (In fact, in 1982, 1985, and 1986 federally chartered S&L failures were responsible for 50 percent or more of government expenses. In 1990 the cost of closing federally chartered S&Ls was 41 percent of the total.)

Meanwhile, major thrifts trading in junk bonds, including many that have failed, have disappeared from the list of the Garn Institute's leading contributors. But several large California S&Ls, as well as Wall Street investment firms that deal heavily in mortgage-related securities and in brokered deposits, continue to be active supporters of the institute.

In May 1991 Garn announced he would not run for reelection to a fourth term in the Senate.

Rick Hohlt resigned—by most accounts he was forced out—as a full-time league employee shortly after the 1989 bailout bill passed, but he was given a consulting contract with the lobby group. He now consults to many thrifts on his own. Even though Hohlt had worked hard to try to defeat the president's bailout plan in 1989, Bush named him to the board of directors of the Student Loan Marketing Association (Sallie Mae), a federally chartered company that creates a secondary market in student loans in the same way that Freddie Mac and Fannie Mae create secondary markets in mortgages. (In the fall of 1991 Hohlt's name appeared in a front-page story in the *New York Times* describing criticism of one of the first deals in "the Bush Administration's showcase program to sell billions of dollars of properties seized from failed thrifts." Hohlt represented a partnership that negotiated to buy $500 million in property with $400 million in government financing that is interest-free for several years. Two field staff members of the RTC complained to their office in Washington that the government stood to lose tens of millions of dollars from the deal. As of early 1992, it was still being negotiated.)

In mid-1990 President Bush nominated Constance Horner, undersecretary at the Department of Health and Human Services, to serve as a director of the National Cooperative Bank, a farm credit agency. It was Horner who, while at the OMB under President Reagan, refused Ed Gray's request for more thrift examiners.

The Senate Banking Committee, headed by Keating Five member Riegle, had to pass on Horner's nomination. Riegle's staff quietly tried to remind the press of Horner's role in the S&L mess, but there was only so much Riegle himself could make out of that connection during her confirmation hearings. After all, the negative information about her came mainly from Ed Gray. If Riegle's committee had challenged Horner's denial of Gray's account (or, for that matter, her claim that she even tried to provide more examiners), it would prove Gray right on a crucial point and perhaps lend credence to his recollection of other meetings. That might have undermined Riegle's efforts

in another arena—the Keating Five hearings—to discredit Gray's recollection of key events. In the end the committee didn't harp too much on Horner's
interference with thrift regulation. She was confirmed.

Ed Gray was resurrected as a hero following the televised hearings into the
Keating Five. He plans to cowrite a book about Congress.

The deficit for fiscal 1992, which ended September 30 of that year, was $290
billion, far and away the largest deficit in history and more than four times
the deficit run when President Reagan and Vice President Bush took office
in 1981.

Acknowledgments

I did most of the interviews and fact gathering for this book from 1986 through 1989, when I covered the S&L industry for the *Washington Post*. At the end of 1989 I took a leave from the newspaper to do more research and to write the bulk of the book. Some information has also come from articles I wrote on the S&L crisis after returning to the *Post* in early 1990.

Writing a history of current or recent events is difficult. Many of the people on whose memories I have had to rely understandably tend to recall events to their own advantage. Luckily, in the case of the S&L scandal, there are many written records with which to compare individual recollections. At the same time, however, written records can sometimes distort what individuals actually did behind the scenes, as anyone familiar with the workings of Congress knows.

Another difficulty is that many of the scores of people I have interviewed over the years still work in government or in private-sector jobs that require contact with government officials. Many therefore have elected to speak to me over the years only if what they told me was not attributed directly to them. The request is understandable. The S&L bailout remains a sore political issue.

With few exceptions, every key figure in this book has been interviewed by me, often on numerous occasions over several years. Rather than identify who did not speak to me on which occasions—a practice that would then imply which others did speak to me and thus identify sources—I have chosen

397

in general not to make the distinction. And usually there was no need, for I have been able to verify most events and conversations through more than one person or through one person and written sources, most of them public documents. When I could not, I try to tell the reader so and provide as much information as possible about who or where the information I use comes from.

I thank the dozens of men and women in the thrift regulatory system, in the industry, and in the organizations that lobby for the industry who have generously and often at risk of their jobs helped me over the years by providing documents and information for stories that otherwise could never have been written.

I also thank the many current and former government officials in the White House and the Office of Management and Budget, in Congress and at the General Accounting Office, the Congressional Budget Office, the Treasury, the Federal Reserve Board, the bank regulatory agencies, and Fannie Mae and Freddie Mac who have spent hours over the years—again, sometimes at peril to their own careers—to explain policies and provide otherwise inaccessible information.

I also am indebted to dozens of journalists who during the last ten years helped move this story from the financial page to the front page.

In addition to colleagues at the *Washington Post,* they include, in no particular order, David Skidmore of the Associated Press; Nancy Miller, formerly of Knight-Ridder Financial News and now of Quick Nikkei News; James O'Shea of the *Chicago Tribune;* Dallas television reporter and magazine writer Byron Harris; John R. Cranford of the *Congressional Quarterly;* Dennis Cauchon of *USA Today;* free-lancer Michael Binstein; authors Paul Muolo, Stephen Pizzo, and Mary Fricker.

Debra Cope, formerly at *National Thrift News* and now at the *American Banker*. Robert Garsson and Jim McTague of the *American Banker*.

David B. Hilder of the *Wall Street Journal* and Leonard Apcar, formerly at the *Journal* and now at the *New York Times;* Nathaniel Nash of the *New York Times;* Allen Pusey of the *Dallas Morning News;* Tom Furlong and Bob Rosenblatt of the *Los Angeles Times*.

I owe special thanks to Robert Wright of the *New Republic,* who edited my March 1989 piece for the magazine, entitled "S&L Hell: Who Will Go There and Why," which was the genesis of this book; to Jack Day, my father, and to Nancy Miller for reading the manuscript; and to Debra Whitefield, for encouragement over the years.

Most of all, I thank Charles, my husband, who edited the manuscript over many months. He deserves much of the credit and none of the blame for this book.

Bibliography

Books

Bodfish, H. Morton, ed. *History of Building and Loan in the United States.* Chicago: United States Building and Loan League, 1931.

Brumbaugh, R. Dan, Jr., *Thrifts under Siege.* Cambridge, Mass.: Ballinger Publishing Co., 1988.

England, Catherine, and Thomas Huertas, eds. *The Financial Services Revolution.* Proceedings of a conference held in February 1987 by the Cato Institute.

Ewalt, Josephine Hedges. *A Business Reborn: The Savings and Loan Story, 1930–1960.* Chicago: American Savings and Loan Institute Press, 1962.

Garcia, Gillian, and Elizabeth Plautz. *The Federal Reserve: Lender of Last Resort.* Cambridge, Mass.: Ballinger Publishing Company, 1988.

Haraf, William S., and Rose Marie Kushmeider, eds. *Restructuring Banking & Financing Services in America.* Washington, D.C.: American Enterprise Institute for Public Policy Research, 1988.

Jackson, Brooks. *Honest Graft: Big Money and the American Political Process.* New York: Alfred A. Knopf, 1988.

Kane, Edward J. *The S&L Insurance Mess: How Did It Happen?* Washington, D.C.: Urban Institute Press, 1989.

Kettl, Donald F. *Leadership at the Fed.* New Haven: Yale University Press, 1986.

Kindleberger, Charles P. *Manias, Panics and Crashes*. New York: Basic Books, 1978.

Klingaman, William K. *1929: The Year of the Great Crash*. New York: Harper & Row Publishers Inc., 1989.

Lewis, Michael M. *Liar's Poker: Rising through the Wreckage of Salomon Brothers*. New York: W. W. Norton, 1989.

Litan, Robert. *What Should Banks Do?* Washington, D.C.: Brookings Institution, 1987.

O'Shea, James. *The Daisy Chain*. New York: Pocket Books, 1991.

Pilzer, Paul Zane, with Robert Deitz. *Other People's Money: How Bad Luck, Worse Judgment and Flagrant Corruption Made a Shambles of a $900 Billion Industry*. New York: Simon & Schuster, 1989.

Pizzo, Stephen; Mary Fricker; and Paul Muolo. *Inside Job: The Looting of America's Savings and Loans*. New York: McGraw-Hill Publishing Co., 1989.

Strunk, Norman, and Fred Case. *Where Deregulation Went Wrong: A Look at the Causes behind Savings and Loan Failures in the 1980s*. Chicago: U.S. League of Savings Institutions, 1988.

Waldman, Michael, and the Staff of Public Citizen's Congress Watch. *Who Robbed America?* New York: Random House, 1990.

White, Lawrence J. *The S&L Debacle: Public Policy Lessons for Bank and Thrift Regulation*. New York: Oxford University Press, 1991.

Papers

Barth, James R., Philip F. Bartholomew, and Michael G. Bradley. *The Determinants of Thrift Institution Resolution Costs*. Research Paper #89-03. November 1989.

———, R. Dan Brumbaugh, Jr., Daniel Sauerhaft, and George H. K. Wang. "Thrift-Institution Failures: Causes and Policy Issues." Prepared for publication in *Proceedings of a Conference on Bank Structure and Competition*, Federal Reserve Bank of Chicago, May 1–3, 1985.

———, R. Dan Brumbaugh, Jr., Daniel Sauerhaft, and George H. K. Wang. "Insolvency and Risk-Taking in the Thrift Industry: Implications for the Future." Prepared for presentation at the Annual Conference of the Western Economic Association, June 30–July 4, 1985.

———, Donald J. Bisenius, R. Dan Brumbaugh, and Daniel Sauerhaft. "Regulation and the Thrift-Industry Crisis." Prepared at the Federal Home Loan Bank Board, October 28, 1991.

"Blueprint for Restructuring America's Financial Institutions, Report of a Task Force." Brookings Institution, 1989.

"The Federal Deposit Insurance System: The First Fifty Years/A History of the FDIC, 1933–1983." Federal Deposit Insurance System, 1984.

"The Federal Reserve System, Purposes and Functions." Published by the Federal Reserve, 1984.

"Mandate for Change: Restructuring the Banking Industry." Federal Deposit Insurance Corporation, 1987.

"Translating Housing Needs into Shelter: Strategies for the 1990s." *Proceedings of Conference Sponsored by Fannie Mae.* January 1989.

"Savings & Loan Crisis: Lessons and a Look Ahead, featuring Representative Charles Schumer, Charles Keating, James Barth, William Black." *Stanford Law & Policy Review,* vol. 2, no. 1 (Spring 1990).

Index

Index